ROBERT BURNS: THE CRITICAL HERITAGE

THE CRITICAL HERITAGE SERIES

GENERAL EDITOR: B. C. SOUTHAM, M.A., B. LITT. (OXON.)
Formerly Department of English, Westfield College, University of London

For a list of books in the series see the back endpaper

ROBERT BURNS

THE CRITICAL HERITAGE

Edited by
DONALD A. LOW
Department of English Studies
University of Stirling

ROUTLEDGE & KEGAN PAUL   LONDON AND BOSTON

First published in 1974
by Routledge & Kegan Paul Ltd
Broadway House, 68–74 Carter Lane,
London EC4V 5EL and
9 Park Street,
Boston, Mass. 02108, U.S.A.
© Donald Low 1974
ISBN 0 7100 7797 1
Library of Congress Catalog Card No. 73–91033

Printed in Great Britain by
Butler & Tanner Ltd,
Frome and London

In Memory of
J. R. L.

General Editor's Preface

The reception given to a writer by his contemporaries and near-contemporaries is evidence of considerable value to the student of literature. On one side we learn a great deal about the state of criticism at large and in particular about the development of critical attitudes towards a single writer; at the same time, through private comments in letters, journals or marginalia, we gain an insight upon the tastes and literary thought of individual readers of the period. Evidence of this kind helps us to understand the writer's historical situation, the nature of his immediate reading-public, and his response to these pressures.

The separate volumes in the *Critical Heritage Series* present a record of this early criticism. Clearly, for many of the highly productive and lengthily reviewed nineteenth- and twentieth-century writers, there exists an enormous body of material; and in these cases the volume editors have made a selection of the most important views, significant for their intrinsic worth or for their representative quality—perhaps even registering incomprehension!

For earlier writers, notably pre-eighteenth century, the materials are much scarcer and the historical period has been extended, sometimes far beyond the writer's lifetime, in order to show the inception and growth of critical views which were initially slow to appear.

In each volume the documents are headed by an Introduction, discussing the material assembled and relating the early stages of the author's reception to what we have come to identify as the critical tradition. The volumes will make available much material which would otherwise be difficult of access and it is hoped that the modern reader will be thereby helped towards an informed understanding of the ways in which literature has been read and judged.

B.C.S.

Contents

CONTENTS

CONTENTS

Abbreviations

The following abbreviations have been used:

BC   *Burns Chronicle.*

Letters   *The Letters of Robert Burns*, ed. J. De Lancey Ferguson, 2 vols, 1931.

Kinsley   *The Poems and Songs of Robert Burns*, ed. James Kinsley, 3 vols, 1968.

Lindsay   Maurice Lindsay, *The Burns Encyclopedia*, 2nd edition (revised and enlarged), 1970.

Snyder   Franklyn B. Snyder, *The Life of Robert Burns*, 1932.

Preface and Acknowledgments

As the history of Burns's reputation is an enormous subject, this edition is restricted, save for its final documents, to criticism written in Great Britain between 1786 and 1837. The period forms the basis of the entire international critical tradition about Burns. My aim has been to provide a more informative documentary record of the crucial early reception of Burns's poetry than has hitherto been available in one book. If the 'genesis of Shakespeare idolatry' is a subject worthy of study in its own right, the outstandingly popular Burns qualifies also. Priority has been given to the first reviews, and to the comments of such major figures as Byron, Carlyle, Coleridge, Jeffrey, Keats, Scott, and Wordsworth: but all shades of critical opinion are represented. To mark the rise of Burns criticism overseas, the collection ends with an important American centenary tribute, that of Ralph Waldo Emerson.

In discussing in the Introduction the continuation of the critical tradition from the mid-nineteenth century until now, I have sought to indicate a number of the more significant ways in which criticism has developed in an international setting, rather than to make a comprehensive survey. In each country the context of criticism has been different. A full synthesis based upon study of Burns's reception in many lands remains desirable.

Burns Supper oratory has its own considerable interest, which is sometimes critical. Unfortunately, the Immortal Memory is a sea without limits! Speeches at a historic meeting in honour of Burns are referred to in No. 52, but it would have been impossible to include more than a fractional sample of the early oratory of the Burns Clubs, of which the first to be formally constituted were Greenock (1801), Paisley (1805), Kilmarnock (1808), and Dunfermline (1812).

Maria Riddell's 'Character Sketch', which has long been recognized as having substantial implications for criticism as well as for biography, is included in this volume (No. 22). Other contemporary descriptions of Burns's personality and appearance are collected in a pamphlet by W. L. Renwick, *Burns as Others saw him* (Edinburgh, 1959), and in *The*

Poems and Songs of Robert Burns, edited by James Kinsley (1968), III, 1534–47.

I should like to thank Mr James Veitch, editor of the *Robert Burns Chronicle*, and the Burns Federation, for permission to reproduce with changes material from my articles 'An unpublished critique of Burns's poetry, 1796' (1970) 'Scott on Burns' (1971).

I wish to thank Mr Tom Crawford and Professor G. Ross Roy for discussing with me specific problems in the history of Burns criticism, and Professor A. F. Falconer for reading more than one draft of my Introduction and suggesting improvements. The members of staff of many libraries, and especially of the Mitchell Library, Glasgow, the National Library of Scotland, and St Andrews University Library, have been generous with time and help. Mr Desmond Donaldson, County Librarian, the Ewart Library, Dumfries, has very kindly searched the volumes of the *Dumfries Weekly Journal* for material relating to Burns. Mrs K. MacFadyen has twice lent her Glasgow flat to let me be near the 4,000-odd items of the Burns Collection in the Mitchell Library! The Revd M. A. MacCorquodale has supplied me with many valuable references, and with a copy of Alexander Campbell's criticism in *Albyn's Anthology*. Above all, my wife's sense of humour, practical encouragement throughout, and constructive criticism have made the completion of this book possible.

Introduction

I

Much of the early criticism of Burns was compounded of praise for his genius, sympathy with his lot, disapproval of the man on moral, social, religious or political grounds, and failure to examine the art of individual poems and songs. Reviewers recognized the originality of *Poems, chiefly in the Scottish Dialect* published in Kilmarnock in 1786 and in Edinburgh in 1787. They paid tribute, and then took fright. The process was repeated over and over again in the half-century which followed.

Henry Mackenzie's review in the *Lounger* set the tone. Burns became 'the Heaven-taught ploughman', and, as Mackenzie's title indicates, the subject most often under discussion was not a body of poetry but a socio-literary phenomenon: 'Surprising effects of Original Genius, exemplified in the Poetical Productions of Robert Burns, an Ayrshire Ploughman'. Critics nearly all agreed that Burns was an inspired poet. Some tried to force him into the mould of their preconceptions of 'the sublime' or 'pathetic', and chose to praise insipid verses in 'To a Mountain Daisy', while completely ignoring his gifts for satire and his aptness in the epistle. But opinion, if undiscriminating, was very favourable: he had genius.

The theme was extended after the poet's death in 1796 to include the conflict between genius and morality. In that year an anonymous obituary notice, which was widely reprinted, made a great deal of Burns's alleged faults, and in 1797 a biography by Robert Heron contained undocumented but plausible suggestions of his dissipation in later years in Dumfries. James Currie's collected edition of 1800, undertaken for the benefit of the poet's widow and family, added new facts, but his essay on Burns's life and writings failed to face or to dispel malicious rumours, thus confirming the terms of moralistic debate. Fresh critical insight was badly needed. This did show itself in part in two lengthy review articles published anonymously in 1809, one by Francis Jeffrey in the *Edinburgh Review* and the other by Walter Scott in the first number of the *Quarterly Review*. However, by dwelling on what they took to be the moral and social weaknesses of Burns, Jeffrey and Scott had the effect of intensifying biographical discussion, which was swinging between the extremes of condemnation and indignant defence, and criticism continued to be hampered.

Myth and counter-myth took the place of sound, perceptive appraisal of his poetry. Burns's sudden fame had spread to England within weeks of the first publication of his poems, and by the time of the Regency he was being variously judged by leading English authors in poems, letters and essays. The strictures of Currie and Jeffrey were given too much attention by Wordsworth, Hazlitt, and others. This extension of the argument about genius and morality, which was kept up absurdly by John Wilson in a new Scottish periodical, *Blackwood's Magazine*, was often even less relevant than previous criticism, because Burns began to be used as a stalking-horse in other men's quarrels. Wordsworth, none the less, helped to give a new direction to one important aspect of Burns criticism because of his belief in realistic self-expression and his insistence on it. By contrast, Jane Austen introduced into her last, uncompleted novel *Sanditon* a pastiche of immoderate talk about Burns's amorous lyrics.

Despite Burns's acknowledgment of his debt to Allan Ramsay and Robert Fergusson, little was done even by Scottish critics to throw light on his relation to earlier Scottish poetry. His achievement as a songwriter was left similarly obscure. Although at the outset his songs were judged to be skilful, hardly anyone troubled to look closely at the technique by which he had made fragments of popular song timeless. Instead, critics continued to regret that he had not followed up his early success with the play he had planned, or with more of the poems. Erotic passion, virtual anonymity, and ardent democratic and national feeling had given the songs an appeal which not even the poems possessed. These very qualities encouraged the belief that the better-known songs were outside the sphere of formal criticism; and that idea was supported by what survived from the eighteenth-century hierarchy of critical 'kinds'. It took Burns's fellow-countryman Carlyle, who was familiar with Scots songs from childhood, and who was also fired by German romantic theory, to redress the balance. By then it was too late. A chance to comment on his recasting and alterations had been missed by those who knew Scots songs as Burns heard them.

The Victorian age opened with Burns's reputation still in the ascendant, despite inadequacies in the critical treatment of his work. Many of his admirers, like Byron's, continued to busy themselves with biographical side issues. But there was another category of readers then as in every period. Those who concentrated on the poetry, rather than on biography or morality, were certainly in a minority; but it is their opinions which retain freshness and particular critical value.

II

BURNS AND HIS CRITICS

Burns's literary career took a very unusual course from initial obscurity (Kilmarnock, 1786) through a blaze of publicity (Edinburgh, 1786–7) to the chosen anonymity of his later work on Scottish song. Contemporary opinions of his poetry were strongly influenced by the different forms in which his poems and songs were first published. Not until 1800, four years after his death, could his work be judged in anything like its entirety (see Appendix A: 'The Publication of Burns's Poems and Songs, 1786–1800').

A study of Burns's changing attitude to criticism shows his pride and impulsiveness. Even more clearly, it points to his independence of judgment. Critics assailed him with bad advice—write in English, cultivate a grand style. Publishers, too, let him down. One, William Creech, was slow in honouring his agreement with Burns, while another, George Thomson, offered notably inept criticism of his songwriting. But Burns knew by instinct and by trial and error where his artistic gifts lay, and, to an astonishing degree, went his own way despite all the pressure.

Poems, chiefly in the Scottish Dialect Kilmarnock 1786

He began by being ambitious, and acutely sensitive to criticism. When the first edition of his *Poems, chiefly in the Scottish Dialect* was in the press of John Wilson, a printer in Kilmarnock, he wrote to a friend,[1]

Be sure to remember a poor Poet militant in your prayers. He looks forward with fear and trembling to that, to him, important moment which stamps the *die*—with—with, perhaps the eternal disgrace of My dear Sir, Your humble, afflicted, tormented,

ROBT. BURNS

Humorous exaggeration does not disguise his anxiety about the fate of a collection which was intended for a regional public, his 'rustic compeers' of Ayrshire and its neighbouring counties. In the first flush of success he wrote,[2]

I am fully persuaded that there is not any class of Mankind so feelingly alive to the titillations of applause as the Sons of Parnassus, nor is it easy to conceive how the heart of the poor Bard dances with rapture, when those, whose character in life gives them a right to be polite Judges, honor him with their approbation.

He was soon to prove fully able to contend with 'polite Judges', but their verdict affected both his feelings and his financial prospects, as remarks throughout his correspondence show.

Did he, in the Kilmarnock edition, as one recent critic has argued, 'strike a pose' as a primitive poet of genius, and was this with a view to disarming criticism?[3] It is necessary to distinguish between different stages in the preparation of the volume. After circulating 'Proposals for. . . . Scotch Poems', he decided to add certain English poems. These, and his preface, show that he expected to have readers of more than one kind. But his original aim remained unchanged. He was to describe it the following year in this way:[4]

For my part, my first ambition was, and still my strongest wish is, to please my Compeers, the rustic Inmates of the Hamlet, while everchanging language and manners will allow me to be relished and understood.

The picture of himself suggested by scattered phrases, single stanzas, and also by entire poems in this predominantly Scottish collection has a realism and humour which has to be set against any false impression that may be created by the preface. He asks for 'rowth o' rhyme'; confesses to 'rantin', 'drinkin'; asserts in his Epistle 'To J. S.' that he 'rhymes for fun'; is found, in the introduction to 'A Vision', 'Stringing blethers up in rhyme'; transmits to his friend Lapraik 'some blethers just clean aff-loof'; and writes his epitaph as a 'whim-inspired fool'. It is these glimpses of spontaneous creativity on the part of a country poet which in their intimacy and earthiness cannot aptly be reconciled with the lofty expectations of learned critics who were seeking further proof of their *primitivist* theories.[5]

Burns undoubtedly misled some readers by a quatrain on the title-page about 'the simple Bard, unbroke by rules of Art', followed by his elegantly written preface. But was it done to deceive? He had absorbed ideas from every quarter, including Rousseau's fashionable concept of the poet as Child of Nature:[6]

> Gie me ae spark o' Nature's fire,
> That's a' the learnin I desire.

4

As Scott was to note, he had 'the *tact* to make his poetry tell by connecting it with the stream of public thought and the sentiment of the age'. Like any young poet, he hoped to reach readers who might help him in his career, and in his preface quite naturally made use of the conventional language of a period in which some form of patronage was necessary to a poor writer. The convention did not accord with his character, any more than it did with Dr Johnson's; but as James Kinsley has pointed out, much of the preface is a vigorous justification of what he had chosen to do.[7] And the verse 'Dedication to G. H.' later in the volume was direct and natural, making up for any awkwardness in the preface. In adding the introductory material Burns was guilty, at worst, of showing 'an excessive susceptibility of immediate impressions —at the same time without *losing* the past', which was to be Byron's definition of the mercurial quality that he identified in himself and described as 'mobility'.[8]

Success in Edinburgh, 1786–87, and some of its consequences

Beginning as a local poet who wrote to please himself and others in his neighbourhood, Burns was by merit and chance thrust into wider fame. The volume he published in Ayrshire in his twenty-seventh year while planning to emigrate to the West Indies was soon known in Edinburgh. Dr Thomas Blacklock, a much older man from the south-west of Scotland living in Edinburgh and respected for his writings, had received a copy of *Poems, chiefly in the Scottish Dialect* from a friend. He promised to pass it on to Hugh Blair, an extremely influential divine, professor and man of letters in the Scottish capital, and suggested that a second edition would sell. This generous encouragement from a blind stranger was not in itself responsible for Burns's decision to stay in Scotland; but it helped, and was to change the course of his life (No. 1).

Edinburgh in the later eighteenth century was a city of cultural distinction. Its outstanding philosopher, David Hume, had died, but there remained very able lawyers, economists, historians, artists, medical men, and social theorists. Some dearth of imaginative writers, made all the more deplorable by the city's failure to recognize the brilliance in vernacular Scots poetry of Robert Fergusson (1750–74), was scarcely noticed, or, if noticed, seemed to be compensated for by a phalanx of literary theorists and essayists, including Hugh Blair and the law lords Monboddo and Kames. Hugh Blair and Henry Mackenzie, whose novel *The Man of Feeling* (1771) rivalled James Macpherson's

Ossianic poems for public acclaim, were arbiters on all literary questions.[9] The authoritative tone of a legal society, and emulation of London, gave to Edinburgh's literary criticism unrivalled prestige north of the border.

Mackenzie's review in the *Lounger* (No. 4) and Blair's equally well-meant suggestions for changes in a second edition of Burns's poems (No. 9) point to a common source of confusion. Speaking Scots themselves, but accustomed to think of English as their country's literary language, they liked Burns's bold vernacular poetry, yet were uncertain about how to say so. In their zeal to act on his behalf, they sought to emphasize the qualities in his work which were likely to win general approval. There were precedents for recognizing the use of Scots for these effects of genre-painting, comedy and pathos, as well of course as the English diction which Burns employed in various poems. Together, these provided evidence of poetic distinction. Within such limits, and especially in the dignified manner of 'The Cotter's Saturday Night', Burns showed 'virtuous sensibility'. It was more effective to put him forward as a poet of the sympathetic emotions than to draw attention to his ecclesiastical satires or his outspoken epistles. Otherwise, he could not be accommodated into current Anglo-Scottish primitivist theory, which in Blair's view had already been vindicated by the ancient poems of Ossian 'discovered' by Macpherson, and which did not rule out the possibility of another rural genius appearing. Burns seemed to be such a genius.

Thus an orthodoxy at once bizarre and prudish impaired criticism. Burns had given many indications in his work of his reading of other poets, including Pope, Shenstone, and Gray. These allusions were not mentioned by his first critics, or at most were referred to with patronizing wonder, which amused James Macaulay, an intelligent observer (No. 10). It was a condition of 'natural genius' that book-learning was largely absent. Burns's frankness, however, was even more embarrassing to the *literati* than his learning. Nowhere is this more clearly illustrated than in Blair's dismissal of 'The Jolly Beggars', which Burns proposed to include in his second edition:

The Whole of What is called the Cantata, the Songs of the Beggars and their Doxies, with the Grace at the end of them, are altogether unfit in my opinion for publication. They are by much too licentious; and fall below the dignity which Mr. Burns possesses in the rest of his poems & would rather degrade them.

These observations are Submitted by one who is a great friend to Mr Burn's Poems and wishes him to preserve the fame of Virtuous Sensibility, & of humorous fun, without offence.

While he silently rejected almost all of Blair's other criticisms, Burns accepted this advice without demur—Blair's response to 'The Jolly Beggars' so obviously indicated the reaction likely to prevail in the capital. The work thus suppressed was a masterpiece, and only by chance did it survive this incident. In 1793 Burns wrote to George Thomson that he had kept no copy of the Cantata.[10]

Blair's attitude indicates what was to be significant for the publication of some of the satires. Surreptitious printing, usually without Burns's consent, first brought a number of poems to the notice of the public.[11] In this way the poet gained an 'underground' reputation, even on occasion notoriety. An extreme instance is provided by James Maxwell's deliberately malicious publication in his *Animadversions* (1788) of the lines showing Burns's Jacobite sympathies, 'Here Stewarts once in triumph reigned'. Because of this slight poem, Burns was called before his superior officers in the Excise and asked to explain himself. In 1789 'Holy Willie's Prayer' first appeared as a pamphlet without giving author, publisher, or place of publication on its title-page. Ten years later it was issued as Burns's work in a Glasgow pamphlet: but it was not included in Currie's collected edition of 1800, and did not find its way into any of the revised issues until 1818. 'The Ayrshire Garland' also came out in 1789, as a broadside. Two further stanzas of the same poem, usually known as 'The Kirk's Alarm', were given in *Poems and Songs by Alexander Tait* the next year. Poems such as these, attacking recognizable people and institutions, would probably have landed Burns in trouble if they had first appeared under his name, and they would certainly have given offence. Understandably, he preferred to show his satires to a few friends rather than publish them. Topical satire in late eighteenth-century Scotland was unacceptable to society— especially when its target was religious hypocrisy.

Contemporaries credited Burns with brilliance in conversation.[12] He was invited into every kind of company during his first winter in Edinburgh (1786–7). His ability to hold his own wherever he went set the seal on his fame, especially among lawyers, who assessed talk as decisively as they did writing. In the words of J. G. Lockhart, a later Edinburgh lawyer, 'They were, perhaps, as proud a set of men as ever enjoyed the tranquil pleasures of unquestioned superiority.'[13] This double success in poetry and polite society made Burns the talking-point of the season. There was more in it than mere current fashion. Those who befriended the poet recognized his worth as a person as well as his literary gift. For this, they earned the poet's deep gratitude. Conspicuous among them were Henry Erskine, Dean of the Faculty of Advocates, Professor Dugald Stewart, and the Earl of Glencairn, who was responsible for the Caledonian Hunt's subscription for a hundred copies of the Edinburgh edition of *Poems, chiefly in the Scottish Dialect*.[14] Later he helped Burns to an Excise appointment:[15]

> But I'll remember thee, Glencairn,
> And a' thou hast done for me!

Despite these examples of disinterested generosity, however, fashion did play a leading part in the lionizing of Burns in Edinburgh, and inevitably it was a capricious one. Burns saw this more clearly than anyone. His action in commemorating the neglected poet Robert Fergusson with an inscribed stone in Greyfriars Churchyard was in itself a reproach to the capital for its coldness. In his Border Journal (1787) he wrote of 'The Greenland Bay of Indifference amid the noise and nonsense of Edinburgh'.[16] 'The town is at present agog with the ploughman poet', wrote Mrs Alison Cockburn on 30 December 1786.[17]

Burns was convinced that his success in Edinburgh could not last, because it was based on the sensational 'novelty' of his reputation as an uneducated poet of genius. He was amused by the excitement he had caused:[18]

For my own affairs, I am in a fair way of becoming as eminent as Thomas a Kempis or John Bunyan; and you may expect henceforth to see my birthday inserted among the wonderful events, in the Poor Robin's and Aberdeen Almanacks, along with the black Monday, & the battle of Bothwel Bridge.

Seldom did he attempt to refute this distorted view of himself. It was not in his immediate interest to do so. Nor did he readily disclose the extent of his learning to people who suspected it. When Mrs Elizabeth Scott charged him with being well educated, he deftly evaded the point in his verse reply.[19] In public, according to Robert Anderson, he deliberately played up to his image:[20]

It was, I know, a part of the machinery, as he called it, of his poetical character to pass for an illiterate ploughman who wrote from pure inspiration. When I pointed out some evident traces of poetical imitation in his verses, privately he readily acknowledged his obligations, and even admitted the advantages he enjoyed in poetical composition from the *copia verborum*, the command of phraseology, which the knowledge and use of the English and Scottish dialects afforded him; but in company he did not suffer his pretensions to pure inspiration to be challenged, and it was seldom done where it might be supposed to affect the success of the subscription for his *Poems*.

What is certain is that Burns often felt apprehensive lest he 'should be ruined by being dragged too suddenly into the glare of polite & learned observation'.[21] There are numerous references in his letters to the possibility that, before long, admiration would give way to neglect or contempt.[22] He wrote to Dr John Moore, for instance, that he could not hope for 'distinguished poetic fame' in English, the language favoured by critics: his originality came from his knowledge of men and of manners not known by 'polite' authors.[23] Having such a clear-sighted estimate of his own abilities, he was made deeply uneasy by suggestions that with the resources of learning and criticism now open to him he could go on to surpass English poets in their own language. The experimental poems of his Edinburgh period, including the cloying 'Address To Edinburgh' in the second edition of his *Poems*, left him dissatisfied. 'I am sick of writing where my bosom is not strongly interested', was his comment on a period when misdirection from critics threatened his independence as a poet.[24]

In his First Commonplace Book (1783-5) Burns had noted the importance of experience as against theory in the making of critics, defining 'a real Critic' as 'one above the biasses of prejudice, but a thorough Judge of Nature', and writing that he had often thought[25]

no man can be a proper critic of Love composition, except he himself, in one, or more instances, have been a warm votary of this passion.

He valued directness and knowledge of the real language of living men far above abstractions. Though he did not trouble to formulate a critical creed, his practice as a writer anticipated Wordsworth's famous statement. His letters and Second Commonplace Book (1787-9) record his increasing disillusionment with 'the Fathers and Brothers of Scientific Criticism' among other influential groups in Edinburgh, variously expressed in jest or earnest according to his mood. One weakness he discovered in his country's leading critics was a preference for genteel, idealized description or didacticism instead of simplicity and naturalness in language. Many of his letters show him to have been long-suffering, but not deceived. He wrote to Mrs Dunlop in March 1787:[26]

I have the advice of some very judicious friends among the Literati here, but with them I sometimes find it necessary to claim the privilege of thinking for myself.

Mrs Dunlop was elderly and had read the Kilmarnock *Poems* with delight and found a new interest in her life in her ensuing correspondence with Burns.[27] Her courage and honesty earned his respect, although he did not always take her literary advice, any more than he did that of her friend Dr Moore. The important role Mrs Dunlop played in his career, and by contrast his view of some critics, are summed up in one of his letters:[28]

Your Criticisms, my honoured Benefactress, are truly the work of a FRIEND.— They are not the blasting depradations of a canker-toothed, caterpillar-Critic; nor are they fair statement of cold impartiality, balancing with unfeeling exactitude the pro & con of an Author's merits: they are the judicious observations of animated Friendship, selecting the beauties of the Piece.

To Moore, who wanted Burns to produce something like Thomson's *Seasons*, only livelier, Burns sent 'a history of MYSELF', the famous autobiographical letter of 2 August 1787 which throws more light on his early career as a poet than any work of criticism.[29]

Among the subjects to which the poet alluded in his letters to Mrs Dunlop were his unsatisfactory dealings with William Creech, printer and later copyright-owner of the Edinburgh edition of *Poems, chiefly in the Scottish Dialect*. In his 'Epistle to Creech' of May 1787 Burns had been able to describe the publisher with good humour as 'Adjutant' of a core of philosophers, poets 'And toothy Critics by the score in bloody raw', but in October 1788 Mrs Dunlop received a copy of a satirical sketch showing that Burns's initial trustfulness had been weakened by a long delay in payment:[30]

> His solid sense by inches you must tell,
> But mete his subtle cunning by the ell.

It is true that in the following March Burns wrote, 'Mr Creech . . . has at last settled, amicably and fully as fairly as could have been expected.'[31]

This has tempted some scholars to defend Creech's business practice: but there is little doubt that he overlooked the difference between hard-headedness and meanness.[32] Apart from his doubtful action in selling the 'third' London edition of 1787 apparently without informing Burns of its existence, his delaying tactics and inability to see beyond considerations of profit stand against him.[33] Moreover, by his later conduct Creech was probably responsible for reducing Burns's interest in further publication. When in 1792 Creech wrote to ask Burns what fresh material he could supply for a new edition of his *Poems*, Burns showed hurt pride in his reply:[34]

A few Books which I very much want, are all the recompence I crave, together with as many copies of this new edition of my own works as Friendship or Gratitude shall prompt me to *present*.

Creech's conscience was not disturbed. He published the new edition in February 1793 and did not inform Burns. On learning of the publication, possibly from a newspaper advertisement, Burns had to write 'begging' (his own word) for his copies.[35]

J. W. Egerer has argued persuasively that Burns was almost completely unaware of the extent of interest in his poems within and beyond Scotland after 1787. Yet his suggestion that[36]

we might have had other lyrics and satires and narratives if Burns had only realized that his dream of a large and appreciative audience was a reality

almost certainly exaggerates the importance of Burns's relationship with his public *en masse* as a factor affecting his desire to write. What always mattered most to him was the response of individuals. The incentive to write 'Tam o' Shanter'—his wish to please Francis Grose—was typical. Similarly, his willingness in 1791 to transcribe a large number of his poems for Robert Riddell in 'The Glenriddell Manuscript' sprang from friendship. In Riddell's home, he was always made welcome by 'The cordiality of Kindness, and the warmth of Friendship'.[37] This incident makes Creech more blameworthy.

The publication of Burns's songs

Burns's true poetic language was not English, as some of his critics would have had it, but Scots, or, for certain purposes, English 'tipped' with Scots; and he was by nature and force of circumstance a poet who wrote best in response to a particular person, event, mood, or tune. These facts show an underlying consistency in a literary career that appears at first to be strangely divided between an early brilliant phase in poetry and a later period of obscurity in collecting, writing, and improving Scots songs. A love of traditional song had been instilled in Burns by his mother. In his First Commonplace Book he wrote ably on the art of words in folksong. A number of love-songs, including one or two of his finest, belong to the early period. The few songs in the Kilmarnock edition, however, were included near the end of the book, and probably were only there to fill up the volume.

This arrangement of his work encouraged the idea that Burns was one to whom song was of minor importance. The handful of songs in the Edinburgh edition of 1787 again was unobtrusive. By then the public notion of him as a poet destined to express himself in various poetic forms of appropriate length and dignity was fixed: nothing that Burns could do would alter it. Feeling trapped by what polite readers expected, and longing to rediscover spontaneous pleasure in his art, he turned increasingly to song-writing. (Too much should not be made of a single incident, but in March 1787 after a 'jury of literati' failed to appreciate one of his songs he wrote to Gavin Hamilton, 'Damn the pedant frigid soul of Criticism for ever and ever!')[38] He brought to it a collector's zeal and his ambition to make a contribution to the living culture of Scotland. This ambition was different from his old desire for distinction. Burns held that Scots song was the nation's self-expression and therefore more important than his personal identity. Song-writing was to be its own reward: he would not accept payment for it.

His contributions to James Johnson's *Scots Musical Museum* from 1787, and to the less sympathetic George Thomson's *Select Collection of Original Scotish Airs* from 1793, fully vindicate his decision to concentrate on song: but to many of his contemporaries it seemed otherwise. Gifted poets are expected to sign their work. Song-collections were not reviewed in the ordinary way, and although the *Scots Musical Museum* became the finest of them all, there had been many others in the period. Burns's cryptic way of indicating the authorship of individual songs by means of a system of initials did little to focus attention on his role as virtual editor and chief contributor. Such notes as 'these marked Z. are old verses, with corrections or additions' concealed his mature lyrical art. The idea grew that his period of significant creation was at an end. In his *Collection of Scottish Songs* (1794) the learned and testy folklorist Joseph Ritson praised Burns as 'a very ingenious critic' of old songs, but remarked that he did not 'appear to his usual advantage in Song: *non omnia possumus*' (No. 20).

Adverse comment did not deflect Burns from his purpose, although he referred ruefully to 'Tam o' Shanter' as his 'standard performance in the poetical line' when he thought of its quality and difference in kind from his other work.[39] Interestingly, the first book-publication of 'Tam o' Shanter' was also casual: the poem appeared as a footnote in the second volume of Grose's *Antiquities of Scotland* in 1791. But whereas 'Tam o' Shanter' was at once praised discerningly by A. F. Tytler (No. 18), and was included by Burns in the 1793 edition of *Poems, chiefly in the Scottish Dialect*, few of his best songs found a place in that edition.

As a song-writer he was free from fashionable attention, but not from inept criticism. George Thomson tried repeatedly to refine Burns's song-writing according to his own standards of genteel taste. Burns tolerated a good deal of interference in the editing of songs, but was energetic in defending his views, as a selection of comments from various letters shows:[40]

Let me tell you, that you are too fastidious in your ideas of Songs & ballads ... Ballad-making is now so completely my hobby-horse, as ever Fortitude was Uncle Toby's ...What pleases me, as simple & naive, disgusts you as ludicrous & low ... These English songs gravel me to death.—I have not that command of the language that I have of my native tongue.—In fact, I think my ideas are more barren in English than in Scottish.

Thomson did not see that his position was one of privilege in that he had the benefit of Burns's artistic collaboration.

In May 1796 Burns informed Thomson that he wished eventually to have his own contributions to the *Scots Musical Museum* and *Select Collection* published in a separate volume:[41]

When your Publication is finished, I intend publishing a Collection, on a cheap plan, of all the songs I have written for you, the *Museum*, &c.—at least of all the songs of which I wish to be called the Author.—I do not propose this so much in the way of emolument, as to do justice to my Muse, lest I should be blamed for trash I never saw, or be defrauded by other claimants of what is justly my own.

Two months later, he died. Currie, Cromek, and other early editors reprinted many of his songs, but it was not until 1817 that there appeared a book with a title broadly in keeping with the terms of Burns's declaration to Thomson: this was *A complete Collection of the Songs of Robert Burns, extracted from his Works and various other Publications.*[42] The manner in which his songs had been published was undoubtedly a major factor in preventing justice from being done to his gifts as a song-writer. The full scope of his knowledge of matters relating to traditional song began to be clear only very much later, with the publication of James C. Dick's *The Songs of Robert Burns* (1903) and his *Notes on Scottish Songs by Robert Burns* (1908).

Reviewing conventions

'Criticism of Burns is only permitted to Scotchmen of purest blood'. Leslie Stephen's remark in his article on Burns in the *Dictionary of National Biography* points to something which was true of an earlier period. Nearly all of Burns's first critics in London were Scotsmen, partly because Scotland supplied a disproportionately large number of Britain's periodical writers, and partly because Burns's poetry was more readily understood by his fellow-Scots than by Englishmen. Without exception, the contemporary critics in Edinburgh were Scots. This makes the poor standard of early reviews and critical essays all the more disappointing. Despite the vernacular revival, which had begun with the publication of anthologies, James Watson's *Choice Collection of Comic and Serious Scots Poems* (1706–11) and Allan Ramsay's *The Ever Green* (1724) and *The Tea-Table Miscellany* (1724–37), the varied heritage of Scottish poetry was very imperfectly known by most reviewers, and by some not at all.

Nevertheless, allowance has to be made for the difficulty reviewers faced in trying to explain the merits of dialect poetry to a public that was schooled like themselves to look down on their native speech. Also, the limits and conventions of reviews and 'critical notices' in magazines of the time have to be kept in mind. If a reviewer succeeded in recommending a book he liked to the public, it scarcely mattered to him or anyone else except the author whether or not the terms of his praise were exact. He was required only to promote or condemn the works which came his way. Lengthy quotations were usually included to illustrate the quality of the book. These quotations, naturally enough, were chosen with the aim of interesting as wide a reading-public as possible. Burns had provided an excellent word-list in *Poems, chiefly in the Scottish Dialect*, which enabled editors and reviewers to gloss extracts helpfully; but their disinclination to select passages containing many unfamiliar words was sometimes increased by a printing problem which the need for glossing imposed.

There was a public demand for sensational information; and any periodical which included poems of marked difficulty ran the risk of a loss in circulation. This situation was partly remedied after 1802, when the *Edinburgh Review* introduced a new type of long review-article in which an author's work could be represented more fully and assessed more closely than before. As early as 1802, however, the habits of concentrating on the sensational in discussion and of quoting conventional or 'purple' passages were endemic in periodical criticism of Burns. The passage of time made Burns's language more difficult even for Scotsmen to understand. As the proportion of English readers of periodicals grew, pressure increased on reviewers to comment on Burns's poetry in a way which they judged a majority of readers would understand.

III

1786–1810

Six hundred and twelve copies of *Poems, chiefly in the Scottish Dialect* were printed. Subscribers received their copies, and the others were quickly sold on the strength of personal recommendation—no 'review copies' were sent to magazine editors. It is not surprising that Burns's earliest readers should have felt indignant when the suggestion was later made that they had failed to show interest in his work. In a letter to the *Edinburgh Evening Courant* in November 1786, 'G. H.' vigorously defended Burns's Ayrshire public against a charge of indifference. It is probable that 'G. H.' was Gavin Hamilton, Burns's friend and early patron, who had every right to feel annoyed on reading that no attempt had 'been made to interest the public in [Burns's] favour' (No. 3).

Burns's *Poems* were immediately popular in his own region; Robert Heron's testimony on the subject is emphatic: 'Old and young, high and low, grave and gay, learned or ignorant, all were alike delighted.' Robert Heron lived in Galloway, adjoining Ayrshire. Someone in his neighbourhood was presented with a copy of Burns's poems by an Ayrshire friend. He pressed it on Heron as 'a work containing some effusions of the most extraordinary genius'. Heron took the book reluctantly, not wishing to offend his friend, and found it enthralling. Ten years later, he wrote the first biography of Burns.

Further from Kilmarnock, an incident took place which is of interest in connection with the first printed notice of Burns. Robert Anderson, James Sibbald's colleague on the *Edinburgh Magazine*, told the story long afterwards to James Currie: [43]

The name of Burns was first mentioned to me by a Mr Cairns, an Ayrshire farmer, who knew him well, with whom I happened to travel between Berwick and Alnwick in the summer before the Poet visited Edinburgh. He spoke of him as a prodigy, and of his poems, lately published at Kilmarnock, in terms of enthusiastic admiration. Not being partial to the productions of the vulgar rhymers in the Scottish dialect, of whom every district has its favourites, I requested him to favour me with a specimen of Burns's poetry, and he readily repeated, among others, passages in the 'Address to a Mouse', which convinced me that the Ayrshire bard was no vulgar rhymer. My curiosity was strongly excited to see the printed collection of his pieces, and Mr Cairns having been so good as to give me an introduction to Mr Bruce, a jeweller in Princes Street, to whom he had brought a copy, on my return to Edinburgh I obtained a sight of it, which I perused with wonder and delight, though its contents were, at times, offensive to taste, and easily prevailed upon the printer of the *Edinburgh Magazine* to insert some pieces in the poetical article of his Miscellany.

Anderson's suspicion of dialect poetry and his opinion that some of Burns's poems were 'offensive to taste' indicate that there were limitations in the new public which awaited the poet. Inevitably, reviews of the Kilmarnock *Poems* expressed ideas about the book which had little to do with Burns's bold use of the vernacular. Aiming to stress the general, as distinct from regional appeal of the poems, reviewers trusted too much to their preconceptions and not enough to observation. Any of Burns's original Ayrshire readers who chanced to read what the city critics wrote about him must have been amazed at this transformation of a 'rhyming billie'.

Sibbald's commendable idea was to arouse interest in Burns by a series of questions and answers (No. 2). His notice, with Anderson's extracts, appears to have served its purpose. He placed Burns's vernacular poems below those of Ramsay and Fergusson, and completely failed to recognize their art, seeing evidence only of 'untutored fancy'. However, Burns's country humour was noted! A comparison with Horace's Ofellus was more realistic than Henry Mackenzie's idealized projection of Burns as a 'Heaven-taught ploughman' (No. 4).

Judged from one point of view—that of public relations—Mackenzie's essay in the *Lounger* was a triumphant success. He knew the preferences of his public; his appeal for readers and patrons succeeded;

and Burns was duly grateful. Mackenzie was sincere in his praise. There is no reason to suppose that he wished to help Burns only because both were freemasons. Nevertheless, from another viewpoint, his was a disastrously inaccurate essay in criticism, which gave rise to endless distortion of Burns's poetry. The whole tendency of Mackenzie's encomium was to emasculate *Poems, chiefly in the Scottish Dialect*. He paid lip-service to humour and satire, but found them too embarrassing to discuss; introduced a comparison with Shakespeare, only to withdraw it at once; repeatedly shrank from Burns's characteristic self-expression and fell back on generalizations. He apologized for the language in which the poet did his best work, and concentrated on the poems of sentiment in English. This was to sacrifice truth, and therefore also Burns's long-term interests as a poet, for instant acclaim.

There are connections between Mackenzie's review and John Logan's less flattering one in the *English Review* (No. 7). Logan, formerly a minister in Edinburgh, had edited the poems of Michael Bruce, whose talents were very highly praised in an essay by Lord Craig in Mackenzie's earlier periodical, the *Mirror*; and Logan had subsequently been accused, though not by Mackenzie, of stealing from Bruce's papers an unusually fine 'Ode to the Cuckoo' which he published as his own composition.[44] Whatever the truth of that matter—the balance of evidence seems to be against Logan—it is interesting to find Logan reviewing Burns, and afterwards justifying his review in a letter to Mackenzie, who had objected that he was biassed. Mackenzie was apparently irritated with Logan for taking a different view from his own, which elsewhere was accepted as critical orthodoxy on Burns.[45]

Logan refused to subscribe to the view that Burns was an untaught poet of genius. Beginning in a caustic manner which anticipates the notorious opening of Jeffrey's 1809 review, he went on to draw attention —very inconveniently for Mackenzie's theory—to signs that Burns had read widely: 'In his serious poems we can trace imitations of almost every English author of celebrity.' Not content with that heresy, he dared to praise the 'Epistle to Rankine', 'in which [Burns] disguises an amour under the veil of partridge-shooting'. This can be contrasted with Hugh Blair's prim dismissal of the poem (No. 9). Logan's views may have been meant to startle opinion in Edinburgh, but he was able to argue coherently for his general estimate of Burns, which was vitiated only in part by his cynicism. His review remains of value because it shows a response to Burns which was stubbornly independent of reviewing fashion.

Writing in the *Monthly Review* in December 1786, James Anderson, like Logan, warned that Burns would not succeed in song-writing, although it was in that that he was destined to excel (No. 5). Anderson, as a student of agriculture, was particularly interested in Burns's descriptions of farming. His was a promising angle from which to approach the poems, one would think; but the resulting criticism is disappointingly general. However, he showed his professional interest amusingly at least when he reviewed the Edinburgh edition by choosing to comment only on 'John Barleycorn' because it contained an 'allegorical account of the whole progress and management of barley'. No other critic could then claim the distinction of reviewing two volumes by Burns. His warm recommendation cannot have gone unnoticed by the *Monthly*'s large and predominantly English reading-public.

There were few reviews of the 1787 edition, and that of 1793 does not seem to have attracted any. The absence of reviews certainly does not signify a lack of public enthusiasm for Burns, as all the other evidence points to a rapid growth of interest in his poetry. But in England his use of Lowland Scots was a serious obstacle, as the poet Cowper pointed out to his Scottish friend Samuel Rose (No. 15). To their credit, some poetry-lovers overcame that obstacle, even when they did not have Wordsworth's advantage of knowing intimately the speech of the north-west of England, which was in certain ways like Burns's Scots (No. 33e). It would be wrong to suppose that everyone was like Cowper's 'very sensible neighbour' in being '*quite ram-feezled*'.[46]

Another reason for the dearth of reviews of the 1787 and 1793 *Poems, chiefly in the Scottish Dialect* probably lies in the policy of William Creech and his London agents. Comment more favourable than Henry Mackenzie's was scarcely to be expected, and Creech was publisher for Mackenzie as well as for Burns. In advertisements he found a neat way of selling both authors at once:[47]

In a few days will be published, Price 6s. in Boards. Elegantly printed in one Volume, Octavo, Illustrated with the Head of the Author the Second Edition of *Poems Chiefly In The Scottish Dialect*. By Robert Burns. Printed for A. Strahan; T. Cadell, in the Strand; and W. Creech, in Edinburgh. N. B. For an account of Robert Burns, and of the Poems, vide *Lounger*, No. 97, vol. iii
Of the above Bookseller may be had,
1. The *Lounger*, By the author of the *Mirror*, 3 Vols. 9s. sewed.

2. The *Mirror*. A periodical Paper published at Edinburgh, 3 vols. 6th Edition, 7s.6d. sewed.
3. *The Man of Feeling*, 3s.

It is unlikely that Creech set out with the specific intention of procuring further reprints in magazines of Mackenzie's essay rather than new reviews of Burns, but that is what happened, and no doubt it suited him well enough. That Burns continued to use the title of the 1786 volume fostered the idea that the editions of 1787 and 1793 were merely re-issues of a book already published. In fact, he had included fresh poems in each edition. About these he was consulted by Creech.

The Edinburgh edition of 1787 contained, with other new material, 'Death and Doctor Hornbook', 'The Brigs of Ayr', 'A Winter Night', and 'Green Grow the Rashes, O'. These poems were not singled out for discussion by reviewers, although they were often reprinted, wholly or in part, in the 'Poetical Miscellanies' of magazines and newspapers. James Anderson, as already mentioned, drew attention to the merits of 'John Barleycorn'. Others who did not have his knowledge of the earlier edition naturally sought to give an idea of the collection as a whole, without paying special attention to the previously unpublished poems. The *Universal Magazine* may have pleased Creech by following up a respectful notice (written by someone whose Scottish geography was not strong—No. 11) with a reprinting of Mackenzie's essay, at the particular request of 'A Friend to Genius' at Eton.

The reviewer in the *Universal* noted 'beautiful sentiments' in the poems. It is not hard to guess at least one passage which he had in mind. Stanza IX of 'The Cotter's Saturday Night' was quoted in the *New Town and Country* and *General* magazines as being 'not only very elegant, but highly poetical'. 'The Cotter's Saturday Night' had established itself as Burns's most popular poem, and reviewers did not hesitate to choose this particular stanza as representative of Burns's best work. It was in English, and could be understood by all. Beyond that, however, these nine lines were enjoyed and admired as a moral summing up of the scene described in the poem. Similar tributes were paid by many critics and readers. Here, the difference in taste from the twentieth century is marked. (Recently, critics have found 'an artificial pose' and 'entirely unnecessary comment' in this part of the poem.[48]) In 1787, and for long afterwards, moralistic writing—however self-conscious—was approved and enjoyed. The reviewer in the *General*

Magazine who regretted that Burns's poems were 'chiefly in Scots' and went on to comment on the excellence of this stanza was typical of the prevailing taste of his age.

The earliest biographical notice of Burns published in a book (as distinct from a magazine) appeared in a *Catalogue of Five Hundred Celebrated Authors of Great Britain; the Whole arranged in Alphabetical Order* (1787):

BURNS, Robert. A ploughman in the county of Ayr in the kingdom of Scotland. He was introduced to notice by a paper in a periodical publication, called the *Lounger*, and his poems were published in the year 1787. Mr. Burns was upon the point of embarking for America, when he was prevented from executing his intention by a letter, exciting him to the further pursuit of his literary career, by doctor Blacklock.

Inaccuracies apart, the implication that Burns owed nearly everything to the *Lounger* and to Blacklock was significant. Many would expect much from a rustic poet for whom, as they were told, so much had been done. Already there were signs of hostility towards Burns and his poetry by a section of the public whose extreme conservatism in religious and moral matters placed them beyond the fringe of even the most eloquent appeal for tolerance. 'A Friend to Virtue' published in 1787 a chapbook parody of 'To a Daisy', which he introduced with this fiercely denunciatory comment:[49]

On reading Burns's poems, and some other productions in his defence, my feelings have been so shocked, that I should think it criminal not to contribute with the virtuous few who have already appeared on the side of injur'd truth.— It is certainly a very agreeable article of licentious faith, that although led astray by fierce passions and wild pleasures, 'Yet the light that led us astray is light from heaven' ... Such articles, together with the contaminating spirit that runs through this work, are calculated to do more injury to religion, and virtue, than all the atheistical, deistical, and heretical books that have been written this last century.

The next year there appeared James Maxwell's *Animadversions*, in which he attacked Burns and Lapraik in execrable verse (No. 17a). Neither of these ephemerae enjoyed national circulation, and for every rhymed lampoon on Burns there could be cited several rhymed tributes, like Helen Craik's of 1789 (No. 17b):

> Here native Genius, gay, unique and strong,
> Shines through each page, and marks the tuneful song.

But this early condemnation of Burns by some readers on moral and religious grounds shows the existence of a more widespread ethical conservatism, which needed only time and the assistance of rumour to emerge in strong criticism of the poet.[50] Tongues wagged about his private life, and eyebrows were raised. Class prejudice, and the echo of Burns's unguarded talk about revolutionary politics also played a part in the forming of disapproving attitudes to his work. Gossip was particularly rife in the months immediately following his death in 1796. Critics could point to an apparently authoritative account of Burns's later years which suggested that drink led to his death and that he neglected his family. George Thomson's widely reprinted obituary notice opened the floodgates (No. 21). Maria Riddell, a spirited friend of Burns, tried to close them again (No. 22), but in vain.

Thomson had never met Burns, but the world in general was not aware of this. In writing the obituary, he relied on imperfect memories of what he had heard about Burns, and on the poet's letters to him. The Kilmarnock edition was described as 'a coarse edition ... published at Dumfries'. In writing the passages which did most damage to the poet's reputation, he distorted the evidence of letters he had received from Burns only weeks before:

Probably he was not qualified to fill a superior station to that which was assigned him. We know that his manners refused to partake the polish of genteel society, that his talents were often obscured and finally impaired by excess, and that his private circumstances were embittered by pecuniary distress ... Like his predecessor Ferguson, though he died at an early age, his mind was previously exhausted; and the apprehensions of a distempered imagination concurred along with indigence and sickness to embitter the last moments of his life.

This part of Thomson's obituary shares with Mackenzie's essay the dubious distinction of being the most influential eighteenth-century contribution to Burns criticism. Like Mackenzie, Thomson sacrificed truth for an immediate object. His aim was to procure help for the widow of the poet and her family, and his appeal, like Mackenzie's sponsorship ten years before, had a welcome measure of success. Thomson had decided that the larger issue of justice to Burns's character would have to wait. It had to. And it was not until 1926, when Sir James Crichton-Brown published *Burns from a New Point of View*, that the poet's death was shown to have been caused by rheumatic fever and heart disease, not alcoholism.[51]

According to Thomson, Burns 'possessed in an extraordinary degree the powers and failings of genius'. This point of view, which quickly gained currency, was to remain dominant in Burns criticism throughout the ensuing period. The poet came to be seen as a figure of symbolic importance by admirers and detractors alike. Maria Riddell, emphasizing the power he displayed and the risks he took in conversation, described him as 'the child of nature, the child of sensibility'. Hers was a brave defence, offering a portrait of the man which was closer in spirit to his writings than that of any other contemporary. She compared him with Sterne, remarking that 'for every ten jokes he got an hundred enemies'.

The *Dumfries Journal*, in which Maria Riddell's 'Character Sketch' appeared, had naturally a particular interest in Burns, but other newspapers also printed essays and poems after his death. Burns had been 'the god of my idolatry' for Charles Lamb, and Lamb's friend Coleridge wrote a poem for a Bristol newspaper to raise money for the Burns family. In it he described Burns as 'Nature's own beloved bard', which is a further indication that the poet's achievement was rapidly acquiring general significance in relation to nature, genius, and morality. Nowhere is this symbolic status plainer than in the comments of Wordsworth (No. 33).

From 1796 criticism increased notably in volume. A tendency to assess Burns in terms of Nature and the theory of Genius, present from the beginning but now more pronounced, often took the place of discussion of particular poems. The essays which raise these wider questions contribute to the evolution of English romantic criticism. Of the other sort, Thomas Tudor Duncan's commentary on Burns has value because it is unusually specific (No. 25). Duncan was not writing as a professional critic; he knew the language and customs of the southwest of Scotland, and he had leisure to set down his opinions fully and freely. The order in which he treated various topics, and the conclusions he reached, throw light on the way in which Burns's poetry was read by a young educated Scotsman in the late eighteenth century.

Very different in approach was Robert Heron's *Memoir* in 1797 (No. 26). Though abler critically, it lacked Duncan's integrity. Heron's interest in Burns and his poems was of long standing, but he followed the lead given by Thomson's obituary and moralized fulsomely, dwelling with evident relish on every feature of the poet's life which he could interpret as a sign of decadence. The importance of this is that his was the first book-length biography, and it gave a further stimulus to the kind of interest which followed Burns's death. On the credit side,

Heron distinguished for the first time a number of the main influences
on the poet; suggested the relative roles in his poetry of common sense,
ardent feeling, morality, and pride; and grouped the poems in two
categories, the first pastorals, the second pieces upon common life and
manners. He preferred the first. The more strictly critical part of his
Memoir made for fuller understanding of both the poems and songs.

William Reid's 'Monody on the Death of Burns' has a prose introduction on Burns's life and poetry made up of extracts from Mackenzie's essay and Thomson's obituary (No. 27). This composite account
shows the fusion of two main parts of the critical tradition. The
'Monody' has an interest of another kind. Reid, a Glasgow bookseller
and devoted student of Burns, could not avoid echoing Thomson's
regret for Burns's 'decline'. But instinctive warmth, and also his feeling
for what is appropriate in the 'Standard Habbie' form raise the latter
part of the poem well above the level of what has gone before, and
produce a remarkable last stanza:

> The Winter nights I've cheer'd by turns,
> Wi' Ramsay, Fergusson, and Burns:
> The first twa cauld are in their urns,
> Their sauls at rest:
> Now weeping Caledonia mourns
> Him last and best.

This expresses admiration for the poet more aptly than many other
poems which were written in his memory during the period immediately after his death, such as William Roscoe's 'Rear high thy
bleak majestic hills', which James Currie included in his collected
edition in 1800. Only James Hogg's 'Sin' Robin's awa'' (No. 72),
written much later, succeeds as well as the 'Monody' in conveying
popular feeling in Scotland after Burns's death.

If Mackenzie and Thomson were responsible for a wrong emphasis
in eighteenth-century Burns criticism, much of the blame for per-
petuating this in the nineteenth century is to be attributed to James
Currie, who prepared the first collected edition of Burns (Liverpool,
1800) (No. 30). Currie had many merits, both as a man of medicine and
of letters. He has not lacked recent apologists who justify his method
of carrying out a task which he saw as primarily one of charity on
behalf of Burns's surviving relatives. R. D. Thornton, in particular, has
rallied to Currie's defence in a fully documented biography of this
'entire stranger' who produced an edition of Burns's poems which

remained the standard one for a quarter of a century. Thornton's impressive case for Currie's valour and honesty can be accepted, though with qualifications. Nevertheless, it is clear that Currie's hatred of alcohol (however understandable in the light of his experience) led him to imply wrongly that drink led to Burns's death. This confirmation of the Thomson-Heron account of Burns's later life naturally harmed the poet's reputation. It appeared to be doubly official as the version of an authorized biographer who was also medically qualified. Moreover, as Charles Lamb scathingly noted, Currie's powers as a writer were severely limited. The life of Burns and 'Observations on the character and conditions of the Scottish peasantry' in his edition were clear and informative, but lacked light and shade. In these sections of his work Currie showed almost too much detachment. The same is true of his 'Criticism on [Burns's] writings', a balanced, yet restricted summing-up of the poet's achievement.

Currie stressed the role of personality in Burns's poems, which he described as 'the effusions of his sensibility'. He was consistent in arguing this case, but gained the emphasis he sought at the cost of over-looking other merits:

If fiction be, as some suppose, the soul of poetry, no one had ever less pretensions to the name of poet than Burns.

Some critics were quick to dispute this. Their claim was that Burns showed invention, the ability to create characters and a situation; 'Tam o' Shanter' was cited as a poem displaying such fiction or invention. What was not refuted, however, was the implication in Currie's criticism that the place of technique in Burns's poetry was secondary. Currie's reading of the poems and songs as a direct record of experience ('the transcript of his own musings on the real incidents of his humble life') moulded the response of early nineteenth-century readers. It was based on sound observation of Burns's quality of spontaneous direct-ness as a poet. Currie recognized genius throughout, but craftsmanship only intermittently. What was due to art was ascribed to inspiration and to force of personality alone.

He drew attention to the combination of humour and tenderness in many of Burns's poems, and praised an important group, the epistles. These broad criticisms were supported by well-chosen illustrations, but were not developed. Currie also introduced several minor themes which were to be taken further by others, for instance the comparison of 'To a Mouse' with 'To a Mountain-Daisy', and of Fergusson's 'The

Farmer's Ingle' with 'The Cotter's Saturday Night'. He endorsed the
view that 'The Cotter's Saturday Night' was Burns's finest poem.

His edition included a large number of Burns's songs, which he
introduced with enthusiasm. He dwelt on Burns's descriptive art in the
songs, rather than on his phrasing or lyrical feeling. In common with
most of his contemporaries he lacked an appropriate critical language
for the subject. To stress Burns's pictorial qualities was natural in view of
inherited ideas about *Ut pictura poesis*, but it was often to miss the point.
On the other hand, what he wrote was direct and comprehensible: he
avoided the dangers of an over-sophisticated approach.[52] Pride in his
Scots nationality helped him to understand that Burns's purpose as a
song-writer had been patriotic. Of Burns's Scots he noted that 'in
pastoral or rural songs, it gives a Doric simplicity, which is very
generally approved'.

Currie's work on Burns broadened the scope of critical comment.
Robert Nares reviewed the edition in two articles in the *British Critic*,
and before long other periodical writers were noting his additions to
the Burns canon. That there was no sudden improvement in the quality
of their discussion, however, seems to be proved by 'T. L.'s 'Strictures
on the writings of Burns' in the *Monthly Register* in 1802. 'T. L.' had
failed to profit from Currie's remarks on Burns's language:

The greater part of his poems are written in the dialect of his country; a dialect,
the least fault of which is, that to every one, except Scotsmen, it is wholly unintelligible. It is true, indeed, that many of the Highland words, having something of simplicity, and occasionally even of strength, are sometimes more
expressive of pastoral imagery, than the more refined dialect of the English.
The terminations, however, of many of the words, having fewer consonants,
are better adapted to the music of poetry. Such are the words 'brae', for the
banks of a river, 'burnie', and many others of the same kind, terminating with
the soft vowels *i* and *e*. But this observation cannot be extended to all, for
surely some of these words, such as 'grounche', 'gutter', 'gowk', and 'gryse',
are such as the muse of poetry would not be very pleased to adopt, and which
none but a Scotsman could undertake to utter. By words like these, the earlier
poems of Burns are not merely defaced, but rendered unintelligible to the
English reader.

This article contained some sweeping and absurd dismissals:

It is not injustice to the Scotch to assert, that in all the long period of their
history, previous to the union, they can scarcely produce one author of pre-
eminent genius, and, with the exception of Boethius and Buchanan, not one
poet.

But 'T.L.' was provocative, both here and subsequently when he compared Burns with Butler, and asserted that 'Tam o' Shanter' (which he described as being 'precisely in the style of Butler') was the second-best poem Burns wrote. The best, he thought, was 'The Cotter's Saturday Night'. Its faults were that it was[53]

too long, and frequently, though less than his other poems, disfigured by the Scotch accent.

He quoted 'it's most beautiful stanza'—the ninth!

In contrast to this patronizing essayist came 'W', who contributed 'General Remarks on the Life and Character of Burns' to the *Scots Magazine* in 1802, and set out to describe the links between Fergusson and Burns that Currie, and Burns himself, had noted. He was not able to complete his work, possibly because the magazine changed editors after his second article had appeared. Like many later readers, 'W' found that the comparison with Fergusson was not always in Burns's favour.

Fergusson was also mentioned by Alexander Chalmers in his introduction to an edition of Burns (1804) which proved very popular, although it did not rival Currie's in authority. Chalmers claimed that Burns surpassed Ramsay and Fergusson, 'by the flights of the sublime and terrible', as well as in humour. David Irving, in a short biography of Burns (1804), saw a general superiority in his poetry over his eighteenth-century Scottish predecessors:

he possesses in an infinitely higher degree the power of captivating the heart, and of arresting the understanding.

He noted 'the arch simplicity, the delicacy, pathos, and even sublimity' of the songs (No. 34).

Cowper had died in 1800, and several commentators on Burns pointed to parallels and contrasts between the poets. Nares, in his review of Currie published in October 1800, was one of the first to make a general statement about their distinction:

among British poets of the end of the eighteenth century, [posterity] may indeed hesitate between Burns and Cowper; but will see no other competitors for the throne of poetical genius. We confine this observation to the dead. The claims of the living cannot yet be determined with perfect impartiality.

Those who wrote at length about Burns and Cowper included Sir Egerton Brydges in 1805 (No. 36), and Josiah Walker in 1811 (No. 45).

Their attempts at comparative appraisal drew attention to significant differences as well as to points of similarity between the two poets. But humour, and a conversational style in poetry, were neglected as topics of criticism. Lamb, who enjoyed both authors, had commented with tantalizing brevity on Cowper and Burns in 1796 (No. 24). Unfortunately, he did not return to the theme.

Of the English poets who knew Burns's work by the first decade of the nineteenth century, Wordsworth and Coleridge were alone in expressing admiration both in prose and verse. Crabbe's son writing of his father says:[54]

Of Burns he was ever as enthusiastic an admirer as the warmest of his own countrymen

—but no comment on Burns by Crabbe has survived. Southey grudged Burns his eminence, and drily scoffed at poetic Scots as an artificial language, 'a sort of Rowleyism' (No. 35b). The half-Scottish Byron was doubtful of whether Burns's fame was deserved, as can be seen in the humour of a passage in *English Bards and Scotch Reviewers* (No. 38), which calls to mind Burns's own remark in a letter of 1789,[55]

my success has encouraged such a shoal of ill-spawned monsters to crawl into public notice, under the title of Scots Poets, that the very term, Scots Poetry, borders on the burlesque.

Although the quality of his poem was uneven, Byron's pride was unmistakable. His outburst

Swains! quit the plough, resign the useless spade!

has something in common with 'The Twa Dogs' in the Kilmarnock edition, with its jests about a young man of fashion:

> At Operas an' Plays parading,
> Mortgaging, gambling, masquerading:
> Or maybe, in a frolic daft,
> To HAGUE or CALAIS takes a waft,
> To mak a *tour* an' tak a whirl,
> To learn *bon ton* an' see the worl'.

Appropriately, Byron was to write many years later about Burns's 'antithetical mind' and of the disparity between his rank as a poet and

the rank of his productions (Nos 49, 61). These two casual but very
penetrating criticisms came from an author not without some Calvinist
training himself, who perhaps recognized in Burns characteristics
he was well placed to understand.

In this earlier period, however, only the poets of *Lyrical Ballads*
paid tribute to Burns in print; and of the two the more consistently
outspoken was Wordsworth. Coleridge was indebted to Lamb and then
to Wordsworth for the stimulus to read Burns. He showed little interest
in Burns's more robust humour or in his love songs.[56] His admiration,
like De Quincey's, almost appears to arise from a sense of duty to his
literary friends or from fashion—rather than from enjoyment. He was,
however, unlike De Quincey in praising Currie, whose acquaintance he
made in 1800 (No. 23c). It may be that Burns's Scots deterred him.
His most important comment on Burns (No. 23f) was made in the
Friend in 1809, and was later repeated in *Biographia Literaria*:

it is the prime merit of genius, and its most unequivocal mode of manifestation,
so to represent familiar objects as to awaken in the minds of others a kindred
feeling concerning them, and that freshness of sensation which is the constant
accompaniment of mental no less than of bodily convalescence.

The illustration from 'Tam o' Shanter' which immediately followed
was often repeated elsewhere in his writings. His linking of Burns's
name with Wordsworth's in this passage is significant both as a major
critical comparison and as an indication that Wordsworth's judgment
of Burns had influenced his own. The clearest evidence for this second
point is Wordsworth's remark to him in a letter of 1799 (No. 29):
'The communications that proceed from Burns come to the mind
with the life and charm of recognitions.'

Wordsworth's praise was passionately sincere. While still in his
teens he had recommended the Kilmarnock edition to his sister (No.
16); and the fervour of Dorothy's description of their visit to Burns's
grave in 1803 is matched by his own urgent tone, in the poems which
he wrote as a result of the visit, and in his later prose (Nos 33, 53, 70).
He never disguised the fact that he saw Burns as a pioneer:

Now I find no manners in Burger; in Burns you have manners everywhere
(1799) ... I thought of Chatterton, the marvellous Boy/, The sleepless Soul
that perished in his pride;/Of Him who walked in glory and in joy/Following
his plough, along the mountain-side;/By our own spirits are we deified (1802)
... [He] showed my youth/How Verse may build a princely throne On humble

truth (1803) . . .Who, but some impenetrable dunce or narrow-minded puritan
in works of art, ever read without delight the picture which he has drawn of the
. . . rustic adventurer, Tam o'Shanter (1816) . . . Familiarity with the dialect of
the counties of Cumberland and Westmorland made it easy for me not only
to understand [Burns's poems] but to feel them (1842).

Affirmations such as these convince one that Wordsworth's basic and
lasting response to Burns's poetry was reverential. This did not prevent
him from appreciating certain sides of Burns's humour, despite his
own habitual seriousness.[57] His comment on the landlord's life in
'Tam o' Shanter' ('conjugal fidelity archly bends to the service of
general benevolence') deserved Lamb's praise; and he also attempted,
unusually, to analyse the comic skill displayed in Burns's first tale,
'Death and Doctor Hornbook'. Wordsworth's criticism of Burns
throws light on both poets. There remains a challenge in his statement,

Tam Shanter I do not deem a character, I question whether there is any individual character in all Burns' writings except his own,

and in the variation,

On the basis of his human character he has reared a poetic one.

Moreover, in his *Letter to a Friend of Burns*, he wrote about the need to
make the biography of authors secondary to literary discussion:

Our business is with their books,—to understand and to enjoy them.

It was to take a century for the majority of Burns's critics to catch up
with the implications of this remark.

Whereas Wordsworth's chief interest was in Burns's poems, Thomas
Moore recognized in his contribution to Scottish song something which
he wished to emulate in his own *Irish Melodies*. Moore's admiration for
Burns was made clear in the letter he wrote to Sir John Stevenson in
1807 when a plan for the *Irish Melodies* had first been proposed to him.
He was later to enlarge on the subject of his relationship to Burns
as a national song-writer in a wide-ranging essay on the art of song
(No. 37b).

Though Burns was thus recognized as a poetic forerunner by Wordsworth and Moore, it was his moral character that continued to be the
principal subject of discussion in Edinburgh. The publication of R. H.

Cromek's *Reliques of Robert Burns* drew from two Edinburgh writers, Francis Jeffrey and Walter Scott, important review-articles which were to have a marked effect on Burns criticism in the following decade (Nos 39, 40). Their literary criticism of his poems and songs was more acute than any that had yet appeared; but it was the explicit and severe moral censure in their essays which caught the attention of most readers.

Jeffrey was given to the dramatic first and last paragraph. His linking of Burns's name with Stephen Duck and Thomas Dermody gave offence in itself; and the tone of his opening commentary must have appeared patronizing in the extreme to those admirers of Burns who did not share the social values of professional and literary Edinburgh. He was no less provocative at the end of the article, where he used the example of Burns's unforced, natural language as a stick with which to beat Wordsworth, whose poetic theory and practice he intensely disliked. As the essay also contained a fierce attack on Burns's alleged lack of chivalry and on his 'perpetual boast of his own independence', its character was quite sensational. Jeffrey's criticism of Burns has been aptly described by David Nichol Smith as 'the most coldly discriminating that has been written by a fellow-countryman'.[58]

Other aspects of his article are noteworthy: his deduction that Burns, though widely read, was not inhibited as a poet by too much learning; his discussion of the poet's humour, powers of description, pathos, and ability in penetrating human character; his argument supporting the opinion that Burns's Scots poetry is better than his English; and finally his eloquent, informed response to the songs. Jeffrey gives a clearly reasoned account of his enthusiasm for Burns's writings and as a critic of Burns he is decisive:

Add to all this, that it is the language of a great body of poetry, with which almost all Scotchmen are familiar; and, in particular, of a great multitude of songs, written with more tenderness, nature, and feeling, than any other lyric compositions that are extant, and we may perhaps be allowed to say, that the Scotch is, in reality, a highly poetical language; and that it is an ignorant, as well as an illiberal prejudice, which would seek to confound it with the barbarous dialects of Yorkshire or Devon.

Readers are left in no doubt about his meaning or about the importance of the subject. Jeffrey's confidence and clarity lend to his criticism an incisiveness which is absent from more temperate essays.

Scott was uniquely qualified to write about Burns's poems and songs. His many remarks in letters and reviews form a considerable body of reminiscence, biographical speculation, and literary criticism, which spans the first thirty years of the nineteenth century. This commentary includes a brief tribute to Burns's skill in emending folksong; a mellow, vividly written account of his meeting with Burns; two comparisons between Burns and Byron, which were not published until after Scott's death; and—his most influential estimate of Burns—the review article on Cromek's *Reliques* in the first number of the *Quarterly Review* in 1809 (No. 40).

In his *Quarterly* essay, Scott described Burns as 'the child of passion and feeling', unquestionably inspired, but lacking essential self-discipline, and in his last years thoroughly dissipated. He took care to explain that there were extenuating circumstances, such as poverty and the lack of political tolerance shown by the men above Burns in the Excise: but he did not question that the poet's later years were degraded, and he held Burns to have been directly responsible for his fate.

There are many adjustments in the essay, which show Scott attempting to strike a just balance. The order of his praise and blame is significant in establishing his complex but austere judgment of Burns the man. In general, criticism of a moral kind tends to dominate. On the first page, for example, Scott writes ruefully of what he takes to be a major truth concerning Burns:

The extravagance of genius with which this wonderful man was gifted, being in his later and more evil days directed to no fixed or general purpose, was, in the morbid state of his health and feelings, apt to display itself in hasty sallies of virulent and unmerited severity: sallies often regretted by the bard himself; and of which, justice to the living and to the dead, alike demanded the suppression.

The rather contorted final clause may be a symptom of inner tension between Scott's literary instinct and his social conscience, but he decides calmly enough to endorse Currie's view that most of Burns's satirical poems should remain unpublished. Indeed, this passage calls to mind that one of Scott's favourite poems was Johnson's *Vanity of Human Wishes*, sombre in tone and profoundly conservative in its moral and religious outlook. Burns, like 'Swedish Charles' in that poem, had

> ... left the name at which the world grew pale,
> To point a moral, or adorn a tale.

It was impossible for Scott to overlook the grim lesson which, he felt, was to be learned from the fate of Burns. Scott's upbringing, his closeness to strict Edinburgh society, his belief in the moral influence of famous example; all these led him to present an unflattering picture of Burns as a man who forgot the responsibilities of genius.

The essay is valuable for its commendation of 'The Jolly Beggars', which had not been included in Currie's edition. In two minor ways, Scott's criticism of the Cantata is curious. He borrowed without acknowledgment from the first publisher of the poem (No. 32) a sentence which was often to be quoted as his own by later critics:

The Jolly Beggars, for humorous description and nice discrimination of character, is inferior to no poem of the same length in the whole range of English poetry.

Moreover, he pretended to write as an Englishman ('doubtless our northern brethren are more familiar . . .'). It is significant that while he mentioned 'Holy Willie's Prayer' as another able poem, which like 'The Jolly Beggars', had not been included in the collected edition, he did not press for this in editions of Burns:

The Cantata already mentioned, is indeed the only one of his productions not published by Dr. Currie, which we consider as not merely justifying, but increasing his renown.

Scott's different attitude to these two poems proves that, while he was fully capable of appreciating both, he could not approve the republication of anything likely to offend against religion. He recognized the 'exquisitely severe' satirical skill of 'Holy Willie's Prayer', but did not commend it as strongly as the Cantata, which presented so radical a criticism of society that it could be enjoyed by Scott and his contemporaries as indulgence in sheer fantasy.

The judicial habit also affects his discussion of Burns's songs. In this essay, his warm admiration breaks out in several places, most notably in the remark that the stanza 'Had we never loved sae kindly . . .' 'contains the essence of a thousand love tales'. And yet Scott's preconceptions prevent him from seeing that Burns's songs were much more important than the 'grand plan of dramatic composition' from which they diverted him. All he can do is make two statements, which are left unreconciled: songs count for comparatively little, but Burns wrote brilliant songs:

this constant waste of his fancy and power of verse in small and insignificant compositions, must necessarily have had no little effect in deterring him from undertaking any grave or important task. Let no one suppose that we undervalue the songs of Burns. When his soul was intent on suiting a favourite air

with words humorous or tender, as the subject demanded, no poet of our
tongue ever displayed higher skill in marrying melody to immortal verse.

Such high praise, offered in spite of his own adverse judgment, can
be compared with a sudden insight recorded in his *Journal* at a time of
personal crisis (11 December 1826).[59]

Long life to thy fame and peace to thy soul, Rob Burns! When I want to express
a sentiment which I feeel strongly, I find the phrase in Shakespeare—or thee.

It is the conflict between Scott's sensibilities and his inherited values
which gives extraordinary interest to his criticism of Burns.

Like Jeffrey, Scott was sound in his comment on Burns's Scots. He
drew attention to a letter in Scots from Burns to William Nicol, and
remarked that the attempt to read a sentence of it 'would break the teeth
of most modern Scotchmen'. This well-chosen illustration of Burns's
knowledge of spoken Scots followed a general assessment of his use of
English and Scots in poetry, which clarified an important issue in
criticism:

although in these flights he naturally and almost unavoidably assumed the
dialect of Milton and Shakespeare, he never seems to have been completely at
his ease when he had not the power of descending into what was familiar to his
ear, and to his habits. In the one case, his use of the English was voluntary, and
for a short time; but when assumed as a primary and indispensable rule of composition, the comparative penury of rhimes, and the want of a thousand emphatic
words which his habitual acquaintance with the Scottish supplied, rendered his
expression confined and embarrassed.

Criticism such as this goes to the heart of the matter, while at the same
time throwing light on Scott's own practice as a creative writer.

The topic of language was also considered by other reviewers of
Cromek's *Reliques*. John Hodgson in the *Monthly Review* took an
entirely different line from Scott, judging Burns's 'best performances'
to be those 'in the purest English', or, if not, in 'Anglo-Scottish'
(No. 43). In the *Eclectic Review*, James Montgomery distinguished
different elements in Burns's Scots, and produced what he rightly
called 'a curious and in some respects a novel view of a very interesting
subject', a theory that the poet's language was nearly always artificially
formed (No. 42):

what is now called the Scottish is in fact only a *written* language; there is not a
poem of Burns (the *mere*, not *pure*, English ones excepted) composed in a
dialect spoken by any class of men in our whole island.

33

Montgomery demonstrated his theory by examples from Burns. If his appraisal of particular poems had been as original as his approach to linguistic matters, his essay would rival those of Jeffrey and Scott in importance. Unfortunately, a rigid puritanism led him to object even to 'Tam o' Shanter', while his conviction that Burns 'stabs at the very heart of religion through the sides of hypocrisy' prevented him from even naming a large group of poems, let alone considering their merits.

Criticism of popular poets occurs in unexpected contexts. In 1809 William Mudford devoted a chapter to Burns in his fictionalized treatise on morals, society, and literature, *Nubilia in Search of a Husband*. It is as well that Mudford pointed out in his preface that he was deliberately experimenting with an elevated prose style. Otherwise, what could one make of an author who wrote that Burns was 'one of the few great geniuses . . . to illuminate the hemisphere of mind'? Mudford's opinions on the poems reflect the consensus of judgment in his day. He was more concerned to defend the principle of independence by which Burns had lived than to enter into detailed discussion of poetry. His position was weakened by concessions to moralizing, but he did take issue with earlier writers, including George Thomson.

IV

1811–1837

It was in the decade 1810–1820 that the practice of celebrating the birth of Burns on 25 January became widely established. There were already several societies of Burns enthusiasts in different parts of Britain.[60] In 1811 the thriving Greenock Burns Club became the object of a clumsy attack in verse by Dr William Peebles, who had been mocked by Burns in 'The Twa Herds', 'The Holy Fair' and 'The Kirk's Alarm'. Peebles, who could not tolerate the thought that men were now meeting to honour the poet's memory, poured scorn on what he called 'Burno-mania' (No. 46). His remonstrance went unheeded. People genuinely enjoyed reading Burns's poems, and his songs were extremely popular. He was held to have written of love in an incomparable way. There were, too, strong patriotic, political, and social reasons for his fame. The author of 'Scots Wha Hae' had pride in Scotland, and that woke pride in others, including exiles. His belief in the equality of man struck a responsive chord, not only among his fellow-Scots, but wherever revolutionary concepts of freedom and brotherhood were held. He had understood the poor and underprivileged, and became known as 'the poet of the people'. Moreover, Burns had written about country life in an age of progressive industrialization which had meant constant movement from the land to large towns and cities. He was 'the poet of nature' as distinct from the sophistication of urbanized materialism and, as such, evoked yearning for what was passing.

These things had much to do with the spread of Burns Clubs and 'Burnomania'. Their effect can be clearly seen not only in the written criticism of the period, but in reports of early Burns Club oratory, of subscription dinners, and of proposals to erect statues.

Josiah Walker contributed to an 1811 edition of Burns a long 'account of his life and character', which was also separately published (No. 45). He had the advantage of having met the poet, and the result of this was a stronger than average interest in every scrap of information concerning Burns's poetry. But Walker was too hidebound by conventional ideas to assess Burns's character in a new way. He quoted with evident approval Hugh Blair's snobbish remark that the poet's politics 'had too much of the smith's shop' about them; and many of his own comments are condescending. However, his criticism of the poems and songs goes into unusual detail. He was one of the first critics to draw attention to the effect of particular words, such as 'hirplin' in the opening passage of 'The Holy Fair':

Of all the terms which any language affords, few could so significantly express the peculiar motion of the hare, when she moves with caution, but without alarm, as the word *hirplin*. In this manner language is extended. A number of words which are little else than synonimes, to persons who are at no pains, or who have no power to define and discriminate, convey to one more anxious for the enjoyment produced by variety and precision of thought, different shades of significance, which he separates with ease. He afterwards employs them to express the meaning which they had conveyed to himself, and they come by his authority and adoption to be legitimated. In almost every page of Burns we may find examples of unusual skill in his choice of words.

Walker supported this contention with varied examples of Burns's skill in words, and of his gifts for metaphor. Walker's discussion of 'Death and Doctor Hornbook' and of 'A Winter Night' was equalled by parts of his commentary on the songs. He grasped that as a song-writer Burns could 'show the whole state of mind by a single experience'.

His suggestion that Burns's art showed little progressive development was to prove influential.

Walker's views were frequently quoted in George Gleig's *A Critique on the Poems of Robert Burns*, published anonymously in Edinburgh in 1812 (No. 47). This was the first, and for a long time the only book exclusively concerned with Burns's poetry. Its appearance twelve years after the first collected edition, and fifteen years after the first biography, points to an order of priority in Burns studies which has seldom changed: there has been a time lag between interest in the man and editorial scholarship, and a longer one between editing and criticism. The author of the *Critique* pointed out that his aim was to satisfy a demand for guidance on the part 'of the country gentleman, the farmer, the artisan, and all those who have moved in the same sphere with the poet': 'Nothing like philosophical criticism' was to be looked for in his book. His was a guidebook, and probably a very popular one. Even when allowance is made for this, the description of Burns as 'an illiterate bard' reveals—and no doubt caused—fundamental confusion. There is critical value, however, in the judgment of 'The Vision', and the author's confirmation that, at this date, 'The Cotter's Saturday Night' was 'universally felt as the most interesting of all [Burns's] poems' is of historical importance.

The author of the *Critique* had sought to enumerate 'the beauties of Burns'. This was a common approach, and poems were often selected for praise on moral grounds alone. Moral judgment at work can be illustrated from the Revd E. Mangin's *View of the Pleasures arising from a Love of Books: in Letters to a Lady* (1814), where 'To a Mountain Daisy' is commended as 'the most faultless and most delightful of all his effusions'. Mangin clearly chose this poem for its 'strain of moral melancholy' and the lesson to be drawn from its reference to the 'artless maid' and the bard apprehensive about his fate. The habit of representing Burns only by inoffensive poems was to grow—influenced, probably, by Thomas Bowdler's publication of his *Family Shakespeare* in 1818. In the Victorian period, it became a very common practice of editors and critics alike.

The next significant episode in the history of Burns's reputation illustrates Coleridge's claim in *Biographia Literaria* that the founding of the *Edinburgh Review* marked 'an important epoch in periodical criticism'. Jeffrey's long essay, and Scott's in the *Quarterly*, proved so influential that several admirers of Burns's poetry published articles defending the poet from the *Edinburgh* and *Quarterly* reviewers specifically. Josiah Walker's *Account of the Life and Character of Robert Burns* contained 'Remarks on Two Late Reviews of the Works of Burns', an anonymous attempt to free Burns's name from 'acrimonious and exaggerated strictures'. In 1815 Alexander Peterkin published his *Review of the Life of Robert Burns, and of Various Criticisms on his Character and Writings*. Peterkin wrote indignantly (No. 51), detected snobbery in the accusation that Burns lacked chivalry, and attacked what he saw as the false moralistic drift of criticism since Currie. Much of his essay was taken up with point-by-point refutation of alleged errors of fact or emphasis in the biographical commentaries of Currie, Irving, Jeffrey, Scott and Walker. He stated his conclusions boldly. Far from being pernicious, Burns's works were 'eminently friendly to good morals'. And Burns had been 'cruelly wronged'. Neither as man nor as poet had he been fairly judged.

Although he did not consider Burns's poetry in detail, Peterkin succeeded in showing that an adequate critical response to it could only be based on a humane (as distinct from fault-finding) approach to Burns's life and poetry. His defence of the poet is an important document because its broad implications included a rejection of moral fault-finding. Peterkin understood that a grudging attitude to literature brings niggardly rewards. He found a ready sympathizer in Wordsworth (No. 53), who was impressed also by the letters Peterkin printed from Gilbert Burns, James Gray, and others who had known Burns and who agreed that Currie's life was unjust. The theme of Wordsworth's *Letter to a Friend of Robert Burns* (1816), summed up in his comment to John Scott,

All men ought to be judged with charity and forbearance after death has put it out of their power to explain the motives of their actions, and especially men of acute sensibility and lively passions,

is closely related to this part of Peterkin's argument (p. 270) about the habit of traducing Burns:

It matters little, whether this evil has arisen from credulity, misinformation, or malicious purpose. It is fit that the error should be corrected,—not merely because it is fair that the dead as well as the living should have justice in every individual instance but because the general interests of society and literature are outraged, if calumny is permitted, in such a case, to circulate in triumphant dogmatism. By calumny we mean injurious accusation without proof. And if ever calumny of the most dastardly kind poisoned public opinion, it has been in the case of Burns.

'The dead as well as the living should have justice.' Wordsworth's main purpose was to render justice to Burns, and he went a considerable way towards realizing it. He was helped by his recognition that Burns's poetry must have the central place when his contribution to literature and society was discussed. But Wordsworth was also anxious to rebut the sweeping criticisms that Jeffrey had brought against his own poetry in his 1809 essay on Burns and in other articles in the *Edinburgh Review*. Inevitably, the section of this pamphlet dealing with 'justice to the living' attracted most notice.

Wordsworth complained that 'the narrow range of [Jeffrey's] comprehension' made him unfit to assess major poetry. This dismissal soon provoked a bitter reply from Hazlitt, Wordsworth's former friend and shrewd critic (No. 56), and a series of self-contradictory pseudonymous articles from John Wilson, another sometime intimate of the Wordsworth household who, unlike Hazlitt, still professed friendship (No. 55). Hazlitt wrote with characteristic honesty, spleen, and brilliance. His way of showing his enthusiasm for 'The Cotter's Saturday Night', for instance, was at once original and direct:

Burns has given the extremes of licentious eccentricity and convivial enjoyment, in the story of this scape-grace [Tam o' Shanter], and of patriarchal simplicity and gravity in describing the old national character of the Scottish peasantry. 'The Cotter's Saturday Night' is a noble and pathetic picture of human manners, mingled with a fine religious awe. It comes over the mind like a slow and solemn strain of music.

The epistles were singled out for praise, which was fitting in view of Hazlitt's stress on Burns's ordinary humanity. Yet the caustic baiting of Wordsworth, which so infuriated Henry Crabb Robinson (No. 48e), detracts from the value of Hazlitt's lecture. There is particular value, therefore, in his comment on Burns in *Select British Poets* (1824), where he does not indulge in invidious comparisons:

One might be tempted to write an elegy rather than a criticism on him. In naïveté, in spirit, in characteristic humour, in vivid description of natural objects and of the natural feelings of the heart, he has left behind him no superior.

Hazlitt here summed up the feelings of more than one generation.

John Wilson had substantial talents, among them a flair for rhetorical utterance and for literary buffoonery, but he had little of Hazlitt's honesty. He was the most plausible periodical writer of the day, and is

a key figure in the process of deterioration in Scottish literary culture
which in the Victorian period was to lead to domination by 'Kailyard'
novelists and poetasters. He and John Gibson Lockhart became
unofficial editors of *Blackwood's Edinburgh Magazine* soon after its
inception in 1817.[61] *Blackwood's* enjoyed wide sales both in Scotland
and England because it contained livelier material than other literary
magazines—even although vicious personal lampooning of such butts
as Scottish Whigs and 'Cockney poets' was a staple element of its
liveliness. Beginning with his articles on Wordsworth and Burns, several
of Wilson's contributions to Burns criticism are represented in this
book (Nos. 55, 59 and 69), on the ground that his views were very
influential, particularly in Scotland, whether given as those of Professor
Wilson, 'Christopher North', or one of his many minor aliases. Wilson
sentimentalized Burns for a new age as thoroughly as Mackenzie
had done in 1786. He made much of nationality, and minimized any
implications in Burns's writings which might disturb conservative
imaginations. There are valuable chance remarks even when his
chicanery is most in evidence, and for that reason alone he cannot
be ignored, but his chief importance is as a representative of a set of
attitudes which strongly affected later Burns criticism. Maurice Lindsay
has written recently,[62]

When cheese is processed, richness of flavour and tang of texture disappear.
What is left is a smooth, tasteless substance, which may be easily spread and
which could not possibly offend the dullest palate. The object of most of Burns's
nineteenth-century editors and commentators was to turn the rich Dunlop of
his life and work into a processed product acceptable to Church and State, and
sufficiently characterless and colourless to enable him to occupy with absolute
decorum the niche of National Bard prepared for him.

Wilson's criticism was of this sort.

Into her last, uncompleted novel *Sanditon* Jane Austen introduced a
passage of dialogue parodying dishonest bluster about Burns (No. 54).
Mirroring the terms of the genius-morality debate accurately, she
subtly reinforced a conservative view of genius by exposing an incoherent rhapsodist ('It were Hyper-criticism, it were Pseudo-philosophy
...') to delicate raillery which reaches its climax in the dismissal
'The Wind I fancy must be Southerly.' Her incidental criticism that
Scott's poetry lacks passion enriches the humour. More neatly than
any sermonizing, the words 'He felt & he wrote & he forgot' convey
qualified liking for Burns's poetry.

Keats's admiration for Burns was robust, and is linked with his dislike of puritanism and the doctrine of thrift as it was forced upon the poor. The letter he wrote to his brother Tom after visiting Burns's tomb shows instinctive antipathy to the pressures in society against which Burns rebelled (No. 57a), while at the same time varying the social criticism expressed three months earlier in *Isabella*:

All I can do is by plump contrasts—Were the fingers made to squeeze a guinea or a white hand? Were the Lips made to hold a pen or a kiss?

Keats's outlook was frankly sensuous, like Burns's own, and the statement that he would sooner be a wild deer or hog than submit to 'the dominion of the kirk' recalls Burns's declaration,[63]

There are only two creatures that I would envy.—A horse in his wild state traversing the forests of Asia,—and an oyster on some of the desert shores of Europe.

Keats anticipated Wordsworth's surprise that Burns was not tempted by the mountains of Arran to extend the scope of his descriptive writings. He felt acutely that Burns was miserable ('We can see horribly clear in the works of such a man his whole life, as if we were God's spies'). In 1819 he was outraged by Wilson's attempt in *Blackwood's* (No. 59) to 'puff' James Hogg by comparing his poetry with Burns's. Implied in his outburst 'The senseless villains' is concern for the living as well as the dead. Hogg's talent was being exploited by *Blackwood's*, while Keats had suffered abuse at the hands of Lockhart.

Lockhart could be as unscrupulous as Wilson in manipulating facts, and in using pseudonyms for dubious ends; but his criticism of Burns is free from the taint of his worst style of writing in *Blackwood's*. The reader of his *Life of Burns* must notice F. B. Snyder's words of warning,[64]

The best that one can say of it ... is that it occasioned Carlyle's review. It is inexcusably inaccurate from beginning to end, at times demonstrably mendacious, and should never be trusted in any respect or detail.

Lockhart's general literary ability, however, is as noteworthy as his handling of the biographical record is unreliable. This is evident from a contrast between Burns and Crabbe in *Peter's Letters to His Kinsfolk* (No. 58), in which he seeks to define Burns's way of identifying himself with his subject in 'The Jolly Beggars'. Burns, he suggests, viewed his beggars from within the group, whereas Crabbe writes of the poor like 'a firm though humane Justice of the Peace'. The *Life of Burns* provides many further examples of Lockhart's ability to penetrate to essentials. He is particularly good on the satires. His understanding of Burns's place in Scottish literary history is exceptional for this date, and, almost alone among early critics, he can convincingly relate the poems and songs to a broad background of Scottish and English literature. Lockhart was the author of *John Bull's Letter to Lord Byron*, a discriminating essay on *Don Juan*. His Burns criticism shows a similar distinction of thought and expression. It is significant that he should refer to Byron's observation that Burns's rank as a poet was entirely different 'from the rank of his productions'. Ignoring the old neo-classic theory of kinds, Lockhart takes his stand as an empirical critic:

That is poetry of the highest order, which exerts influence of the most powerful order on the hearts and minds of mankind.

For good measure, he produces an argument to show the inadequacy of Dr Johnson's appraisal of pastoral. His evidence is Burns's poetry.

While the quality of Lockhart's work makes it stand out, several other Scots-born writers contributed significantly in this period to the continuously expanding discussion of Burns. Among them, Thomas Campbell offered a sensible defence against Jeffrey, praising certain poems in a forthright manner (No. 60); James Hogg championed Burns both in conversations which were re-created in *Blackwood's* series 'Noctes Ambrosianae' and elsewhere (Nos 69, 72); and Allan Cunningham, in addition to linking a description of the funerals of Burns and Byron, started to develop criticism of the songs based on knowledge—not always exact—of Burns's local sources of inspiration (Nos 65, 71). The diversity of approach shown by these three writers proves that, while there was general agreement in Scotland about Burns's quality as a poet, many aspects of his work were only beginning to be explored.[65]

It was in a review of Lockhart's *Life of Burns* by Carlyle that one Scottish tradition in criticism of Burns found its fullest expression (No. 67). This long essay was yet another reply to Jeffrey, who included it in the *Edinburgh Review*—prompted by a mood which combined renewed confidence in his own judgment, exasperation at Carlyle's Germanic English, and a measure of contrition. Carlyle saw Burns's life as tragic, and followed Scott in holding the poet ultimately responsible for his fate. His essential message was simple and severe:

Burns took neither his calling as a poet nor his duties in life seriously
enough. With this may be compared a statement at the beginning of
Scott's 1812 fragment of Autobiography (which Carlyle could not
have seen):[66]

From the lives of some poets a most important moral lesson may doubtless be
derived, and few sermons can be read with so much profit as the Memoirs of
Burns, of Chatterton, or of Savage.

Carlyle's sense of mission led him to enunciate the moral lesson he
found in the life of Burns in stark terms. But if parts of his lay sermon
now appear to be over-zealous, his aim was to speak the truth in love;
and the evidence is present throughout of his love of Burns's writings,
as well as of his indignation at the poet's sufferings.

He began by admitting that it was hard to 'measure [Burns] by any
true standard', a point which was to be taken up fifty years later by
Matthew Arnold. Burns, in Carlyle's opinion, had possessed unlimited
potential, but it was never fulfilled. He should be assessed for the spirit
of his writings, his 'indispensable air of Trust', rather than in terms of
craftsmanship. The imperfections of his work made such an approach
necessary, and it was also clear that his poetry received its distinctive
quality from his life and character, and not from art:

Never in one instance was it permitted him to grapple with any subject with the
full collection of his strength, to fuse and mould it in the concentrated fire of
his genius. To try by the strict rules of Art such imperfect fragments, would be
at once unprofitable and unfair . . . We can look on but few of these pieces as, in
strict critical language, deserving the name of Poems: they are rhymed eloquence, rhymed pathos, rhymed sense; yet seldom essentially melodious, aerial,
poetical.

Carlyle here draws attention to an important truth about Burns, the
unusual degree to which his poetry depends on the projection of his
personality. But it was misleading to suggest that poems can be satis-
factorily discussed except as works of art, and equally confusing to
maintain that Burns's poetry consisted exceptionally of 'imperfect
fragments' which needed to be exempted from formal criticism. The
strength and weakness of Carlyle's essay largely result from these
premises.

He is very sound on Burns's 'clearness of sight', and on the general
link between the poems of affection and the satires. Indignation, he

observes, is 'an inverted Love'. His commentary on 'The Jolly Beggars' advances criticism, being both clear and musically informed. (As James Hogg noted—No. 72—his downgrading of 'Tam o' Shanter' is at least provocative.) Carlyle seems to agree with Stendhal's remark that 'Burns was at least half a musician', and is able to relate the songs to his own knowledge of folksong in the south-west of Scotland. He responds to the atmosphere of 'Macpherson's Farewell', for instance, with a spontaneous feeling of pleasure which springs from familiarity with the words when sung:

But who, except Burns, could have given words to such a soul; words that we never listen to without a strange half-barbarous, half-poetic fellow-feeling?

On the other hand, Burns's humour sometimes escapes him, and Carlyle's doctrine of the poet as hero, coupled with disregard for art, tends to reduce individual poems in his eyes to the level of moral illustrations. The chief merit of his essay lies in its courageous general criticism.[67] It was to be left to others to 'discover' neglected poems, a process well illustrated by Cunningham's commendation of the superb 'Elegy on Matthew Henderson' in 1834 (No. 71).

To De Quincey, when looking back in 1837, two decisive events in the history of Burns's reputation appeared to be Currie's publication of the first collected edition in 1800, and the 'oblique collision between Lord Jeffrey and Mr. Wordsworth' in 1816 (No. 73).[68] He argued that Wordsworth's intervention renewed interest in Burns, to which other factors contributed:

[Mr. Cunningham] having since brought fresh research and the illustrative power of the arts to bear upon the subject, and all this having gone on concurrently with the great modern revolution in literature—that is, the great extension of a *popular* interest, through the astonishing reductions of price—the result is, that Burns has, at length, become a national and, therefore, in a certain sense, a privileged subject; which, in a perfect sense, he was *not*, until the controversial management of his reputation had irritated the public attention. Dr. Currie did not address the same alert condition of the public feeling, nor, by many hundred degrees, so *diffused* a condition of any feeling which might imperfectly exist, as a man must consciously address in these days, whether as the biographer or the critic of Burns.

De Quincey was generalizing too readily from his personal knowledge of Cunningham, Currie, and Wordsworth. Nevertheless, there is

43

considerable force in the observation of a man who had lived through the great age of English romantic poetry and 'the modern revolution in literature' that Burns 'with his peculiarly wild and almost ferocious spirit of independence, came a generation too soon'.

IV

THE AMERICAN RECEPTION

Burns's poetry became popular in the United States of America almost as soon as in the United Kingdom. Individual poems were reprinted in many American newspapers and, beginning with the 1787 Edinburgh *Poems, chiefly in the Scottish Dialect*, most British editions were advertised by American booksellers within a few weeks of publication. Three editions of the *Poems* were published in America before 1800: in Philadelphia and in New York, in 1788, and in Philadelphia in 1798. These sold widely. Although Johnson's *Scots Musical Museum* was on sale, also, little attention was given at first to Burns's songs. After 1800, however, numerous American editions of Burns's works incorporated the songs and poems collected by Currie and other editors in Britain.[69] In this way the pattern of the British reception repeated itself.

The history of Burns's early American reputation has been explored by Anna M. Painter.[70] Three things stand out from her detailed account: the considerable publishing enterprise shown by two small groups of expatriate Scots in the eastern seaboard cities of New York and Philadelphia; their dependence throughout on critical articles which had already appeared in British magazines; and—by implication—the willingness of American readers to welcome the works of a poet whose language must often have seemed foreign to them.

It was this last feature which was to count for most in the long run. The New York edition of 1788 printed in full in the fragment 'When Guildford good our Pilot stood' the names of men prominent in the British army during the Revolutionary War, which Burns had slightly disguised by the omission of some letters—a clear indication of American interest in the poet's particular relevance in the new republic. George Washington owned this edition.[71] Later, Burns's egalitarian and democratic sentiments found ready assent in the minds of generations of readers in the United States. A specifically American sense of identity with Burns became very clear as the nineteenth century wore on. The idea that the poet belonged in spirit with 'The Land of the Free' was pithily expressed by Oliver Wendell Holmes:[72]

Burns ought to have passed ten years of his life in America, for those words of his:
    'A man's a man for a' that'
show that true American feeling belonged to him as much as if he had been born in sight of the hill before me as I write—Bunker Hill.

No doubt it occurred to Burns's earliest American readers that his praise of independence vindicated their own recent historic choice. Fellow-feeling with Burns was instinctive, and it was to grow, not to lessen, with the passing of time. Thus in 1957 Hardin Craig wrote, 'In the United States we have no national poet unless, by virtue of our language and our cultural inheritance, Shakespeare and Burns belong to us'.[73]

However, several decades passed before the national attitude towards Burns expressed itself strongly in criticism. This was largely because the Scottish immigrants who took the lead in spreading knowledge of his work looked for help to criticism written in the British Isles. Archibald McLean, who published the New York edition of 1788, had come from Glasgow in 1783, the year when peace was established. In advertising 'Burn's [sic] Poems, the famous North-British Muse' in his *Independent Journal*, he quoted at length from Henry Mackenzie's article in the *Lounger*, including the passage about Burns as 'Heaven-taught ploughman'.[74] By doing so, he perpetuated in the United States the prevailing British image of Burns, and created a precedent for critical dependence. Peter Stewart and George Hyde, his Scots-born rivals in Philadelphia who beat him to the post as first American publishers of Burns, relied instead on the article in the *Monthly Review* of December 1786. Their advertisements in the *Pennsylvania Packet* and elsewhere of the works of 'The Celebrated Ayrshire Ploughman' drew attention first of all to Burns's comic brilliance, rather than to his command of sentiment.[75] For this, one feels, they deserved to win the race for first publication! But Stewart and Hyde, no less than McLean, helped to form a habit of relying on what was written about Burns in the British Isles.

The persistence of that habit is shown by an article 'On the Poetry of Burns' by James F. Otis in the *Southern Literary Messenger* of March 1836, which bibliographers commonly cite as an exceptionally early American critical discussion of Burns. After introducing his subject in two paragraphs about the general nature of poetry, Otis goes on to reproduce biographical and critical comment by Currie and Carlyle. He offers a note of explanation.[76]

This paper was written at the request of a literary society of which the author was a member, and the facts are gathered principally from Currie. Some extracts from the poet's own letters, and from an eloquent review of Lockhart's Burns, which appeared a few years since in the *Edinburgh Review*, are interwoven, and the whole made up as an essay to be 'read not printed'.

Such modest dependence on the views of men from Burns's part of Scotland is typical of early American commentary on Burns.

As Burns's fame continued to grow in the United States and in Canada throughout the nineteenth century, it was natural that people of Scottish descent should be most active in promoting knowledge of his poetry and of the legend associated with his name. But at no time was North American enthusiasm for Burns confined to a single ethnic group. The centenary Burns celebrations of 1859 produced notable tributes, including a speech by Ralph Waldo Emerson in Boston on 25 January which is perhaps the finest example of early comment on Burns by a distinguished American man of letters. It is included in this collection to represent the development of Burns criticism overseas (No. 756). Emerson fully appreciated the universality of Burns.

Since 1859, and especially in the present century, much valuable scholarly and critical work on Burns has appeared in the United States (see below, p. 51). It is reasonable to assume that its quality is partly due to the fact that it came after a long period during which Burns's poetry was read with unselfconscious enjoyment in North America.

V

THE CRITICAL TRADITION AFTER 1837

In view of the pattern established in the first fifty years of Burns criticism, it is not surprising that since 1837 the main critical tradition in Great Britain has been Scottish. Important exceptions exist, such as Matthew Arnold's influential judgment in 'The Study of Poetry', 1880, but there have been no modern English, Irish, or Welsh contributions to Burns studies to compare with the work of, say, F. B. Snyder or J. De Lancey Ferguson in the United States.

A long line of Scots-born critics have added to the discussion of

Burns's poems and songs, sometimes significantly, sometimes in unconscious repetition of their predecessors. Original criticism, as distinct from bardolatry, has been rare; but many readers have made good use of the commentaries supplied by successive editors of Burns, including Robert Chambers (1861), W. Scott Douglas (1877–9), William Wallace (1896), and W. E Henley and T. F. Henderson (1896). James Kinsley's fully annotated 1968 edition has already stimulated new interpretations.[77]

Particularly interesting comment has been made by expatriate writers, and by others returning to Scotland after a period of absence. In 1879 R. L. Stevenson drew on an exile's experience when he administered a rebuke to J. C. Shairp, Professor of Poetry at Oxford, and one of innumerable moralistic critics of Burns in the Victorian age. Stevenson directed attention to 'the unity of [Burns's] nature', noting a vigour and directness in the writing which Shairp had found embarrassing:[78]

The man here presented is not that Burns, *teres atque rotundus*—a burly figure in literature, as, from our present vantage of time, we have begun to see him: this, on the other hand, is Burns as he may have appeared to a contemporary clergyman, whom we shall conceive to have been a kind and indulgent but orderly and orthodox person, anxious to be pleased, but too often hurt and disappointed by the behaviour of his red-hot protégé and solacing himself with the explanation that the poet was 'the most inconsistent of men' . . . Indeed, we can only be sorry and surprised that Principal Shairp should have chosen a theme so uncongenial. When we find a man writing on Burns, who likes neither 'Holy Willie', nor the 'Beggars', nor the 'Ordination', nothing is adequate to the situation but the old cry of Géronte: 'Que diable allait-il faire dans cette galère?'

Stevenson is an important transitional figure in Burns criticism, as in other Scottish literary traditions. Brief though his essay is, it is uncompromising in its insistence that Burns should be viewed realistically, as a scathing satirist who was 'among the least impersonal of artists'.

Stevenson's impatience with conventional attitudes partly anticipates the iconoclastic severity of 'Hugh MacDiarmid' (C. M. Grieve), who examined Scotland's cultural heritage afresh after the First World War. MacDiarmid went on to write the only major poetry in Scots since Burns's own, and to wage unceasing war as a prose-writer on those whose views he could not accept. The Burns cult by turns amused and disgusted him, because he judged that many of those who professed to care for Burns had no real concern for poetry, let alone for poets.

In *A Drunk Man looks at the Thistle* (1926) he tried to rescue Burns from his admirers:[79]

> No' wan in fifty kens a wurd Burns wrote
> But misapplied is a'body's property,
> And gin there was his like alive the day
> They'd be the last a kennin' haund to gi'e—
>
> Croose London Scotties wi' their braw shirt fronts
> And a' their fancy freen's, rejoicin'
> That similah gatherings in Timbuctoo,
> Bagdad—and Hell, nae doot—are voicin'
>
> Burns' sentiments o' universal love,
> In pidgin' English or in wild-fowl Scots,
> And toastin' ane wha's nocht to them but an
> Excuse for faitherin' Genius wi' *their* thochts.

To MacDiarmid it appeared that

> As Kirks wi' Christianity hae dune,
> Burns Clubs wi' Burns—wi' a' thing it's the same,
> The core o' ocht is only for the few,
> Scorned by the mony, thrang wi'ts empty name.

He returned to the subject in *At the Sign of the Thistle* (1934), with a short story of devastating ribaldry, later entitled 'The Last Great Burns Discovery', and a polemical essay on 'The Burns Cult', containing astringent comment, and showing even more markedly than T. S. Eliot's Milton criticism the partisan judgment of 'a poetic practitioner' with strong political beliefs. MacDiarmid principally attacked the Burns cult, noting that

It has produced mountains of rubbish about him—to effectively bury the dynamic spirit—but not a single good critical study.

However, he also pointed to a number of shortcomings in Burns's poetry:[80]

It has been said that repetition of the same lines or phrases accounts for seventy-five per cent of Burns's work; certainly his great work is a small portion of the remaining twenty-five per cent—and not the portion most generally known.

48

Most of his work has dated very badly; it is full of eighteenth-century conventionalism and the minutiae of dead and even at the time local controversies. It marked the end of a phase—not a fresh start in Scots letters. It contains surprisingly little history, little sense of Scotland's destiny, and as to his love-songs they might all have been written to the same lay figure, for any particularity they contain. He has the typical voluptuary's aversion from realism in this respect.

Clearly a biased and provocative statement! But MacDiarmid succeeded in his aim of stimulating a more critical approach to Burns. His nationalism and communism led him to emphasize, perhaps to overemphasize, the revolutionary political spirit of certain poems by Burns. This possible distortion of history can be defended on the ground that many other critics have portrayed Burns wrongly as a conformist.

In an essay on Burns in *Latitudes* (1924), Edwin Muir claimed that the only contemporary verdict on him free from 'a touch of cant . . . something morally or socially superior' was that of Allan Cunningham's father, which he quoted:[81]

Few men had so much of the poet about them, and few poets so much of the man: the man was probably less pure than he ought to have been, but the poet was pure and bright to the end.

Muir's own criticism was founded on an appreciation of the poet's merits. He stressed the 'sense of completeness' which is communicated by Burns's poetry. Later, Muir showed an unusually tolerant understanding of Burns's popular reputation when he wrote on 'The Burns Myth' (1947):[82]

For a Scotsman to see Burns simply as a poet is well-nigh an impossibility. Burns is so deeply imbedded in Scottish life that he cannot be detached from it, from what is best in it and what is worst in it, and regarded as we regard Dunbar or James Hogg or Walter Scott. He is more a personage to us than a poet, more a figurehead than a personage, and more a myth than a figurehead . . . here is a poet for everybody, a poet who has such an insight into ordinary thoughts and feelings that he can catch them and give them poetic shape, as those who merely think or feel them cannot. This was Burns's supreme art. It seems to be simple. People are inclined to believe that it is easier to express ordinary thoughts and feelings in verse than complex and unusual ones. The problem is an artificial one, for in the end a poet does what he has a supreme gift for doing. Burns's gift lay here; it made him a myth; it predestined him to become the Rabbie of Burns Nights. When we consider Burns we must therefore include the Burns

Nights with him, and the Burns cult in all its forms: if we sneer at them we sneer at Burns. They are his reward, or punishment (whichever the fastidious reader may prefer to call it) for having had the temerity to express the ordinary feelings of his people, and having become a part of their life. What the Burns Nights ignore is the perfection of Burns' art, which makes him one of the great poets. But there is so much more involved that this, his real greatness, can be assumed and taken for granted.

The Burns cult has been a frequent topic of other modern Scottish authors, and the first unexpurgated edition of *The Merry Muses of Caledonia* (1959) was the work of James Barke, a novelist, and a poet, Sydney Goodsir Smith. But the fullest analysis of Burns's poems and songs has come from academic critics. David Daiches is the author of two valuable studies, *Robert Burns* (1950, rev. 1966) and *Robert Burns and his World* (1971). Another work of critical distinction is Thomas Crawford's *Burns: A Study of the Poems and Songs* (1960, 2nd ed. 1965), in which for the first time biography is firmly relegated to the background. David Craig in his *Scottish Literature and the Scottish People 1680-1830* (1961) includes a stimulating section on Burns. Since 1892 the *Burns Chronicle*, the annual journal of the Burns Federation, has published a wide variety of articles dealing with all aspects of the poet's life and writings.

VI

BURNS AS A WORLD POET

Burns, whose chief ambition was to entertain a regional public, has become world-famous. His poems and songs owe their universal popularity to his distinctive humour and his celebration of love, and also to his democratic spirit and to the appeal of country things.

Part of the history of the poet's reputation can be traced in editions of his poems published abroad, and in translations.[83] Several translations into French were made between 1825 and 1840, and part or all of the poet's work was first translated into the following languages by the dates indicated: German (1839), Flemish (1852), Swedish (1854), Danish (1867), Russian (1875), Italian (1878), Czech (1892), Hungarian (1892), Japanese (1906), Norwegian (1923), Icelandic (1924), Rumanian (1925), Esperanto (1926), Faroese (1945), Spanish (1954), Hebrew (1956), Polish (1956), Bulgarian (1957), Chinese (1961), Korean (1961), Albanian (1962). Burns's poetry was known in several countries before being translated—the first short articles in Russian magazines were published in the 1820s, for example—but usually translation has proved very important in spreading knowledge of his work.[84]

Modern critics of Burns have accordingly been of many nations. Auguste Angellier's *Robert Burns* (2 vols, Paris, 1893) is an outstanding early example of original criticism from outside Britain.[85] Balanced intelligently between biography and analysis of the poetry, his work marks a new stage of professionalism in the study of Burns; but he does not leave behind the capacity to generalize shown by earlier critics. Hans Hecht's *Burns* (Heidelberg, 1919, translated 1926 [enlarged] and 1950, second edition) was described by the American scholar Franklyn B. Snyder as 'the best brief life of Burns'. Snyder's own *Life of Robert Burns* (1932, 1968) deserves to be called the most scholarly biography on a full scale yet to have been published; and, like Hecht, he showed sound judgment in his remarks on Burns's poetry. J. De Lancey Ferguson, who edited Burns's *Letters* (2 vols, Oxford, 1931), combined meticulous scholarship with the ability to keep before his readers a broad interpretation of Burns's character and literary gifts. His book *Pride and Passion: Burns* (New York, 1939, 1964) remains one of the most illuminating introductions to the poet. The high standard of American scholarship on Burns is being maintained by scholars like F. L. Beaty, G. Ross Roy (a Canadian, domiciled in the United States), and John C. Weston.

Beyond Europe and North America, there have been numerous essays of very considerable interest, as well as longer studies. To name three writers from many: Madame A. E. Elistratova has produced a detailed critique for Russian readers in *Robert Burns* (Moscow, 1957), while the translations of Samuel Marshak have been widely read in the Soviet Union; and Toshio Namba has described the enthusiastic reception of Burns's poetry in Japan (*Studies in Scottish Literature* I, 1964). This list could easily be extended.

The need now is for the kind of criticism which will go beyond the old boundaries without becoming merely modish. Burns's poetry should be fully related to that of his English contemporaries, including Blake and Cowper. Raymond Bentman's recent claim that Burns is best viewed as a romantic poet deserves an answer; and, in this connection, Scott's comparison of Burns and Byron needs to be taken further.[86] Burns's songs have not fared so well at the hands of critics as his poems. It would be best if they were to be reappraised by persons at home in the criticism of both music and poetry. The complex background of folksong on which Burns drew has also to be kept constantly in mind. *The Merry Muses of Caledonia* has yet to be discussed in relation to the main body of Burns's poetry. Another subject for further study is the interplay in Burns of folk humour, lyricism, and literary irony. A useful comparison could be made with Lewis Grassic Gibbon's trilogy *A Scots Quair* (1932–4).

The history of Burns criticism proves that it is all too easy to be sidetracked from consideration of his poetic art into irrelevant discussion of his life. Nevertheless, it would be a great mistake to write about the poems and songs as if they had little or nothing to do with Burns the man. The relationship between his personal experience and what he wrote was very close indeed; it is seen most clearly in the epistles and in some of the love poems. Nor can Burns's poetry be fully understood without some knowledge of its original social context. It shows one man's response to a particular society at a particular time. A recent warning by Richard Hoggart deserves to be kept in mind by students of Burns: 'A work of art, no matter how much it rejects or ignores its society, is deeply rooted within it. It has massive cultural meanings. There is no such thing as "a work of art in itself" '.[87]

Finally, it is salutary to recall Edwin Muir's remark that 'if we sneer at the Burns cult, we sneer at Burns'. Burns was a country poet who wrote spontaneously from experience of life and who did not depend primarily on the stimulus that comes from books. This fact, sometimes overlooked by bookish critics, has never been forgotten in the Burns cult. The 'Epistle To Lapraik', in which art conceals art, has lost none of its relevance:

> I am nae *Poet*, in a sense,
> But just a *Rhymer* like by chance,
> An' hae to Learning nae pretence,
>   Yet, what the matter?
> Whene'er my Muse does on me glance,
>   I jingle at her.
>
> Your Critic-folk may cock their nose,
> And say, 'How can you e'er propose,
> 'You wha ken hardly *verse* frae *prose*,
>   'To mak a *sang*?'
> But by your leaves, my learned foes,
>   Ye're maybe wrang.
>
> What's a jargon o' your Schools,
> Your Latin names for horn an' stools;

If honest Nature made you *fools*,
  What sairs your Grammars?
Ye'd better taen up *spades* and *shools*,
  Or *knappin-hammers*.

A set o' dull, conceited Hashes,
Confuse their brains in *Colledge-classes*!
They *gang in* Stirks, and *come out* Asses,
  Plain truth to speak;
An' syne they think to climb Parnassus
  By dint o' Greek!

Gie me ae spark o' Nature's fire,
That's a' the learning I desire;
Then tho' I drudge thro' dub an' mire
  At pleugh or cart,
My Muse, tho' hamely in attire,
  May touch the heart.

NOTES

1 To David McWhinnie [17 April 1786]. *Letters* I, p. 25.
2 To Mrs Dunlop, 15 November 1786. *Letters* I, p. 49.
3 A. M. Kinghorn, 'The literary and historical origins of the Burns myth', *Dalhousie Review* (1959), xxxix, p. 78.
4 To John Moore, January 1787. *Letters* I, p. 70.
5 For a survey of primitivist doctrine, and of theories of genius, see M. H. Abrams, *The Mirror and the Lamp: Romantic Theory and the Critical Tradition* (1958), Norton edition, pp. 83–4, 104–5, 184–201, and 350 n.46.
6 Cf. F. L. Beaty, 'Ae spark o' Nature's fire', *English Language Notes* (1964), iv.
7 Kinsley, pp. 972–3.
8 *Don Juan* XVI, 97 and note.
9 In January 1783 Burns wrote to his former teacher John Murdoch that he prized *The Man of Feeling* 'next to the Bible'. *Letters* I, p. 14.
10 To George Thomson [September 1793]. *Letters* II, p. 202. On the editorial problem set by 'The Jolly Beggars', see Kinsley, pp. 1150–2.
11 See Appendix A and Egerer, *passim*.
12 See No. 22, and Kinsley, pp. 1534–47.
13 *Life Of Robert Burns*, 3rd ed., corrected, 1830, p. 137.
14 An annotated list (names A–F only) of subscribers to the Edinburgh edition of 1787 is given in *BC* (1959, 1961–3), viii, x–xii.
15 'Lament for James, Earl of Glencairn', ll. 79–80.
16 'Journal of the Border Tour', ed. De L. Ferguson, in *Burns, his associates and Contemporaries*, ed. R. T. Fitzhugh (1943), p. 111.
17 Quoted in *BC* (1908), xvii, p. 49.

18 To Gavin Hamilton, 7 December 1786. *Letters* I, p. 55.

19 Kinsley 147A and B, 'The Guidwife of Wauchope-House to Robert Burns, the Airshire Bard. Feb. 1787', and 'The Answer' [March 1787].

20 To James Currie, 28 September 1799. *BC* (1925), xxxiv, p. 12.

21 To John Ballantine, 13 December 1786. *Letters* I, p. 57.

22 e.g. *Letters* I, pp. 58–9, 69, 71, 86, 237.

23 To John Moore, January 1787. *Letters* I, p. 70.

24 To Mrs Dunlop, 12 February 1788. *Letters* I, p. 183.

25 *Robert Burns's Commonplace Book 1783–1785*, ed. D. Daiches (1965), p. 11.

26 To Mrs Dunlop, 22 March 1787. *Letters* I, 80. Robert Anderson noted that Burns 'steadily resisted the attempts of emendatory criticism'. *BC* (1925), xxxiv, p. 16.

27 See *Robert Burns And Mrs Dunlop*, ed. W. Wallace (1898).

28 To Mrs Dunlop, 27 September 1788. *Letters* I, p. 261.

29 *Letters* I, pp. 104–16. Ramsay of Ochertyre also urged Burns to emulate Thomson by writing 'Scottish Georgics'; Kinsley, p. 1539.

30 To Mrs Dunlop, 23 October 1788. Cf. Kinsley, no. 355, l. 55n.

31 To Mrs Dunlop, 25 March 1789. *Letters* I, p. 317.

32 See Stephen Parks, 'Justice to William Creech', *Publications of the Bibliographical Society of America* (1966), lx, pp. 453–64.

33 Robert Arbuthnot (1728–1803) wrote to James Beattie on 25 March 1799, 'Creech thinks of nothing but acquiring money a Science in which he has I believe succeeded very well being worth it is said £30,000.' (Aberdeen University Library, letter C772.)

34 To William Creech, 16 April 1792. *Letters* II, p. 114.

35 To William Creech, 28 February 1793. *Letters* II, p. 151.

36 J. W. Egerer, 'Burns and "Guid Black Prent" ', *The Age Of Johnson: Essays Presented to C. B. Tinker* (1949), p. 279.

37 Preface, Glenriddell Manuscript.

38 To Gavin Hamilton, 8 March 1787. *Letters* I, p. 79.

39 To Mrs Dunlop, 11 April 1791. *Letters* II, p. 68.

40 *Letters* II, pp. 126, 166, 210, 268.

41 To George Thomson [*c*. 18 May 1796]. *Letters* II, p. 321.

42 Egerer, no. 197.

43 Letter to James Currie, 27 October 1799. *BC* (1925), xxxiv, p. 13.

44 H. W. Thompson, *A Scottish Man of Feeling* (1931), pp. 215–16.

45 Mackenzie's essay interested a Frenchman, F. Prevost, who wrote to him from London on 26 April 1787 asking for information about 'Burn' (Thompson, *op. cit.*, p. 227). This is one of the earliest indications of foreign interest in Burns.

46 In 1790 Robert Munro, a graduate of Oxford, commented on 'the rare union of great simplicity and great knowledge of human nature' in Burns's work. (Quoted in *BC* (1908), xvii, p. 55.)

47 Quoted by Egerer, p. 14.

48 D. Daiches, *Robert Burns*, rev. ed. (1966), p. 146; T. Crawford, *Burns: A Study of the Poems and Songs*, 2nd ed. (1965), p. 179.

49 Quoted by Snyder, p. 231.

50 Envy of Burns as an author led John Home, the author of *Douglas*, to state in 1788, 'The encouragement that fellow has met with is a perfect disgrace to the nation.' Commenting on this on 6 November 1789, a journalist added 'Burns's reputation is vastly faded.' Quoted in *BC* (1940), new series, xv, p. 16.

51 Cf. *Annals Of Medical History* (1928), x, pp. 47ff. *British Medical Journal*, 30 December 1944; R. T. Fitzhugh, *Robert Burns: the Man and the Poet* (1971), pp. 414–29.

52 David Daiches has suggested that 'the typical young American critic of the last twenty-five years is acutely embarrassed by such a simple lyrical utterance as, say, Burns's "A Red Red Rose", and just does not know what to do with it.' Daiches, *English Literature* (1964), p. 83.

53 *Monthly Register* (1802).

54 *The Poetical Works Of The Rev. George Crabbe* (1834), I, p. 172.

55 To Mrs Dunlop, 4 March 1789. *Letters* I, pp. 311–12.

56 'Coleridge had none of the triumphant earthiness which made Hazlitt appreciate Burns so fully; on the contrary, he wished to emphasize the moral significance even of Rabelais.' T. M. Raysor, *Coleridge: Shakespearean Criticism*, 2nd ed. (1960), I, p. xxx.

57 The similarity between 'Tam o' Shanter' and 'The Waggoner' is one of the topics discussed by Russell Noyes in 'Wordsworth And Burns', *PMLA* (1944), lix, pp. 813–32.

58 *Jeffrey's Literary Criticism*, ed. D. N. Smith (1910), p. 39.

59 *The Journal of Sir Walter Scott 1825–26*, ed. J. G. Tait (1939), p. 290.

60 See J. MacVie, *The Burns Federation: A Bi-Centenary Review* (1959).

61 For attributions of *Blackwood's* articles I have used A. L. Strout, *A Bibliography of Articles in Blackwood's Magazine 1817–1825* (Lubbock Texas, 1959), and W E. Houghton, ed., *The Wellesley Index to Victorian Periodicals* (Toronto, 1966), vol. 1.

62 Lindsay, vi.

63 *Letters* I, p. 146.

64 Snyder, p. 488. But see the defence of Lockhart's *Life of Burns* in F. R. Hart, *Lockhart as Romantic Biographer* (1971), chapter 3.

65 Comparison with other 'peasant poets' became a regular feature of Burns criticism in periodicals. In the *London Magazine* in 1820 (i, p. 325), John Scott pointed out that Burns had received more schooling than John Clare, to whom he had been likened. The first of many comparisons between Burns and Béranger occurs in a review of Béranger's *Chansons* in the *Foreign Quarterly Review* (July 1833), xii, pp. 28–49.

66 J. G. Lockhart, *The Life of Sir Walter Scott* (1902 'Edinburgh' edition), I, pp. 1–2.

67 The essay quickly proved influential in Europe. In his edition of Burns (Leipzig, 1835), Adolphus Wagner praised Carlyle's effort to contribute to general (supranational) literature through his work on Burns.

68 De Quincey had in 1809 drawn the attention of the Wordsworths to Jeffrey's essay on Burns with its 'scurrilous trash about Mr. Wordsworth' (J. E. Jordan, *De Quincey to Wordsworth: A Biography of a Relationship* (1962), p. 100).

69 For titles and details of these editions, see J. W. Egerer, *A Bibliography of Robert Burns* (1964).

70 Anna M. Painter, 'American Editions of the poems of Burns before 1800', *Library* (1932), 14th series, xii. This article includes information about poems printed in newspapers and magazines.

71 Painter, *op. cit.*, p. 450. Originally it was planned that the New York edition would be a subscription edition, like that of Edinburgh (1787), but there were not enough subscribers and it was sold instead in the usual way. Washington appears to have been among the original subscribers.

72 Quoted in *The World's Memorials of Robert Burns*, collected and described by Edward Goodwillie (Detroit, 1911), p. 169.

73 Hardin Craig, 'Burns and the English-speaking world', *BC* (1957), 3rd series, vi, p. 17.

74 Painter, *op. cit.*, pp. 438–9.

75 *Ibid.*, p. 444.

76 *Southern Literary Messenger* (March 1836), p. 238.

77 *Critical Essays on Robert Burns*, ed. D. A. Low, 1974, includes new essays by G. Ross Roy, Ian M. Campbell, David Murison, Alexander Scott, John D. Baird, David Daiches, and Cedric Thorpe Davie.

78 'Some Aspects of Robert Burns', *Cornhill Magazine* (October 1879), pp. 408–9.

79 *Collected Poems of Hugh MacDiarmid*, rev. ed. (1967), pp. 64, 66.

80 *At the Sign of the Thistle* (1934), pp. 169, 175.

81 *Latitudes* (1924), p. 1.

82 'The Burns Myth', in W. Montgomerie, ed., *Burns: New Judgements*, pp. 5–8.

83 The dates in this paragraph are based on *New Cambridge Bibliography of English Literature*, vol. II. 1660–1800 (1971), columns 1997–2000.

84 Comparative study might begin with American, French, German, and Russian essays of the 1830s. The first Australian edition was published in 1832.

85 There is no complete translation of Angellier's work, but important passages are translated by Mrs Jane Burgoyne in *BC* (1969–73), 3rd series, xviii–xxii.

86 R. Bentman, 'The Romantic Poets and critics on Robert Burns', *Texas Studies In Literature and Languages* (1964), vi. Some contrasts between Burns

and Byron are noted by W. W. Robson in 'Byron as Poet', British Academy, (1958).

87 R. Hoggart, 'Contemporary cultural studies', *Contemporary Criticism*, ed. M. Bradbury and D. Palmer (1970), p. 163.

Note on the Text

The materials printed in this volume follow the original texts in all important respects. Typographical errors in the originals have been silently corrected. Line-references to Burns's poems and songs are to James Kinsley's edition (see p. xvii). Wherever possible, important documents have been printed nearly in their entirety, but repetitive comment and extraneous biographical discussion have been cut. These omissions are indicated in the text. Editorial footnotes are numbered, while original footnotes are indicated by asterisks (*), daggers (†), etc.

POEMS, CHIEFLY IN THE SCOTTISH DIALECT

Kilmarnock 1786

1. Thomas Blacklock writes from the capital

September 1786

Letter of 4 September 1786 to Rev. George Lawrie, minister of Loudon. Snyder, pp. 153–4.

Dr Thomas Blacklock (1721–91), who had published a volume of poems in 1746, took a keen interest in literature despite being blind. This letter was sent by Lawrie to Gavin Hamilton, who gave it to Burns. The poet wrote to Dr John Moore in August 1787, 'I had composed my last song I should ever measure in Caledonia, "The gloomy night is gathering fast", when a letter from Dr. Blacklock to a friend of mine overthrew all my schemes by rousing my poetic ambition.—The Doctor belonged to a set of Critics for whose applause I had not even dared to hope.—His idea that I would meet with every encouragement for a second edition fired me so much that away I posted to Edinburgh without a single acquaintance in town, or a single letter of introduction in my pocket' (*Letters* I, p. 115) (see Introduction, p. 5).

I ought to have acknowledged your favor long ago, not only as a testimony of your kind remembrance, but as it gave me an opportunity of sharing one of the finest, and, perhaps, one of the most genuine entertainments, of which the human mind is susceptible. A number of avocations retarded my progress in reading the poems; at last, however, I have finished that pleasing perusal. Many instances have I seen of nature's force and beneficence, exerted under numerous and formidable disadvantages; but none equal to that, with which you have been

61

kind enough to present me. There is a pathos and delicacy in his serious poems; a vein of wit and humour in those of a more festive turn, which cannot be too much admired, nor too warmly approved; and I think I shall never open the book without feeling my astonishment renewed and increased. It was my wish to have expressed my approbation in verse; but whether from declining life or a temporary depression of spirits, it is at present out of my power to accomplish that agreeable intention.

Mr. Stewart, professor of morals in this university, had formerly read me three of the poems, and I had desired him to get my name inserted among the subscribers: but whether this was done or not I never could learn. I have little intercourse with Dr. Blair, but will take care to have the poems communicated to him by the intervention of some mutual friend. It has been told me by a gentleman, to whom I showed the performances, and who sought a copy with diligence and ardour, that the whole impression is already exhausted. It were therefore much to be wished, for the sake of a young man, that a second edition, more numerous than the former, could immediately be printed; as it appears certain that its intrinsic merit, and the exertion of the author's friends, might give it a more universal circulation than any thing of the kind which has been published within my memory.

2. Unsigned notice in *Edinburgh Magazine*

iv (October 1786), 284–8

The *Edinburgh Magazine, or Literary Miscellany* of November and December 1786 reprinted poems by Burns. In January 1787 the poet wrote to thank James Sibbald, its publisher, for 'the warmth with which you have befriended an obscure man, and young Author, in your three last Magazines' (*Letters* I, p. 62). Sibbald (1745–1803) probably wrote this, the earliest review of Burns. His helper Robert Anderson (1750–1830) wrote to James Currie in 1799, 'I . . . easily prevailed upon the printer of the *Edinburgh Magazine* to insert some pieces in the poetical article of his Miscellany . . . The circulation of these extracts, co-operating with the interesting account of Burns in the *Lounger*, prepared the way for his favourable reception in Edinburgh' (*BC* (1923), xxxii, and (1925), xxxiv).

When an author we know nothing of solicits our attention, we are but too apt to treat him with the same reluctant civility we show to a person who has come unbidden into company. Yet talents and address will gradually diminish the distance of our behaviour, and when the first unfavourable impression has worn off, the author may become a favourite, and the stranger a friend. The poems we have just announced may probably have to struggle with the pride of learning and the partiality of indulgence; yet they are entitled to particular indulgence.

Who are you, Mr. Burns? will some surly critic say. At what university have you been educated? what languages do you understand? what authors have you particularly studied? whether has Aristotle or Horace directed your taste? who has praised your poems, and under whose patronage are they published? In short, what qualifications entitle you to instruct or entertain us? To the questions of such a catechism, perhaps honest Robert Burns would make no satisfactory answers. 'My good Sir', he might say, 'I am a poor country man; I was bred up at the school of Kilmarnock; I understand no languages but my own; I have studied Allan Ramsay and Ferguson. My poems have been praised at many a fire-side; and I ask no patronage for them, if they deserve none. I have not looked on mankind *through the spectacle of books*. An ounce of mother wit, you know, is worth a pound of clergy; and Homer and Ossian, for any thing that I have heard, could neither write nor read.' The author is indeed a striking example of native genius bursting through the obscurity of poverty and the obstructions of laborious life. He is said to be a common ploughman; and when we consider him in this light, we cannot help regretting that wayward fate had not placed him in a more favoured situation. Those who view him with the severity of lettered criticism, and judge him by the fastidious rules of art, will discover that he has not the doric simplicity of Ramsay, nor the brilliant imagination of Ferguson; but to those who admire the exertions of untutored fancy, and are blind to many faults for the sake of numberless beauties, his poems will afford singular gratification. His observations on human characters are acute and sagacious, and his descriptions are lively and just. Of rustic pleasantry he has a rich fund; and some of his softer scenes are touched with inimitable delicacy. He seems to be a boon companion, and often startles us with a dash of libertinism, which will keep some readers at a distance. Some of his subjects are serious, but those of the humorous kind are the best. It is not meant, however, to enter into a minute investigation of his merits, as the copious extracts we have subjoined will enable our readers to judge for themselves. The Character Horace gives to Ofellus is particularly applicable to him.

Rusticus abnormis sapiens, crassaque Minerva.[1]

[quotes 'Address to the Deil']

We regret that we have not room to insert the poems of *Hallow-E'en*, *The Cotter's Saturday Night*, and the *Epistle to a Brother Poet*; and must remain content with a few miscellaneous extracts from the poems in general.

[quotes 'Epistle to J. L*****k', ll. 43–78, 'The Holy Fair', stanzas IX–XI, XXI–XXII, XXVI–XXVII, 'Hallow-E'en', stanzas VII–VIII, XIII–XIV, XVII–XXVII]

---

1 'a peasant, a philosopher unschooled and of rough mother-wit'. Horace, *Satires* II.ii.3. Loeb translation.

3. Correspondence in *Edinburgh Evening Courant*

November 1786

(a) Letter by 'Allan Ramsay', *Edinburgh Evening Courant*, 13 November 1786.

TO THE EDITOR, 'EDINBURGH EVENING COURANT'.

Sir,

It is an old saying 'That a prophet hath no honour in his own country'; and I am of opinion that the same adage may be applied in many instances with equal propriety to authors.

Amongst the British poets, Gay and Thomson (whose writings do honour to themselves, to their country, and to human nature) are striking examples of the neglect which is but too frequently the attendant on modest merit. This part of the kingdom has not produced many poets, and therefore, when a rarity of the kind appears, it becomes the business of those whose fortune and situation enable them to promote the cultivation of genius to lend him assistance to such a laudable pursuit.

Within these few weeks I have been highly gratified by perusing a collection of poems in the Scottish dialect, the production of a common farmer in Ayrshire of the name of Burns. His language is nervous, and his sentiments would do honour to a much more enlightened scholar. In short, he appears to be not only a keen satirist, but a man of great feeling and sensibility.

The county of Ayr is perhaps superior to any in Scotland in the number of its Peers, Nabobs, and wealthy Commoners, and yet not one of them has upon this occasion stepped forth as a patron to this man, nor has any attempt been made to interest the public in his favour. His poems are read, his genius is applauded, and he is left to his fate. It is a reflection on the county and a disgrace to humanity.

To this self-taught poet I am an entire stranger, but his productions have afforded me so much pleasure that if this hint should raise an emulation in that county to rescue from penury a genius which, if unprotected, will probably sink into obscurity, I will most cheerfully contribute towards it, and I know many others who will follow the example. Should my efforts to serve this man with the laity be ineffectual, I propose as a *dernier resort* to address the clergy of that county, many of whom he hath taken particular notice of in his poems. I am, etc.,

ALLAN RAMSAY.

Dunbartonshire, Nov. 7, 1786.

(b) Reply by 'G.H.', *Edinburgh Evening Courant*, 15 November 1786. 'G.H.' who defended Burns's Ayrshire subscribers, was probably Gavin Hamilton, dedicatee of the Kilmarnock edition. Hamilton, who knew the size of the edition, had taken forty copies to distribute among his friends (see Introduction, p. 15).

Sir,

I beg you will inform Allan Ramsay of Dunbartonshire that Mr. Burns, the person whom he mentions in your paper of Monday last, published an edition of his poems consisting of 600 copies, the greatest part of which were subscribed for, or bought up by, the gentlemen of Airshire, many of whom have taken particular notice of the Author. Allan Ramsay's reflection upon the county does therefore little credit either to his information upon the subject or to the politeness of his stile.

G. H.

Glasgow, 14th Nov., 1786.

4. Henry Mackenzie, unsigned essay in *Lounger*

97 (9 December 1786)

Frequently reprinted during and after Burns's lifetime, this was by far the most influential contemporary account of his poetry. Its immediate effect was to create intense public interest in the poet, who had newly arrived in Edinburgh. The view of Burns as 'a Heaven-taught ploughman' caused lasting confusion (see Introduction, p. 16). Henry Mackenzie (1745–1831), comptroller of taxes for Scotland, was the author of *The Man Of Feeling*, which Burns prized 'next to the Bible'. He edited two periodicals, the *Mirror* (1770) and the *Lounger* (1785–6). In 1814 Scott dedicated *Waverley* to Mackenzie, describing him as 'our Scottish Addison'.

Surprising effects of Original Genius, exemplified in the Poetical Productions of Robert Burns, *an Ayrshire Ploughman.*

To the feeling and the susceptible there is something wonderfully pleasing in the contemplation of genius, of that supereminent reach of mind by which some men are distinguished. In the view of highly superior talents, as in that of great and stupendous natural objects, there is a sublimity which fills the soul with wonder and delight, which expands it, as it were, beyond its usual bounds, and which, investing our nature with extraordinary powers, and extraordinary honours, interests our curiosity, and flatters our pride.

This divinity of genius, however, which admiration is fond to worship, is best arrayed in the darkness of distant and remote periods, and is not easily acknowledged in the present times, or in places with which we are perfectly acquainted. Exclusive of all the deductions which envy or jealousy may sometimes be supposed to make, there is a familiarity in the near approach of persons around us, not very consistent with the lofty ideas which we wish to form of him who has led captive our imagination in the triumph of his fancy, overpowered our feelings

67

with the tide of passion, or enlightened our reason with the investigation of hidden truths. It may be true, that 'in the olden time' genius had some advantages which tended to its vigour and its growth; but it is not unlikely that, even in these degenerate days, it rises much oftener than it is observed; that in 'the ignorant present time' our posterity may find names which they will dignify, though we neglected, and pay to their memory those honours which their contemporaries had denied them.

There is, however, a natural, and indeed a fortunate vanity in trying to redress this wrong which genius is exposed to suffer. In the discovery of talents generally unknown, men are apt to indulge the same fond partiality as in all other discoveries which they themselves have made; and hence we have had repeated instances of painters and of poets, who have been drawn from obscure situations, and held forth to public notice and applause, by the extravagant encomiums of their introductors, yet in a short time have sunk again to their former obscurity; whose merit, though perhaps somewhat neglected, did not appear to have been much undervalued by the world, and could not support, by its own intrinsic excellence, that superior place, which the enthusiasm of its patrons would have assigned it.

I know not if I shall be accused of such enthusiasm and partiality, when I introduce to the notice of my readers a poet of our own country, with whose writings I have lately become acquainted; but if I am not greatly deceived, I think I may safely pronounce him a genius of no ordinary rank. The person to whom I allude, is *Robert Burns*, an Ayrshire Ploughman, whose poems were some time ago published in a country town in the west of Scotland, with no other ambition, it would seem, than to circulate among the inhabitants of the county where he was born, to obtain a little fame from those who had heard of his talents. I hope I shall not be thought to assume too much, if I endeavour to place him in a higher point of view, to call for a verdict of his country on the merit of his works, and to claim for him those honours which their excellence appears to deserve.

In mentioning the circumstances of his humble station, I mean not to rest his pretensions solely on that title, or to urge the merits of his poetry when considered in relation to the lowness of his birth, and the little opportunity of improvement, which his education could afford. These particulars, indeed, might excite our wonder at his productions; but his poetry, considered abstractedly, and without the apologies arising from his situation, seems to me fully intitled to command our feelings, and to obtain our applause. One bar, indeed, his birth and education have opposed to his fame, the language in which most of his poems are written. Even in Scotland, the provincial dialect which Ramsay and he have used, is now read with a difficulty which greatly damps the pleasure of the reader; in England it cannot be read at all, without such a constant reference to a glossary, as nearly to destroy that pleasure.

Some of his productions, however, especially those of the grave style, are almost English. From one of those I shall first present my readers with an extract, in which I think they will discover a high tone of feeling, a power and energy of expression, particularly and strongly characteristic of the mind and the voice of a poet. 'Tis from his poem intitled the 'Vision', in which the genius of his native county, Ayrshire, is thus supposed to address him:

[quotes 'The Vision', ll. 205–40]

Of strains like the above, solemn and sublime, with that rapt and inspired melancholy in which the Poet lifts his eye 'above this visible diurnal sphere,' the Poems intitled, 'Despondency', the 'Lament', 'Winter, a Dirge', and the Invocation to 'Ruin', afford no less striking examples. Of the tender and the moral, specimens equally advantageous might be drawn from the elegiac verses, intitled, 'Man was made to mourn', from 'The Cottar's Saturday Night', the Stanzas 'To a Mouse', or those 'To a Mountain-Daisy', on turning it down with the plough in April 1786. This last poem I shall insert, not from its superior merit, but because its length suits the bounds of my Paper.

[quotes 'To a Mountain-Daisy']

I have seldom met with an image more truly pastoral than that of the lark, in the second stanza. Such strokes as these mark the pencil of the poet, which delineates Nature with the precision of intimacy, yet with the delicate colouring of beauty and of taste.

The power of genius is not less admirable in tracing the manners, than in painting the passions, or in drawing the scenery of Nature. That intuitive glance with which a writer like *Shakespeare* discerns the characters of men, with which he catches the many changing hues of life, forms a sort of problem in the science of mind, of which it is easier to see the truth than to assign the cause. Though I am very far from meaning to compare our rustic bard to Shakespeare, yet whoever will read his lighter and more humorous poems, his 'Dialogue of the Dogs'.

his 'Dedication to G— H—, Esq.'; his 'Epistles to a young Friend', and 'to W. S—n', will perceive with what uncommon penetration and sagacity this Heaven-taught ploughman, from his humble and un-lettered station, has looked upon men and manners.

Against some passages of those last-mentioned poems it has been objected, that they breathe a spirit of libertinism and irreligion. But, if we consider the ignorance and fanaticism of the lower class of people in the country where these poems were written, a fanaticism of that pernicious sort which sets *faith* in opposition to *good works*, the fallacy and danger of which, a mind so enlightened as our Poet's could not but perceive;[1] we shall look upon his lighter Muse, not as the enemy of religion, (of which in several places he expresses the justest sentiments), but as the champion of morality, and the friend of virtue.

There are, however, it must be allowed, some exceptionable parts of the volume he has given to the public, which caution would have suppressed, or correction struck out; but Poets are seldom cautious, and our Poet had, alas! no friends or companions from whom correc-tion could be obtained. When we reflect on his rank in life, the habits to which he must have been subject, and the society in which he must have mixed, we regret perhaps more than wonder, that delicacy should be so often offended in perusing a volume in which there is so much to interest and to please us.

Burns possesses the spirit as well as the fancy of a poet. That honest pride and independence of soul which are sometimes the muse's only dower, break forth on every occasion in his works. It may be, then, I shall wrong his feelings, while I indulge my own, in calling the attention of the public to his situation and circumstances. That con-dition, humble as it was, in which he found content, and wooed the muse, might not have been deemed uncomfortable; but grief and mis-fortunes have reached him there; and one or two of his poems hint, what I have learnt from some of his countrymen, that he has been obliged to form the resolution of leaving his native land, to seek under a West Indian clime that shelter and support which Scotland has denied him. But I trust means may be found to prevent this resolution from

---

[1] When the review was reprinted in the *Scots Magazine*, this passage read: 'we shall not look upon his lighter muse as the enemy of religion (of which in several places he expresses the justest sentiments), though she has been somewhat unguarded in her ridicule of hypocrisy.

In this, as in other respects, it must be allowed that there are exceptionable parts of the volume he has given to the Public, which caution would have suppressed, or correction struck out.'

taking place; and that I do my country no more than justice, when I suppose her ready to stretch out her hand to cherish and retain this native poet, whose 'wood-notes wild' possess so much excellence. To repair the wrongs of suffering or neglected merit; to call forth genius from the obscurity in which it had pined indignant, and place it where it may profit or delight the world; these are exertions which give to wealth an enviable superiority, to greatness and to patronage a laudable pride.

5. James Anderson, unsigned review in *Monthly Review*

lxxxv (December 1786), 439–48

James Anderson, Ll.D. (1739–1808), an economist and student of 'scientific farming', wrote on agriculture in the *Monthly Review* for several years. He was a friend of Thomas Blacklock. In 1790 Burns subscribed to his literary and scientific magazine, the *Bee* (see No. 14 and Introduction, p. 18).

Poeta nascitur, non fit, is an old maxim, the truth of which has been generally admitted;[1] and although it be certain that in modern times many verses are manufactured from the brain of their authors with as much labour as the iron is drawn into form under the hammer of the smith, and require to be afterwards smoothed by the file with as much care as the burnishers of Sheffield employ to give the last finish to their wares; yet after all, these verses, though ever so smooth, are nothing but *verses*, and have no genuine title to the name of *Poems*. The humble bard, whose work now demands our attention, cannot claim a place among these polished *versifiers*. His simple strains, artless and unadorned, seem to flow without effort, from the native feelings of the

1 'A poet is born, not made'.

heart. They are always nervous, sometimes inelegant, often natural, simple, and sublime. The objects that have obtained the attention of the Author are humble; for he himself, born in a low station, and following a laborious employment, has had no opportunity of observing scenes in the higher walks of life, yet his verses are sometimes struck off with a delicacy, and artless simplicity, that charms like the bewitching though irregular touches of a Shakespear. We much regret that these poems are written in some measure in an unknown tongue, which must deprive most of our Readers of the pleasure they would otherwise naturally create; being composed in the Scottish dialect, which contains many words that are altogether unknown to an English reader; beside, they abound with allusions to the modes of life, opinions, and ideas, of the people in a remote corner of the country, which would render many passages obscure, and consequently uninteresting, to those who perceive not the forcible accuracy of the picture of the objects to which they allude. This work, therefore, can only be fully relished by the natives of that part of the country where it was produced; but by such of *them* as have a taste sufficiently refined to be able to relish the beauties of nature, it cannot fail to be highly prized.

By what we can collect from the poems themselves, and the short preface to them, the Author seems to be struggling with poverty, though cheerfully supporting the fatigues of a laborious employment. He thus speaks of himself in one of the poems:

> The star that rules my luckless lot,
> Has fated me the russet coat,
> And damn'd my fortune to the groat:
>   But, in requit,
> Has blest me with a random shot
>   Of country wit.

He afterwards adds,

[quotes 'To J.S****', ll. 67–84]

Fired with the subject, he then bursts into a natural, warm, and glowing description of youth—

[quotes 'To J.S****', ll. 85–96]

'None of the following works' [we are told in the Preface] 'were ever composed with a view to the press. To amuse himself with the little creations of his own fancy, amid the toil and fatigues of a laborious life; to transcribe the various feelings, the loves, the griefs, the hopes, the fears in his own breast; to find some kind of counterpoise to the struggles of a world, always an alien scene, a task uncouth to the poetical mind; these were his motives for courting the Muses, and in these he found poetry its own reward.'

These poems are chiefly in the comic strain. Some are of the descriptive cast; particularly 'Hallow-e'en', which contains a lively picture of the magical tricks that still are practised in the country at that season. It is a valuable relic, which, like Virgils eighth *Eclogue*, will preserve the memory of these simple incantations long after they would otherwise have been lost. It is very properly accompanied with notes, explaining the circumstances to which the poem alludes. Sometimes the poems are in the elegiac strain, among which class the Reader will find much of nature in the lines to a mouse, on turning up her nest with the plough, in Nov. 1785—and those to a mountain-daisy, on turning one down with the plough, in April 1786. In these we meet with a strain of that delicate tenderness, which renders the *Idylls* of Madam Deshouliers so peculiarly interesting.[1] Some of the poems are in a more serious strain; and as these contain fewer words that are not pure English than the others, we shall select one as a specimen of our Author's manner.

The poem we have selected exhibits a beautiful picture of that simplicity of manners, which still, we are assured, on the best authority, prevails in those parts of the country where the Author dwells. That it may be understood by our Readers, it is accompanied by a Glossary and Notes, with which we have been favoured by a friend, who thoroughly understands the language, and has often, he says, witnessed with his own eyes, that pure simplicity of manners which are delineated with the most faithful accuracy in this little performance. We have used the freedom to modernise the orthography a little, wherever the measure would permit, to render it less disgusting to our Readers south of the Tweed.

[quotes 'The Cotter's Saturday Night', stanzas I–XX]

These stanzas are SERIOUS. But our Author seems to be most in his own element when in the sportive, humorous strain. The poems of this cast, as hath been already hinted, so much abound with provincial

[1] Antoinette Deshoulières (1638–94), French lyric poetess.

phrases, and allusions to local circumstances, that no extract from them would be sufficiently intelligible to our English readers.

The modern ear will be somewhat disgusted with the measure of many of these pieces, which is faithfully copied from that which was most in fashion among the ancient Scottish bards; but hath been, we think with good reason, laid aside by later Poets. The versification is in general easy; and it seems to have been a matter of indifference to our Author in what measure he wrote. But if ever he should think of offering any thing more to the Public, we are of opinion his performances would be more highly valued were they written in measures less antiquated. The few Songs, Odes, Dirges, &c. in this collection, are very poor in comparison of the other pieces. The Author's mind is not sufficiently stored with brilliant ideas to succeed in that line.

In justice to the Reader, however, as well as the Author, we must observe that this collection may be compared to a heap of wheat carelessly winnowed. Some grain of a most excellent quality is mixed with a little chaff, and half ripened corn. How many splendid volumes of poems come under our review, in which, though the mere chaff be carefully separated, not a single atom of perfect grain can be found, all being light and insipid. We never reckon our task fatiguing, when we can find, even among a great heap, a single pearl of price; but how pitiable is our lot, when we must toil and toil, and can find nothing but tiresome uniformity, with neither fault to rouse, nor beauty to animate the jaded spirits!

6. Unsigned notice in *New Annual Register*

From *The New Annual Register, or General Repository of History, Politics, and Literature, for the Year 1786.*

Burns's *Poems, chiefly in the Scottish Dialect* are the productions of a man in a low station in life, which he composed 'to amuse himself with the little creations of his own fancy, amid the toil and fatigues of labour; to transcribe the various feelings, the loves, the griefs, the hopes, the fears in his own breast.' And many of them are elegant, simple, and pleasing. Those that are written in a more serious strain have much poetical merit; but the humorous and satirical pieces appear to have been most congenial to the author's feelings, and turn of mind. Such as are of the descriptive kind contain faithful and pleasing delineations of the simplicity of manners, and engaging scenes to be found in a country life. Upon the whole, we think that our rural bard is justly entitled to the patronage and encouragement which have been liberally extended towards him.

7. John Logan questions the legend

February 1787

John Logan (1748–88), a versatile if rather unscrupulous man of letters, had been a parish minister in Scotland. In 1785 he moved to London where he managed the *English Review* (see Introduction, p. 17).

(a) Unsigned review, *English Review* (February 1787), ix, pp. 89–93

In an age that is satiated with literary pleasures nothing is so grateful to the public taste as novelty. This ingredient will give a gust to very indifferent fare and lend a flavour to the produce of the home-brewed vintage. Whatever excites the jaded appetite of an epicure will be prized, and a red herring from Greenock or Dunbar will be reckoned a *délice*. From this propensity in human nature a musical child, a rhyming milkwoman, a learned pig, or a Russian poet will 'strut their hour upon the stage', and gain the applause of the moment. From this cause, and this alone, Stephen Duck, the thresher, and many other *nameless* names have glittered and disappeared like those bubbles of the atmosphere which are called *falling* stars.[1]

Robert Burns, the Ayrshire ploughman, whose Poems are now before us, does not belong to this class of *obscurorum virorum*. Although he is by no means such a poetical prodigy as some of his *malicious* friends have represented, he has a genuine title to the attention and approbation of the public, as a *natural*, though not a *legitimate*, son of the muses.

The first poems in this collection are of the humorous and satirical kind, and in these our author appears to be most at home. In his serious poems we can trace imitations of almost every English author of celebrity,* but his humour is entirely his own. His 'Address to the

---

[1] Stephen Duck (1705–50) whose *Poems On Several Subjects* went through seven editions in their year of first publication 1730.

* Robert Burns, though he has been represented as an ordinary ploughman, was a farmer, or what they call a tenant in Scotland, and rented land which he cultivated with

Deil' (Devil), 'The Holy Fair' (a country sacrament), and his 'Epistle' in which he disguises an amour under the veil of partridge-shooting, are his masterpieces in this line; and happily in these instances his humour is neither local nor transient, for the devil, the world, and the flesh will always keep their ground. 'The Vision' is perhaps the most poetical of all his performances. Revolving his obscure situation, in which there was nothing to animate pursuit or gratify ambition, comparing his humble lot with the more flourishing condition of mercantile adventurers, and vowing to renounce the unprofitable trade of verse for ever, there appeared to him a celestial figure; not one of the nine muses, celebrated in fiction, but the real muse of every inspired poet, the GENIUS of his native district and frequented scenes. This is an elegant and happy imagination. The form of Nature that first met his enamoured eyes is the muse of the rural poet. The mountains, the forests, and the streams are the living volumes that impregnate his fancy and kindle the fire of genius. The address of this rural deity to him marks the character and describes the feelings of a poet.

[quotes 'The Vision', ll. 199–234]

'Hallowe'en', or 'Even', gives a just and literal account of the principal spells and charms that are practised on that anniversary among the peasants of Scotland, from the desire of prying into futurity, but it is not happily executed. A mixture of the solemn and burlesque can never be agreeable.

'The Cotter's (Cottager's) Saturday Night' is, without exception, the best poem in the collection. It is written in the stanza of Spenser, which probably our bard acquired from Thomson's 'Castle of Indolence' and Beattie's 'Minstrel'. It describes one of the happiest and most affecting scenes to be found in a country life, and draws a domestic picture of rustic simplicity, natural tenderness, and innocent passion that must please every reader whose feelings are not perverted.

The Odes 'To a Mouse on turning up her Nest' and 'To a Mountain Daisy' are of a similar nature, and will strike every reader for the elegant fancy and the vein of sentimental reflection that runs through them. As the latter contains few provincial phrases we shall present it to the reader.

[quotes 'To a Mountain-Daisy']

his own hands. He is better acquainted with the English poets than most English authors that have come under our review.

77

The stanza of Mr. Burns is generally ill-chosen, and his provincial dialect confines his beauties to one half of the island. But he possesses the genuine characteristics of a poet; a vigorous mind, a lively fancy, a surprising knowledge of human nature, and an expression rich, various and abundant. In the plaintive or pathetic he does not excel; his love-poems (though he confesses, or rather professes, a *penchant* to the *belle passion*) are execrable; but in the midst of vulgarity and common-place, which occupy one half of the volume, we meet with many striking beauties that make ample compensation. One happy touch on the Eolian harp from fairy fingers awakes emotions in the soul that make us forget the antecedent mediocrity or harshness of that natural music.

The liberal patronage which Scotland has extended to this self-taught bard reflects honour on the country. If Mr. Burns has flourished in the shade of obscurity, his country will form higher expectations from him when basking in the sunshine of applause. His situation, how-ever, is critical. He seems to possess too great a facility of composition and is too easily satisfied with his own productions. Fame may be procured by novelty, but it must be supported by merit. We have thrown out these hints to our young and ingenious author because we discern faults in him which, if not corrected, like the *fly in the apothecary's ointment*, may give an unfortunate tincture and colour to his future compositions.

(b) Extract from a letter to Henry Mackenzie, 28 February 1787 (*BC* (1944), xix; and cf. H. W. Thompson, *A Scottish Man of Feeling* (1931), pp. 226–7)

Give me leave to assure you that you have been misinformed with regard to the Critique it contains on the poems of Burns. That article is not a very good one, but it is impartial, and I dare say Mr. Burns will be very pleased with the praise that he has received. His humorous poems are not preferred to his serious; it is only said that in the former he is more at his ease, at home and original than in the latter. It is very remarkable that the poems you deservedly distinguish, the 'Mouse', the 'Mountain Daisy', the 'Vision', and the 'Cottar's Saturday Night', are highly praised. Still, however, I can hardly allow him the merit of a native vein for the plaintive and pathetic. 'The Cottar's Sat. Night' draws tears, but exhibits only natural affection and tenderness heightened by devotion. That is not the pathetic. Mr. Burns is a clever fellow, a Man of Observation, and a Country Libertine, but I am much mistaken if he has anything of the Penseroso in his character. The 'Mouse' and the 'Mountain Daisy' contain the plaintive of reflection, not of feeling. His love poems, that is his bawdy songs, are said to be execrable, which is perhaps a strong expression, but no man should avow rakery who does not possess an estate of 500 £ a year. I read his works under considerable disadvantage. I received three letters from Edinburgh full of irrational and unbounded panegyric, representing him as a poetical phenomenon that owed nothing but to Nature and his own Genius. When I opened the book I found that he was as well acquainted with the English poets as I was, and I could point you out a hundred imitations. There is a kind of Imposture not infrequent among poets of conveying Modern ideas in a dialect of Antiquity. If Chatterton's poems had been published according to the Modern Orthography, they would not have found so many readers and admirers. I have given Burns' poems to several English gentlemen who cannot discern their beauties. When that rage and Mania which seizes Edinburgh at least once a year has subsided, I am confident that your own opinion will coincide with Mine.

Notwithstanding what I have written, my opinion of Burns' merit is perhaps as high as what is entertained at Edinburgh. I do not think however, that he is so much an Original as has been represented, and, indeed, I do not recollect a new image of nature in all his works, except one in the Ode to the 'Mountain Daisy'. An enthusiastic lover always discovers new and concealed beauties in his Mistress.

8. Unsigned notice in *Critical Review*

1st ser. lxiii (May 1787), 387–8

We have had occasion to examine a number of poetical productions, written by persons in the lower ranks of life, and who had hardly received any education; but we do not recollect to have ever met with a more signal instance of true and uncultivated genius, than in the author of these Poems. His occupation is that of a common plough-man; and his life has hitherto been spent in struggling with poverty. But all the rigours of fortune have not been able to repress the frequent efforts of his lively and vigorous imagination. Some of these poems are of a serious cast; but the strain which seems most natural to the author, is the sportive and humorous. It is to be regretted, that the Scottish dialect, in which these poems are written, must obscure the native beauties with which they appear to abound, and renders the sense often unintelligible to an English reader. Should it, however, prove true, that the author has been taken under the patronage of a great lady in Scotland, and that a celebrated professor has interested himself in the cultivation of his talents, there is reason to hope, that his distinguished genius may yet be exerted in such a manner as to afford more general delight. In the mean time, we must admire the generous enthusiasm of his untutored muse; and bestow the tribute of just applause on one whose name will be transmitted to posterity with honour.

9. Hugh Blair suggests changes in the poems

1787

Undated notes about the Kilmarnock *Poems* and about other material which Burns thought of including in his Edinburgh edition (*BC* (1932), n.s. vii).

Dr Hugh Blair (1718–1800) was from 1758 minister of the High Church, Edinburgh, and from 1762 Professor of Rhetoric and Belles Lettres in Edinburgh University. Blacklock had written, 'His taste is too highly polished and his genius too regular in its emotions to make allowances for the sallies of a more impetuous ardour' (Snyder, p. 203). Burns accepted only the first and fourth of these suggested emendations. He was grateful to Blair, but saw his shortcomings clearly (*Letters* I, p. 88; II, p. 340) (see Introduction, p. 6).

['A Dedication To G— H— Esq.;', line 49] The line—*And och—that's nae Regen-n*—ought to be omitted as Mr. Burns agreed.
[*Ibid.*, ll. 68ff.] The Paragraph beginning with this line, *O ye what leave the springs o' C-lv-n*—had much better I think be omitted. The Poem will be better without it, & it will give offence by the ludicrous views of the punishments of Hell.
['Epistle to J. R.—', stanzas 7ff.] The Description of shooting the hen is understood, I find, to convey an indecent meaning: tho' in reading the poem, I confess, I took it literally, and the indecency did not strike me. But if the Author meant to allude to an affair with a Woman, as is supposed, the whole Poem ought undoubtedly to be left out of the new edition. ['The Holy Fair', stanza 12] The line—*wi' tidings of Sal-v-n*—ought to be alter'd, as it gives just offence. The Author may easily contrive some other Rhyme in place of the word *Sal-v-n*.
['Address to the Deil', stanza 11] The stanza of—*There mystic knots make great abuse*—had better be left out, as indecent.
['A Dream', stanza 13] The stanza—*Young Royal Tarry Breeks, I learn*—is also coarse and had better be omitted.

['Epitaph For G. H. Esq.;'] The last line—*May I be saved or d—d*—is very exceptionable. The general thought may remain, *may I be with him wherever he is*—but may be d—d with him, is too much, & ought undoubtedly to be altered.

Of the proposed additions to the New Edition some are very good. The best, I think, are—'John Barleycorn'—'Death & Dr. Hornbook' —'The Winter Night'—the verses left in a friend's house where the Author slept.

There are a few which in my opinion ought not to be published.

The two stanzas to the tune of 'Gilliecrankie', which refer to the death of Zimir and Cozbi as related in the book of Numbers, are beyond doubt quite inadmissible.

The Verses entitled 'The Prophet' and 'God's Complaint', from the 15th Ch. of Jeremiah, are also inadmissible. They would be considered burlesquing the Scriptures.

The Whole of What is called the Cantata, the Songs of the Beggars and their Doxies,[1] with the Grace at the end of them, are altogether unfit in my opinion for publication. They are by much too licentious; and fall below the dignity which Mr. Burns possesses in the rest of his poems & would rather degrade them.

These observations are Submitted by one who is a great friend to Mr. Burn's Poems and wishes him to preserve the fame of Virtuous Sensibility, & of humorous fun, without offence.

[1] Refers to 'Love and Liberty' ('The Jolly Beggars').

10. James Macaulay questions the legend

1787

Stanzas 5–12, 'Rhyming Epistle to Mr. R– B–, Ayrshire', *Edinburgh Evening Courant*, 23 June 1787. James Macaulay was an Edinburgh printer. This epistle was included in his *Poems on Various Subjects, in Scots and English*, 1788 (see Introduction, p. 6).

But still for a' the blast that's made,
I doubt you are some sleekit blade,
That never handled shool[1] or spade,
    Or yet the pleugh,
Unless it were to hae it said—
    An' that's enough:

For by the scraps o' French an' Latin,
That's flung athort your buik fu' thick in,
It's easy seen you've aft been flitting
    Frae school to school;
An' nae thanks to your head an' wittin',
    Tho' you're nae fool.

I'm no for riving aff your brow,
The laurel folk may think you due;
But, gin a while you left the pleu'
    To tend the College,
What need you smoor[2] the thing that's true,
    Wi' a' your knowledge?

The prints—newspapers an' reviews,
Frae time to time may aft you rouse,
An' say you're *Heaven-taught*—your views
    Are clear an' fair,
An' a' your ain, gi'en by THE MUSE
    O'er the Banks o' Ayr.

---

[1] *shool*: shovel.   [2] *smoor*: smother.

But, waesuck,[1] that'll no gae down
Wi' ilka chiel about this town
That struts in black, an' eke a gown;
    Na, na, they canna
Believe that poets fa' aroun',
    Like flakes o' manna!

In days o' yore, folk aft were fleec'd;
But miracles lang syne hae ceas'd
Among the gentry here, at least.
    Wha ne'er can think
A bard direct frae Heav'n can feast,
    An' write, an' *drink*.

In a' think that's in our possession,
We may discern a due progression,
Whilk forces frae us this confession,
    Man didna fa',
Down frae the lift[2] without transgression
    Or yet a flaw.

You've surely notic'd this yoursel',
Afore we read, we aye maun spell;
An' till the chucky[3] leave the shell
    Whar it was hidden,
It canna soun' the morning bell
    Upo' your midden.

The grain you t'ither day did saw
Ayont the knowe, was smoor'd wi' snaw,
An' summer suns maun gar it blaw,
    Ere it be ready
For Autumn's sonsy lassies braw
    To mak it *teddy*.[4]

Ilk think in Nature has a time,
When any may say, it's in its prime,
An' disna in a hurry climb
    To real perfection.
But maun gae thro' its ilka clime,
    An' ain direction.

[1] *waesuck*: alas.   [2] *lift*: sky.   [3] *chucky*: young chick.
[4] *teddy*: ready for carting to the stock-yard.

It's just the same, (for ought I ken),
Among the folk that lifts the pen,
To write on kingdoms, brutes, or men;
   Ane's brains sae stappit,[1]
Mony a owk[2] on lear[3] we spen',
   To clear our *caput*.

This being than a settled case,
Ne'er try to put things out o' place;
But own your intellects you brace
   Wi' solid lore,
As mony a ane, wi' honest face,
   Has done afore.

---

[1] *stappit*: steeped.   [2] *owk*: week.   [3] *lear*: learning.

POEMS, CHIEFLY IN THE SCOTTISH DIALECT

Edinburgh 1787

---

11. Notices in *Universal Magazine*

May 1787

(a) Unsigned notice, *Universal Magazine*, lxxx (May 1787), pp. 260–2

These Poems, the author of which is in the humble situation of a plough-man, in the Highlands of Scotland, possess uncommon excellence, whether we consider them as adorned with beautiful sentiments, picturesque imagery, or harmonious versification. They are introduced by a list of subscribers for more than two thousand eight hundred copies, and by a dedication 'to the noblemen and gentlemen of the Caledonian Hunt,' which is distinguished by a dignity and spirit worthy of bards in more exalted situations.

We shall select, as a specimen, the poem entitled 'A Winter Night', and part of an 'Epistle to Davie, a Brother Poet'. An explanation of the Scotch words, in alphabetical order, is in a note at the end.

[quotes 'A Winter Night'; 'Epistle to Davie', stanzas IV–X]

(b) On reading this, 'A Friend to Genius', sent from Eton on 11 June a copy of Mackenzie's 'Judicious Critique', which was reprinted in the Supplement to the *Universal Magazine*, lxxx, pp. 352–5 (see Introduction, p. 19)

Extraordinary ACCOUNT *of* ROBERT BURNS, *the* Ayrshire Ploughman.
To the EDITOR *of the* UNIVERSAL MAGAZINE.

SIR,

The two Poems which you inserted in your Magazine for May last, must have excited a Curiosity in your Readers to know something of the extraordinary Genius that produced them. I have, therefore, great Satisfaction in sending you the following Account, with a judicious Critique on the Poems, which I met with in the 97th Number of the *Lounger*, a very ingenious periodical Paper lately published at Edinburgh by the Authors of the *Mirror*, and now collected, like that entertaining Work, into three Pocket Volumes. I am happy to add that the benevolent Wishes of the Author, at the Conclusion, have been seconded by a very noble Subscription in Favour of this untutored Bard.

I am, &c. A Friend to Genius.

Eton, June 11.

12. Unsigned notice in
New Town and Country Magazine

August 1787

Robert Burns, we are informed, is a ploughman, but blessed by Nature with a powerful genius. His subjects are not, as might have been expected, confined to the objects which surrounded him; he is satirical as well as pastoral, and humorous as well as pathetic. These poems being 'chiefly in the Scottish dialect', it must necessarily confine their beauties to a small circle of readers; however, the author has given good specimens of his skill in English. The following stanza is not only very elegant, but highly poetical.

> O happy love! where love like this is found!
> O heart-felt raptures! bliss beyond compare!
> I've paced much this weary, *mortal round,*

ROBERT BURNS

And sage EXPERIENCE bids me this declare—
'If Heaven a draught of heavenly pleasure spare,
  'One *cordial* in this melancholly *Vale*,
' 'Tis when a youthful, loving *modest* Pair,
'In other's arms, breathe out the tender tale,
'Beneath the milk-white thorn that scents the ev'ning gale'.

13. Unsigned notice in *General Magazine and Impartial Review*

i (1787), 79–80

By general report we learn, that R.B. is a *plough-boy*, of small education, but blessed by nature with a powerful genius. His subjects are not, as might have been expected, confined to the objects which surround him: he is satirical as well as pastoral, and humorous as well as elegiac. Thus he speaks of a certain great character:

For you, young Potentate o' W—,
  I tell your *Highness* fairly,
Down Pleasure's stream, wi' swelling sails,
  I'm tauld ye're driving rarely;
But some day ye may gnaw your nails,
  An' curse your folly sairly,
That e'er ye brak Diana's pales,
  Or rattl'd dice wi' *Charlie*
    By night or day.

And thus of a popular orator:

Yon ill-tongu'd tinkler, *Charlie Fox*,
May taunt you wi' his jeers an' mocks;
But gie him 't het, my hearty cocks!
  E'en cowe the cadie!
An' send him to his dicing box,
  An' sportin' lady.

88

It is greatly to be lamented that these poems are 'chiefly in the Scottish dialect', as it must necessarily confine their beauties to a small circle of readers, and as the author has given good specimens of his skill in the English; probably in the *humorous* pieces the spirit might evaporate with the dialect; but in the serious compositions we should have been more highly gratified had the language been of a piece with the following stanza, which we quote not only as very elegant, but highly poetical:

> O happy love! where love like this is found!
>   O heart-felt raptures! bliss beyond compare!
> I've paced much this weary, *mortal round*,
>   And sage EXPERIENCE bids me this declare—
> 'If Heaven a draught of heavenly pleasure spare,
>   'One *cordial* in this melancholly *Vale*,
> ' 'Tis when a youthful, loving, *modest* Pair,
>   'In other's arms, breathe out the tender tale,
> 'Beneath the milk-white thorn that scents the ev'ning gale.'

We are happy to observe prefixed to this collection of natural genius and strong sense, a list of subscribers, at once so numerous and respectable, as to do honour to the author's countrymen, and whose bounty we trust will enable him to preserve that independence of mind, and to indulge himself in those flights of imagination which he appears to possess in an eminent degree, and which constitutes the genuine poet of nature.

14. James Anderson, unsigned notice in *Monthly Review*

lxxvii (December 1787), 491

(See No. 5 and Introduction, p. 19.)

We are glad to find, by the numerous and respectable list of subscribers prefixed to the volume before us, that this Bard of Nature has no reason to complain that 'a poet is not honoured in his own country'. It appears that he has been very liberally patronized by an indulgent Public; and we rejoice to see that he may now have it in his power to tune his oaten reed at his ease. Whether this change in his circumstances will prove beneficial to the cause of literature, or productive of greater happiness to the individual, time alone can discover; but we sincerely wish it may prove favourable to both.

Having given a pretty full account of the first edition of these poems, in our Review for December last, we only announce the present publication as an article of some curiosity, and mention that in this edition, several new poems are added, which bear evident marks of coming from the same hand with the former collection. The most entertaining of these additions appeared, to us, to be, 'John Barleycorn, a Ballad', which gives a very entertaining allegorical account of the whole progress and management of barley, from its being sown in the ground, to its affording a warm, exhilarating liquor. The thought of it is not altogether new; but it is delivered in a style of great pleasantry, and native humour. As this piece is written *in English*, it will be relished alike by the southern and the northern reader.

15. William Cowper on Burns

July and August 1787

Extracts from letters of 24 July and 27 August 1787 to Samuel Rose. Rose, a student at Glasgow University, had urged the English poet Cowper to read Burns (*Correspondence of William Cowper*, ed. T. Wright (1904), IV, pp. 145–8). (See Introduction, p. 18.)

(a) William Cowper to Samuel Rose, 24 July 1787

I have . . . read Burns's poems, and have read them twice; and though they be written in a language that is new to me, and many of them on subjects much inferior to the author's ability, I think them on the whole a very extraordinary production. He is I believe the only poet these kingdoms have produced in the lower rank of life since Shakespeare (I should rather say since Prior,) who need not be indebted for any part of his praise to a charitable consideration of his origin, and the disadvantages under which he has laboured. It will be pity if he should not hereafter divest himself of barbarism, and content himself with writing pure English, in which he appears perfectly qualified to excel. He who can command admiration, dishonours himself if he aims no higher than to raise a laugh.

(b) William Cowper to Samuel Rose, 27 August 1787

Poor Burns loses much of his deserved praise in this country through our ignorance of his language. I despair of meeting with any Englishman who will take the pains that I have taken to understand him. His candle is bright, but shut up in a dark lantern. I lent him to a very sensible neighbour of mine; but his uncouth dialect spoiled all; and before he had half read him through he was quite *ram-feezled*.[1]

[1] exhausted.

16. Dorothy Wordsworth on Burns

6, 16 December 1787

Extract from a letter to Jane Pollard, referring to the Kilmarnock edition. *The Letters of William and Dorothy Wordsworth*, ed. E. De Selincourt, 2nd ed., I *The Early Years 1785–1805*, rev. C. L. Shaver (1967), p. 13 (see also Nos 29, 33, 44, 53, 70, and Introduction, pp. 28–9, 37–8).

When I last wrote I forgot to thank you for those verses you were so kind as to transcribe for me. My Br Wm was here at the time I got your Letter, I told him that you had recommended the book[1] to me, he had read it and admired many of the pieces very much; and promised to get it me at the book-club, which he did. I was very much pleased with them indeed, the one which you mentioned to me is I think very comical, I mean the address to a Louse: there is one, to a mountain daisy, which is very pretty.

[1] 'the book': Kilmarnock edition.

17. Verse attack and verse tribute

1788, 1789

(a) Extract from 'On the Ayr-shire Ploughman Poet, or Poetaster, R.B.', in *Animadversions on Some Poets and Poetasters of the Present Age Especially R—T B—S, and J—N L—K. With a Contrast of Some of the Former Age. By James Maxwell, Poet in Paisley* (Paisley, 1788).

J—N L—K is John Lapraik, who exchanged rhymed epistles with Burns (see Introduction, p. 20).

Of all British poets that yet have appear'd,
None e'er at things sacred so daringly sneer'd,
As he in the west, who but lately is sprung
From behind the plough-tails, and from raking of dung.
A champion for Satan, none like him before,
And his equal, pray God, we may never see more;
For none have like him, been by Satan inspir'd,
Which makes his rank nonsense by fools so admir'd.
He is to this land and this age a disgrace,
And mostly to those who his poems embrace.
His jargon gives rakes and vile harlots delight,
But all sober people abhor the vile sight.
He makes of the scriptures a ribaldry joke;
By him are the laws both of God and man broke.
   The prophet Isaiah (divinely inspir'd)
Who hath been by wise-men so greatly admir'd.
The Jewish and Heathen, and Christians too,
Have thought that his language did all men outdo:
Yet this stupid blockhead upon him so falls,
That only wild raptures his diction he calls.*
   The song of the captives at Babylon streams;
At their lamentation he only makes games;
Because on the willows their harps silent hung,
While they by the Heathen endured such wrong;

* 'The Cotter's Saturday-Night'.

93

This infidel mocks at the Psalmist so sly,
Like fiddles and baby-clouts hung up to dry.*
   The most solemn ordinance Christ hath ordain'd,†
Which hath in his church, since his passion, remain'd,
This infidel scoffer calls that but a Fair,
To which rakes and harlots together repair,
To make lewd appointments of carnal delight;
Thus is it described by this hellish wight.
'Tis true by too many 'tis grossly abus'd,
By whom, like a fair or a market 'tis us'd:
Too many, like him and his jilts there attend,
Which greatly the hearts of the faithful offend:
But surely no bus'ness such cattle have there,
To make it appear like a market or fair.
   Nor is this the half that in truth may be said,
Tho' some take his part, who make preaching their trade.
For some of our clergy his Poems esteem,
And some of our elders think no man like him.
But let them esteem him, and value his lies,
By consequence then they the scriptures despise.
Tho' some of that function he favours indeed,
Who seem true adherents to his hellish creed.

(b) Verse by Helen Craik, dated 'Oct. 1789' inscribed on reverse of frontispiece portrait of Burns in a copy of the 1787 edition now in the Burns Collection, Mitchell Library, Glasgow.

Helen Craik (1750?–1825) was a lady of literary interests who lived near Dumfries.

Here native Genius, gay, unique and strong,
Shines through each page, and marks the tuneful song;
Rapt Admiration her warm tribute pays,
And Scotia proudly echoes all she says;
Bold Independence, too, illumes the theme
And claims a manly privilege to Fame.
—Vainly, O Burns! wou'd rank and riches shine,
Compar'd with in-born merit great as thine,
These Chance may take, as Chance has often giv'n,
But Pow'rs like thine can only come from Heav'n.

* His Poem called 'The Ordination'.
† His poem which he calls 'The Holy Fair'.

94

18. A. F. Tytler on 'Tam o' Shanter'

March 1791

Extract from letter of 12 March 1791 to Burns. *The Life and Works of Robert Burns*, ed. R. Chambers, rev. W. Wallace, 1896, III, pp. 55–6.

Alexander Fraser Tytler (1747–1813), later Lord Woodhouselee, was an Edinburgh advocate, professor, and man of letters. On 11 March 1791 he received a sheet of Grose's *Antiquities* on which was printed 'Tam o' Shanter'. He already knew Burns, and wrote this letter giving his opinion of the poem. Burns deleted four lines on the advice given here when 'Tam o' Shanter' was reprinted in the 2-volume Edinburgh edition of 1793 (see Introduction, p. 13).

Edinburgh, 12th March 1791

I have seldom in my life tasted of higher enjoyment from any work of genius than I have received from this composition; and I am much mistaken if this poem alone, had you never written another syllable, would not have been sufficient to have transmitted your name down to posterity with high reputation. In the introductory part, where you paint the character of your hero and exhibit him at the ale-house *ingle*, with his tippling cronies, you have delineated nature with a humour and *naïveté* that would do honour to Matthew Prior; but when you describe the infernal orgies of the witches' sabbath and the hellish scenery in which they are exhibited, you display a power of imagination that Shakespeare himself could not have exceeded. I know not that I have ever met with a picture of more horrible fancy than the following:

> Coffins stood round, like open presses,
> That shaw'd the dead in their last dresses;
> And, by some devilish cantraip sleight,
> Each in its cauld hand held a light.

95

But when I came to the succeeding lines, my blood ran cold within me:

> A knife a father's throat had mangled—
> Whom his ain son o' life bereft—
> *The grey hairs yet stack to the heft.*

And here, after two following lines, 'Wi' mair of horrible and awefu', &c., the descriptive part might perhaps have been better closed than the four lines which succeed, which, though good in themselves, yet, as they derive all their merit from the satire they contain, are here rather misplaced among the circumstances of pure horror. The initiation of the young witch is most happily described—the effect of her charms exhibited in the dance on Satan himself—the apostrophe, 'Ah little thought thy reverend grannie!' the transport of Tam, who forgets his situation and enters completely into the spirit of the scene—are all features of high merit in this excellent composition. The only fault it possesses is that the winding-up, or conclusion, of the story is not commensurate to the interest which is excited by the descriptive and characteristic painting of the preceding parts. The preparation is fine, but the result is not adequate. But for this, perhaps, you have a good apology—you stick to the popular tale.[1]

And now that I have got out my mind and feel a little relieved of the weight of that debt I owed you, let me end this desultory scroll by an advice: You have proved your talent for a species of composition in which but a very few of our own poets have succeeded. Go on— write more tales in the same style—you will eclipse Prior and La Fontaine; for with equal wit, equal power of numbers and equal naïveté of expression, you have a bolder and more vigorous imagination.

---

[1] Burns replied: (*Letters* II, p. 70. Ellisland, April 1791)
As to the faults you detected in the piece, they are truly there: one of them, the hit at the lawyer and priest, I shall cut out; as to the falling off in the catastrophe, for the reason you justly adduce it cannot easily be remedied. Your approbation, sir, has given me such additional spirits to persevere in this species of poetic composition, that I am already revolving two or three stories in my fancy. If I can bring these floating ideas to bear any kind of embodied form, it will give me an additional opportunity of assuring you how much I have the honour to be, &c.

19. Robert Heron on three poems

1793

Extract from Robert Heron, *Observations made in a Journey through the Western Counties of Scotland* (Perth, 1793), II, pp. 349–50.

Robert Heron (1764–1807) had been a minor acquaintance of Burns in Edinburgh, and was to write the first full-scale *Memoir* of the poet, published in 1797. Hans Hecht comments that the few pages from which this passage is taken 'look like a first draft of the Memoir' (H. Hecht, *Robert Burns*, 2nd ed., rev. (1950), p. 253) (see No. 26, and Introduction, p. 15).

The Poems which thus brought Mr. Burns into fashion,—for a winter, have all considerable merit. Some of them I think the first pieces of their kind in ours, or in any language with which I am acquainted. 'The Cotter's Saturday Night', which is really a faithful description from the life, proves, that the manners of our rustics can afford subjects for pastoral poetry more elevated and more amiable than those which are exhibited in Gay's 'Shepherd's Week'; that Pastoral Poetry needs not to employ itself upon fictitious manners and modes of life, but may, with higher poetical advantages, paint the humble virtues, the simple pleasures, the inartificial manners of our peasantry, such as they actually exist. The Poem on the rustic rites and festivity of the 'Hallowe'en' is finely fanciful, and most divertingly comic; but, the subject was indeed rich in materials for the man of fancy, and humour. A later composition of Mr. Burns's, a Tale, intituled 'Alloway Kirk',[1] in which the vulgar ideas concerning witchcraft are happily introduced, has very high merit of the same cast as that of 'Hallowe'en'. As a Tale, it wants indeed, the inimitable, arch simplicity of the *Tales* of Fontaine. But, it has beauties of a higher kind. I have been more entertained by it than by any of Prior's. Burns seems to have thought, with Boccacce and Prior, that some share of indelicacy was a necessary ingredient in a Tale. Pity that he should have debased so fine a piece, by any thing, having even the

[1] 'Tam o' Shanter'.

remotest relation to obscenity! Many of his other poems are perhaps superior to these in merit; although these be my favourites. In all of them we find that originality of sentiment and of imagery which none can display, but he who looks around, on nature and on life, with the eye of a man of genius.

20. Joseph Ritson: Burns and song

1794

Ritson (1752–1804), an able English antiquary of a combative temperament, published his *Collection of Scottish Songs* in two volumes in 1794. He referred in I, LXXIV–LXXV, to Burns's contributions to James Johnson's *Scots Musical Museum* (see Introduction, p. 12).

Robert Burns, a natural poet of the first eminence, does not, perhaps, appear to his usual advantage in Song: *non omnia possumus*. The political 'fragment', as he calls it ['When *Guildford* good our Pilot stood'] inserted in the Second Volume of the present collection, has, however, much merit in some of the satirical stanzas, and could it have been concluded with the spirit with which it is commenced, would indisputably have been intitled to great praise; but the character of his favourite minister seems to have operated like the touch of a torpedo; and after vainly attempting something like a panegyric, he seems under the necessity of relinquishing the task. Possibly the bard will one day see occasion to complete his performance as a uniform satire.*

* Mr. Burns, as good a poet as Ramsay, is, it must be regretted an equally licentious unfaithful publisher of the performances of others. Many of the original, old, ancient, genuine songs inserted in Johnson's *Scots Musical Museum* derive not a little of their merit from passing through the hands of this very ingenious critic.

21. George Thomson, an unsigned obituary notice in *London Chronicle*

28–30 July 1796

'Memoirs of the Late Robert Burns, the Scotch Poet', an unsigned article, almost certainly written by George Thomson; text here from J. De Lancey Ferguson, 'The earliest obituary of Burns', *Modern Philology* (November 1934), xxxii, pp. 179–84.

George Thomson (1757–1851), correspondent of Burns and publisher of *A Select Collection of Original Scotish Airs* (1793–1818), did much harm to Burns's reputation by insinuating in this obituary, which was often reprinted, that alcoholism caused the poet's early death (see Introduction, pp. 21–2).

Burns was literally a ploughman, but neither in that state of servile dependence or degrading ignorance which the situation might bespeak in this country. He had the common education of a Scottish peasant, perhaps something more, and that spirit of independence, which, though banished in that country from the scenes of aristocratic influence, is sometimes to be found to a high degree in the humblest classes of society. He had genius, starting beyond the obstacles of poverty, and which would have distinguished itself in any situation. His early days were occupied in procuring bread by the labour of his own hands, in the honourable task of cultivating the earth; but his nights were devoted to books and the muse, except when they were wasted in those haunts of village festivity, and in the indulgences of the social bowl, to which the Poet was but too immoderately attached in every period of his life. He wrote, not with a view to encounter the public eye, or in the hope to procure fame by his productions, but to give vent to the feelings of his own genius—to indulge the impulse of an ardent and poetical mind. Burns, from that restless activity, which is the peculiar characteristic of his countrymen, proposed to emigrate to Jamaica, in order to seek his fortune by the exertion of those talents

99

of which he felt himself possessed. It was upon this occasion that one of his friends suggested to him the idea of publishing his poems, in order to raise a few pounds to defray the expenses of his passage. The idea was eagerly embraced. A coarse edition of his poems was first published at Dumfries. They were soon noticed by the gentlemen in the neighbourhood. Proofs of such uncommon genius in a situation so humble, made the acquaintance of the author eagerly sought after. His poems found their way to Edinburgh; some extracts, and an account of the author were inserted in the periodical paper, the *Lounger*, which was at that time in the course of publication. The voyage of the author was delayed in the hope that a suitable provision would be made for him by the generosity of the public. A subscription was set on foot for a new edition of his works, and was forwarded by the exertions of some of the first characters in Scotland. The subscription contains a greater number of respectable names than almost have ever appeared to any similar production, but as the book was set at a low price, we have reason to know that the return to the author was not very considerable. Burns was brought to Edinburgh for a few months, everywhere invited and caressed, and at last one of his patrons procured him the situation of an Exciseman, and an income somewhat less than 50 l. per ann. We know not whether any steps were taken to better this humble income. Probably he was not qualified to fill a superior station to that which was assigned him. We know that his manners refused to partake the polish of genteel society, that his talents were often obscured and finally impaired by excess, and that his private circumstances were embittered by pecuniary distress. Such, we believe, is the character of a man, who in his compositions had discovered the force of native humour, the warmth and tenderness of passion, and the glowing touches of a descriptive pencil—a man who was the pupil of nature, the poet of inspiration, and who possessed in an extraordinary degree the powers and failings of genius. Of the former, his works will remain a lasting monument; of the latter, we are afraid that his conduct and his fate afford but too melancholy proofs. Like his predecessor Ferguson, though he died at an early age, his mind was previously exhausted; and the apprehensions of a distempered imagination concurred along with indigence and sickness to embitter the last moments of his life. He has left behind a wife, with five infant children, and in the hourly expectation of a sixth, without any resource but what she may hope from the public sympathy, and the regard due to memory of her husband. Need we say anything more to awaken the feelings of Benevolence? Burns, who himself erected a monument to the memory of his unfortunate predecessor Ferguson, has left in his distressed and helpless family an opportunity to his admirers and the public, at once to pay a tribute of respect to the genius of a Poet, and to erect a substantial monument of their own beneficence.

22. 'Candidior', character sketch in *Dumfries Journal*

August 1796

'Character Sketch' by 'Candidior' [Maria Riddell]; revised text here from J. Currie, ed., *The Works of Robert Burns*, 2nd ed. (1801), I, pp. 247–59. (Only a trial sheet of the original article survives, cf. *Studies In Scottish Literature* (1968), v, pp. 194–7.)

Maria Riddell (1772–1808) knew Burns well in the last five years of his life. This defence of his character was judged by Henley and Henderson to be 'so admirable in tone, and withal so discerning and impartial in understanding, that it remains the best thing written of him by a contemporary critic' (*The Poetry of Robert Burns* (1896), II, p. 421) (see Introduction, p. 22).

The attention of the public seems to be much occupied at present with the loss it has recently sustained in the death of the Caledonian poet Robert Burns; a loss calculated to be severely felt throughout the literary world, as well as lamented in the narrower sphere of private friendship. It was not therefore probable that such an event should be long un-attended with the accustomed profusion of posthumous anecdotes and memoirs which are usually circulated immediately after the death of every rare and celebrated personage: I had however conceived no intention of appropriating to myself the privilege of criticising Burns' writings and character, or of anticipating on the province of a biographer.

Conscious indeed of my own inability to do justice to such a subject, I should have continued wholly silent, had misrepresentation and calumny been less industrious; but a regard to truth, no less than affection for the memory of a friend, must now justify my offering to the public a few at least of those observations which an intimate acquaintance with Burns, and the frequent opportunities I have had of observing equally his happy qualities and his failings for several years past, have enabled me to communicate.

It will actually be an injustice done to Burns' character, not only by future generations and foreign countries, but even by his native Scotland, and perhaps a number of his contemporaries, that he is generally talked of, and considered, with reference to his poetical talent *only*: for the fact is, even allowing his great and original genius its due tribute of admiration, that poetry (I appeal to all who have had the advantage of being personally acquainted with him) was actually not his *forte*. Many others perhaps may have ascended to prouder heights in the region of Parnassus, but none certainly ever outshone Burns in the charms— the sorcery, I would almost call it, of fascinating conversation, the spontaneous eloquence of social argument, or the unstudied poignancy of brilliant repartee; nor was any man, I believe, ever gifted with a larger portion of the '*vivida vis animi*'.[1]

His personal endowments were perfectly correspondent to the qualifications of his mind; his form was manly; his action, energy itself; devoid in great measure perhaps of those graces, of that polish, acquired only in the refinement of societies where in early life he could have no opportunities of mixing; but where, such was the irresistible power of attraction that encircled him, though his appearance and manners were always peculiar, he never failed to delight, and to excel. His figure seemed to bear testimony to his earlier destination and employments. It seemed rather moulded by nature for the rough exercises of agriculture, than the gentler cultivation of the Belles Lettres. His features were stamped with the hardy character of independence, and the firmness of conscious, though not arrogant, pre-eminence; the animated expressions of countenance were almost peculiar to himself; the rapid lightnings of his eye were always the harbingers of some flash of genius, whether they darted the fiery glances of insulted and indignant superiority, or beamed with the impassioned sentiment of

1 'lively force of mind'.

fervent and impetuous affections. His voice alone could improve upon the magic of his eye; sonorous, replete with the finest modulations, it alternately captivated the ear with the melody of poetic numbers, the perspicuity of nervous reasoning, or the ardent sallies of enthusiastic patriotism. The keenness of satire was, I am almost at a loss whether to say his forte or his foible; for though nature had endowed him with a portion of the most pointed excellence in that dangerous talent, he suffered it too often to be the vehicle of personal, and sometimes unfounded, animosities. It was not always that sportiveness of humour, that 'unwary pleasantry,' which *Sterne* has depictured with touches so conciliatory, but the darts of ridicule were frequently directed as the caprice of the instant suggested, or as the altercations of parties and of persons happened to kindle the restlessness of his spirit into interest or aversion. This however, was not invariably the case; his wit (which is no unusual matter indeed,) had always the start of his judgment, and would lead him to the indulgence of raillery uniformly acute, but often unaccompanied with the least desire to wound. The suppression of an arch and full-pointed bon-mot from a dread of offending its object, the sage of Zuric very properly classes as a virtue *only to be sought for in the Calendar of Saints*: if so, Burns must not be too severely dealt with for being rather deficient in it. He paid for this mischievous wit as dearly as any one could do. ' 'Twas no extravagant arithmetic' to say of him, as was said of Yorick, 'that for every ten jokes he got an hundred enemies;' but much allowance will be made by a candid mind for the splenetic warmth of a spirit whom 'distress had spited with the world,' and which, unbounded in its intellectual sallies and pursuits, continually experienced the curbs imposed by the waywardness of his fortune. The vivacity of his wishes and temper was indeed checked by almost habitual disappointments, which sat heavy on a heart, that acknowledged the ruling passion of independence, without having ever been placed beyond the grasp of penury. His soul was never languid or inactive, and his genius was extinguished only with the last sparks of retreating life. His passions rendered him, according as they disclosed themselves in affection or antipathy, an object of enthusiastic attachment, or of decided enmity; for *he* possessed none of that negative insipidity of character, whose love might be regarded with indifference, or whose resentment could be considered with contempt. In this it should seem, the temper of his associates took the tincture from his own; for *he* acknowledged in the universe but two classes of objects, those of adoration the most fervent, or of aversion the most uncontrollable;

and it has been frequently a reproach to him, that unsusceptible of indifference, often hating, where he ought only to have despised, he alternately opened his heart and poured forth the treasures of his understanding to such as were incapable of appreciating the homage; and elevated to the privileges of an adversary, some who were unqualified in all respects for the honor of a contest so distinguished.

It is said, that the celebrated Dr. Johnson professed to 'love a good hater,' a temperament that would have singularly adapted him to cherish a prepossession in favor of our bard, who perhaps fell but little short even of the surly Doctor in this qualification, as long as the disposition to ill-will continued; but the warmth of his passions was fortunately corrected by their versatility. He was seldom, indeed never implacable in his resentments, and sometimes it has been alleged, not inviolably faithful in his engagements of friendship. Much indeed has been said about his inconstancy and caprice, but I am inclined to believe, that they originated less in a levity of sentiment, than from an extreme impetuosity of feeling, which rendered him prompt to take umbrage; and his sensations of pique, where he fancied he had discovered the traces of neglect, scorn, or unkindness, took their measure of asperity from the overflowings of the opposite sentiments which preceded them, and which seldom failed to regain its ascendency in his bosom on the return of calmer reflexion. He was candid and manly in the avowal of his errors, and *his avowal* was a *reparation*. His native *fierté* never forsaking him for a moment, the value of a frank acknowledgment was enhanced tenfold towards a generous mind, from its never being attended with servility. His mind organized only for the stronger and more acute operations of the passions, was impracticable to the efforts of superciliousness that would have depressed it into humility, and equally superior to the encroachments of venal suggestions that might have led him in to the mazes of hypocrisy.

It has been observed, that he was far from averse to the incense of flattery, and could receive it tempered with less delicacy than might have been expected, as he seldom transgressed extravagantly in that way himself: where he paid a compliment it might indeed claim the power of intoxication, as approbation from him was always an honest tribute from the warmth and sincerity of his heart. It has been sometimes represented, by those who it should seem had a view to depreciate, though they could not hope wholly to obscure that native brilliancy, which the powers of this extraordinary man had invariably bestowed on every thing that came from his lips or pen, that the history of the

Ayrshire ploughboy was an ingenious fiction, fabricated for the purposes
of obtaining the interests of the great, and enhancing the ,merits of
what in reality required no foil. 'The Cotter's Saturday Night', 'Tam
o' Shanter', and the 'Mountain Daisy', besides a number of later
productions where the maturity of his genius will be readily traced,
and which will be given to the public as soon as his friends have
collected and arranged them, speak sufficiently for themselves; and had
they fallen from a hand more dignified in the ranks of society than that
of a peasant, they had perhaps bestowed as unusual a grace there, as
even on the humbler shade of rustic inspiration from whence they
really sprung.

To the obscure scene of Burns' education, and to the laborious
though honorable station of rural industry, in which his parentage
enrolled him, almost every inhabitant of the South of Scotland can
give testimony. His only surviving brother, Gilbert Burns, now guides
the ploughshare of his forefathers in Ayrshire, at a farm near Mauchline,
and our poet's eldest son (a lad of nine years of age, whose early
dispositions already prove him to be in some measure the inheritor of
his father's talents as well as indigence) has been destined by his family
to the humble employments of the loom.

That Burns had received no classical education, and was acquainted
with the Greek and Roman authors only through the medium of
translations, is a fact of which all who were in the habits of conversing
with him might readily be convinced. I have indeed seldom observed
him to be at a loss in conversation, unless where the dead languages and
their writers have been the subjects of discussion. When I have pressed
him to tell me, why he never applied himself to acquire the Latin, in
particular, a language which his happy memory would have so soon
enabled him to be master of, he used only to reply, with a smile, that
he had already learnt all the Latin he desired to know, and that was
'Omnia vincit amor,' a sentence that from his writings and most favorite
pursuits, it should undoubtedly seem that he was most thoroughly
versed in; but I really believe his classic erudition extended little, if
any, farther.

The penchant Burns had uniformly acknowledged for the festive
pleasures of the table, and towards the fairer and softer objects of nature's
creation, has been the rallying point from whence the attacks of
his censors have been uniformly directed, and to these it must be confessed he shewed himself no stoic. His poetical pieces blend with alternate
happiness of description, the frolic spirit of the flowing bowl, or melt

the heart to the tender and impassioned sentiments in which beauty always taught him to pour forth his own. But who would wish to reprove the feelings he has consecrated with such lively touches of nature? and where is the rugged moralist that will persuade us so far to 'chill the genial current of the soul,' as to regret that Ovid ever celebrated his Corinna, or that Anacreon sung beneath his vine?

I will not however undertake to be the apologist of the irregularities even of a man of genius, though I believe it is as certain that genius never was free from irregularities, as that their absolution may in great measure be justly claimed, since it is perfectly evident that the world had continued very stationary in its intellectual acquirements, had it never given birth to any but men of plain sense. Evenness of conduct, and a due regard to the decorums of the world, have been so rarely seen to move hand in hand with genius, that some have gone as far as to say, though there I cannot wholly acquiesce, that they are even incompatible; besides, the frailties that cast their shade over the splendor of superior merit, are more conspicuously glaring than where they are the attendants of mere mediocrity. It is only on the gem we are disturbed to see the dust, the pebble may be soiled and we never regard it. The eccentric intuitions of genius too often yield the soul to the wild effervescence of desires, always unbounded, and sometimes equally dangerous to the repose of others as fatal to its own. No wonder then if virtue herself be sometimes lost in the blaze of kindling animation, or that the calm monitions of reason are not invariably found sufficient to fetter an imagination, which scorns the narrow limits and restrictions that would chain it to the level of ordinary minds. The child of nature, the child of sensibility, unschooled in the rigid precepts of philosophy, too often unable to control the passions which proved a source of frequent errors and misfortunes to him, Burns made his own artless apology in language more impressive than all the argumentatory vindications in the world could do, in one of his own poems, where he delineates the gradual expansion of his mind to the lessons of the 'tutelary muse,' who concludes an address to her pupil, almost unique for simplicity and beautiful poetry, with these lines:

I saw thy pulse's madd'ning play
Wild send thee pleasure's devious way;
Misled by Fancy's meteor ray,
    By passion driven;

But yet the light that led astray,
Was *light from heaven*!'

['The Vision', ll. 235-40]

I have already transgressed beyond the bounds I had proposed to myself, on first committing this sketch to paper, which comprehends what at least I have been led to deem the leading features of Burns' mind and character; a literary critique I do not aim at; mine is wholly fulfilled if in these pages I have been able to delineate any of those strong traits that distinguished him, of those talents which raised him from the plough, where he passed the bleak morning of his life, weaving his rude wreaths of poesy with the wild field flowers that sprung around his cottage, to that enviable eminence of literary fame, where Scotland will long cherish his memory with delight and gratitude; and proudly remember, that beneath her cold sky a genius was ripened, without care of culture, that would have done honor to climes more favorable to those luxuriances—that warmth of coloring and fancy in which he so eminently excelled.

From several paragraphs I have noticed in the public prints, ever since the idea of sending this sketch to some one of them was formed, I find private animosities have not yet subsided, and that Envy has not yet exhausted all her shafts. I still trust, however, that honest fame will be permanently affixed to Burns' character, which I think it will be found he *has* merited by the candid and impartial among his countrymen. And where a recollection of the imprudencies that sullied his brighter qualifications interpose, let the imperfections of all human excellence be remembered at the same time; leaving those inconsistencies, which alternately exalted his nature into the seraph, and sunk it again into the man, to the tribunal which *alone* can investigate the labyrinths of the human heart—

Where they alike in trembling hope *repose*,
—The bosom of his father and his *God*.

GRAY'S ELEGY.

Annandale, August 7, 1796

107

23. Coleridge on Burns

1796–1817

(See Introduction, p. 28.)

(a) 'To a Friend [Charles Lamb] who had declared his Intention of writing no more Poetry' [1796], ('First published in a Bristol newspaper in aid of a subscription for the family of Robert Burns'.) *Poems*, ed. E. H. Coleridge (1912), II, p. 158

... Nature's own belovéd bard ...

(b) To John Thelwall, 17 December 1796. *Letters of S. T. Coleridge*, ed. E. L. Griggs (1956), I, p. 278

... Bowles, the most tender, and, with the exception of Burns, the only *always-natural* poet in our Language ...

(c) To Thomas Poole, 24 July 1800. *Ibid.*, p. 608. Coleridge had just met Currie. Contrast Lamb's opinion of the *Life*, No. 24 (e)

I would have you by all means order the late Edition in four Volumes of Burns's Works—the Life is written by Currie, and a masterly specimen of philosophical Biography it is.

(d) [February 1805] *Notebooks of S. T. Coleridge*, ed. Kathleen Coburn (1957–), p. II, 2431 f.5. Miss Coburn suggests that Coleridge may refer to 'Afton Water' or 'The Banks o' Doon'. Or the allusion may be to 'Halloween', stanza XXV, which had been praised by Currie

. . . for impassioned and *particularized* Description (see Burns' description of a Brook, and Wordsworth's Poetry in a hundred places) . . .

(e) The *Friend*, 15 February 1810; text here from edition by Barbara E. Rooke (1969), I, p. 293. The lady who told Coleridge this story was probably Anna Dorothea Benson: see *Letters of Burns* (1931), II, p. 153

I cannot here refuse myself the pleasure of recording a speech of the Poet Burns, related to me by the lady to whom it was addressed. Having been asked by her, why in his more serious Poems he had not changed the two or three Scotch words which seemed only to disturb the purity of the style? the Poet with great sweetness, and his usual happiness in reply, answered why in truth it would have been better, but—

> The rough bur-thistle spread wide
> Amang the bearded bear,
> I turn'd the weeder-clips aside
> An spar'd the symbol dear.

An author may be allowed to quote from his own poems, when he does it with as much modesty and felicity as Burns did in this instance.

(f) Extract from the *Friend*, 14 September 1809, as condensed by Coleridge in *Biographia Literaria*, 1817; text here from *Biographia Literaria*, ed. G. Watson (1956), p. 49

To carry on the feelings of childhood into the powers of manhood; to combine the child's sense of wonder and novelty with the appearances which every day for perhaps forty years had rendered familiar:

> With sun and moon and stars throughout the year
> And man and woman;

this is the character and privilege of genius, and one of the marks which distinguish genius from talents. And therefore it is the prime merit of genius, and its most unequivocal mode of manifestation, so to represent familiar objects as to awaken in the minds of others a kindred feeling concerning them, and that freshness of sensation which is the constant accompaniment of mental no less than of bodily convalescence. Who has not a thousand times seen snow fall on water? Who has not watched it with a new feeling from the time that he has read Burns' comparison of sensual pleasure:

> To snow that falls upon a river
> A moment white—then gone for ever!

In poems, equally as in philosophic disquisitions, genius produces the strongest impressions of novelty while it rescues the most admitted truths from the impotence caused by the very circumstance of their universal admission. Truths of all others the most awful and mysterious, yet being at the same time of universal interest, are too often considered as *so* true, that they lose all the life and efficiency of truth and lie bed-ridden in the dormitory of the soul side by side with the most despised and exploded errors.

(g) Extract from *Biographia Literaria* (1817). Text from edition by G. Watson (1956), p. 255

When I think how many and how much better books than Homer, or even than Herodotus, Pindar or Eschylus, could have read, are in the power of almost every man, in a country where almost every man is instructed to read and write; and how restless, how difficultly hidden, the powers of genius are, and yet fine even in situations the most favorable, according to Mr. Wordsworth, for the formation of a pure and poetic language, in situations which ensure familiarity with the grandest objects of the imagination, but one Burns among the shepherds of Scotland, and not a single poet of humble life among those of *English* lakes and mountains; I conclude that Poetic Genius is not only a very delicate but a very rare plant.

But be this as it may, the feelings with which

> I think of Chatterton, the marvellous boy,
> The sleepless soul that perish'd in his pride:
> Of Burns, that walk'd in glory and in joy
> Behind his plough upon the mountain-side,

are widely different from those with which I should read a poem where the author, having occasion for the character of a poet and a philosopher in the fable of his narration, had chosen to make him a chimney-sweeper; and then, in order to remove all doubts on the subject, had invented an account of his birth, parentage and education, with all the strange and fortunate accidents which had concurred in making him at once poet, philosopher and sweep! Nothing but biography can justify this.

24. Charles Lamb on Burns

1796–1826

Extracts from letters to various correspondents, 1796–1826. *The Letters of Charles Lamb, to which are added those of his Sister, Mary Lamb*, ed. E. V. Lucas (1935) (see Introduction, p. 27).

(a) To S. T. Coleridge, postmark 1 June 1796. Lucas, I, p. 9

That is a capital line in your 6th no.[1]: 'This dark frieze-coated, hoarse, teeth-chattering Month'—they are exactly such epithets as Burns would have stumbled on, whose poem on the ploughed up daisy you seem to have had in mind.

(b) To Coleridge, 10 June 1796. Lucas, I, p. 13

[Southey's 'Joan of Arc'] is alone sufficient to redeem the character of the age we live in from the imputation of degenerating in Poetry, were there no such beings extant as Burns and Bowles, Cowper and— fill up the blank how you please, I say nothing.

---

[1] Refers to Coleridge's 'Lines on observing a Blossom on the First Of February 1796', printed in the *Watchman*, vi, 11 April 1796.

(c) To Coleridge, 10 December 1796. Lucas, I, p. 73

Publish your *Burns* when and how you like, it will be new to me,[1]—
my memory of it is very confused, and tainted with unpleasant
associations. Burns was the god of my idolatry, as Bowles of yours.
I am jealous of your fraternising with Bowles, when I think you
relish him more than Burns or my old favourite, Cowper. But you
conciliate matters when you talk of the 'divine chit-chat' of the latter:
by the expression I see you thoroughly relish him.

(d) To Robert Southey, 20 March 1799. Lucas, I, p. 152

The three first stanzas [of 'The Spider'] are delicious; they seem to me
a compound of Burns and Old Quarles, those kind of home-strokes,
where more is felt than strikes the ear; a terseness, a jocular pathos,
which makes one feel in laughter. The measure, too is novel and
pleasing. I could almost wonder Rob. Burns in his lifetime never
stumbled upon it.

(e) To Coleridge, ? 28 July 1800, Lucas, I, p. 193

Have you seen the new edition of Burns? his posthumous works and
letters? I have only been able to procure the first volume which contains
his life—very confusedly and badly written, and interspersed with dull
pathological and *medical* discussions. It is written by a Dr. Currie.
Do you know the well-meaning doctor? Alas, *ne sutor ultra crepitum*![2]

---

[1] Refers to Coleridge's, 'To a Friend who had declared his Intention of writing no more
Poetry' (*Poems of S. T. Coleridge*, ed. E. H. Coleridge (1912), II, p. 158).
[2] 'Let the cobbler stick to his rattling.' Lamb's punning variation on *crepidam* ('sandal,
last', Pliny, *Historia Naturalis*, XXXV, 85), as edited by Lucas.

(f) To William Wordsworth, 26 April 1816. Lucas, II, p. 190

. . . the Letter [*To A Friend Of Robert Burns*, No. 53a] I read with unabated satisfaction. Such a thing was wanted, called for. The parallel of Cotton with Burns I heartily approve; Iz Walton hallows any page in which his reverend name appears. 'Duty archly bending to purposes of general benevolence' is exquisite.

(g) To John Bates Dibdin [30 June 1826]. Lucas, III, p. 49

I never knew an enemy to puns, who was not an ill-natured man. Your fair critic in the coach reminds me of a Scotchman who assured me that he did not see much in Shakespeare. I replied, I dare say *not*. He felt the equivoke, looked awkward, and reddish, but soon returned to the attack, by saying that he thought Burns was as good as Shakespeare. I said that I had not doubt he was—to a *Scotchman*. We exchanged no more words that day.

25. Thomas Duncan on Burns

1796

From a letter dated 10 October 1796, lacking signature and name of addressee, Cowie Bequest, Burns Collection, Mitchell Library, Glasgow.

This letter, which expresses an admiring reader's response to the poetry of Burns shortly after his death, was probably written by Thomas Tudor Duncan (1776–1858), in 1796 a tutor in a Liverpool family, to his kinsman James Currie, who had begun to plan the first collected edition of Burns (*BC* (1970), 3rd ser. xix) (see Introduction, p. 22).

Thus have I endeavoured to communicate to you some idea of the pleasure with which I was affected by the poems of Burns. I have been more willing to discuss the subject of his beauties than to point out his faults, partly, I believe, from a consciousness that I had formerly wronged him in my opinion, & from a wish to make him even an ideal reparation. Hence this letter has more the appearance of elaborate eulogium than of impartial strictures. For the sake of form, then, I shall make a few observations on what appears to me censurable in the writings of our poet.

If I were required to cancel any particular department of these, I should fix upon that which comprehends the epitaphs or epigrams. Some of the latter are bitingly severe, others—to me, at least, they appear so—extremely insipid.

Another fault, too, I have found with our author—that he does not *always* suit the measure of his verses to the subject on which they treat. The elegy on Capt. M. H. for instance, is composed in a metre which custom has appropriated to humour & which is therefore perfectly incongruous with the gravity of the language. Its effect was, to me, extremely unpleasant. For the same or a similar reason I feel dissatisfied with some of the religious pieces. We know but too well that our vulgar Scotch version of the psalms is anything but elegant or sublime — & yet Burns has been so injudicious as to adopt the same metre for his imitations of them. To the unprejudiced stranger these poems may appear in their true colours— & I believe their intrinsic merit entitles them to admiration—but, to a Scotch presbyterian, (if I may be allowed to judge of others by myself,)

> The man in life wherever placed,
> Hath happiness in store

will ever recal the remembrance of

> That man hath perfect blessedness
> Who walketh not astray.

This unhappy association, if it, indeed, exists, is certainly extremely unfavorable to the bard. The nobleness of his sentiments is concealed under the meanness of their dress.

On some occasions the modest sex have reason to except against the indelicacy of our poet's humour. [But] in the later editions of his works, there have been few passages which give cause for serious offence.

It may not be unworthy of remark, too, that the *rhyming* part of Burns' versification is frequently faulty. Thus we find *legs, rigs, & naigs* coupled together in the same stanza— & *blame* with *limb* in another. So little scrupulous is Burns in this respect that even when the accent lies on the penultimate of a word, he seems perfectly satisfied if he couples it with another which coincides with it only in the sound of the *last* syllable—as *bóther, téther; cóllie, bíllie; scónner, dínner*. It is true that he was more fettered in the choice of his rhymes than most poets, as he frequently employs a species of versification which requires four lines with the same termination in the same stanza.

But, after all, the blemishes here enumerated are but as specks in the disk of the Sun. The dazzling lustre of the grand whole deters the eye from too minute a scrutiny into its defects.

With all his beauties to recommend him, however, Burns still labours under various disadvantages, disadvantages which will prevent him from ever being universally read with that relish to which his intrinsic merit entitles him to aspire.

It is one misfortune— & a radical one—that the most beautiful of his poems are composed in a dialect which is little understood beyond the boundaries of his native kingdom— & which is more—a dialect which, even there, is daily getting more & more into disuse among those who are most capable of reaping pleasure from the sentiments they contain.

On our own account perhaps we have reason to rejoice, but, for the sake of our Southern neighbors, we certainly ought to regret that some of these poems are full of allusions to, & others are actually founded on *local* superstitions & *local customs*. Such poems cannot be so exquisitely pleasing to strangers as to those who have witnessed such customs & observed the effects of such superstitions—nor can their interest be so much excited in perusing them.

The marked partiality, too, which our countryman discovers for his native land will tend to prejudice *weak* & *bigotted* minds against his works, tho' with the generous & enlightened of every country it must rather militate in his favor.

Burns has been accused, too, by the ministerialist of Jacobinism. He has been condemned by the godly for Infidelity. If the term Jacobinism be synonymous with Patriotism, he who prides himself in the title of 'Patriot-bard' is justly accused. If to rend the cloak of Hypocrisy be a sin as heinous as to trample upon [MS badly torn] . . .

Nor has envy been lacking . . .
with her baleful breath, his well earned fame . . .   [MS. torn]
of his works he was assailed by a whole . . .   [MS. torn]
exerted themselves to the utmost to blacken . . .
the spirit of party to oppose his success. How inconsistent, this, with the generous sentiments of Burns himself! How differently he would have acted in similar circumstances we may judge from his epistle to his brother bard W.S-n. Would he not have exclaimed with enthusiasm

> Come let us lay our heads together
>   In love fraternal!
> May Envy wallop in a tether—
>   Black fiend infernal!

Poetry pleases in proportion as it presents an accurate picture of what we have seen or experienced—or, in short, of what we are able with ease to figure to our imaginations. In proportion to the difficulty which we find in comprehending the images, in such proportion is the diminution of that delight with which they ought to inspire us.

26. Robert Heron, memoir in *Monthly Magazine*

June 1797

Extract from Robert Heron, *A Memoir of the Life of the Late Robert Burns*, Edinburgh 1797; text here from H. Hecht, *Robert Burns*, 2nd ed., rev. 1950, pp. 251ff. The *Memoir* first appeared, signed 'H', in the *Monthly Magazine* (June 1797), iii, pp. 213-16 and 552-62. It was reprinted in the *Edinburgh Magazine* (1797), *Philadelphia Monthly Magazine* (1798), and elsewhere (see No. 19, and Introduction, p. 22).

He returned from labour to learning, and from learning went again to labour; till his mind began to open to the charms of taste and knowledge; till he began to feel a passion for books and for the subjects of books, which was to give a colour to the whole thread of his future life. On nature, he soon began to gaze with new discernment, and with new enthusiasm. His mind's eye opened to perceive affecting beauty and sublimity, where, by the mere gross peasant, there was nought to be seen, but water, earth, and sky, but animals, plants, and soil: even as the eyes of the servant of Elisha were suddenly enlightened to behold his master and himself guarded from the Syrian bands, by horses and chariots of fire, to all but themselves, invisible.

What might perhaps first contribute to dispose his mind to poetical efforts, is, a particular practice in the devotional piety of the Scottish peasantry. It is still common for them to make their children get by heart the psalms of David, in that version of homely rhymes, which is used in their churches. In the morning, and in the evening of every day; or, at least on the evening of every Saturday and Sunday; these psalms are sung in solemn family-devotion, a chapter of the bible is read, an extemporary prayer is fervently uttered. The whole books of the sacred scriptures are continually in the hands of almost every peasant. And it is impossible, that there should not be occasionally some souls among them, awakened to the divine emotions of genius, by that rich assemblage which these books present, of almost all that is interesting in incidents, or picturesque in imagery, or affectingly sublime or tender in sentiments and character. It is impossible that those rude rhymes, and the simple artless music with which they are accompanied, should not occasionally excite some ear to a fond perception of the melody of verse. That Burns had felt these impulses, will appear undeniably certain to whoever shall carefully peruse his 'Cottar's Saturday Night'; or shall remark, with nice observation, the various fragments of *scripture* sentiment, of *scripture* imagery, of *scripture* language, which are scattered throughout his works.

Still more interesting to the young peasantry, are those ancient ballads of love and war, of which a great number are yet popularly known and sung in Scotland. While the prevalence of the Gaelic language in the northern parts of this country, excluded from those regions the old Anglo-Saxon songs and minstrels: These songs and minstrels were, in the mean time, driven by the Norman conquests and establishments, out of the southern counties of England; and were forced to wander, in exile, towards its northern confines, or even into the southern districts of the Scottish kingdom. Hence, in the old English songs, is every eminent bard still related to have been of the *north country*; but, on the contrary, in the old Scottish songs, it is always the *south country*, to which every favourite minstrel is said to belong. Both these expressions are intended to signify one district, a district comprehending precisely the southern counties of Scotland, with the most northern counties of England. In the south of Scotland, almost all the best of those ballads are still often sung by the rustic maid or matron at her spinning wheel. They are listened to, with ravished ears, by old and young. Their rude melody; that mingled curiosity and awe, which are naturally excited by the very idea of their antiquity; the exquisitely tender and natural complaints sometimes poured forth in them; the gallant deeds of knightly heroism, which they sometimes celebrate; their wild tales of demons, ghosts and fairies, in whose existence superstition alone has believed; the manners which they represent; the obsolete, yet picturesque and expressive language in which they are often clothed; give them wonderful power to transport every imagination, and to agitate every heart. To the soul of Burns, they were like a happy breeze touching the strings of an Æolian harp, and calling forth the most ravishing melody.

Beside all this, the 'Gentle Shepherd', and the other poems of *Allan Ramsay*, have long been highly popular in Scotland. They fell early into the hands of Burns. And while the fond applause which they received, drew his emulation; they presented to him likewise treasures of phraseology, and models of versification. *Ruddiman's Weekly Magazine* was, during this time, published; was supported chiefly by the original communications of correspondents; and found a very extensive sale. In it, Burns read, particularly, the poetry of *Robert Ferguson*, written chiefly in the Scottish dialect, and exhibiting many specimens of uncommon poetical excellence. The 'Seasons' of *Thomson*, too, the 'Grave' of *Blair*, the far-famed 'Elegy' of *Gray*, the 'Paradise Lost' of *Milton*, the wild strains of *Ossian*, perhaps the 'Minstrel' of *Beattie*, were so commonly read, even among those with whom Burns would naturally associate, that poetical curiosity, although less ardent than his, could, in such circumstances, have little difficulty in procuring them.

With such means to give his imagination a poetical bias, and to favour the culture of his taste and genius, Burns gradually became a poet. He was not one of those forward children, who, from a mistaken impulse, begin prematurely to write and to rhyme, and hence, never attain to excellence. Conversing familiarly for a long while, with the works of those poets who were known to him: Contemplating the aspect of nature, in a district which exhibits an uncommon assemblage of the beautiful and the ruggedly grand, of the cultivated and the wild: Looking upon human life with an eye quick and keen, to remark as well the stronger and leading, as the nicer and subordinate features of character: It was thus that he slowly and unconsciously acquired a poetical temper of soul, and a poetic cast of thought. He was distinguished among his fellows, for extraordinary intelligence, good sense, and penetration, long ere they suspected him to be capable of writing verses. His mind was mature, and well stored with such knowledge as lay within his reach; he had made himself master of powers of language, superior to those of almost any former writer in the Scottish dialect; before he conceived the idea of surpassing *Ramsay* and *Ferguson*.

In the mean time, beside the studious bent of his genius, there were other features in his opening character, which might seem to mark him for a poet. He began early in life to regard with sullen disdain and aversion, all that was sordid in the pursuits and interests of the peasants among whom he was placed. He became discontented with the humble labours to which he saw himself confined, and with the poor subsistence that was all he could earn by them. He was excited to look upon the rich and great, whom he saw around him, with an emotion between envy and contempt; as if something had still whispered to his heart, that there was injustice in the exterior inequality between his fate and theirs. While such emotions arose in his mind, he conceived an inclination,—very common among the young men of the more uncultivated parts of Scotland, to go abroad to *America* or the *West Indies*, in quest of a better fortune.—His heart was, at the same time, expanded with passionate ardour, to meet the impressions of love and *friendship*. With several of the young peasantry, who were his fellows in labour, he contracted an affectionate intimacy. He eagerly sought admission into the brotherhood of *Free Masons*; which is recommended to the young men of this country, by nothing so much as by its seeming to extend the sphere of agreeable acquaintance, and to knit closer the bonds of friendly endearment. In some *Mason Lodges* in his neighbourhood, Burns had soon the fortune, whether good or bad, to gain the notice of several gentlemen who were better able than his fellow-peasants, to estimate the true value of such a mind as his. One or two of them might be men of convivial dispositions, and of religious notions rather licentious than narrow; who encouraged his talents, by occasionally inviting him to be the companion of their looser hours; and who were at times not ill pleased to direct the force of his wit and humour against those sacred things which they affected outwardly to despise as mere *bugbears*, while perhaps they could not help inwardly trembling before them as realities. For a while, the native rectitude of his understanding, and the excellent principles in which his infancy had been educated, withstood every temptation to intemperance or impiety. Alas! it was not always so.—He was even in the first years of his rising youth, an ardent lover; feeling the passion, not affected, light and sportive; but solemn, anxious, fervent, absorbing the whole soul; such as it is described by Thomson in his enrapturing poem on 'Spring'. When his heart was first struck by the charms of village beauty; the *love* he felt was pure, tender, and sincere, as that of the youth and maiden in his own 'Cottar's Saturday Night'. If the ardour of his passion hurried him afterwards to triumph over the chastity of the maid he loved; the tenderness of his heart, the manly honesty of his soul, soon made him offer, with eager solicitude, to repair by marriage the injury of love.

About this time in the progress of his life and character, did he first begin to be publicly distinguished as a poet. A *masonic* song, a satirical epigram, a rhyming epistle to a friend, attempted with success; taught him to know his own powers, and gave him confidence to try tasks more arduous, and which should command still higher applause. The annual celebration of the *Sacrament of the Lord's Supper*, in the rural parishes of Scotland, has much in it of those old *Popish* festivals, in which superstition, traffic, and amusement, used to be strangely intermingled. Burns saw, and seized, in it, one of the happiest of all subjects, to afford scope for the display—of that strong and piercing sagacity by which he could almost intuitively distinguish the reasonable from the absurd, and the becoming from the ridiculous;—of that picturesque power of fancy, which enabled him to represent scenes, and persons, and groupes, and looks, attitudes, and gestures, in a manner almost as lively and impressive, even in words, as if all the artifices and energies of the pencil had been employed;—of that knowledge which he had necessarily acquired of the manners, passions, and prejudices of the rustics around him, of whatever was ridiculous no less than of whatever was affectingly beautiful, in rural life. A thousand prejudices of *Popish*, and perhaps too of ruder *Pagan* superstition, have from time immemorial been connected in the minds of the *Scottish* peasantry, with the annual recurrence of the *Eve of the Festival of all the Saints*, or *Hallowe'en*. These were all intimately known to Burns, and had made a powerful impression upon his imagination and feelings. Choosing them for the subject of a poem, he produced a piece, which is, almost to frenzy, the delight of those who are best acquainted with its subject; and which will not fail to preserve the memory of the prejudices and usages which it describes, when they shall, perhaps, have ceased to give one merry evening in the year to the cottage fire-side. The simple joys, the honest love, the sincere friendship, the ardent devotion of the cottage; whatever in the more solemn part of the rustic's life is humble and artless, without being mean or unseemly; or tender and dignified, without aspiring to stilted grandeur, or to un- natural, buskined pathos; had deeply impressed the imagination of the rising poet; had in some sort wrought itself into the very texture of the fibres of his soul. He tried to express in verse what he most tenderly felt, what he most enthusiastically imagined; and composed the 'Cottar's Saturday's Night'.

These pieces, the true effusions of genius, informed by reading and observation, and promoted by its own native ardour, as well as by friendly applause; were soon communicated from one to another among

the most discerning of Burns's acquaintance; and were, by every new
reader, perused and re-perused with an eagerness of delight and approbation, which would not suffer him long to withhold them from the
press. A *subscription* was proposed; was earnestly promoted by some
gentlemen, who were glad to interest themselves in behalf of such
signal poetical merit; was soon crowded with the names of a considerable number of the inhabitants of Ayrshire; who, in the proffered
purchase, sought not less to gratify their own passion for *Scottish*
poesy, than to encourage the wonderful ploughman.

At the manufacturing village of Kilmarnock were the poems of
Burns, for the first time, printed. The whole edition was quickly
distributed over the country.

They were every where received with eager admiration and delight.
They eminently possessed all those qualities which never fail to render
any literary work quickly and permanently popular. They were
written in a phraseology, of which all the powers were universally
felt; and which, being at once, *antique, familiar*, and now *rarely written*,
was hence fitted for all the dignified and picturesque uses of poetry,
without being disagreeably obscure. The imagery, and the sentiment
were, at once, faithfully natural, and irresistibly impressive and interesting. Those topics of satire and scandal in which the rustic delights;
that *humorous* imitation of character, and that *witty* association of ideas
familiar and striking but not naturally allied to one another, which
have force to shake his sides with laughter; those fancies of superstition
at which he still wonders and trembles; those affecting sentiments and
images of true religion, which are at once dear and awful to his heart;
were all represented by Burns with all a poet's magic power. Old and
young, high and low, grave and gay, learned or ignorant, all were
alike delighted, agitated, transported. I was at that time resident in
Galloway, contiguous to *Ayrshire*: and I can well remember, how
that even plough-boys and maid-servants would have gladly bestowed
the wages which they earned the most hardly, and which they wanted
to purchase necessary clothing, if they might but procure the works of
Burns. A copy happened to be presented from a gentleman in Ayrshire
to a friend in my neighbourhood. He put it into my hands, as a work
containing some effusions of the most extraordinary genius. I took it,
rather that I might not disoblige the lender, than from any ardour of
curiosity or expectation. 'An unlettered ploughman, a poet!' said I,
with contemptuous incredulity. It was on a Saturday evening. I
opened the volume, by accident, while I was undressing, to go to bed.

I closed it not, till a late hour on the rising Sunday morn, after I had read over every syllable it contained. And,

Ex illo Corydon, Corydon est tempore nobis! Virg, Ec. 7.[1]

The most remarkable quality he displayed, both in his writings and his conversation, was, certainly, an enlarged, vigorous, keenly discerning, Comprehension of Mind. Whatever be the subject of his verse; he seems still to grasp it with giant force; to wield and turn it with easy dexterity; to view it on all sides, with an eye which no turn of outline and no hue of colouring can elude; to mark all its relations to the group of surrounding objects; and then to select what he chooses to represent to our imaginations, with a skilful and happy propriety, which shows him to have been, at the same time, master of all the rest. It will not be very easy for any other mind, however richly stored with various knowledge; for any other imagination, however elastic and inventive; to find any new and suitable topic that has been omitted by Burns, in celebrating the subjects of all his greater and more elaborate poems. It is impossible to consider, without astonishment, the amazing fertility of invention which is displayed, under the regulation of a sound judgment, and a correct taste, in the pieces intitled the 'Twa Dogs': the 'Address to the De'il'; 'Scotch Drink'; the 'Holy Fair'; 'Hallowe'en': the 'Cottar's Saturday Night'; 'To a Haggis'; 'To a Louse': 'To a Mountain Daisy': 'Tam O'Shanter'; on 'Captain Grose's Peregrinations': 'The humble Petition of Bruar water'; 'The Bard's Epitaph'. Shoemakers, footmen, threshers, milk-maids, peers, stay-makers, have all written verses, such as deservedly attracted the notice of the world. But in the poetry of these people, while there was commonly some genuine effusion of the sentiments of agitated nature, some exhibition of such imagery as at once impressed itself upon the heart; there was also ever much to be excused in consideration of their ignorance, their want of taste, their extravagance of fancy, their want or abuse of the advantages of a liberal education. Burns has no pardon to demand for defects of this sort. He might scorn every concession which we are ready to grant to his peculiar circumstances, without being, on this account, reduced to relinquish any part of his claims to the praise of poetical excellence. He touches his lyre, at all times, with the hand of a master. He demands to be ranked, not with the Woodhouses, the Ducks, the Ramsays, but with the Miltons, the Popes, the Grays. No poet was ever more largely

---

[1] 'From that day it has been Corydon, Corydon every time with us.' Vergil, *Eclogues*, VII, l. 70. Tr. E. V. Rieu (1949).

endowed with that strong common sense which is necessarily the very source and principle of all fine writing.

The next remarkable quality in this man's character, seems to have consisted in native strength, Ardour, and delicacy of Feelings, passions, and affections, *Si vis me flere; dolendum primum est ipsi tibi*.[1] All that is valuable in poetry, and, at the same time, peculiar to it, consists in the effusion of particular, not general, *sentiment*, and in the picturing out of particular *imagery*. But education, reading, a wide converse with men in society, the most extensive observation of external nature, however useful to improve, cannot even all combined, confer the power of comprehending either *imagery* or *sentiment* with such force and vivacity of conception, as may enable one to impress whatever he may choose upon the souls of others, with full, irresistible, electric energy. This is a power which nought can bestow, save native soundness, delicacy, quickness, ardour, force of those parts of our bodily organization, of those energies in the structure of our minds, on which depend all our sensations, emotions, appetites, passions, and affections. Who ever knew a man of high original genius, whose senses were imperfect, his feelings dull and callous, his passions all languid and stagnant, his affections without ardour, and without constancy? Others may be artisans, speculatists, imitators in the fine arts. None but the man who is thus richly endowed by nature, can be a poet, an artist, an illustrious inventor in philosophy. Let any person *first* possess this original soundness, vigour, and delicacy of the primary energies of mind; and *then* let him receive some impression upon his imagination which shall excite a passion for this or that particular pursuit: he will scarcely fail to distinguish himself by illustrious efforts of exalted and original genius. Without having, *first*, those simple ideas which belong, respectively, to the different senses; no man can ever form for himself the complex notions, into the composition of which such simple ideas necessarily enter. Never could Burns, without this delicacy, this strength, this vivacity of the powers of bodily sensation, and of mental feeling, which I would here claim as the indispensible native endowments of true genius; without these, never could he have poured forth these sentiments, or pourtrayed those images, which have so powerfully impressed every imagination, and penetrated every heart. Almost all the sentiments and images diffused throughout the poems of Burns, are fresh from the mint of nature. He sings what he had himself beheld with interested attention,—what he had himself felt with keen emotions of pain or pleasure.

[1] 'If you wish me to weep, you yourself must grieve first.' Horace, *Ars Poetica*, l. 102.

You actually see what he describes: you more than sympathize with his joys: your bosom is inflamed with all his fire: your heart dies away within you, infected by the contagion of his despondency. He exalts, for a time, the genius of his reader to the elevation of his own; and, for the moment, confers upon him all the powers of a poet. Quotations were endless. But any person of discernment, taste, and feeling, who shall carefully read over Burns's book, will not fail to discover, in its every page, abundance of those sentiments and images to which this observation relates.—It is originality of genius, it is soundness of perception, it is delicacy of passion, it is general vigour and impetuosity of the whole mind, by which such effects are produced. Others have sung, in the same Scottish dialect, and in similar rhymes, many of the same topics which are celebrated by Burns. But, what with Burns awes or fascinates; in the hands of others only disgusts by its deformity, or excites contempt by its meanness and uninteresting simplicity.

A third quality which the life and the writings of Burns show to have belonged to his character, was, a quick and correct Discernment of the distinctions between RIGHT and WRONG, between TRUTH and FALSEHOOD and this, accompanied with a passionate preference of whatever was *right* and *true*, with an indignant abhorrence of whatever was *false* and morally *wrong*. It is true that he did not always steadily distinguish and eschew the evils of drunkenness and licentious love; it is true that these, at times, seem to obtain even the approbation of his muse. But there remains in his works enough to show, that his cooler reason, and all his better feelings, earnestly rejected those gay vices, which he could sometimes, unhappily, allow himself to practise, and would sometimes recommend to others, by the charms which his imagination lent them. What was it but the clear and ardent discrimination of justice from injustice, which inspired that indignation with which his heart often burned, when he saw those exalted by fortune, who were not exalted by their merits? His 'Cottar's Saturday Night', and all his graver poems, breathe a rich vein of the most amiable, yet manly, and even delicately correct, morality. In his pieces of satire, and of lighter humour, it is still upon the accurate and passionate discernment of falsehood, and of moral turpitude, that his ridicule turns. Other poets are often as remarkable for the incorrectness, or even the absurdity of their general truths, as for interesting sublimity or tenderness of sentiment, or for picturesque splendour of imagery. Burns is not less happy in teaching general truths, than in that display of sentiment and imagery, which more peculiarly belongs to the province of the poet. Burns's morality deserves this high praise; that it is not a system merely of *discretion*; it is not founded upon any scheme of superstition; but seems to have always its source, and the test by which it is to be tried, in the most diffusive benevolence, and in a regard for the universal good.

The only other leading feature of character that appears to be strikingly displayed in the life and writings of Burns, is a *lofty-minded* CONSCIOUSNESS *of his own* TALENTS *and* MERITS. Hence, the fierce and contemptuous asperity of his satire; the sullen and gloomy dignity of his complaints, addressed, not so much to alarm the soul of pity, as to reproach injustice, and to make fortunate baseness shrink abashed; that general gravity and elevation of his sentiments, which admits no humbly insinuating sportiveness of wit, which scorns all compromise between the *right* and the *expedient*, which decides with the authoritative voice of a judge from whom there is no appeal, upon characters, principles, and events, whenever they present themselves to notice. From his works, as from his conversation and manners, *pride* seems to have excluded the effusion of *vanity*. In the composition, or correctness of his poetry, he never suffered the judgment, even of his most re-spectable friends, to dictate, to him. This line in one of his poems, ('When I *look back* on *prospects drear*') was criticised; but he would not condescend either to reply to the criticism, or to alter the expression. Not a few of his smaller pieces are sufficiently trivial, vulgar, and hackneyed in the thought, are such as the pride of genius should have disdained to write, or, at least, to publish. But there is reason to believe that he despised such pieces, even while he wrote and published them; that it was rather in regard to the effects they had already produced upon hearers and readers, than from any overweening opinion of their intrinsic worth, he suffered them to be printed. His wit is always dignified. He is not a merry-andrew in a motley coat, sporting before you for your diversion: but a hero, or a philosopher, deigning to admit you to witness his relaxations; still exercising the great energies of his soul: and little caring, at the moment, whether you do, or do not, cordially sympathize with his feelings.

His poems may be all distributed into the two classes of *pastorals* and *pieces upon common life and manners*. In the former class, I include all those in which rural imagery, and the manners and sentiments of rustics, are chiefly described. In the latter I would comprehend his epigrams, epistles, and, in short, all those pieces in which the imagery and sentiments are drawn from the condition and appearances of common life, without any particular reference to the country. It is in the first class, that the most excellent of his poems are certainly to be found. Those few pieces which he seems to have attempted in that miserable strain, called *the Della Crusca* style, appear to me to be the least commendable of all his writings. He usually employs those forms of *versification*, which have been used chiefly by the former writers of poetry in the Scottish dialect, and by some of the elder English poets. His *phraseology* is evidently drawn from those books of English poetry which were in his hands, from the writings of former Scottish poets, and from those unwritten stores of the Scottish dialect, which became known to him, in the conversation of his fellow-peasants. Some other late writers in the Scottish dialect seem to think, that not to write English is certainly, to write Scottish. Burns, avoiding this error, hardly ever transgressed the propriety of English grammar, except in compliance with the long-accustomed variations of the genuine Scottish dialect.

From the preceding detail of the particulars of this poet's life, the reader will naturally and justly infer him to have been an honest, proud and warm-hearted man; of high passions, a sound understanding, a vigorous and excursive imagination. He was never known to descend to any act of deliberate meanness. In Dumfries, he retained many respectable friends, even to the last. It may be doubted whether he have not, by his writings, exercised a greater power over the minds of men, and by consequence, on their conduct, upon their happiness and misery, upon the general system of life, than has been exercised by any half dozen of the most eminent statesmen of the present age. The power of the statesmen, is but shadowy, so far as it acts upon externals, alone. The power of the writer of genius, subdues the heart and understanding, and having thus made the very springs of action its own, through them moulds almost all life and nature at its pleasure. Burns has not failed to command one remarkable sort of homage, such as is never paid but to great original genius. A crowd of poetasters started up to imitate him, by writing verses as he had done, in the Scottish dialect. But, O *imitatores! servum pecus!*[1] To persons to whom the Scottish dialect, and the customs and manners of rural life in Scotland, have no charm; I shall possibly appear to have said too much about Burns. By those who passionately admire him, I shall, perhaps, be blamed, as having said too little.

[1] O imitators, slavish herd.

27. William Reid, unsigned verse tribute

1797

Stanzas 18–20, 'Monody on The Death of Robert Burns', unsigned poem by William Reid, *Poetry; Original and Selected*, Brash and Reid chapbooks (Glasgow [1797]), II, p. 8.

The poem is attributed to Reid in *Works of Robert Burns*, ed. the Ettrick Shepherd [James Hogg] and William Motherwell (Glasgow, 1836), V, p. 282 (see Introduction, p. 23).

But let us not, as chatt'ring fools,
Proclaim his fau'ts, like envy's tools,
Wha seek out darkness just like owls,
　　Dark, dark indeed,
But a' his failings co'er wi' mools,[1]
　　Now since he's dead.

As bright a genius death has torn
Frae us, as Scotia did adorn,
Like Pheobus whan he springs at morn,
　　Clear was his head;
What news could mak' us mair forlorn,
　　Than Robin's dead?

The Winter nights I've cheer'd by turns,
Wi' Ramsay, Fergusson, and Burns:
The first twa cauld are in their urns,
　　Their sauls at rest:
Now weeping Caledonia mourns,
　　Him last and best.

[1] *mools:* grave-clods.

28. Alexander Campbell on Burns

1798, 1816

Alexander Campbell (1764–1829) was described by Sir Walter Scott, whom he tried to tutor in music, as 'a warm-hearted man . . . of many accomplishments, but dashed with *bizarrerie* of temper'. The book from which this extract is taken was modelled on Thomas Warton's *History of English Poetry*.

(a) Extract from *An Introduction to the History of Poetry In Scotland* (Edinburgh, 1798), pp. 306–8.

When a few copies of [the Kilmarnock edition] made their appearance in Edinburgh, soon after it was published, the readers of this sort of poetry were astonished, and each enquired at the other, who this Robert Burns might be? and when it was known that this Elisha of the last of the Scottish bards was a ploughman in Ayrshire, his poetical productions were looked on as prodigies of genius. The whole literary world was taken by surprise, and even the fashionable circles caught the contagion. From the cottage to the palace, nothing was heard but the praises of our 'second Ramsay, our second Fergusson': nay, by some he was deemed greater than either of these poets. Critiques appeared in periodical works, and in the newspapers of the day: but, when novelty had ceased to admire, and envy had been hushed in silence, the real merits of our poet were more dispassionately considered. The consequence was, that his works became more and more relished, the oftener they were perused; and, it is believed, will stand the test of fair criticism, as long as the standard of taste is referable to nature and feeling. The life of Burns is already before the public. It is written by Mr. Robert Heron, of Edinburgh. The public are anxiously looking forward to the time, when a more circumstantial account of the life and writings of our favourite poet, shall come from the pen of the

Historian Medica[1] and his friend, so well known as a physician and philosopher.

It was the peculiar felicity of Burns, on his first entrance on the literary stage, to be patronized and supported, even to a degree, rarely the lot of the most consumate talents. It became, for a time, the *rage*, to use a fashionable phrase, to talk of him, to recite his pieces, and boast of having spent an evening in company with the Ayrshire bard.

(b) Extract from *Albyn's Anthology* (Edinburgh, 1816), Preface.

In A.D. 1786 *Poems, chiefly in the Scottish Dialect* by ROBERT BURNS were printed by John Wilson, Kilmarnock, in one volume octavo; in which appeared specimens of those verses (to well-known Scottish melodies), that filled every reader with wonder and admiration. BURNS has fixed the standard of song-writing or vocal poetry. His masterly lyrics breathe the tender pathos of TIBULLUS, the rural sweetness of the Doric Muse, and all the ardour of PINDAR and animation of HOMER himself. To what purpose would a waste of words be, in a fruitless attempt to dilate on the grasp and versatility of his poetical talent? Volumes have been written; and the subject is still new—it is inexhaustible. The late MR. JAMES JOHNSON, music engraver, happily for himself and the world, fell in with BURNS, about the time that industrious artist commenced his *Scots Musical Museum*, a work of no small merit;* and, cordially embracing the spirited speculation, he gave a loose to his Muse, by which Johnson's *Museum* became the repository of Scottish song, till another more splendid work attracted his attention, which now became divided; till at length he was seduced, and MR. GEORGE THOMSON finally triumphed, as is sufficiently well known. . . .

After the appearance of BURNS' Poems, all the town and country presses teemed with publications of this sort; and since JOHNSON's *Scots Museum* and THOMSON's *Collection of Original Scottish Airs*, appeared, many similar publications have issued from the press, both in Scotland and England.

[1] James Currie.

* The late Mr. Stephen Clerk, organist, was the person who harmonised the greater number of the melodies adapted to BURNS' verses in the Scots museum. This gentleman was the intimate friend of BURNS: consequently he laboured CON AMORE. The fact is they were congenial spirits and enjoyed the moment sacred to conviviality and the muses. Clerk was an uncommonly sensible and accomplished man, and certainly the first organist of his day north of the Tweed.

29. Wordsworth: 'the presence of human life in Burns'

February 1799

Extract from letter of 27 February 1799 to S. T. Coleridge. *The Letters of William and Dorothy Wordsworth*, ed. E. De Selincourt, 2nd ed., I *The Early Years 1787–1805*, rev. C. L. Shaver (1967), pp. 255–6 (see Nos 16, 33, 44, 53, 70 and Introduction, pp. 28–9, 37–8).

I do not so ardently desire character in poems like Burger's,[1] as manners, not transitory manners reflecting the wearisome unintelligible obliquities of city-life, but manners connected with the permanent objects of nature and partaking of the simplicity of those objects. Such pictures must interest when the original must cease to exist. The reason will be immediately obvious if you consider yourself as lying in a valley on the side of mount Etna reading one of Theocritus's Idylliums or on the plains of Attica with a comedy of Aristophanes on your hand. Of Theocritus and his spirit perhaps three fourths remain, of Aristophanes a mutilated skeleton; at least I suppose so for I never read his works but in a most villainous translation. But I may go further read Theocritus in Ayrshire or Merionethshire and you will find perpetual occasions to recollect what you see daily in Ayrshire or Merionethshire read Congreve Vanbrugh and Farquhar in London and though not a century is elapsed since they were alive and merry, you will meet with whole pages that are uninteresting and incomprehensible. Now I find no manners in Burger; in Burns you have manners everywhere. Tam Shanter I do not deem a character, I question whether there is any individual character in all Burns' writings except his own. But every where you have the presence of human life. The communications that proceed from Burns come to the mind with the life and charm of recognitions. But Burns also is energetic solemn and sublime in sentiment, and profound in feeling. His 'Ode to Despondency' I can never read without the deepest agitation.

[1] Gottfried August Bürger (1747–94).

30. James Currie on Burns

1800

'Criticism on the writings of Burns', *The Works of Robert Burns, with an Account of his Life* (Liverpool, 1800), I, pp. 267–336.

James Currie (1756–1805), a Scottish doctor living in Liverpool, prepared the first collected edition of Burns in the four years following the poet's death. His introductory 'Remarks on the Character and Condition of the Scottish Peasantry' and 'Life of Burns' proved influential, as did this essay, which was often reprinted in later editions (see Introduction, p. 23).

After this account of the life and personal character of Burns, it may be expected that some inquiry should be made into his literary merits. It will not however be necessary to enter very minutely into this investigation. If fiction be, as some suppose, the soul of poetry, no one had ever less pretensions to the name of poet than Burns. Though he has displayed great powers of imagination, yet the subjects on which he has written, are seldom, if ever, imaginary; his poems, as well as his letters, may be considered as the effusions of his sensibility, and the transcript of his own musings on the real incidents of his humble life. If we add, that they also contain most happy delineations of the characters, manners, and scenery that presented themselves to his observation, we shall include almost all the subjects of his muse. His writings may therefore be regarded as affording a great part of the data on which our account of his personal character has been founded; and most of the observations we have applied to the man, are applicable, with little variation, to the poet.

The impression of his birth, and of his original station in life, was not more evident on his form and manners, than on his poetical productions. The incidents which form the subjects of his poems, though some of them highly interesting and susceptible of poetical imagery, are incidents in the life of a peasant who takes no pains to disguise the lowliness of his condition, or to throw into shade the circumstances

132

attending it, which more feeble or more artificial minds would have endeavoured to conceal. The same rudeness and inattention appears in the formation of his rhymes, which are frequently incorrect, while the measure in which many of the poems are written has little of the pomp or harmony of modern versification, and is indeed, to an English ear, strange and uncouth. The greater part of his earlier poems are written in the dialect of his country, which is obscure, if not unintelligible to Englishmen, and which though it still adheres more or less to the speech of almost every Scotchman, all the polite and the ambitious are now endeavouring to banish from their tongues as well as their writings. The use of it in composition naturally therefore calls up ideas of vulgarity to the mind. These singularities are encreased by the character of the poet, who delights to express himself with a simplicity that approaches to nakedness, and with an unmeasured energy that often alarms delicacy, and sometimes offends taste. Hence in approaching him, the first impression is perhaps repulsive: there is an air of coarseness about him, which is difficultly reconciled with our established notions of poetical excellence.

As the reader however becomes better acquainted with the poet, the effects of his peculiarities lessen. He perceives in his poems, even on the lowest subjects, expressions of sentiment, and delineations of manners, which are highly interesting. The scenery he describes is evidently taken from real life; the characters he introduces, and the incidents he relates, have the impression of nature and truth. His humour, though wild and unbridled, is irresistibly amusing, and is sometimes heightened in its effects by the introduction of emotions of tenderness, with which genuine humour so happily unites. Nor is this the extent of his power. The reader, as he examines farther, discovers that the poet is not confined to the descriptive, the humourous, or the pathetic; he is found, as occasion offers, to rise with ease into the terrible and the sublime. Every where he appears devoid of artifice, performing what he attempts with little apparent effort, and impressing on the offspring of *his fancy the stamp of his understanding*. The reader capable of forming a just estimate of poetical talents, discovers in these circumstances marks of uncommon genius, and is willing to investigate more minutely its nature and its claims to originality.

The humour of Burns is of a richer vein than that of Ramsay or Fergusson, both of whom, as he himself informs us, he had 'frequently in his eye, but rather with a view to kindle at their flame, than to servile imitation.' His descriptive powers, whether the objects on which they are employed be comic or serious, animate or inanimate, are of the highest order. A superiority of this kind is essential to every species of poetical excellence. In one of his earlier poems his plan seems to be to inculcate a lesson of contentment on the lower classes of society, by shewing that their superiors are neither much better nor happier than themselves; and this he chuses to execute in the form of a dialogue between two dogs. He introduces this dialogue by an account of the persons and characters of the speakers. The first, whom he has named *Caesar*, is a dog of condition:

> His locked, letter'd, braw brass collar,
> Shew'd him the gentleman and scholar.

High-bred though he is, he is however full of condescension.

> At kirk or market, mill or smiddie,
> Nae tawted tyke, though e'er sae duddie,
> But he had stan't, as glad to see him,
> *And stroan't on stanes an hillocks wi' him.*

The other, *Luath*, is a 'ploughman's collie,' but a cur of a good heart and a sound understanding.

> His honest, sonsie, baws'nt face,
> Ay gat him friends in ilka place.
> His breast was white, his towsie back
> Weel clad wi' coat o' glossy black;
> *His gawcie tail, wi' upward curl,*
> *Hung o'er his hurdies wi' a swirl.*

Never were *twa dogs* so exquisitely delineated. Their gambols before they sit down to moralize, are described with an equal degree of happiness; and through the whole dialogue, the character, as well as the different condition of the two speakers, is kept in view. The speech of *Luath*, in which he enumerates the comforts of the poor, gives the following account of their merriment on the first day of the year.

[quotes 'The Twa Dogs', ll. 129–38]

Of all the animals who have moralized on human affairs since the days of Æsop, the dog seems best entitled to this privilege, as well from his superior sagacity, as from his being more than any other the friend and associate of man. The dogs of Burns, excepting in their talent for moralizing, are downright dogs; and not the Horses of Swift, or the *Hind and Panther* of Dryden, men in the shape of brutes. It is this circumstance that heightens the humour of the dialogue. The 'twa dogs' are constantly kept before our eyes, and the contrast between their form and character as dogs, and the sagacity of their conversation, heightens the humour, and deepens the impression of the poet's satire. Though in this poem the chief excellence may be considered as humour, yet great talents are displayed in its composition; the happiest powers of description, and the deepest insight into the human heart.* It is seldom however that the humour of Burns appears in so simple a form. The liveliness of his sensibility frequently impels him to introduce into subjects of humour, emotions of tenderness or of pity, and where occasion admits, he is sometimes carried on to exert the higher powers of imagination. In such instances he leaves the society of Ramsay and of Fergusson, and associates himself with the masters of English poetry, whose language he frequently assumes.

Of the union of tenderness and humour, examples may be found in the 'Death and Dying Words of poor Maillie', in the auld 'Farmer's New-Year's Morning Salutation to his Mare Maggie', and in many of his other poems. The praise of whisky is a favourite subject with Burns. To this he dedicates his poem of 'Scotch Drink'. After mentioning its cheering influence in a variety of situations, he describes, with singular liveliness and power of fancy, its stimulating effects on the blacksmith working at his forge.

> Nae mercy, then, for airn or steel;
> The brawnie, bainie, ploughman chiel,
> Brings hard owre-hip, wi' sturdy wheel,
>   The strong fore-hammer,
> Till block an' studdie ring and reel
>   Wi' dinsome clamour.

---

* When this poem first appeared, it was thought by some very surprising, that a peasant who had not had an opportunity of associating even with a simple gentleman, should have been able to pourtray the character of high-life with such accuracy. And when it was recollected that he had probably been at the races of Ayr, where nobility as well as gentry are to be seen, it was concluded that the race-ground had been the field of his observation. This was sagacious enough—but it did not require such instruction to inform Burns, that human nature is essentially the same in the high and the low; and a genius which comprehends the human mind, easily comprehends the accidental varieties introduced by situation.

On another occasion,* chusing to exalt whisky above wine, he
introduces a comparison between the natives of more genial climes,
to whom the vine furnishes their beverage, and his own countrymen
who drink the spirit of malt. The description of the Scotsman is
humorous.

> But bring a Scotsman frae his hill,
> Clap in his cheek a Highland gill,
> Say, such is royal George's will,
>   An' there's the foe,
> He has nae thought but how to kill
>   Twa at a blow.

Here the notion of danger rouses the imagination of the poet. He
goes on thus:

> Nae cauld, faint-hearted doubtings tease him;
> Death comes—wi' fearless eye he sees him;
> Wi' bluidy hand a welcome gies him;
>   An' when he fa's,
> His latest draught o' breathin lea'es him
>   In faint huzzas.

Again however, he sinks into humour, and concludes the poem with
the following most laughable, but most irreverent apostrophe.

> Scotland, my auld, respected mither!
> Tho' whiles ye moistify your leather,
> 'Till whare ye sit, on craps o' heather,
>   Ye tine your dam;
> *Freedom* and *whisky* gang thegither,
>   Tak aff your dram!

Of this union of humour with the higher powers of imagination,
instances may be found in the poem entitled 'Death and Dr. Hornbook',
and in almost every stanza of the 'Address to the Deil', one of the
happiest of his productions. After reproaching this terrible being with
all his 'doings' and misdeeds, in the course of which he passes through
a series of Scottish superstitions, and rises at times into a high strain
of poetry, he concludes this address, delivered in a tone of great

* The 'Author's earnest Cry and Prayer to the Scotch Representatives in Parliament'.

familiarity, not altogether unmixed with apprehension, in the following words.

> But, fare you weel, auld Nickie-ben!
> O wad you tak a thought an' men'!
> Ye aiblins might—I dinna ken—
> Still hae a stake—
> I'm wae to think upo' yon den
> Ev'n for your sake!

Humour and tenderness are here so happily intermixed, that it is impossible to say which preponderates.

Fergusson wrote a dialogue between the *Causeway* and the *Plainstones** of Edinburgh. This probably suggested to Burns his dialogue between the old and the new bridge over the river Ayr.† The nature of such subjects requires that they shall be treated humourously, and Fergusson has attempted nothing beyond this. Though the *Causeway* and the *Plainstones* talk together, no attempt is made to personify the speakers. A 'cadie'‡ heard the conversation, and reported it to the poet.

In the dialogue between the 'Brigs of Ayr,' Burns himself is the auditor, and the time and occasion on which it occurred is related with great circumstantiality. The poet, 'pressed by care,' or 'inspired by whim', had left his bed in the town of Ayr, and wandered out alone in the darkness and solitude of a winter night, to the mouth of the river where the stillness was interrupted only by the rushing sound of the influx of the tide. It was after mid-night. The Dungeon-clock had struck two, and the sound had been repeated by Wallace-Tower.§ All else was hushed. The moon shone brightly, and

> The chilly frost, beneath the silver beam,
> Crept gently-crusting, o'er the glittering stream.

In this situation the listening bard hears the 'clanging sugh' of wings moving through the air, and speedily he perceives two beings, reared, the one on the Old, the other on the New Bridge, whose form and attire he describes, and whose conversation with each other he rehearses. These genii enter into a comparison of the respective edifices

---

* The *middle of the street*, and the *side-way*.   † *The Brigs of Ayr.*
‡ A messenger.   § The two steeples of Ayr.

over which they preside, and afterwards, as is usual between the old and young, compare modern characters and manners with those of past times. They differ as may be expected, and taunt and scold each other in broad Scotch. This conversation, which is certainly humorous, may be considered as the proper business of the poem. As the debate runs high, and threatens serious consequences, all at once it is interrupted by a new scene of wonders.

[quotes 'The Brigs of Ayr', ll. 194–201, 213–16]

Next follow a number of other allegorical beings, among whom are the four Seasons, Rural Joy, Plenty, Hospitality, and Courage.

> Benevolence, with mild, benignant air,
> A female form, came from the tow'rs of Stair:
> Learning and Worth in equal measures trode,
> From simple Catrine, their long-loved abode:
> Last, white-robed Peace, crowned with a hazle-wreath,
> To rustic Agriculture did bequeath
> The broken iron-instrument of death;
> At sight of whom our Sprites forgat their kindling wrath.

This poem, irregular and imperfect as it is, displays various and powerful talents, and may serve to illustrate the genius of Burns. In particular it affords a striking instance of his being carried beyond his original purpose by the powers of imagination.

In Fergusson's poem, the *Plainstones* and *Causeway* contrast the characters of the different persons who walked upon them. Burns probably conceived that by a dialogue between the Old and New Bridge, he might form a humorous contrast between ancient and modern manners in the town of Ayr. Such a dialogue could only be supposed to pass in the stillness of night, and this led our poet into a description of a midnight scene, which excited in a high degree the powers of his imagination. During the whole dialogue the scenery is present to his fancy, and at length it suggests to him a fairy dance of aerial beings, under the beams of the moon, by which the wrath of the Genii of the *Brigs of Ayr* is appeased.

Incongruous as the different parts of this poem are, it is not an incongruity that displeases, and we have only to regret that the poet did not bestow a little pains in making the figures more correct, and in smoothing the versification.

The epistles of Burns, in which may be included his 'Dedication to

G. H. Esq.' discover, like his other writings, the powers of a superior understanding. They display deep insight into human nature, a gay and happy strain of reflection, great independence of sentiment and generosity of heart. It is to be regretted, that in his 'Holy Fair', and in some of his other poems, his humour degenerates into personal satire, and is not sufficiently guarded in other respects. The 'Halloween' of Burns is free from every objection of this sort. It is interesting not merely from its humorous description of manners, but as it records the spells and charms used on the celebration of a festival, now even in Scotland falling into neglect, but which was once observed over the greater part of Britain and Ireland.* These charms are supposed to afford an insight into futurity, especially on the subject of marriage, the most interesting event of rural life. In the 'Halloween', a female in performing one of the spells, has occasion to go out by moonlight, to dip her shift-sleeve into a stream *running towards the South*. It was not necessary for Burns to give a description of this stream. But it was the character of his ardent mind to pour forth not merely what the occasion required, but what it admitted; and the temptation to describe so beautiful a natural object by moon-light, was not to be resisted—

> Whyles owre a linn the burnie plays
> As thro' the glen it wimpl't;
> Whyles round a rocky scar it strays;
> Whyles in a wiel it dimpl't;
> Whyles glitter'd to the nightly rays,
> Wi' bickering, dancing dazzle;
> Whyles cookit underneath the braes,
> Beneath the spreading hazle,
> Unseen that night.

Those who understand the Scottish dialect will allow this to be one of the finest instances of description, which the records of poetry afford. Though of a very different nature, it may be compared in point of excellence with Thomson's description of a river swollen by the rains of winter, bursting through the streights that confine its torrent, 'boiling, wheeling, foaming, and thundering along.'†

In pastoral, or to speak more correctly, in rural poetry, of a serious nature, Burns excelled equally as in that of a humorous kind, and using less of the Scottish dialect in his serious poems, he becomes more

* In Ireland it is still celebrated. It is not quite in disuse in Wales.
† See Thomson's 'Winter'.

generally intelligible. It is difficult to decide whether the 'Address to a Mouse whose nest was turned up with the plough', should be considered as serious or comic. Be this as it may, the poem is one of the happiest, and most finished of his productions. If we smile at the 'bickering brattle' of this little flying animal, it is a smile of tenderness and pity. The descriptive part is admirable; the moral reflections beautiful, and arising directly out of the occasion; and in the conclusion there is a deep melancholy, a sentiment of doubt and dread, that rises to the sublime. The 'Address to a Mountain Daisy, turned down with the plough', is a poem of the same nature, though somewhat inferior in point of originality, as well as in the interest produced. To extract out of incidents so common, and seemingly so trivial as these, so fine a train of sentiment and imagery, is the surest proof, as well as the most brilliant triumph, of original genius. 'The Vision' is two cantos, from which a beautiful extract is taken by Mr. Mackenzie, in the 97th number of the *Lounger*, is a poem of great and various excellence. The opening, in which the poet describes his own state of mind, retiring in the evening, wearied from the labours of the day, to moralize on his conduct and prospects, is truely interesting. The chamber, if we may so term it, in which he sits down to muse, is an exquisite painting.

> There, lanely, by the ingle-cheek
> I sat and ey'd the spewing reek,
> That filled, wi'hoast-provoking smeek,
>   The auld, clay biggin;
> An' heard the restless rattons squeak
>   About the riggin.

To reconcile to our imagination, the entrance of an aerial being into a mansion of this kind, required the powers of Burns—he however succeeds. Coila enters, and her countenance, attitude, and dress, unlike those of other spiritual beings, are distinctly pourtrayed. To the painting on her mantle, on which is depicted the most striking scenery, as well as the most distinguished characters, of his native county, some exceptions may be made. The mantle of Coila, like the cup of Thyrsis,* and the shield of Achilles, is too much crowded with figures, and some of the objects represented upon it, are scarcely admissible, according to the principles of design. The generous temperament of Burns led him into these exuberances. In his second edition he enlarged the number of

---

* See the first 'Idyllium' of Theocritus.

figures originally introduced, that he might include objects to which he was attached by sentiments of affection, gratitude, or patriotism. The second *Duan* or canto of this poem, in which Coila describes her own nature and occupations, particularly her superintendence of his infant genius, and in which she reconciles him to the character of a bard, is an elevated and solemn strain of poetry, ranking in all respects, excepting the harmony of numbers, with the higher productions of the English muse. The concluding stanza, compared with that already quoted, will show to what a height Burns rises in this poem, from the point at which he set out.

> *And wear thou this*—she solemn said,
> And bound the *holly* round my head;
> The polish'd leaves, and berries red,
>   Did rustling play;
> And, like a passing thought, she fled
>   In light away.

In various poems Burns has exhibited the picture of a mind under the deep impressions of real sorrow. The 'Lament', the 'Ode to Ruin', 'Despondency', and 'Winter a Dirge', are of this character. In the first of these poems the 8th stanza, which describes a sleepless night from anguish of mind, is particularly striking. Burns often indulged in those melancholy views of the nature and condition of man, which are so congenial to the temperament of sensibility. The poem entitled, 'Man was made to Mourn', affords an instance of this kind, and the 'Winter Night', is of the same description. This last is highly characteristic, both of the temper of mind, and of the condition of Burns. It begins with a description of a dreadful storm on a night in winter. The poet represents himself as lying in bed, and listening to its howling. In this situation he naturally turns his thought to the *ourie** Cattle, and the *silly*†
Sheep, exposed to all the violence of the tempest.
Having lamented their fate, he proceeds in the following manner.

> Ilk happing bird—wee, helpless thing!
> That, in the merry months o' spring,
> Delighted me to hear thee sing,
>   What comes o' thee?
> Whare wilt thou cow'r thy chittering wing,
>   An' close thy e'e?

* *Ourie*, out-lying, *Ourie Cattle*, Cattle that are unhoused all winter.
† *Silly* is in this, as in other places, a term of compassion and endearment.

Other reflections of the same nature occur to his mind; and as the mid-night moon 'muffled with clouds' casts her dreary light on his window, thoughts of a darker and more melancholy nature croud upon him. In this state of mind, he hears a voice pouring through the gloom, a solemn and plaintive strain of reflection. The mourner compares the fury of the elements with that of man to his brother man, and finds the former light in the balance.

> See stern oppression's iron grip,
>   Or mad ambition's gory hand,
> Sending like blood-hounds from the slip,
>   Woe, want, and murder, o'er the land.—

He pursues this train of reflection through a variety of particulars, in the course of which he introduces the following animated apostrophe.

> O ye! who, sunk in beds of down,
>   Feel not a want but what yourselves create,
>   Think, for a moment, on his wretched fate,
>   Whom friends and fortune quite disown!
> Ill-satisfy'd keen Nature's clam'rous call,
>   Stretch'd on his straw he lays him down to sleep,
> While thro' the ragged roof and chinky wall,
>   Chill, o'er his slumbers, piles the drifty heap!

The strain of sentiment which runs through this poem is noble, though the execution is unequal, and the versification is defective.

Among the serious poems of Burns, 'The Cotter's Saturday Night' is perhaps entitled to the first rank. 'The Farmer's Ingle' of Fergusson evidently suggested the plan of this poem, as has already been mentioned; but after the plan was formed, Burns trusted entirely to his own powers for the execution. Fergusson's poem is certainly very beautiful. It has all the charms which depend on rural characters and manners happily pourtrayed, and exhibited under circumstances highly grateful to the imagination. 'The Farmer's Ingle' begins with describing the return of evening. The toils of the day are over, and the farmer retires to his comfortable fire-side. The reception which he and his men-servants receive from the careful housewife, is pleasingly described. After their supper is over, they begin to talk on the rural events of the day.

'Bout kirk and market eke their tales gae on,
How *Jock* woo'd *Jenny* here to be his bride;
And there how *Marion* for a bastart son,
Upo' the cutty-stool was forced to ride.
The waefu' scauld o' our *Mess John* to bide.

The 'Gudame' is next introduced as forming a circle round the fire, in the midst of her grand-children, and while she spins from the rock, and the spindle plays on her 'russet lap', she is relating to the young ones, tales of witches and ghosts. The poet exclaims,

O mock na this my friends! but rather mourn,
Ye in life's brawest spring wi' reason clear,
Wi' eild our idle fancies a' return,
And dim our dolefu' days wi' bairnly fear;
The mind's aye *cradled* when the *grave* is near.

In the mean time the farmer, wearied with the fatigues of the day, stretches himself at length on the *settle*, a sort of rustic couch which extends on one side of the fire, and the cat and house-dog leap upon it to receive his caresses. Here, resting at his ease, he gives his directions to his men-servants for the succeeding day. The housewife follows his example, and gives her orders to the maidens. By degrees the oil in the cruise begins to fail; the fire runs low; sleep steals on his rustic group; and they move off to enjoy their peaceful slumbers. The poet concludes by bestowing his blessing on the 'husbandman and all his tribe.'

This is an original and truely interesting pastoral. It possesses every thing required in this species of composition. We might have perhaps said, every thing that it admits, had not Burns written his 'Cotter's Saturday Night'.

The cottager returning from his labours, has no servants to accompany him, to partake of his fare, or to receive his instructions. The circle which he joins, is composed of his wife and children only; and if it admits of less variety, it affords an opportunity for representing scenes that more strongly interest the affections. The younger children running to meet him, and clambering round his knee; the elder, returning from their weekly labours with the neighbouring farmers, dutifully depositing their little gains with their parents, and receiving their father's blessing and instructions; the incidents of the courtship of Jenny, their eldest daughter, 'woman grown;' are circumstances of the most interesting kind, which are most happily delineated: and after

143

their frugal supper, the representation of these humble cottagers forming a wider circle round their hearth, and uniting in the worship of God, is a picture the most deeply affecting of any which the rural muse has ever presented to the view. Burns was admirably adapted to this delineation. Like all men of genius he was of the temperament of devotion, and the powers of memory co-operated in this instance with the sensibility of his heart, and the fervour of his imagination.* 'The Cotter's Saturday Night' is tender and moral, it is solemn and devotional, and rises at length into a strain of grandeur and sublimity, which modern poetry has not surpassed. The noble sentiments of patriotism with which it concludes, correspond with the rest of the poem. In no age or country have the pastoral muses breathed such elevated accents, if the 'Messiah' of Pope be excepted, which is indeed a pastoral in form only. It is to be regretted that Burns did not employ his genius on other subjects of the same nature, which the manners and customs of the Scottish peasantry would have amply supplied. Such poetry is not to be estimated by the degree of pleasure which it bestows; it sinks deeply into the heart, and is calculated, far beyond any other human means, for giving permanence to the scenes and the characters it so exquisitely describes.

Before we conclude, it will be proper to offer a few observations on the lyric productions of Burns. His compositions of this kind are chiefly songs, generally in the Scottish dialect, and always after the model, of the *Scottish Songs*, on the general character and moral influence of which, some observations have already been offered. We may hazard a few more particular remarks.

Of the historic or heroic ballards of Scotland, it is unnecessary to speak. Burns has no where imitated them, a circumstance to be regretted, since in this species of composition, from its admitting the more terrible as well as the softer graces of poetry, he was eminently qualified to have excelled. The Scottish songs which served as a model to Burns, are almost without exception pastoral, or rather rural. Such of them as are comic, frequently treat of a rustic courtship, or a country wedding; or they describe the differences of opinion which arise in married life. Burns has imitated this species, and surpassed his models. The song beginning 'husband, husband, cease your strife' may be cited in support of this observation.† His other comic songs are of equal

* The reader will recollect that the Cotter was Burns's father.
† The dialogues between husbands and their wives, which form the subjects of the Scottish songs, are almost all ludicrous and satirical, and in these contests the lady is

merit. In the rural songs of Scotland, whether humorous or tender, the sentiments are given to particular characters, and very generally, the incidents are referred to particular scenery. This last circumstance may be considered as the distinguishing feature of the Scottish songs, and on it a considerable part of their attraction depends. On all occasions the sentiments, of whatever nature, are delivered in the character of the person principally interested. If love be described, it is not as it is observed, but as it is felt; and the passion is delineated under a particular aspect. Neither is it the fiercer impulses of desire that are expressed, as in the celebrated ode of Sappho, the model of so many modern songs; but those gentler emotions of tenderness and affection, which do not entirely absorb the lover; but permit him to associate his emotions with the charms of external nature, and breathe the accents of purity and innocence, as well as of love. In these respects the love-songs of Scotland are honourably distinguished from the most admired classical compositions of the same kind; and by such associations a variety, as well as liveliness, is given to the representation of this passion, which are not to be found in the poetry of Greece or Rome, or perhaps of any other nation. Many of the love-songs of Scotland describe scenes of rural courtship; many may be considered as invocations from lovers to their mistresses. On such occasions a degree of interest and reality is given to the sentiments, by the spot designed to these happy interviews being particularized. The lovers perhaps meet at the *Bush aboon Traquair*, or on the *Banks of Etrick*; the nymphs are invoked to wander among the wilds of *Roslin*, or *the woods of Invermay*. Nor is the spot merely pointed out; the scenery is often described as well as the characters, so as to present a compleat picture to the fancy.* Thus the maxim

---

generally victorious. From the collections of Mr. Pinkerton we find that the comic muse of Scotland delighted in such representations from very early times, in her rude dramatic efforts, as well as in her rustic songs.

* One or two examples may illustrate this observation. A Scottish song, written about a hundred years ago, begins thus.

> On Etrick banks, on a summer's night,
>   At gloaming, when the sheep drove hame,
> I met my lassie, braw and tight,
>   Come wading barefoot a' her lane:
>
> My heart grew light, I ran, I flang
>   My arms about her lily neck,
> And kiss'd and clasped there fu' lang,
>   My words they were na mony, feck.

The lover, who is a Highlander, goes on to relate the language he employed with this Lowland maid to win her heart, and to persuade her to fly with him to the Highland hills,

of Horace, *ut pictura poesis*,[1] is faithfully observed by these rustic bards, who are guided by the same impulse of nature and sensibility which influenced the father of epic poetry, on whose example the precept of the Roman poet was perhaps founded. By this means the imagination is employed to interest the feelings. When we do not conceive distinctly, we do not sympathize deeply in any human affection; and we conceive nothing in the abstract.

Abstraction, so useful in morals, and so essential in science, must be abandoned when the heart is to be subdued by the powers of poetry or of eloquence. The bards of a ruder condition of society, paint individual objects; and hence among other causes, the easy access they obtain to the heart. Generalization is the vice of poets whose learning overpowers their genius; of poets of a refined and scientific age.

The dramatic style which prevails so much in the Scottish songs, while it contributes greatly to the interest they excite, also shows that they have originated among a people in the earlier stages of society. Where this form of composition appears in songs of a modern date, it indicates that they have been written after the ancient model.*

---

there to share his fortune. The sentiments are in themselves beautiful. But we feel them with double force, while we conceive that they were addressed by a lover to his mistress, whom he met all alone, on a summer's evening, by the banks of a beautiful stream, which some of us have actually seen, and which all of us can paint to our imagination. Let us take another example. It is now a nymph that speaks. Hear how she expresses herself.

> How blythe each morn was I to see
> My swain come o'er the hill!
> He skipt the burn, and flew to me,
> I met him with gude will.

Here is another picture drawn by the pencil of nature. We see a shepherdess standing by the side of a brook, watching her lover as he descends the opposite hill. He bounds lightly along; he approaches nearer and nearer; he leaps the brook, and flies into her arms. In the recollection of these circumstances, the surrounding scenery becomes endeared to the fair mourner, and she bursts into the following exclamation.

> O the broom, the bonnie bonnie broom,
> The broom of the Cowden-Knowes!
> I wish I were with my dear swain,
> With his pipe and my ewes.

Thus the individual spot of this happy interview is pointed out, and the picture is completed.

[1] 'poetry [will be] like painting'.

* That the dramatic form of writing characterizes the productions of an early, or what amounts to the same thing, of a rude stage of society, may be illustrated by a reference to the most ancient compositions that we know of, the Hebrew scriptures and the writings of Homer. The form of dialogue is adopted in the old Scottish ballads even in narration,

The Scottish songs are of very unequal poetical merit, and this inequality often extends to the different part of the same song. Those that are humorous, or characteristic of manners, have in general the merit of copying nature; those that are serious, are tender and often sweetly interesting, but seldom exhibit high powers of imagination, which indeed do not easily find a place in this species of composition. The alliance of the words of the Scottish songs with the music, has in some instances given to the former a popularity, which otherwise they would not have obtained.

The association of the words and the music of these songs, with the more beautiful parts of the scenery of Scotland, contributes to the same effect. It has given them not merely popularity, but permanence; it has imparted to the works of man some portion of the durability of the works of nature. If from our imperfect experience of the past, we may judge with any confidence respecting the future, songs of this description are of all others least likely to die. In the changes of language they may no doubt suffer change; but the associated strain of sentiment and of music, will perhaps survive, while the clear stream sweeps down the vale of Yarrow, or the yellow broom waves on the Cowden-Knowes.

The first attempts of Burns in song-writing were not very successful. His habitual inattention to the exactness of rhimes, and to the harmony

---

whenever the situations described become interesting. This sometimes produces a very striking effect, of which an instance may be given from the ballad of 'Edom o' Gordon', a composition apparently of the sixteenth century. The story of the ballad is shortly this— The castle of Rhodes, in the absence of its lord, is attacked by the robber Edom o' Gordon. The lady stands on her defence, beats off the assailants, and wounds Gordon, who in his rage orders the castle to be set on fire. That his orders are carried into effect, we learn from the expostulation of the lady, who is represented as standing on the battlements, and remonstrating on this barbarity. She is interrupted—

> O then bespak hir little son,
>   Sate on his nourice' knee;
> Says, 'mither dear, gi' owre this house,
>   'For the reek it smithers me.'
> 'I wad gie a' my gowd, my childe,
>   'Sae wad I a' my fee,
> For ae blast o' the westlin wind,
>   To blaw the reek frea thee.'

The circumstantiality of the Scottish love-songs, and the dramatic form which prevails so generally in them, probably arises from their being the descendents and successors of the ancient ballads. In the beautiful modern song of 'Mary of Castle-Cary,' the dramatic form has a very happy effect. The same may be said of 'Donald and Flora,' and 'Come under my Plaidie,' by the same author, Mr. Macniel.

of numbers, arising probably from the models on which his versification was formed, were faults likely to appear to more disadvantage in
this species of composition, than in any other; and we may also remark,
that the strength of his imagination, and the exuberance of his sensibility, were with difficulty restrained within the limits of gentleness,
delicacy and tenderness, which seem to be assigned to the love-songs of
his nation. Burns was better adapted by nature for following in such
compositions, the model of the Grecian, than of the Scottish muse. By
study and practice he however surmounted all these obstacles. In his
earlier songs there is some ruggedness; but this gradually disappears in
his successive efforts; and some of his latter compositions of this kind,
may be compared in polished delicacy, with the finest songs in our
language, while in the eloquence of sensibility they surpass them all.

The songs of Burns, like the models he followed and excelled, are
often dramatic and for the greater part amatory; and the beauties of
rural nature are every where associated with the passions and emotions
of the mind. Disdaining to copy the works of others, he has not, like
some poets of great name, admitted into his descriptions exotic
imagery. The landscapes he has painted, and the objects with which
they are embellished, are in every single instance, such as are to be
found in his own country. In a mountainous region, especially when it
is comparatively rude and naked, the most beautiful scenery will always
be found in the vallies, and on the banks of the wooded streams. Such
scenery is peculiarly interesting at the close of a summer-day. As we
advance northwards, the number of the days of summer indeed
diminishes; but from this cause, as well as from the mildness of the
temperature, the attraction of the season increases, and the summer-
night becomes still more beautiful. The greater obliquity of the sun's
path on the ecliptic, prolongs the grateful season of twilight, to the midnight hours, and the shades of the evening seem to mingle with the
morning's dawn. The rural poets of Scotland, as may be expected,
associate in their songs the expressions of passion, with the most
beautiful of their scenery, in the fairest season of the year, and generally
in those hours of the evening when the beauties of nature are most
interesting.*

To all these adventitious circumstances, on which so much of the

* A lady, of whose genius the editor entertains high admiration, (Mrs. Barbauld) has
fallen into an error in this respect. In her prefatory address to the works of Collins, speaking of the natural objects that may be employed to give interest to the descriptions of
passion, she observes, 'they present an inexhaustible variety, from the song of Solomon,
breathing of Cassia, Myrrh, and Cinnamon, to the Gentle Shepherd of Ramsay, whose

effect of poetry depends, great attention is paid by Burns. There is scarcely a single song of his, in which particular scenery is not described, or allusions made to natural objects, remarkable for beauty or interest; and though his descriptions are not so full as are sometimes met with in the older Scottish songs, they are in the highest degree appropriate and interesting. Instances in proof of this might be quoted from the 'Lea-Rig,' 'Highland Mary,' the 'Soldier's Return,' 'Logan Water,' from that beautiful pastoral 'Bonnie Jean,' and a great number of others. Occasionally the force of his genius carries him beyond the usual boundaries of Scottish song, and the natural objects introduced, have more of the character of sublimity. An instance of this kind is noticed by Mr. Syme, and many others might be adduced.

> Had I a cave on some wild, distant shore,
> Where the winds howl to the wave's dashing roar:
> There would I weep my woes,
> There seek my lost repose,
> Till grief my eyes should close,
> Ne'er to wake more.

In one song, the scene of which is laid in a winter-night, the 'Wan moon' is described as 'setting behind the white waves;' in another the 'storms' are apostrophized, and commanded to 'rest in the cave of their slumbers.' On several occasions, the genius of Burns loses sight entirely of his archetypes, and rises into a strain of uniform sublimity. Instances of this kind appear in 'Libertie,' 'A Vision,' and in his two war-songs, 'Bruce to his Troops,' and the 'Song of Death.' These last are of a description of which we have no other in our language. The martial songs of our nation are not military, but naval. If we were to seek a comparison of these songs of Burns, with others of a similar nature, we must have recourse to the poetry of ancient Greece, or of modern Gaul.

damsels carry their milking pails through the frost and snows of their less genial, but not less pastoral Country.' The damsels of Ramsay do not walk in the midst of frost and snow. —Almost all the scenes of the Gentle Shepherd are laid in the open air, amidst beautiful natural objects, and at the most genial season of the year. Ramsay introduces all his acts with a prefatory description to assure us of this. The fault of the climate of Britain is not, that it does not afford us the beauties of summer, but that the season of such beauties is comparatively short, and even uncertain. There are days and nights, even in the northern division of the Island, which equal, or perhaps surpass what are to be found in the latitude of Sicily or of Greece.

Burns has made an important addition to the songs of Scotland. In his compositions the poetry equals and sometimes surpasses the music. He has enlarged the poetical scenery of his country. Many of her rivers and mountains, formerly unknown to the muse, are now consecrated by his immortal verse. The Doon, the Lugar, the Ayr, the Nith, and the Cluden—will in future, like the Yarrow, the Tweed, and the Tay, be considered as classic streams, and their borders will be trod with new and superior emotions.

The greater part of the songs of Burns were written after he removed into the County of Dumfries. Influenced perhaps by habits formed in early life, he usually composed while walking in the open air. When engaged in writing these songs, his favorite walks were on the banks of the Nith, or of the Cluden, particularly near the ruins of Lincluden Abbey; and this beautiful scenery he has very happily described under various aspects, as it appears during the softness and serenity of evening, and during the stillness and solemnity of the moon-light night.

There is no species of poetry, the productions of the drama not excepted, so much calculated to influence the morals, as well as the happiness of a people, as those popular verses which are associated with national airs, and which being learnt in the years of infancy, make a deep impression on the heart, before the evolution of the powers of the understanding. The compositions of Burns of this kind now presented in a collected form to the world, make a most important addition to the popular songs of his nation. Like all his other writings, they exhibit independence of sentiment; they are peculiarly calculated to increase those ties which bind generous hearts to their native soil, and to the domestic circle of their infancy; and to cherish those sensibilities, which under due restriction, form the purest happiness of our nature. If in his unguarded moments he composed some songs on which this praise cannot be bestowed, let us hope that they will speedily be forgotten. In several instances, where Scottish airs were allied to words objectionable in point of delicacy, Burns has substituted others of a purer character. On such occasions, without changing the subject, he has changed the sentiments. A proof of this may be seen in the air, 'John Anderson my Joe,' which is now united to words that breathe a strain of conjugal tenderness, that is as highly moral as it is exquisitely affecting.

Few circumstances could afford a more striking proof of the strength of Burns's genius, than the general circulation of his poems in England, notwithstanding the dialect in which the greater part are written, and which might be supposed to render them here uncouth or obscure. In some instances he has used this dialect on subjects of a sublime nature; but in general he confines it to sentiments or description of a tender or humorous kind; and where he rises into elevation of thought, he assumes a purer English stile. The singular faculty he possessed of mingling in the same poem, humorous sentiments and descriptions, with imagery of a sublime and terrific nature, enabled him to use this variety of dialect on some occasions with striking effect. His poem of 'Tam o' Shanter,' affords an instance of this. There he passes from a scene of the lowest humour, to situations of the most awful and terrible kind. He is a musician that runs from the lowest to the highest of his keys, and the use of the Scottish dialect, enables him to add two additional notes to the bottom of his scale.

Great efforts have been made by the inhabitants of Scotland of the superior ranks, to approximate in their speech to the pure English standard; and this has made it difficult to write in the Scottish dialect, without exciting in them some feelings of disgust, which in England are scarcely felt. An Englishman who understands the meaning of the Scottish works, is not offended, nay, on certain subjects he is perhaps pleased with the rustic dialect, as he may be with the Doric Greek of Theocritus.

But a Scotchman inhabiting his own country, if a man of education, and more especially if a literary character, has banished such words from his writings, and has attempted to banish them from his speech; and being accustomed to hear them from the vulgar daily, does not easily admit of their use in poetry, which requires a stile elevated and ornamental. A dislike of this kind is, however, accidental, not natural. It is of the species of disgust which we feel at seeing a female of high birth in the dress of a rustic; which, if she be really young and beautiful, a little habit will enable us to overcome. A lady who assumes such a dress puts her beauty indeed to a severer trial. She rejects—she indeed opposes the influence of fashion; she possibly abandons the grace of elegant and flowing drapery; but her native charms remain, the more striking perhaps because the less adorned; and to these she trusts for fixing her empire on those affections over which fashion has no sway. If she succeeds a new association arises. The dress of the beautiful rustic becomes itself beautiful, and establishes a new fashion for the young and the gay. And when in after ages, the contemplative observer shall view her picture in the gallery that contains the portraits of the beauties of successive centuries, each in the dress of her respective day, her drapery will not deviate more than that of her rivals, from the standard of his taste, and he will give the palm to her who excels in the lineaments of nature.

Burns wrote professedly for the peasantry of his country, and by them their native dialect is universally relished. To a numerous class of the natives of Scotland of another description, it may also be considered as attractive in a different point of view. Estranged from their native soil, and spread over foreign lands, the idiom of their country unites with the sentiments and the descriptions on which it is employed, to recall to their minds the interesting scenes of infancy and youth—to awaken many pleasing, many tender recollections. Literary men, residing at Edinburgh or Aberdeen, cannot judge on this point for one hundred and fifty thousand of their expatriated countrymen.*

To the use of the Scottish dialect in one species of poetry, the composition of songs, the taste of the public has been for some time reconciled. The dialect in question excels, as has already been observed, in the copiousness and exactness of its terms for natural objects; and in pastoral or rural songs, it gives a Doric simplicity, which is very generally approved. Neither does the regret seem well founded which some persons of taste have expressed, that Burns used this dialect in so many other of his compositions. His declared purpose was to paint the manners of rustic life among his 'humble compeers,' and it is not easy to conceive, that this could have been done with equal humour and effect, if he had not adopted their idiom. There are some indeed who will think the subject too low for poetry. Persons of this sickly taste will find their delicacies consulted in many a polite and learned author; let them not seek for gratification in the rough and vigorous lines, in the unbridled humour, or in the overpowering sensibility of this bard of nature.

To determine the comparative merit of Burns would be no easy task. Many persons afterwards distinguished in literature, have been born in as humble a situation of life, but it would be difficult to find any other, who, while earning his subsistence by daily labour, has written verses

---

* These observations are excited by some remarks of respectable correspondents of the description alluded to. This calculation of the number of Scotchmen living out of Scotland is not altogether arbitrary, and it is probably below the truth. It is in some degree founded on the proportion between the number of the sexes *in Scotland*, as it appears from the invaluable Statistics of Sir John Sinclair.—For Scotchmen of this description more particularly, Burns seems to have written his song beginning, 'Their groves o' Sweet myrtle,' a beautiful strain, which it may be confidently predicted, will be sung with equal or superior interest, on the banks of the Ganges or of the Mississippi, as on those of the Tay or the Tweed.

which have attracted and retained universal attention, and which are likely to give the author a permanent and distinguished place among the followers of the muses. If he is deficient in grace, he is distinguished for ease, as well as energy; and these are indications of the higher order of genius. The father of Epic poetry exhibits one of his heroes as excelling in strength, another in swiftness—to form his perfect warrior these attributes are combined. Every species of intellectual superiority admits perhaps of a similar arrangement. One writer excels in force; another in ease—he is superior to them both, in whom both these qualities are united. Of Homer himself it may be said, that like his own Achilles, he surpasses his competitors in mobility as well as strength.

The force of Burns lay in the powers of his understanding and in the sensibility of his heart; and these will be found to infuse the living principle into all the works of genius which seem destined to immortality. His sensibility had an uncommon range. He was alive to every species of emotion. He is one of the few poets that can be mentioned, who have at once excelled in humour, in tenderness, and in sublimity; a praise unknown to the ancients, and which in modern times is only due to Ariosto, to Shakespear, and perhaps to Voltaire. To compare the writings of this Scottish peasant, with the works of these Giants in literature, might appear presumptious; yet it may be asserted, that he has displayed *the foot of Hercules*. How near he might have approached them by proper culture, with lengthened years, and under happier auspices, it is not for us to calculate. But while we run over the melancholy story of his life, it is impossible not to heave a sigh at the asperity of his fortune; and as we survey the records of his mind, it is easy to see, that out of such materials have been reared the fairest and the most durable of the monuments of genius.

31. Robert Nares, unsigned review of Currie's edition in *British Critic*

xvi (October 1800), 366–79 and xvii (April 1801), 416–22

Robert Nares, later Archdeacon of Stafford, was one of the editors of the *British Critic*, which was founded in 1793 as a by-product of a 'Society For The Reformation Of Principles By Appropriate Literature'. Maria Riddell (No. 22) wrote to Currie on 16 January 1801, 'Are you satisfied with the *British Critic*? I trust you are. Nares promised to Review your publication himself. That secured, I guess'd, *à peu près* the Opinion he would profess of it' (*BC* (1923), p. 84).

In 1795, when we were first threatened with invasion, he appeared in the ranks of the Dumfries volunteers, and contributed to rouse the martial genius of his countrymen, by the following animated and almost sublime war-song.

[quotes 'Orananaoig, or, The song of death']

The whole power of such a poem depends upon the fire and enthusiasm which it breathes, and which it communicates. Whoever was to examine it for incorrect language, or inharmonious verses, would rather show his own bad taste than the faults of the author. It belongs to ardent passion to be negligent, ragged, and naked in expression; to despise ornament, to disregard small circumstances, to hurry forward to its object. These lines most powerfully express the feelings of triumphant death. They display the sadness of victory, combined with its glory. They exhibit the loftiest attitude of human nature, the unconquerable enthusiasm, the heroic pride, the gloomy grandeur, of those who breathe out their last in songs of triumph. There is a dark sublimity in this exaltation over death, in this contempt for the most awful of objects, which more than any other human sentiment has a sovereign power over the heart of man. If they have not elegance, it is because they are above it . . . 'The Lament of Mary Queen of

Scots' is a poem of singular merit. Whether the merits of that unfortunate Princess will endure impartial discussion, in plain prose, may
perhaps well be doubted; but her sufferings are certainly a beautiful
subject for poetry. Her miseries seem however hitherto rather to have
biassed the judgment of historians than to have animated the genius of
poets. Burns was too zealous a Scotchman, and too much of a Jacobite,
not to have all his feelings roused by her fate; and the following lines,
of exquisite sensibility, will show how strongly he could feel and paint
her wrongs.

[quotes 'Lament of Mary Queen of Scots', ll. 33-56]

If the author of these charming verses had been still alive, we should
have counselled him to remove the little appearance of Scotch phraseology, which may repel some readers from the perusal of the poem. It
is in this poem only an *appearance*, by which some English readers may
be disgusted, and no poetical advantage can be gained. In the above
stanzas there are scarcely any Scotch words. The author has only disguised a few English words in Scotch orthography; and as the majority
of the words, and even some entire stanzas, are perfectly English, the
result is a useless and unpleasant jumble of dialects. In those comic poems
which paint the manners of the Scotch peasantry, there is a peculiar
propriety in the use of the Scottish dialect; and wherever that dialect
can boast expressions more significant, more tender, or more elegant,
than the English (which happens sometimes, though less frequently
than provincial partiality may suppose) a Scottish peasant may certainly
avail himself of these advantages of his native speech, which he will
write better and more easily, because it is his native speech. But for
such a confused mixture of mere Scotch spelling with English words,
as we see in the above extract, there is no such plea. Let us advise
writers of Scotch verse to use their provincial language only where it
has a real superiority, sufficient to compensate the disadvantage of
sometimes deterring, and always displeasing and perplexing English
readers. But to return from such minute criticism to the contemplation
of the genius of Burns, which never perhaps appeared more conspicuous than in the following noble Song, which seems to us to
deserve a high place in the first class of lyric poems.

[quotes 'Robert Bruce's march to Bannockburn']

Those who consider the artifices of style as the principal merit of
poetry, will probably wonder at the high place which we have assigned

to this little Song. Still less can we expect the concurrence of those paradoxical critics, who transmute faults into merits, who deem obscurity a great poetical excellence, and even an indispensable quality of the higher ode. We have no hope of, and indeed we have scarce a wish for the concurrence of such readers or judges of poetry. But those who regard the power of inspiring passion as the noblest excellence of an ode; who know that passion has no leisure for elegance; that it is hardly reconcilable with that refinement of thought, or profusion of imagery, which are the principal causes of obscurity; that impassioned language is simple, negligent, abrupt, vehement, full of repetition, confined to its object, and, though often disorderly, yet more than clear, because peculiarly significant; those who have formed such a taste, and adopted such a standard of excellence in lyric poetry, will perhaps not blame us for saying, that we think this song scarcely inferior in spirit and energy to any English Ode that has appeared since 'Alexander's Feast.' The fire which breathes through this Song seemed too great to have been inspired by retrospective patriotism, by the defeat of an invasion which occurred near five centuries ago. We suspected that more recent events must have contributed to kindle such a flame, and the suspicion is changed into certainty, by a passage in one of the poet's letters . . . So complete and deplorable was his delusion, that he thought he was doing honour to the ancient heroes of his native land, when he confounded them with the slaves of Robespierre, whom he thought the soldiers of liberty! and on whose arms he implored the benediction of God. Yet it never ought to be forgotten, that in the midst of this wretched delusion, Burns was preserved by the natural vigour of his understanding, and by the honest feelings of his heart, from those detestable excesses into which so many men of more knowledge and prouder pretensions have fallen. His democracy had not so debased and besotted his mind, that he could contemplate with pleasure, or even with patience, the idea of a French force employed in *reforming* the government of Great Britain. He was far below the level of those *Patriots*, who implored the aid of the oppressors of Switzerland for the delivery of Ireland! As a specimen of the natural strength of a constitution, not totally subdued even by the revolutionary plague, we insert the following song, distinguished by the usual spirit of Burns, admirably appropriate to the occasion for which it was written, and too animated to leave any doubt of the sincerity of the honest and generous, though deluded poet.

[quotes 'The Dumfries Volunteers']

Vigour and animation are qualities so essential to original genius, that we scarcely wonder at discovering them, even under the most disadvantageous circumstances in such a man as Burns. But it is truly wonderful that we find so much tenderness, and even so much elegance, in the writings of this uninstructed and unpolished rustic. The roughness of his education, and the still more fatal grossness of his debauchery, had not destroyed the sensibility and native gracefulness of his mind. Several of his poems, especially some of his posthumous songs, show not only that splendour of fancy and vivacity of comic power, which attracted the admiration of men of taste to his first publication; but demonstrate also a tenderness and delicacy, which are seldom found in laborious poverty, and scarcely ever in tumultuous dissipation. Our selections have already afforded ample proof of the spirit and grandeur of the conceptions of this great poet. The following Song will show that his talent was not confined to the higher poetry.

[quotes 'The bonny wee thing']

The simplicity of tenderness is as much displayed in this little Song, as the simplicity of vehemence in the general odes, which we formerly quoted. One Song in this collection has a peculiar interest. It is the last which the unfortunate poet lived to finish.

[quotes 'Here's a health to ane I lo'e dear']

The full merit of this excellent Song will be most felt by those who have had the misfortune to load their memory with tasteless unfeeling common places, which, by the help of smooth versification, have usurped the title of amorous poetry. Let any passage of the most tolerable of these cold triflers be compared with the third and fourth lines of his Song, the comparison will assuredly leave no doubt of the great superiority of Burns.

Our Scottish readers would scarcely pardon us, if we were not to insert the following proof of the patriotism of our poet.

[quotes 'Their groves o' sweet myrtle . . . ']

It would be easy to multiply extracts, but enough has been cited to justify our opinion, and that of the public is already declared. We will venture to pronounce that the judgment of the present age will, in this case, be confirmed by the remotest posterity; who, among British poets of the end of the eighteenth century, may indeed hesitate between

Burns and Cowper; but will see no other competitors for the throne of poetical genius. We confine this observation to the dead. The claims of the living cannot yet be determined with perfect impartiality.

32. Thomas Stewart: 'The Jolly Beggars'

1800, 1801

Stewart was a Glasgow bookseller and Burns enthusiast.

(a) Extract from unsigned foreword 'To the public', *The Poetical Miscellany, Containing Posthumous Poems, Songs, Epitaphs and Epigrams. By Robert Burns, the Ayrshire Poet.* Stewart and Meikle (Glasgow, 1800)

Among the original productions of Burns, the editor cannot avoid a particular notice of the JOLLY BEGGARS, which, of itself, is sufficient to give celebrity to any collection. The pleasing variety of recitative and songs, affording specimens of almost every measure of verse; the appropriate humour of the respective characters; the natural description of the manners and enjoyments of 'the wandering train'; and the simplicity of the ancient Scottish dialect which it displays, rank it among the foremost sallies of our favourite Poet.

(b) Extract from unsigned 'Advertisement', *Poems Ascribed to Robert Burns, the Ayrshire Bard*, Stewart (Glasgow, 1801)

An analysis of this admirable *jeu d'esprit* ['The Jolly Beggars'] might furnish materials for a long essay. At present, suffice it to say, that for humorous description, and nice discrimination of character, it is inferior to no poem of the same length, in the whole range of English poetry.—The recitative part is possessed of very considerable merit, but the songs constitute its chief excellence: they are sufficiently familiar and witty, without falling too low, or rising too much above the simplicity of a song; the measure is judiciously varied, and always adapted to the subject . . . An approach to licentiousness in some pieces, exposed Burns, when alive, to the scoffs of the illiberal, which still insult his ashes. But let the self-sufficient, who asperse the memory of a son of genius for some slight deviations from decorum remember to appreciate his merits also, and to be more attentive to a declaration sanctioned by greater than human authority, that 'to the pure all things are pure'.

33. William and Dorothy Wordsworth on Burns

1802–42

See Nos 16, 29, 44, 53, 70, and Introduction, pp. 28–9, 37–8.

(a) Stanza VII, 'Resolution and Independence'; written 3 May–4 July 1802, published in *Poems in Two Volumes* (1807)

> I thought of Chatterton, the marvellous Boy,
> The sleepless Soul that perished in his pride;
> Of Him who walked in glory and in joy
> Following his plough, along the mountain-side;
> By our own spirits are we deified:
> We Poets in our youth begin in gladness:
> But thereof come in the end despondency and madness.

(b) Extracts from Dorothy Wordsworth, 'Recollections of a Tour made in Scotland A.D. 1802', *Journals of Dorothy Wordsworth*, ed. E. De Selincourt (1941), I, pp. 198–202

August 18th, Thursday. Went to the churchyard where Burns is buried, a bookseller accompanied us. He showed us the outside of Burns's house, where he had lived the last three years of his life, and where he died. It has a mean appearance, and is in a bye situation, whitewashed— dirty about the doors, as almost all Scotch houses are—flowering plants in the windows.

Went on to visit his grave. He lies at a corner of the churchyard, and his second son, Francis Wallace, beside him; there is no stone to mark the spot; but a hundred guineas have been collected, to be expended on some sort of monument. 'There', said the Bookseller, pointing to a pompous monument, 'there lies Mr. Such-a-one' (I have forgotten his name), 'a remarkably clever man; he was an attorney, and hardly ever lost a cause he undertook. Burns made many a lampoon upon him, and there they rest, as you see'. We looked at the grave with melancholy and painful reflections, repeating to each other his own verses:—

[quotes 'A Bard's Epitaph', ll. 13–24]

. . . We were glad to leave Dumfries, which is no agreeable place to them who do not love the bustle of a town that seems to be rising up to wealth. We could think of little else but poor Burns, and his moving about on that 'unpoetic ground'. In our road to Brownhill, the next stage, we passed Ellisland at a little distance on our right, his farm-house. We might there have had more pleasure in looking round, if we had been nearer to the spot; but there is no thought surviving in connection with Burns's daily life that is not heart-depressing . . . I cannot take leave of the country which we passed through to-day, without mentioning that we saw the Cumberland mountains within half a mile of Ellisland, Burns's house, the last view we had of them . . . we talked of Burns, and of the prospect he must have had, perhaps from his own door, of Skiddaw and his companions, indulging ourselves in fancy that we *might* have been personally known to each other, and he have looked upon those objects with more pleasure for our sakes.

(c) 'At the Grave of Burns, 1803', ll. 19–48; partly written before 1807, published in Wordsworth's *Poems, Chiefly of Early And Late Years* (1842)

Fresh as the flower, whose modest worth
He sang, his genius 'glinted' forth,
Rose like a star that touching earth,
   For so it seems,
Doth glorify its humble birth
    With matchless beams.

The piercing eye, the thoughtful brow,
The struggling heart, where be they now?—
Full soon the Aspirant of the plough,
   The prompt, the brave,
Slept, with the obscurest, in the low
    And silent grave.

I mourned with thousands, but as one
More deeply grieved, for He was gone
Whose light I hailed when first it shone,
   And showed my youth
How Verse may build a princely throne
   On humble truth.

Alas! where'er the current tends,
Regret pursues and with it blends—
Huge Criffel's hoary top ascends
   By Skiddaw seen,—
Neighbours we were, and loving friends
   We might have been;

True friends though diversely inclined;
But heart with heart and mind with mind,
Where the main fibres are entwined,
   Through Nature's skill,
May even by contraries be joined
   More closely still.

(d) 'Thoughts suggested the day following, on the banks of the Nith, near the poet's residence', ll. 31–48; completed in 1839, published in 1842 volume

How oft inspired must he have trod
These pathways, yon far-stretching road!
There lurks his home; in that Abode,
   With mirth elate,
Or in his nobly-pensive mood,
   The Rustic sate.

Proud thoughts that image overawes,
Before it humbly let us pause,
And ask of Nature from what cause
   And by what rules
She trained her Burns to win applause
   That shames the Schools.

Through busiest street and loneliest glen
Are felt the flashes of his pen;
He rules 'mid Winter snows, and when
   Bees fill their hives;
Deep in the general heart of men
   His power survives.

(e) Note written by Wordsworth in 1842 on MS. of 'At the Grave of Burns' and 'Thoughts suggested the day following', *Poetical Works of William Wordsworth*, ed. E. De Selincourt, 1946, II, pp. 441–2

With the Poems of Burns I became acquainted almost immediately upon their first appearance in the volume printed at Kilmarnock in 1786. Their effect upon my mind has been sufficiently expressed above. Familiarity with the dialect of the border counties of Cumberland and Westmorland made it easy for me not only to understand but to feel them. It was not so with his contemporary or rather his predecessor Cowper, as appears from one of his letters. This is to be regretted; for the simplicity, the truth and vigour of Burns would have strongly recommended him, notwithstanding occasional coarseness, to the sympathies of Cowper, and ensured the approval of his judgment. It gives me pleasure, venial I trust, to acknowledge at this late day my obligations to these two great authors, whose writings, in conjunctions with Percy's *Reliques*, powerfully counteracted the mischievous influence of Darwin's dazzling manner, the extravagance of the earlier dramas of Schiller, and that of other German writers upon my taste and nature tendencies.[1] May these few words serve as a warning to youthful Poets who are in danger of being carried away by the inundation of foreign literature, from which our own is at present suffering so much, both in style and points of far greater moment. True it is that in the poems of Burns, as now collected, are too many reprehensible passages; but their immorality is rather the ebullition of natural temperament and a humour of levity than a studied thing: whereas in these foreign Writers, and in some of our own country not long deceased (and in an eminent deceased Poet of our own age), the evil, whether of voluptuousness, impiety, or licentiousness, is courted upon system, and therefore is greater, and less pardonable.

[1] *changed to*: both then and at a later period, when my taste and natural tendencies were under an injurious influence from the dazzling manner of Darwin, and the extravagance of the earlier Dramas of Schiller, and that of other German writers.

34. David Irving on Burns

1804

Extract from 'The life of Robert Burns', by David Irving, in his
The Lives of the Scottish Poets (1804), II, pp. 487–501.

Irving (1778–1860) had published a *Life of Robert Fergusson* while
still a student at Edinburgh University in 1799. In 1820 he was
appointed Librarian of the Faculty of Advocates. His *History of
Scottish Poetry* appeared posthumously in 1861.

The most beautiful of his poems are professedly written in the Scottish
dialect; but in general they are not deeply tinctured with provincial
idioms; many of the stanzas are almost purely English. His verses,
though not very polished or melodious, are commonly distinguished
by an air of originality which atones for every deficiency. His rhymes
are often imperfect, and his expressions indelicate; he passes from ease
to negligence, and from simplicity to coarseness. But these peculiarities
we may ascribe to his early habits of association.

The poems of Burns, though most remarkable for the quality of
humour, exhibit various instances of the true sublime: the vigour of his
imagination, and the soundness of his understanding, enabled him to
attain a variety of excellence which can only be traced in the productions of original genius. Some of his subjects are sufficiently mean; but
he never fails to illumine them with brilliant flashes of intellect. His
flights however are sudden and irregular: the strong impulses of his
mind were not sufficiently chastened and directed by the wholesome
discipline of the schools. His compositions, however beautiful in
detached parts, are very often defective in their general plan.

The most exquisite of his serious poems is 'The Cotter's Saturday
Night'. The characters and incidents which the poet here describes in so
interesting a manner, are such as his father's cottage presented to his
observation; they are such as may every where be found among the
virtuous and intelligent peasantry of Scotland. 'I recollect once he told

me,' says Professor Stewart, 'when I was admiring a distant prospect in one of our morning walks, that the sight of so many smoking cottages gave a pleasure to his mind, which none could understand who had not witnessed like himself, the happiness and the worth which they contained.' With such impressions as these upon his mind, he has succeeded in delineating a charming picture of rural innocence and felicity. The incidents are well selected, the characters skilfully distinguished, and the whole composition is remarkable for the propriety and sensibility which it displays. To transcribe every beautiful passage which the poem contains, would be to transcribe almost every stanza: the following may be selected on account of its moral as well as its poetical effect:

[quotes 'The Cotter's Saturday Night', stanzas VII–X]

His stanzas 'To a Mountain Daisy, on turning one down with the plough,' have always been acknowledged as beautiful and interesting. His address 'To a Mouse, on turning her up in her nest with the plough,' evinces the fertility of his genius, and the unbounded benevolence of his heart. These two poems derive additional interest from the attitude in which the writer is himself presented to our view; we behold him engaged in the labours of the field, and moving in his humble sphere with all the dignity of honest independence and conscious genius. The exordium of his very poetical production entitled 'The Vision' is also rendered interesting by the same circumstance; it exhibits Burns in the retirement of his homely cottage:

[quotes 'The Vision', ll. 1–24]

Others of his serious poems are distinguished by beauties of no vulgar kind. Many passages rise to sublimity: and his moral reflections are often solemn, pathetic, and perspicacious.

But it is perhaps in his humorous and satirical poems that he appears to most advantage. Nature had endowed him with an uncommon degree of sagacity; and his perpetual disappointments and mortifications rendered him a more keen observer of the follies of mankind. His satire however, when he refrains from personalities, is seldom unmerciful: his general opinion of human nature was by no means unfavourable; and he commonly exposes vice and folly with a kind of gay severity.

'Halloween' exhibits a humorous and masterly description of some of the remarkable superstitions of his countrymen. The incidents are selected and the characters discriminated with his usual fel·city. His

'Address to the Deil', as well as 'Death and Dr. Hornbook', is distinguished by an original vein of satirical humour. 'The Holy Fair' is entitled to every praise except that of scrupulous decency. The subsequent stanzas may serve to discover with what efficacy Burns could wield the shafts of ridicule:

[quotes 'The Holy Fair', stanzas XII–XVI]

'The Ordination' is another ecclesiastical satire, remarkable for its wit and humour. The following verses are pregnant with meaning:

> There, try his mettle on the creed,
>   And bind him down wi' caution,
> That *stipend* is a carnal weed
>   He taks but for the fashion.

'Holy Willie's Prayer,' which is excluded from Dr. Currie's edition, and the 'Address to the Unco Guid, or the Rigidly Righteous,' are wholesome satires on hypocrisy; but the former is reprehensible for the extreme indecency which it occasionally exhibits. 'The Twa Dogs,' the 'Dream,' and the 'Dedication to Gavin Hamilton, Esq.' may also be classed among his happier efforts.

The tale entitled 'Tam o' Shanter' displays a rich vein of humorous description, and even high powers of invention . . . One of the most striking passages which the works of Burns contain, is to be found in this production:

[quotes 'Tam o' Shanter', ll. 109–40]

The songs of Burns, which are chiefly of the pastoral and rural kind, are frequently distinguished by strokes of genuine poetry. The versification indeed is not always sufficiently smooth: but the arch simplicity, the delicacy, pathos, and even sublimity, which they so often display, leave the author nearly without a rival in this department of literature. The songs which I shall here select as specimens, are written in the military spirit. The first is entitled 'Robert Bruce's Address to his Army:'

[quotes 'Robert Bruce's march to Bannockburn']

The following song is supposed to be sung by the wounded and dying of a victorious army. It was composed during the late war with France.

[quotes 'Orananaoig, or, The song of death']

The last of these specimens is sufficient to evince that Burns could employ the English language with considerable efficacy: but the advice which he received from Dr. Moore can hardly be considered as altogether judicious. 'It is evident,' says his correspondent, 'that you already possess a great variety of expression and command of the English language; you ought therefore to deal more sparingly for the future in the provincial dialect: why should you, by using *that*, limit the number of your admirers to those who understand the Scottish, when you can extend it to all persons of taste who understand the English language.' The situation and studies of Burns had prepared him for excelling in Scottish poetry; but it is far from being evident that he was qualified to contend with the mighty masters of the English lyre. It was therefore with sufficient prudence that he chiefly confined himself to a department in which he was without a rival. His superiority to Ramsay and Fergusson is manifest; he possesses in an infinitely higher degree the power of captivating the heart, and of arresting the understanding.

35. Southey's letters on Burns

1804-5

Extracts from letters to John Rickman and Grosvenor Charles Bedford. *New Letters of Robert Southey*, ed. Kenneth Curry (1965), I, pp. 370, 378-9 (see Introduction, p. 27).

(a) To John Rickman, 14 December 1804

When I am dead it will be 'poor Southey'—some kind hearted friend will do for me what Currie has done for Burns and Hayley for Cowper, and what I leave behind will be both more and better than has sufficed in those cases for great profit and great popularity. This is putting the case at the worst, but if it please God to let me live and do well I have not the slightest doubt in the course of the next seven years, of realizing what will secure me from the necessity of future task work, even if none of the lucky accidents of life should turn up in my favour.

(b) To Grosvenor Charles Bedford, 6 April 1805

Make a Mem. that from the poems of Robert Fergusson born at Edinburgh 1750-1774—Hyems transcribes the poems 'Against repining at Fortune'—'Ode to the Gowdspink' and 'The Farmers Ingle'.[1] I would say of him that—of one who died so young it would be hard and unjust to judge severely that there would have been no lack of talents if his moral stamina had been sounder, and that Burns's admiration for him and Allan Ramsay seems to have been taken up like his attachment to the Stuarts, as a national prejudice, in this instance strengthened by a natural feeling for the unhappy fate of one whose faults so nearly resembled his own.

[1] Relates to Southey's editing of *Specimens of the Later English Poets* (3 vols, 1807).

I have some brief things to say about Scotch poetry as to the language which will best come in under Allan Ramsay. The language is no more *spoken* there than here. It is a sort of Rowleyism, composed of all the Scotch words they can collect—as Chatterton raked in glossaries, which has this advantage that passes for wit if you see the author meant to be witty, because you cannot tell whether he is or no, and allows him to introduce all the beastliest phrases and images in cant language, for which, if they had been in plain English or plain Scotch the book would have been deservedly thrown behind the fire.[1]

36. Sir Egerton Brydges on Burns

September 1805

Extract from an article dated 23 September 1805 by Sir Egerton Brydges, in his *Censura Literaria* (1815), viii, 2nd ed., pp. 36–59.

A prolific minor writer, Sir Egerton Brydges (1762–1837) had visited Burns. His account of the meeting is included in M. Lindsay's *Burns Encyclopedia*, 2nd ed., rev. (1970).

The genius of Burns was more sublime than that of Cowper. Both excelled in the familiar: but yet the latter was by nature as well as education more gentle, more easy, and delicate: he had also more of tenuity, while Burns was more concise, more bold, and energetic. They both also abounded in humour, which possessed the same characteristics in each; one mild, serene, and smiling; the other daring and powerful, full of fire and imagery. The poems of one fill the heart and the fancy with the soft pleasures of domestic privacy, with the calm and innocent

1 Southey did not include any work by Fergusson, Ramsay or Burns in the *Specimens of the Later English Poets* (1807). Hyems is a soubriquet for Winter, printer of the *Specimens*.

occupations of rural solitude, the pensive musings of the moralist, and the chastised indignation of pure and simple virtue: the poems of the other breathe by turns Grief, Love, Joy, Melancholy, Despair and Terror; plunge us in the vortex of passion, and hurry us away on the wings of unrestrained and undirected fancy.

Cowper could paint the scenery of Nature and the simple emotions of the heart with exquisite simplicity and truth. Burns could array the morning, the noon, and the evening in new colours; could add new graces to female beauty, and new tenderness to the voice of love. In every situation in which he was placed, his mind seized upon the most striking circumstances, and combining them anew, and dressing them with all the fairy trappings of his imagination, he produced visions such as none but 'poets dream.' Wherever he went, in whatever he was employed, he saw every thing with a poet's eye, and clothed it with a poet's tints.

The hearts and tempers of these bards seem to have been cast in moulds equally distinct: while Cowper shrunk from difficulties and was palsied with dangers, we can conceive Burns at times riding with delight in the whirlwind, performing prodigies of heroism, and foremost in the career of a glorious death. We can almost suppose in his athletic form and daring countenance, had he lived in times of barbarism, and been tempted by hard necessity to forego his principles, such an one as we behold at the head of a banditti in the savage scenery of Salvator Rosa, gilding the crimes of violence and depredation by acts of valour and generosity! In Cowper, on the contrary we view a man only fitted for the most refined state of society, and for the bowers of peace and security.

There is a relative claim to superiority on the side of Burns, on which I cannot lay so much stress as many are inclined to do. I mean his want of education, while the other enjoyed all the discipline and all the advantages of a great public school. If the addiction to the Muses, and the attainment of poetical excellence were nothing more than an accidental application of general talents to a particular species of intellectual occupation, how happens it that among the vast numbers educated at Westminster, or Eton, or Winchester, or Harrow, among whom there must be very many of very high natural endowments, and where day after day, and year after year, they are habituated to poetical composition by every artifice of emulation, and every advantage of precept and example, so few should attain the rank of genuine poets, while Burns in a clay-built hovel, amid the labours of the plough and the flail, under the anxiety of procuring his daily bread, with little instruction and few books, and surrounded only by the humblest society, felt an irresistible impulse to poetry, which surmounted every obstacle, and reached a felicity of expression, a force of sentiment, and a richness of imagery scarce ever rivalled by an union of ability, education, practice, and laborious effort? Thinking therefore that poetical talent is a bent impressed by the hand of Nature, I cannot give the greatest weight to subsequent artificial circumstances; but yet I must admit that in the case of Burns they were so unfavourable that no common natural genius could have overcome them.

On the contrary, there were some points in the history of Burns more propitious to the bolder features of poetry, than in that of Cowper. He wrote in the season of youth, when all the passions were at their height; his life was less uniform, and his station was more likely to encourage energy and enthusiasm, than the more polished and insipid ranks, to which the other belonged. In the circles of fashion, fire and impetuosity are deemed vulgar; and with the roughnesses of the human character all its force is too often smoothed away. An early intercourse with the upper *nobility* is too apt to damp all the generous emotions, and make one ashamed of romantic hopes and sublime conceptions. From blights of this kind the early situation of Burns protected him. The heaths and mountains of Scotland, among which he lived, braced his nerves with vigour, and cherished the bold and striking colours of his mind.

But it seems to me vain and idle to speculate upon education and outward circumstances, as the causes or promoters of poetical genius. It is the inspiring breath of Nature alone, which gives the powers of the genuine bard, and creates a ruling propensity, and a peculiar cast of character which will rise above every impediment, but can be substituted by neither art nor labour. To write mellifluous verses in language which may seem to the eye and the ear adorned with both imagery and elegance, may be a faculty neither unattainable, nor even uncommon. But to give that soul, that predominance of thought, that illuminated tone of a living spirit, which spring in so inexplicable a manner from the chords of the real lyre, is beyond the reach of mere human arrangement, without the innate and very rare gift of the Muse. That gift has regard neither to rank, station, nor riches. It shone over the cradles of Surry, and Buckhurst, amid the splendour of palaces, and the lustre of coronets; it shone over those of Milton, and Cowley, and Dryden, and Gray, and Collins, amid scenes of frugal and unostentatious competence and mediocrity; it shone over that of Burns, in the thatched hovel, the chill abode of comfortless penury and humble labour.

If there be any who doubt whether, in the exercise of this gift, Burns contributed to his own happiness, let them hear the testimony of himself. 'Poesy,' says he to Dr. Moore, 'was still a darling walk for my mind; but it was only indulged in according to the humour of the hour. I had usually half a dozen, or more pieces on hand; I took up one or other as it suited the momentary tone of the mind, and dismissed the work as it bordered on fatigue. My passions, when once lighted up, raged like so many devils, till they got vent in rhyme, and then the conning over my verses, like a spell, soothed all into quiet!' In truth, with regard to happiness, or misery, the impulse of the true poet towards his occupation is generally irresistible, even to the neglect of all, to which prudence and self-interest imperiously dictate his attention. Thus placed in the conflict of opposite attractions he too often falls a victim to the compunctions of mental regret, and the actual stripes of worldly adversity. But the dye is cast; even the misery, which is endured in such a cause, is dear to him; and the hope that his memory will live, and the pictures of his mind be cherished when his bones are mouldering in the dust, is a counterpoise to more than ordinary sufferings!

I do not mean to encourage the idea, that the imprudences,* and much less the immoralities, of Burns, were absolutely inseparable from

---

* I include not pecuniary imprudences, for which, I think, he has been unjustly censured. He had expended in nine years the subscription money of his poems—but how had he expended it? Partly in an unsuccessful farm; partly in assisting his friends, and partly in aid of his slender income. His contempt for money, especially as he had suffered from infancy the effects of actual penury, was highly noble and generous. I cannot agree with some critics, that he had no cause to complain of want of due patronage. Was the mean place of an exciseman, with a salary of from 35 l. to 50 l. a year proper for Burns after his merits were acknowledged, and his literary genius deemed a national honour? Is it wonderful, that upon such an income, such a man, who was encouraged to give up his mind to poetry, which rendered him unfit to improve it, was uneasy and discontented? He died out of debt;—but he had saved nothing!—Unpardonable imprudence!!! We are told, indeed, that an increase of income would only have increased the indulgence of his intemperance—a very generous mode of reconciling us to the hardships of his lot;—and as if intemperance was generally found to increase with affluence! Considering how immense is the present patronage of government, I must consider the neglect of Burns, whose powers had been duly appreciated, a stigma upon the age; and it is but candid to believe that more easy circumstances of fortune would have materially tended to soften the most objectionable habits of his last years, and perhaps have prolonged his life. Many points of this subject remain untouched; but the limits of this Number call on me to stop my pen.

the brilliance of his talents, or the sensibilities of his heart. I am not justifying, I only attempt to plead for them, in mitigation of the harsh and narrow censures of malignity and envy. I call on those of dull heads and sour tempers to judge with candour and mercy, to respect human frailties, more especially when redeemed by accompanying virtues, and to enter not into the garden of Fancy with implements too coarse, lest in the attempt to destroy the weeds, they pluck up also all the flowers.

September, 23, 1805.

37. Thomas Moore: Burns and song

1807, 1841

Thomas Moore (1779-1852), Irish poet, friend and then biographer of Byron, was well qualified to comment on Burns as a writer of national song (see Introduction, p. 29).

(a) Extract from a letter to Sir John Stevenson [February 1807], *The Letters of Thomas Moore*, ed. W. S. Dowden (1964), I, pp. 116-17

The task which you propose to me, of adapting words to these [traditional Irish] airs, is by no means easy. The poet, who would follow the various sentiments which they express, must feel and understand that rapid fluctuation of spirits, that unaccountable mixture of gloom and levity, which composes the character of my countrymen, and has deeply tinged their music. Even in their liveliest strains we find some melancholy note intrude—some minor third or flat seventh—which throws its shade as it passes, and makes even mirth interesting. If Burns had been an Irishman (and I would willingly give up all our claims upon Ossian for him,) His heart would have been proud of such music, and his genius would have made it immortal.

(b) Extract from *The Poetical Works of Thomas Moore collected by Himself* (1841), V, preface, X–XV

Having thus got on Scottish ground, I find myself awakened to the remembrance of a name which, whenever song-writing is the theme, ought to rank second to none in that sphere of poetical fame. Robert Burns was wholly unskilled in music; yet the rare art of adapting words successfully to notes, of wedding verse in congenial union with melody, which, were it not for his example, I should say none but a poet versed in the sister-art ought to attempt, has yet, by him, with the aid of music, to which my own country's strains are alone comparable, been exercised with so workmanly a hand, as well as with so rich a variety of passion, playfulness, and power, as no song-writer, perhaps, but himself, has ever yet displayed.

That Burns, however untaught, was yet, in ear and feeling, a musician, is clear from the skill with which he adapts his verse to the structure and character of each different strain. Still more strikingly did he prove his fitness for this peculiar task, by the sort of instinct with which, in more than one instance, he discerned the real and innate sentiment which an air was calculated to convey, though always before associated with words expressing a totally different feeling. Thus the air of a ludicrous old song, 'Fee him, father, fee him', has been made the medium of one of Burns's most pathetic effusions; while, still more marvellously, 'Hey tuttie tattie' has been elevated by him into that heroic strain, 'Scots, wha hae wi' Wallace bled;'—a song which in a great national crisis, would be of more avail than all the eloquence of a Demosthenes.*

It was impossible that the example of Burns, in these, his higher

* I know not whether it has ever been before remarked, that the well-known lines in one of Burns's most spirited songs,

> 'The title's but the guinea's stamp,
> The man's the gold for a' that'

may possibly have been suggested by the following passage in Wycherley's play, the *Country Wife*.—'I weigh the *man*, not his *title*; 'tis not the King's *stamp* can make the metal better'.

inspirations, should not materially contribute to elevate the character of English song-writing, and even to lead to a re-union of the gifts which it requires, if not, as of old, in the same individual, yet in that perfect sympathy between poet and musician which almost amounts to identity, and of which we have seen, in our own times, so interesting an example in the few songs bearing the united names of these two sister muses, Mrs. Arkwright and the late Hemans.

Very different was the state of the song-department of English poesy at the time when first I tried my novice hand at the lyre. The divorce between song and sense had then reached its utmost range; and to all verses connected with music, from a Birth-day Ode down to the *libretto* of the last new opera, might fairly be applied the solution Figaro gives of the quality of the words of songs, in general,—'Ce qui ne vaut pas la peine d'étre dit, on le chante' . . .

How far my own labours in this field—if, indeed, the gathering of such idle flowers may be so designated—have helped to advance, or even kept pace with the progressive improvement I have here described, it is not for me to presume to decide. I only know that in a strong and inborn feeling for music lies the source for whatever talent I may have shown for poetical composition; and that it was the effort to translate into language the emotions and passions which music appeared to me to express, that first led to my writing any poetry at all deserving of the name. Dryden has happily described music as being 'inarticulate poetry'; and I have always felt, in adapting words to an expressive air, that I was but bestowing upon it the gift of articulation, and thus enabling it to speak to others all that was conveyed, in its wordless eloquence, to myself.

38. Byron on Burns

1809

English Bards and Scotch Reviewers (1809), with Byron's notes, lines 765–818 (see Nos 49, 61, and Introduction, p. 27).

When some brisk youth, the tenant of a stall,
Employs a pen less pointed than his awl,
Leaves his snug shop, forsakes his store of shoes,
St. Crispin quits, and cobbles for the muse,
Heavens! how the vulgar stare! how crowds applaud!
If chance some wicked wag should pass his jest,
'Tis sheer ill-nature—don't the world know best?
Genius must guide when wits admire the rhyme,
And Capel Lofft declares 'tis quite sublime.*
Hear, then, ye happy sons of needless trade!
Swains! quit the plough, resign the useless spade!
Lo! Burns and Bloomfield, nay, a greater far,
Gifford was born beneath an adverse star,
Forsook the labours of a servile state,
Stemm'd the rude storm, and triumph'd over fate:
Then why no more? if Phoebus smiled on you,
Bloomfield! why not on brother Nathan too?†
Him too the mania, not the muse, has seized;
Not inspiration, but a mind diseased:
And now no boor can seek his last abode,
No common be enclosed without an ode.
Oh! since increased refinement deigns to smile
On Britain's sons, and bless our genial isle,
Let poesy go forth, pervade the whole,
Alike the rustic, and mechanic soul!

---

* Capel Lofft, Esq., the Maecenas of shoemakers, and preface-writer-general to distressed versemen; a kind of gratis accoucheur to those who wish to be delivered of rhyme, but do not know how to bring forth.
† See Nathaniel Bloomfield's ode, elegy, or whatever he or any one else chooses to call it, on the enclosures of 'Honington Green'.

Ye tuneful cobblers! still your notes prolong,
Compose at once a slipper and a song;
So shall the fair your handywork peruse,
Your sonnets sure shall please—perhaps your shoes.
May Moorland weavers boast Pindaric skill,★
And tailors' lays be longer than their bill!
While punctual beaux reward the grateful notes,
And pay for poems—when they pay for coats.

To the famed throng now paid the tribute due,
Neglected genius! let me turn to you.
Come forth, oh Campbell! give thy talents scope;
Who dares aspire if thou must cease to hope?
And thou, Melodious Rogers! rise at last,
Recall the pleasing memory of the past;†
Arise! let blest remembrance still inspire,
And strike to wonted tones thy hallow'd lyre;
Restore Apollo to his vacant throne,
Assert thy country's honour and thine own.
What! must deserted Poesy still weep
Where her last hopes with pious Cowper sleep?
Unless, perchance, from his cold bier she turns,
To deck the turf that wraps her minstrel, Burns!
No! though contempt hath mark'd the spurious brood,
The race who rhyme from folly, or for food,
Yet still some genuine sons 'tis hers to boast,
Who, least affecting, still affect the most:
Feel as they write, and write but as they feel—
Bear witness Gifford, Sotheby, Macneil.‡

★ Vide 'Recollections of a Weaver in the Moorlands of Staffordshire'.
† It would be superfluous to recall to the mind of the reader the authors of 'The
Pleasures of Memory' and 'The Pleasures of Hope', the most beautiful didactic poems in
our language, if we except Pope's 'Essay on Man': but so many poetasters have started up,
that even the names of Campbell and Rogers are become strange.
‡ Gifford, author of the *Baviad* and *Maeviad*, the first satires of the day, and translator
of Juvenal. Sotheby, translator of Wieland's 'Oberon' and Virgil's *Georgics*, and author of
'Saul', an epic poem. Macneil, whose poems are deservedly popular, particularly 'Scotland's Scaith', and the 'Waes of War', of which ten thousand copies were sold in one
month.

R. H. CROMEK,
RELIQUES OF ROBERT BURNS

1808

---

39. Francis Jeffrey, from an unsigned review in *Edinburgh Review*

xiii (January 1809), 249–76

Jeffrey (1773–1850), an Edinburgh lawyer who became first editor of the *Edinburgh Review* in 1802, was frequently criticized for his severe argument that Burns had no sense of chivalry. Later he modified his views and accepted Carlyle's review of Lockhart's *Life of Burns* for inclusion in the *Edinburgh Review*. He wrote in 1837 to William Empson, 'You south Saxons cannot value [Burns] rightly, and miss half the pathos, and more than half the sweetness' (see Introduction, p. 30).

Burns is certainly by far the greatest of our poetical prodigies—from Stephen Duck down to Thomas Dermody. *They* are forgotten already; or only remembered for derision. But the name of Burns, if we are not mistaken, has not yet 'gathered all its fame'; and will endure long after those circumstances are forgotten which contributed to its first notoriety. So much indeed are we impressed with a sense of his merits; that we cannot help thinking it a derogation from them to consider him as a prodigy at all; and are convinced that he will never be rightly estimated as a poet, till that vulgar wonder be entirely repressed which was raised on his having been a ploughman. It is true, no doubt, that he was born in an humble station, and that much of his early life was devoted to severe labour, and to the society of his fellow-labourers.

178

But he was not himself either uneducated or illiterate; and was placed perhaps in a situation more favourable to the development of great poetical talents, than any other which could have been assigned him. He was taught, at a very early age, to read and write; and soon after acquired a competent knowledge of French, together with the elements of Latin and Geometry. His taste for reading was encouraged by his parents and many of his associates; and, before he had ever composed a single stanza, he was not only familiar with many prose writers, but far more intimately acquainted with Pope, Shakespeare and Thomson, than nine tenths of the youth that leave school for the university. These authors, indeed, with some old collections of songs, and the lives of Hannibal and of Sir William Wallace, were his habitual study from the first days of his childhood; and, cooperating with the solitude of his rural occupations, were sufficient to rouse his ardent and ambitious mind to the love and the practice of poetry. He had as much scholarship, we imagine, as Shakespeare, and far better models to form his ear to harmony, and train his fancy to graceful invention.

We ventured, on a former occasion, to say something of the effects of regular education, and of the general diffusion of literature, in repressing the vigour and originality of all kinds of mental exertion. That speculation was perhaps carried somewhat too far; but if the paradox have proof any where, it is in its application to poetry. Among well educated people, the standard writers of this description are at once so venerated and so familiar, that it is thought equally impossible to rival them, and to write verses without attempting it. If there be one degree of fame which excites emulation, there is another which leads to despair; nor can we conceive any one less likely to add one to the short list of original poets, than a young man of fine fancy and delicate taste, who has acquired a high relish for poetry, by perusing the most celebrated writers, and conversing with the most intelligent judges. The head of such a person is filled, of course, with all the splendid passages of antient and modern authors, and with the fine and fastidious remarks which have been made even on these passages. When he turns his eyes, therefore, on his own conceptions, they can scarcely fail to appear rude and contemptible. He is perpetually haunted and depressed by the ideal presence of those great masters and their exacting critics. He is aware to what comparisons his productions will be subjected among his own friends and associates; and recollects the derision with which so many rash adventurers have been chased back to their obscurity. Thus, the merit of his great predecessors chills, instead of encouraging his ardour; and the illustrious names which have already reached to the summit of excellence, act like the tall and spreading trees of the forest, which overshadow and strangle the saplings which have struck root in the soil below,—and afford shelter to nothing but creepers and parasites.

There is, no doubt, in some few individuals, 'that strong divinity of soul,'—that decided and irresistible vocation to glory, which, in spite of all these obstructions, calls out, perhaps, once or twice in a century, a bold and original poet from the herd of scholars and academical literati. But the natural tendency of their studies, and by far the most common operation, is to repress originality, and discourage enterprise, and either to change those whom nature meant for poets, into mere readers of poetry, or to bring them out in the form of witty parodists, or ingenious imitators. Independent of the reasons which have been already suggested, it will perhaps be found too, that necessity is the mother of invention in this as well as in the more vulgar arts; or, at least, that inventive genius will frequently slumber in inaction, where preceding ingenuity has in part supplied the wants of the owner. A solitary and uninstructed man, with lively feelings and an inflammable imagination, will be easily led to exercise those gifts, and to occupy and relieve his mind in poetical composition; but if his education, his reading and his society supply him with an abundant store of images and emotions, he will probably think but little of these internal resources, and feed his mind contentedly with what has been provided by the industry of others.

To say nothing, therefore, of the distractions and the dissipation of mind that belong to the commerce of the world, nor of the cares of minute accuracy and high finishing which are imposed on the professed scholar, there seem to be deeper reasons for the separation of originality and accomplishment; and for the partiality which has led poetry to choose almost all her favourites among the recluse and uninstructed. A youth of quick parts, in short, and creative fancy,—with just so much reading as to guide his ambition, and rough hew his notions of excellence,—if his lot be thrown in humble retirement, where he has no reputation to lose, and where he can easily hope to excel all that he sees around him, is much more likely, we think, to give himself up to poetry, and to train himself to habits of invention, than if he had been encumbered by the pretended helps of extended study and literary society.

If these observations should fail to strike of themselves, they may perhaps derive additional weight from considering the very remarkable fact, that almost all the great poets of every country have appeared in an early stage of their history, and in a period comparatively rude and unlettered. Homer went forth like the morning star before the dawn of literature in Greece; and almost all the great and sublime poets of modern Europe are already between two and three hundred years old. Since that time, although books and readers, and opportunities of reading, are multiplied a thousand fold, we have improved chiefly in point and terseness of expression, in the art of raillery, and in clearness and simplicity of thought. Force, richness and variety of invention, are now at least as rare as ever. But the literature and refinement of the age does not exist at all for a rustic and illiterate individual; and, consequently, the present time is to him what the rude times of old were to the vigorous writers which adorned them.

But though, for these and for other reasons, we can see no propriety in regarding the poetry of Burns chiefly as the wonderful work of a peasant, and thus admiring it much in the same way as if it had been written with his toes; yet there are peculiarities in his works which remind us of the lowness of his origin, and faults for which the defects of his education afford an obvious cause, if not a legitimate apology. In forming a correct estimate of these works; it is necessary to take into account those peculiarities.

The first is, the undisciplined harshness and acrimony of his invective. The great boast of polished life is the delicacy, and even the generosity of its hostility,—that quality which is still the characteristic as it is the denomination of a gentleman,—that principle which forbids us to attack the defenceless, to strike the fallen, or to mangle the slain,—and enjoins us, in forging the shafts of satire, to increase the polish exactly as we add to their keenness or their weight. For this, as well as for other things, we are indebted to chivalry; and of this Burns had none. His ingenious and amiable biographer has spoken repeatedly in praise of his talents for satire,—we think, with a most unhappy partiality. His epigrams and lampoons appear to us, one and all, unworthy of him;— offensive from their extreme coarseness and violence,—and contemptible from their want of wit or brilliancy. They seem to have been written, not out of playful malice or virtuous indignation, but out of fierce and ungovernable anger. His whole raillery consists in railing; and his satirical vein displays itself chiefly in calling names and in swearing. We say this mainly with a reference to his personalities. In many of his more general representations of life and manners, there is no doubt much that may be called satirical, mixed up with admirable humour, and description of inimitable vivacity.

There is a similar want of polish, or at least of respectfulness, in the general tone of his gallantry. He has written with more passion, perhaps, and more variety of natural feeling, on the subject of love, than any other poet whatsoever,—but with a fervour that is sometimes indelicate, and seldom accommodated to the timidity and 'sweet austere composure' of women of refinement. He has expressed admirably the feelings of an enamoured peasant, who, however refined or eloquent he may be, always approaches his mistress on a footing of equality; but has never caught that tone of chivalrous gallantry which uniformly abases itself in the presence of the object of its devotion. Accordingly, instead of suing for a smile, or melting in a tear, his muse deals in nothing but locked embraces and midnight rencontres; and, even in his complimentary effusions to ladies of the highest rank, is for straining them to the bosom of her impetuous votary. It is easy, accordingly, to see from his correspondence, that many of his female patronesses shrunk from the vehement familiarity of his admiration; and there are even some traits in the volumes before us, from which we can gather, that he resented the shyness and estrangement to which these feelings gave rise, with at least as little chivalry as he had shown in producing them.

But the leading vice in Burns's character, and the cardinal deformity indeed of all his productions, was his contempt, or affectation of contempt, for prudence, decency and regularity; and his admiration of thoughtlessness, oddity, and vehement sensibility;—his belief, in short, in *the dispensing power* of genius and social feeling, in all matters of morality and common sense. This is the very slang of the worst German plays, and the lowest of our town-made novels; nor can any thing be more lamentable, than that it should have found a patron in such a man as Burns, and communicated to a great part of his productions a character of immorality, at once contemptible and hateful. It is but too true, that men of the highest genius have frequently been hurried by their passions into a violation of prudence and duty; and there is something generous, at least, in the apology which their admirers may make for them, on the score of their keener feelings and habitual want of reflection. But this apology, which is quite unsatisfactory in the mouth of another, becomes an insult and an absurdity whenever it proceeds from their own. A man may say of his friend, that he is a noble-hearted fellow,—too generous to be just, and with too much spirit to be always prudent and regular. But he cannot be allowed to say even this of himself; and still less to represent himself as a hairbrained sentimental soul, constantly carried away by fine fancies and visions of love and philanthropy, and born to confound and despise the cold-blooded sons of prudence and sobriety. This apology evidently destroys itself; for it shows that conduct to be the result of deliberate system, which it affects at the same time to justify as the fruit of mere thoughtlessness and casual impulse. Such protestations, therefore, will always be treated, as they deserve, not only with contempt, but with incredulity; and their magnanimous authors set down as determined profligates, who seek to disguise their selfishness under a name somewhat less revolting. That profligacy is almost always selfishness, and that the excuse of impetuous feeling can hardly ever be justly pleaded for those who neglect the ordinary duties of life, must be apparent, we think, even to the least reflecting of those sons of fancy and song. It requires no habit of deep thinking, nor any thing more, indeed, than the information of an honest heart, to perceive that it is cruel and base to spend, in vain superfluities, that money which belongs of right to the pale industrious tradesman and his famishing infants; or that it is a vile prostitution of language, to talk of that man's generosity or goodness of heart, who sits raving about friendship and philanthropy in a tavern, while his wife's heart is breaking at her cheerless fireside, and his children pining in solitary poverty.

This pitiful cant of careless feeling and eccentric genius, accordingly, has never found much favour in the eyes of English sense and morality. The most signal effect which it ever produced, was on the muddy brains of some German youth, who left college in a body to rob on the highway, because Schiller had represented the captain of a gang as so very noble a creature.—But in this country, we believe, a predilection for that honourable profession must have preceded this admiration of the character. The style we have been speaking of, accordingly, is now the heroics only of the hulks and the house of correction; and has no chance, we suppose, of being greatly admired, except in the farewell speech of a young gentleman preparing for Botany Bay.

It is humiliating to think how deeply Burns has fallen into this debasing error. He is perpetually making a parade of his thoughtlessness, inflammability and imprudence, and talking with much complacency and exultation of the offence he has occasioned to the sober and correct part of mankind. This odious slang infects almost all his prose, and a very great proportion of his poetry; and is, we are persuaded, the chief, if not the only source of the disgust with which, in spite of his genius, we know that he is regarded by many very competent and liberal judges. His apology, too, we are willing to believe, is to be found in the original lowness of his situation, and the slightness of his acquaintance with the world. With his talents and powers of observation, he could not have seen *much* of the beings who echoed this raving, without feeling for them that distrust and contempt which would have made him blush to think he had ever stretched over them the protecting shield of his genius.

Akin to this most lamentable trait of vulgarity, and indeed in some measure arising out of it, is that perpetual boast of his own independence, which is obtruded upon the readers of Burns in almost every page of his writings. The sentiment itself is noble, and it is often finely expressed; —but a gentleman would only have expressed it when he was insulted or provoked; and would never have made it a spontaneous theme to those friends in whose estimation he felt that his honour stood clear. It is mixed up too in Burns with too fierce a tone of defiance; and indicates rather the pride of a sturdy peasant, than the calm and natural elevation of a generous mind.

The last of the symptoms of rusticity which we think it necessary to notice in the works of this extraordinary man, is that frequent mistake of mere exaggeration and violence, for force and sublimity, which has defaced so much of his prose composition, and given an air of heaviness and labour to a good deal of his serious poetry. The truth is, that his *forte* was in humour and in pathos—or rather in tenderness of feeling; and that he has very seldom succeeded, either where mere wit and sprightliness, or where great energy and weight of sentiment were requisite. He had evidently a very false and crude notion of what constitutes *strength* of writing; and instead of that simple and brief directness which stamps the character of vigour upon every syllable, has generally had recourse to a mere accumulation of hyperbolical expressions, which incumber the diction instead of exalting it, and show the determination to be impressive, without the power of executing it. This error also we are inclined to ascribe entirely to the defects of his education. The value of simplicity in the expression of passion, is a lesson, we believe, of nature and of genius;—but its importance in mere grave and impressive writing, is one of the latest discoveries of rhetorical experience.

With the allowances and exceptions we have now stated, we think

Burns entitled to the rank of a great and original genius. He has in all his compositions great force of conception; and great spirit and animation in its expression. He has taken a large range through the region of Fancy, and naturalized himself in almost all her climates. He has great humour,—great powers of description,—great pathos,—and great discrimination of character. Almost every thing that he says has spirit and originality; and every thing that he says well, is characterized by a charming facility, which gives a grace even to occasional rudeness, and communicates to the reader a delightful sympathy with the spontaneous soaring and conscious inspiration of the poet.

Considering the reception which these works have met with from the public, and the long period during which the greater part of them have been in their possession, it may appear superfluous to say any thing as to their characteristic or peculiar merit. Though the ultimate judgment of the public, however, be always sound, or at least decisive, as to its general result, it is not always very apparent upon what grounds it has proceeded; nor in consequence of what, or in spite of what, it has been obtained. In Burns's works there is much to censure, as well as much to praise; and as time has not yet separated his ore from its dross, it may be worth while to state, in a very general way, what we presume to anticipate as the result of this separation. Without pretending to enter at all into the comparative merit of particular passages, we may venture to lay it down as our opinion,—that his poetry is far superior to his prose; that his Scottish compositions are greatly to be preferred to his English ones; and that his Songs will probably outlive all his other productions. A very few remarks on each of these subjects will comprehend almost all that we have to say of the volumes now before us.

The prose works of Burns, consist almost entirely of his letters. They bear, as well as his poetry, the seal and the impress of his genius; but they contain much more bad taste, and are written with far more apparent labour. His poetry was almost all written primarily from feeling, and only secondarily from ambition. His letters seem to have been nearly all composed as exercises, and for display. There are few of them written with simplicity or plainness; and though natural enough as to the sentiment, they are generally very strained and elaborate in the expression. A very great proportion of them, too, relate neither to facts nor feelings peculiarly connected with the author or his correspondent—but are made up of general declamation, moral reflections, and vague discussions,—all evidently composed for the sake of effect, and frequently introduced with long complaints of having nothing to say, and of the necessity and difficulty of letter-writing.

By far the best of these compositions, are such as we should consider as exceptions from this general character,—such as contain some specific information as to himself, or are suggested by events or observations directly applicable to his correspondent. One of the best, perhaps, is that addressed to Dr. Moore, containing an account of his early life, of which Dr. Currie has made such a judicious use in his Biography . . .

Before proceeding to take any particular notice of his poetical compositions, we must apprise our Southern readers, that all his best pieces are written in Scotch; and that it is impossible for them to form any adequate judgment of their merits, without a pretty long residence among those who still use that language. To be able to translate the words, is but a small part of the knowledge that is necessary. The whole genius and idiom of the language must be familiar; and the characters, and habits, and associations of those who speak it. We beg leave too, in passing, to observe, that this Scotch is not to be considered as a provincial dialect, the vehicle only of rustic vulgarity and rude local humour. It is the language of a whole country,—long an independent kingdom, and still separate in laws, character and manners. It is by no means peculiar to the vulgar; but is the common speech of the whole nation in early life,—and with many of its most exalted and accomplished individuals throughout their whole existence; and, if it be true that, in later times, it has been, in some measure, laid aside by the more ambitious and aspiring of the present generation, it is still recollected, even by them, as the familiar language of their childhood, and of those who were the earliest objects of their love and veneration. It is connected, in their imagination, not only with that olden time which is uniformly conceived as more pure, lofty and simple than the present, but also with all the soft and bright colours of remembered childhood and domestic affection. All its phrases conjure up images of school-day innocence and sports, and friendships which have no pattern in succeeding years. Add to all this, that it is the language of a great body of poetry, with which almost all Scotchmen are familiar; and, in particular, of a great multitude of songs, written with more tenderness, nature, and feeling, than any other lyric compositions that are extant, and we may perhaps be allowed to say, that the Scotch is, in reality, a highly poetical language; and that it is an ignorant, as well as an illiberal prejudice, which would seek to confound it with the barbarous dialects of Yorkshire or Devon. In composing his Scottish poems, therefore, Burns did not make an instinctive and necessary use of the only dialect he could employ. The last letter which we have quoted, proves, that before he had penned a single couplet, he could write in the dialect of England with far greater purity and propriety than nine-tenths of those who are called well educated in that country. He wrote in Scotch, because the writings which he most aspired to imitate were composed in that language; and it is evident, from the variations preserved by Dr. Currie, that he took much greater pains with the beauty and purity of his expressions in Scotch than in English; and, every one who understands both, must admit, with infinitely better success.

But though we have ventured to say thus much in praise of the Scottish poetry of Burns, we cannot presume to lay many specimens of it before our readers; and, in the few extracts we may be tempted to make from the volumes before us, shall be guided more by a desire to exhibit what may be intelligible to all our readers, than by a feeling of what is in itself of the highest excellence.

We have said that Burns is almost equally distinguished for his tenderness and his humour:—we might have added, for a faculty of combining them both in the same subject, not altogether without parallel in the older poets and balladmakers, but altogether singular, we think, among modern critics. The passages of pure humour are entirely Scottish,—and untranslateable. They consist in the most picturesque representations of life and manners, enlivened, and even exalted by traits of exquisite sagacity, and unexpected reflection. His tenderness is of two sorts; that which is combined with circumstances and characters of humble, and sometimes ludicrous simplicity; and that which is produced by gloomy and distressful impressions acting on a mind of keen sensibility. The passages which belong to the former description are, we think, the most exquisite and original, and, in our estimation, indicate the greatest and most amiable turn of genius; both as being accompanied by fine and feeling pictures of humble life, and as requiring that delicacy, as well as justness of conception, by which alone the fastidiousness of an ordinary reader can be reconciled to such representations. The exquisite description of 'the Cotter's Saturday Night' affords, perhaps, the finest example of this sort of pathetic. Its whole beauty cannot, indeed, be discerned but by those whom experience has enabled to judge of the admirable fidelity and completeness of the picture. But, independent altogether of national peculiarities, and even in spite of the obscurity of the language, we are persuaded that it is impossible to peruse the following stanzas without feeling the force of tenderness and truth.

[quotes 'The Cotter's Saturday Night,' stanzas II–IV, VI–VIII, XII–XIII l. 110, XVIII]

The charm of the fine lines written on turning up a mouse's nest with the plough, will also be found to consist in the simple tenderness of the delineation.

[quotes 'To A Mouse,' ll. 19–36]

The verses to a Mountain Daisy, though more elegant and picturesque, seem to derive their chief beauty from the same sentiment.

[quotes 'To A Mountain Daisy,' ll. 1–18, 25–30]

There are many touches of the same kind in most of the popular and beautiful poems in this collection, especially in the 'Winter Night'—the address to his old Mare—the address to the Devil, &c.;—in all which, though the greater part of the piece be merely ludicrous and picturesque, there are traits of a delicate and tender feeling, indicating that unaffected softness of heart which is always so enchanting. In the humorous address to the Devil, which we have just mentioned, every Scottish reader must have felt the effect of this relenting nature in the following stanzas.

[quotes 'To the Deil', ll. 85–95, 121–6]

The finest examples, however, of this simple and unpretending tenderness, are to be found in those songs which are likely to transmit the name of Burns to all future generations. He found this delightful trait in the old Scottish ballads which he took for his model, and upon which he has improved with a felicity and delicacy of imitation altogether unrivalled in the history of literature. Sometimes it is the brief and simple pathos of the genuine old ballad; as,

> But I look to the West when I lie down to rest,
>   That happy my dreams and my slumbers may be;
> For far in the West lives he I love best,
>   The lad that is dear to my baby and me.

Or, as in this other specimen—

[quotes 'Drumossie moor, Drumossie day']

Sometimes it is animated with airy narrative, and adorned with images of the utmost elegance and beauty. As a specimen taken at random, we insert the following stanzas.

[quotes 'There was a lass, and she was fair', ll. 5–24]

Sometimes, again, it is plaintive and mournful—in the same strain of unaffected simplicity.

[quotes 'Address to the Woodlark']

We add the following from Mr. Cromek's new volume; as the original form of the very popular song given at p. 325 of Dr. Currie's 4th volume.

[quotes 'The Banks o' Doon' [A], ll. 1–20]

Sometimes the rich imagery of the poet's fancy almost overcomes the leading sentiment.

[quotes 'Again rejoicing Nature sees', stanzas III–VI]

The sensibility which is thus associated with simple imagery and gentle melancholy, is to us the most winning and attractive. But Burns has also expressed it when it is merely the instrument of torture—of keen remorse and tender agonizing regret. There are some strong traits of the former feeling, in the poems entitled the 'Lament,' 'Despondency,' &c., when, looking back to the times

When love's luxurious pulse beat high.

he bewails the consequences of his own irregularities. There is something cumbrous and inflated, however, in the diction of these pieces. We are infinitely more moved with his 'Elegy upon Highland Mary'. Of this first love of the poet, we are indebted to Mr. Cromek for a brief, but very striking account, from the pen of the poet himself. In a note on an early song inscribed to this mistress, he had recorded in a manuscript book—

'My Highland lassie was a warm-hearted, charming young creature as ever blessed a man with generous love. After a pretty long tract of the most ardent reciprocal attachment, we met, by appointment, on the second Sunday of May, in a sequestered spot by the Banks of Ayr, where we spent the day in taking a farewel, before she should embark for the West-Highlands, to arrange matters among her friends of our projected change of life. At the close of Autumn following, she crossed the sea to meet me at Greenock; where she had scarce landed when she was seized with a malignant fever, which hurried my dear girl to the grave in a few days,—before I could even hear of her illness.

Mr. Cromek, has added, in a note, the following interesting particulars; though without specifying the authority upon which he details them.

This adieu was performed with all those simple and striking ceremonials which rustic sentiment has devised to prolong tender emotions and to inspire awe. The lovers stood on each side of a small purling brook; they laved their hands in its limpid stream, and, holding a bible between them, pronounced their vows to be faithful to each other. They parted—never to meet again!

The anniversary of *Mary Campbell's* death (for that was her name), awakening in the sensitive mind of *Burns* the most lively emotion, he retired from his family, then residing on the farm of Ellisland, and wandered, solitary, on the banks of the Nith, and about the farm yard, in the extremest agitation of mind, nearly the whole of the night: His agitation was so great, that he threw himself on the side of a corn stack, and there conceived his sublime and tender elegy—his address 'To Mary in Heaven'.

The poem itself is as follows.
[quotes 'Thou lingering Star with lessening ray']

Of his pieces of humour, the tale of Tam o' Shanter is probably the best: though there are traits of infinite merit in 'Scotch Drink,' the 'Holy Fair,' and 'Hallow E'en,' and several of the Songs; in all of which, it is very remarkable, that he rises occasionally into a strain of beautiful description or lofty sentiment, far above the pitch of his original conception. The poems of observation on life and characters, are the 'Twa Dogs,' and the various Epistles,—all of which show very extraordinary sagacity and powers of expression. They are written, however, in so broad a dialect, that we dare not venture to quote any part of them. The only pieces that can be classed under the head of pure fiction, are the 'Two Bridges of Ayr,' and the 'Vision.' In the last, there are some vigorous and striking lines. We select the passage in which the Muse describes the early propensities of her favourite, rather as being more intelligible, than as superior to the rest of the poem.

[quotes 'The Vision', ll. 211–40]

There is another fragment, called a 'Vision,' which belongs to a higher order of poetry. If Burns had never written any thing else, the power of description, and the vigour of the whole composition, would have entitled him to the remembrance of posterity.

[quotes 'As I stood by yon roofless tower', ll. 9–32]

Some verses, written for a Hermitage, sound like the best parts of Grongar Hill. The reader may take these few lines as a specimen.

> As thy day grows warm and high,
> Life's meridian flaming nigh,
> Dost thou spurn the humble vale?
> Life's proud summits would'st thou scale?
> Dangers, eagle-pinioned, bold,
> Soar around each cliffy hold,
> While cheerful peace, with linnet song,
> Chants the lowly dells among.

There is a little copy of 'Verses upon a Newspaper,' written in the same condensed style, and only wanting translation into English to be worthy of Swift.[1]

The finest piece, of the strong and nervous sort, however, is undoubtedly the address of Robert Bruce to his army at Bannockburn, beginning, 'Scots, wha hae wi' Wallace bled.' 'The Death-Song,' beginning,

> Farewell, thou fair day, thou green earth and ye skies,
> Now gay with the bright-setting sun,

is to us less pleasing. There are specimens, however, of such vigour and emphasis scattered through his whole works, as are sure to make themselves and their author remembered; for instance, that noble description of a dying soldier.

> Nae cauld, faint-hearted doubtings tease him:
> Death comes; wi' fearless eye he sees him;
> Wi' bluidy hand a welcome gi'es him;
>   An' whan he fa's,
> His latest draught o' breathin lea'es him
>   In faint huzzas.

---

[1] 'Kind Sir, I've read your paper through' . . . Kinsley, no. 282.

The whole song of 'For a' that,' is written with extraordinary spirit. The first stanza ends,

> For rank is but the guinea stamp;
> The *man's* the goud, for a' that.

—All the songs, indeed, abound with traits of this kind. We select the following at random.

> O woman, lovely, woman fair!
> An angel form's faun to thy share,
> 'Twad been o'er meikle to've gi'en thee mair,
> I mean an angel mind.

We dare not proceed further in specifying the merits of pieces which have been so long published. Before concluding upon this subject, however, we must beg leave to express our dissent from the poet's amiable and judicious biographer, in what he says of the general harshness and rudeness of his versification. Dr. Currie, we are afraid, was not Scotchman enough to comprehend the whole prosody of the verses to which he alluded. Most of the Scottish pieces are more carefully versified than the English; and we appeal to our Southern readers, whether there be any want of harmony in the following stanza.

> Wild beats my heart to trace your steps,
>   Whose ancestors, in days of yore,
> Thro' hostile ranks and ruin'd gaps
>   Old *Scotia's* bloody lion bore;
> Ev'n *I* who sing in rustic lore,
>   Haply *my sires* have left their shed,
> And fac'd grim danger's loudest roar.
>   Bold-following where *your* fathers led!

The following is not quite English; but it is intelligible to all readers of English, and may satisfy them that the Scottish song-writer was not habitually negligent of his numbers.

[quotes 'Their groves o' sweet myrtle']

If we have been able to inspire our readers with any portion of our own admiration for this extraordinary writer, they will readily forgive us for the irregularity of which we have been guilty, in introducing so long an account of his whole works, under colour of the additional volume of which we have prefixed the title to this article. The truth is, however, that unless it be taken in connexion with his other works, the present volume has little interest, and could not be made the subject of any intelligible observations. It is made up of some additional letters, of middling merit,—of complete copies of others, of which Dr. Currie saw reason to publish only extracts,—of a number of remarks, by Burns, on old Scottish songs,—and finally, of a few additional poems and songs, certainly not disgraceful to the author, but scarcely fitted to add to his reputation. The world, however, is indebted, we think, to Mr. Cromek's industry for this addition to so popular an author;—and the friends of the poet, we are sure, are indebted to his good taste, moderation and delicacy, for having confined it to the pieces which are now printed. Burns wrote many rash—many violent, and many indecent things; of which we have no doubt many specimens must have fallen into the hands of so diligent a collector. He has, however, carefully suppressed everything of this description, and shown that tenderness for his author's memory, which is the best proof of the veneration with which he regards his talents. We shall now see if there be any thing in the volume which deserves to be particularly noticed . . .

The observations on Scottish songs, which fill nearly 150 pages, are, on the whole, minute and trifling; though the exquisite justness of the poet's taste, and his fine relish of simplicity in this species of composition, is no less remarkable here than in his correspondence with Mr. Thomson. Of all other kinds of poetry, he was so indulgent a judge, that he may almost be termed an indiscriminate admirer. We find, too, from these observations, that several songs and pieces of songs, which he printed as genuine antiques, were really of his own composition.

The common-place book, from which Dr. Currie had formerly selected all that he thought worth publication, is next given entire by Mr. Cromek. We were quite as well, we think, with the extracts;— at all events, there was no need for reprinting what had been given by Dr. Currie;—a remark which is equally applicable to the letters of which we had formerly extracts.

Of the additional poems which form the concluding part of the volume, we have but little to say. We have little doubt of their authenticity; for, though the editor has omitted, in almost every instance, to specify the source from which they were derived, they certainly bear the stamp of the author's manner and genius. They are not, however, of his purest metal, nor marked with his finest die:

Several of them have appeared in print already; and the songs are, as usual, the best. This little lamentation of a desolate damsel, is tender and pretty.

[quotes 'O how can I be blythe and glad', ll. 9–20]

We now reluctantly dismiss this subject. We scarcely hoped, when we began our critical labours, that an opportunity would ever occur of speaking of Burns as we wished to speak of him: and therefore, we feel grateful to Mr. Cromek for giving us this opportunity. As we have no means of knowing, with precision, to what extent his writings are known and admired in the southern part of the kingdom, we have perhaps fallen into the error of quoting passages that are familiar to most of our readers, and dealing out praise which every one of them has previously repeated. We felt it impossible, however, to resist the temptation of transcribing a few of the passages which struck us on turning over the volumes; and reckon with confidence on the gratitude of those to whom they are new,—while we are not without hopes of being forgiven by those who have been used to admire them.

We shall conclude with two general remarks—the one national, the other critical. The first is, that it is impossible to read the productions of Burns, along with his history, without forming a higher idea of the intelligence, taste, and accomplishments of the peasantry, than most of those in the higher ranks are disposed to entertain. Without meaning to deny that he himself was endowed with rare and extraordinary gifts of genius and fancy, it is evident, from the whole details of his history, as well as from the letters of his brother, and the testimony of Mr. Murdoch and others to the character of his father, that the whole family, and many of their associates, who have never emerged from the native obscurity of their condition, possessed talents, and taste, and intelligence, which are little suspected to lurk in those humble retreats. His epistles to brother poets, in the rank of farmers and shopkeepers in the adjoining villages,—the existence of a book-society and debating-club among persons of that description, and many other incidental traits in his sketches of his youthful companions,—all contribute to show, that not only good sense, and enlightened morality, but litera-ture, and talents for speculation, are far more generally diffused in society than is generally imagined; and that the delights and the benefits of these generous and humanizing pursuits, are by no means confined to those whom leisure and affluence have courted to their enjoyment. That much of this is peculiar to Scotland, and may be properly referred to our excellent institutions for parochial education, and to the natural sobriety and prudence of our nation, may certainly be allowed: but we have no doubt that there is a good deal of the same principle in England, and that the actual intelligence of the lower orders will be found, there also, very far to exceed the ordinary estimates of their superiors. It is pleasing to know, that the sources of rational enjoyment are so widely disseminated; and, in a free country, it is comfortable to think, that so great a proportion of the people is able to appreciate the advantages of its condition, and fit to be relied on in all emergencies where steadiness and intelligence may be required.

Our other remark is of a more limited application; and is addressed chiefly to the followers and patrons of that new school of poetry, against which we have thought it our duty to neglect no opportunity of testifying. Those gentlemen are outrageous for simplicity; and we beg leave to recommend to them the simplicity of Burns. He has copied the spoken language of passion and affection, with infinitely more fidelity than they have ever done, on all occasions which properly admitted of such adaptation: but he has not rejected the helps of elevated language and habitual associations, nor debased his composition by an affectation of babyish interjections, and all the puling expletives of an old nurserymaid's vocabulary. They may look long enough among his nervous and manly lines, before they find any 'Good lacks!'—'Dear hearts!'—or 'As a body may say,' in them; or any stuff about dancing daffodils and sister Emmelines. Let them think, with what infinite contempt the powerful mind of Burns would have perused the story of Alice Fell and her duffle cloak,—of Andrew Jones and the half-crown,—or of Little Dan without breeches, and his thievish grandfather. Let them contrast their own fantastical personages of hysterical schoolmasters and sententious leech-gatherers, with the authentic rustics of Burns's 'Cotter's Saturday Night', and his inimitable songs; and reflect on the different reception which these personifications have met with from the public. Though they will not be reclaimed from their puny affectations by the example of their learned predecessors, they may, perhaps, submit to be admonished by a self-taught and illiterate poet, who drew from Nature far more directly than they can do, and produced something so much liker the admired copies of the masters whom they have abjured.

40. Walter Scott, from an unsigned review in *Quarterly Review*

i (February 1809), 19–36

Scott played a large part in founding the *Quarterly Review*, a Tory rival to the *Edinburgh Review*. This was the second article in the first issue (see No. 50, and Introduction, pp. 30–3).

We opened a book bearing so interesting a title with no little anxiety. Literary reliques vary in species and value almost as much as those of the catholic or of the antiquary. Some deserve a golden shrine for their intrinsic merit, some are valued from the pleasing recollections and associations with which they are combined, some, reflecting little honour upon their unfortunate author, are dragged by interested editors from merited obscurity. The character of Burns, on which we may perhaps hazard some remarks in the course of this article, was such as to increase our apprehensions. The extravagance of genius with which this wonderful man was gifted, being in his later and more evil days directed to no fixed or general purpose, was, in the morbid state of his health and feelings, apt to display itself in hasty sallies of virulent and unmerited severity: sallies often regretted by the bard himself; and of which, justice to the living and to the dead, alike demanded the suppression. Neither was this anxiety lessened, when we recollected the pious care with which the late excellent Dr. Currie had performed the task of editing the works of Burns. His selection was limited, as much by respect to the fame of the living, as of the dead. He dragged from obscurity none of those satirical effusions, which ought to be as ephemeral as the transient offences which called them forth. He excluded every thing approaching to licence, whether in morals or in religion, and thus rendered his collection such, as doubtless Burns himself, in his moments of sober reflection, would have most highly approved. Yet applauding, as we do most highly applaud, the leading principles of Dr. Currie's selection, we are aware that they sometimes led him into fastidious and over-delicate rejection of the bard's most spirited and happy effusions. A thin octavo published at Glasgow in 1801, under the title of 'Poems ascribed to Robert Burns, the Ayrshire bard,' furnishes valuable proofs of this assertion. It contains, among a good deal of rubbish, some of his most brilliant poetry. A cantata in particular, called 'The Jolly Beggars,' for humorous description and nice discrimination of character, is inferior to no poem of the same length in the whole range of English poetry. The scene indeed is laid in the very lowest department of low life, the actors being a set of strolling vagrants, met to carouse, and barter their rags and plunder for liquor in a hedge ale-house. Yet even in describing the movements of such a group, the native taste of the poet has never suffered his pen to slide into any thing coarse or disgusting. The extravagant glee and outrageous frolic of the beggars are ridiculously contrasted with their maimed limbs, rags, and crutches—the sordid and squalid circumstances of their appearance are judiciously thrown into the shade. Nor is the art of the poet less conspicuous in the individual figures, than in the general mass. The festive vagrants are distinguished from each other by personal appearance and character, as much as any fortuitous assembly in the higher orders of life. The group, it must be observed, is of Scottish character, and doubtless our northern brethren are more familiar with its varieties than we are: yet the distinctions are too well marked to escape even the South'ron. The most prominent persons are a maimed soldier and his female companion, a hackneyed follower of the camp, a stroller, late the consort of an Highland ketterer or sturdy beggar,—'but weary fu' the waefu' woodie!'—Being now at liberty, she becomes an object of rivalry between a 'pigmy scraper with his fiddle' and a strolling tinker. The latter, a desperate bandit, like most of his profession, terrifies the musician out of the field, and is preferred by the damsel of course. A wandering ballad-singer, with a brace of doxies, is last introduced upon the stage. Each of these mendicants sings a song in character, and such a collection of humourous lyrics, connected by vivid poetical description, is not, perhaps, to be paralleled in the English language. As the collection and the poem are very little known in England, and as it is certainly apposite to the Reliques of Robert Burns, we venture to transcribe the concluding ditty, chaunted by the ballad-singer at the request of the company, whose 'mirth and fun have now grown fast and furious,' and set them above all sublunary terrors of jails, stocks, and whipping posts. It is certainly far superiot to any thing in the *Beggars Opera*, where alone we could expect to find its parallel.

[quotes 'Love and Liberty'—'A Cantata', ll. 242–81]

We are at a loss to conceive any good reason why Dr. Currie did not introduce this singular and humourous cantata into his collection. It is true, that in one or two passages the muse has trespassed slightly upon decorum, where, in the language of Scottish song,

> High kilted was she
> As she gaed ower the lea.

Something however is to be allowed to the nature of the subject, and something to the education of the poet: and if from veneration to the names of Swift and Dryden, we tolerate the grossness of the one, and the indelicacy of the other, the respect due to that of Burns, may surely claim indulgence for a few light strokes of broad humour. The same collection contains 'Holy Willie's Prayer,' a piece of satire more exquisitely severe than any which Burns afterwards wrote, but unfortunately cast in a form too daringly profane to be received into Dr. Currie's Collection.

Knowing that these, and hoping that other compositions of similar spirit and tenor, might yet be recovered, we were induced to think that some of them, at least, had found a place in the collection now given to the public by Mr. Cromek. But he has neither risqued the censure nor laid claim to the applause, which might have belonged to such an undertaking. The contents of the volume before us are more properly gleanings than reliques, the refuse and sweepings of the shop, rather than the commodities which might be deemed contraband. Yet even these scraps and remnants contain articles of curiosity and value, tending to throw light on the character of one of the most singular men by whose appearance our age has been distinguished.

The first portion of the volume contains nearly two hundred pages of letters addressed by Burns to various individuals, written in various tones of feeling and modes of mind, in some instances exhibiting all the force of the writer's talents, in others only valuable because they bear his signature. The avidity with which the reader ever devours this species of publication, has been traced to the desire of seeing the mind and opinions of celebrated men in their open and undisguised moments, and of perusing and appreciating their thoughts, while the gold is yet rude ore, ere it is refined and manufactured into polished sentences or sounding stanzas. But notwithstanding these fair pretences, we doubt if this appetite can be referred to any more honourable source than the love of anecdote and private history. In fact, letters, at least those of a general and miscellaneous kind, very rarely contain the real opinions of the writer. If an author sits down to the task of formally composing a work for the use of the public, he has previously considered his subject, and made up his mind both on the opinions he is to express, and on the mode of supporting them. But the same man usually writes a letter only because the letter must be written, is probably never more at a loss than when looking for a subject, and treats it when found, rather so as to gratify his correspondent, than communicate his own feelings. The letters of Burns, although containing passages of great eloquence, and expressive of the intense fire of his disposition, are not exceptions from this general rule. They bear occasionally strong marks of affectation, with a tinge of pedantry rather foreign from the bard's character and education . . .

These passages however, in which the author seems to have got the better of the man, in which the desire of shining and blazing, and thundering supersedes the natural expressions of feeling, and passion, are less frequent in the letters of Burns than perhaps of any other professed writer. Burns was in truth the child of passion and feeling. His character was not simply that of a peasant exalted into notice by uncommon literary attainments, but bore a stamp which must have distinguished him in the highest as in the lowest situation in life. To ascertain what was his natural temper and disposition, and how far it was altered or modified by the circumstances of birth, education, and fortune, might be a subject for a long essay; but to mark a few distinctions is all that can be here expected from us.

We have said that Robert Burns was the child of impulse and feeling. Of the steady principle which cleaves to that which is good, he was unfortunately divested by the violence of those passions which finally wrecked him. It is most affecting to add that while swimming, struggling, and finally yielding to the torrent, he never lost sight of the beacon which ought to have guided him to land, yet never profited by its light.

We learn his opinion of his own temperament in the following emphatic burst of passion.

'God have mercy on me! a poor d–mned, incautious, duped, unfortunate fool! The sport, the miserable victim, of rebellious pride, hypochondriac imagination, agonizing sensibility, and bedlam passions!'

'Come stubborn pride and unshrinking resolution, accompany me through this to me miserable world!' In such language did this powerful but untamed mind express the irritation of prolonged expectation and disappointed hope, which slight reflection might have pointed out as the common fate of mortality. Burns neither acknowledged adversity as the 'tamer of the human breast,' nor knew the golden curb which discretion hangs upon passion. He even appears to have felt a gloomy pleasure in braving the encounter of evils which prudence might have avoided, and to have thought that there could be no pleasurable existence between the extremes of licentious frenzy and of torpid sensuality. 'There are two only creatures that I would envy.—A horse in his wild state traversing the forests of Asia,—and an oyster on some of the desert shores of Europe. The one has not a wish without enjoyment; the other has neither wish nor fear.' When such a sentiment is breathed by such a being, the lesson is awful: and if pride and ambition were capable of being taught, they might hence learn that a well regulated mind and controlled passions are to be prized above all the glow of imagination, and all the splendour of genius.

We discover the same stubborn resolution rather to endure with patience the consequences of error, than to own and avoid it in future, in the poet's singular choice of a pattern of fortitude.

'I have bought a pocket Milton, which I carry perpetually about with me, in order to study the sentiments—the dauntless magnanimity; the intrepid, unyielding independence, the desperate daring, and noble defiance of hardship, in that great personage, SATAN.'

Nor was this a rash or precipitate choice, for in a more apologetic mood he expresses the same opinion of the same personage.

'My favorite feature in Milton's Satan is his manly fortitude in supporting what cannot be remedied—in short, the wild, broken fragments of a noble, exalted mind in ruins. I meant no more by saying he was a favorite hero of mine.'

With this lofty and unbending spirit were connected a love of independence and a hatred of controul amounting almost to the sublime rant of Almanzor.

> He was as free as Nature first made man,
> Ere the base laws of servitude began,
> When wild in woods the noble savage ran.

In general society Burns often permitted his determination of vindicating his personal dignity to hurry him into unjustifiable resentment of slight or imagined neglect. He was ever anxious to maintain his post in society, and to extort that deference which was readily paid to him by all from whom it was worth claiming. This ill-judged jealousy of precedence led him often to place his own pretensions to notice in competition with those of the company who, he conceived, might found theirs on birth or fortune. On such occasions it was no easy task to deal with Burns. The power of his language, the vigour of his satire, the severity of illustration with which his fancy instantly supplied him, bore down all retort. Neither was it possible to exercise over the poet that restraint which arises from the chance of further personal consequences. The dignity, the spirit, the indignation of Burns was that of a plebeian, of a high-souled plebeian indeed, of a citizen of Rome or Athens, but still of a plebeian untinged with the slightest shade of that spirit of chivalry which since the feudal times has pervaded the higher ranks of European society. This must not be imputed to cowardice, for Burns was no coward. But the lowness of his birth, and habits of society, prevented rules of punctilious delicacy from making any part of his education; nor did he, it would seem, see any thing so rational in the practice of duelling, as afterwards to adopt or to affect the sentiments of the higher ranks upon that subject. A letter to Mr. Clarke, written after a quarrel upon political topics, has these remarkable, and we will add manly expressions.

From the expressions Capt. —— made use of to me, had I had nobody's welfare to care for but my own, we should certainly have come, according to the manners of the world, to the necessity of murdering one another about the business. The words were such as, generally, I believe, end in a brace of pistols; but I am still pleased to think that I did not ruin the peace and welfare of a wife and a family of children in a drunken squabble.

In this point therefore, the pride and high spirit of Burns differed from those of the world around him. But if he wanted that chivalrous sensibility of honour which places reason upon the sword's point, he had delicacy of another sort, which those who boast most of the former do not always possess in the same purity. Although so poor as to be ever on the very brink of absolute ruin, looking forwards now to the situation of a foot-soldier, now to that of a common beggar, as no unnatural consummation of his evil fortune, Burns was in pecuniary transactions, as proud and independent as if possessed of a prince's revenue. Bred a peasant, and preferred to the degrading situation of a common exciseman, neither the influence of the low minded crowd around him, nor the gratification of selfish indulgence, nor that contempt of futurity, which has characterised so many of his poetical brethren, ever led him to incur or endure the burden of pecuniary obligation. A very intimate friend of the poet, from whom he used occasionally to borrow a small sum for a week or two, once ventured to hint that the punctuality with which the loan was always replaced at the appointed time was unnecessary and unkind. The consequence of this hint was the interruption of their friendship for some weeks, the bard disdaining the very thought of being indebted to a human being one farthing beyond what he could discharge with the most rigid punctuality. It was a less pleasing consequence of this high spirit that Burns was utterly inaccessible to all friendly advice. To lay before him his errors, or to point out their consequences, was to touch a string that jarred every feeling within him. On such occasions, his, like Churchill's was

> The mind which starting, heaves the heartfelt groan,
> And hates the form she knows to be her own.

It is a dreadful truth, that when racked and tortured by the well-meant and warm expostulations of an intimate friend, he at length started up in a paroxysm of frenzy, and drawing a sword cane, which he usually wore, made an attempt to plunge it into the body of his adviser—the next instant he was with difficulty withheld from suicide.

Yet this ardent and irritable temperament had its periods, not merely of tranquillity, but of the most subduing tenderness. In the society of men of taste, who could relish and understand his conversation, or whose rank in life was not so much raised above his own as to require, in his opinion, the assertion of his dignity, he was eloquent, impressive, and instructing. But it was in female circles that his powers of expression displayed their utmost fascination. In such, where the respect demanded by rank was readily paid as due to beauty or accomplishment; where he could resent no insult, and vindicate no claim of superiority, his conversation lost all its harshness, and often became so energetic and impressive, as to dissolve the whole circle into tears. The traits of sensibility which, told of another, would sound like instances of gross affectation, were so native to the soul of this extraordinary man, and burst from him so involuntarily, that they not only obtained full credence as the genuine feelings of his own heart, but melted into unthought of sympathy all who witnessed them. In such a mood they were often called forth by the slightest and most trifling occurrences; an ordinary engraving, the wild turn of a simple Scottish air, a line in an old ballad, were, like 'the field mouse's nest' and 'the uprooted daisy,' sufficient to excite the sympathetic feelings of Burns. And it was wonderful to see those, who, left to themselves, would have passed over such trivial circumstances without a moment's reflection, sob over the picture, when its outline had been filled up by the magic art of his eloquence.

The political predilections, for they could hardly be termed principles, of Burns, were entirely determined by his feelings. At first appearance, he felt, or affected, a propensity to jacobitism. Indeed a youth of his warm imagination and ardent patriotism, brought up in Scotland thirty years ago, could hardly escape this bias. The side of Charles Edward was the party, not surely of sound sense and sober reason, but of romantic gallantry and high achievement. The inadequacy of the means by which that prince attempted to regain the crown, forfeited by his fathers, the strange and almost poetical adventures which he underwent, the Scottish martial character honoured in his victories, and degraded and crushed in his defeat, the tales of the veterans who had followed his adventurous standard, were all calculated to impress upon the mind of a poet a warm interest in the cause of the house of Stuart. Yet the impression was not of a very serious cast; for Burns himself acknowledges in one of these letters that 'to tell the matter of fact, except when my passions were heated by some accidental cause, my jacobitism was merely by way of *vive la bagatelle*'. The same enthusiastic ardour of disposition swayed Burns in his choice of political tenets, when the country was agitated by revolutionary principles. That the poet should have chosen the side on which high talents were most likely to procure celebrity; that he, to whom the factitious distinctions of society were always odious, should have listened with complacence to the voice of French philosophy, which denounced them as usurpations on the rights of man, was precisely the thing to be expected. Yet we cannot but think that if his superiors in the Excise department had tried the experiment of soothing rather than of irritating his feelings, they might have spared themselves the disgrace of rendering desperate the possessor of such uncommon talents. For it is but too certain that from the moment his hopes of promotion were utterly blasted, his tendency to dissipation hurried him precipitately into those excesses which shortened his life. We doubt not that in that awful period of national discord he had done and said enough to deter, in ordinary cases, the servants of government from countenancing an avowed partizan of faction. But this partizan was Burns!—Surely the experiment of lenity might have been tried, and perhaps successfully. The conduct of Mr. Graham of Fintray, our poet's only shield against actual dismission, and consequent ruin, reflects the highest credit upon that gentleman. We may dismiss these reflections on the character of Burns with his own beautiful lines.

> I saw thy pulse's maddening play,
> Wild send thee pleasure's devious way,
>   By passion driven:
> But yet the light that led astray,
>   Was light from heaven.

The second part of this volume contains a number of memoranda by Burns, concerning the Scottish songs and music published by Johnstone, in 6 volumes 8vo.—Many of these appear to us exceedingly trifling. They might indeed have adorned with great propriety, a second edition of the work in question, or any other collection of Scottish songs; but, separated from the verses to which they relate, how can any one be interested in learning that 'Down the Burn Davie' was the composition of David Maigh, keeper of blood hounds to the Laird of Riddell; that 'Tarry woo' was, in the opinion of Burns, a 'very pretty song,' or even that the author of 'Polwarth on the Green' was 'Captain John Drummond MacGrigor, of the family of Bochaldie'? Were it of consequence, we might correct the valuable information thus conveyed, in one or two instances, and enlarge it in many others. But it seems of more importance to mark the share which the poet himself took in compiling or embellishing this collection of traditional poetry, especially as it has not been distinctly explained either by Dr. Currie or Mr. Cromek. Tradition, generally speaking, is a sort of perverted alchemy which converts gold into lead. All that is abstractedly poetical, all that is above the comprehension of the merest peasant, is apt to escape in frequent recitation; and the *lacunae*, thus created, are filled up either by lines from other ditties, or from the mother wit of the reciter or singer. The injury, in either case, is obvious and irreparable. But with all these disadvantages, the Scottish songs and tunes preserved for Burns that inexpressible charm which they have ever afforded to his countrymen. He entered into the idea of collecting their fragments with all the zeal of an enthusiast; and few, whether serious or humorous, past through his hands without receiving some of those magic touches, which, without greatly altering the song, restored its original spirit, or gave it more than it had ever possessed. So dexterously are these touches combined with the ancient structure, that the *rifacciamento*, in many instances, could scarcely have been detected, without the avowal of the Bard himself. Neither would it be easy to mark his share in the individual ditties. Some he appears entirely to have re-written; to others he added supplementary stanzas; in some he retained only the leading lines and the chorus, and others he merely arranged and ornamented. For the benefit of future antiquaries, however, we may observe that many of the songs, claimed by the present editor as the exclusive composition of Burns, were, in reality, current long before he was born. Let us take one of the best examples of his skill in imitating the old ballad.—'M'Pherson's Lament' was a well known song many years before the Ayrshire Bard wrote those additional verses which constitute its principal merit. This noted freebooter was executed at Inverness, about the beginning of the last century. When he came to the fatal tree, he played the tune to which he has bequeathed his name upon a favourite violin, and holding up the instrument, offered it to any one of his clan who would undertake to play the tune over his body at his lyke-wake: as none answered, he dashed it to pieces on the executioner's head, and flung himself from the ladder. The following are the wild stanzas, grounded, however, upon some traditional remains,* which Burns has put into the mouth of this desperado.

[quotes 'McPherson's Farewell']

How much Burns delighted in the task of eking out the ancient melodies of his country, appears from the following affecting passage in a letter written to Mr. Johnstone, shortly before his death.

You are a good, worthy, honest fellow, and have a good right to live in this world—because you deserve it. Many a merry meeting this publication has given us, and possibly it may give us more, though, alas! I fear it. This protracting, slow, consuming illness which hangs over me, will, I doubt much, my ever dear friend, arrest my sun before he has well reached his middle career, and will turn over the Poet to far other and more important concerns than studying the

---

* We have heard some of these recited, particularly one, which begins—

> Now farewell house and farewell friends,
>   And farewell wife and bairns;
> There's nae repentance in my heart,
>   The fiddle's in my arms—

brilliancy of wit, or the pathos of sentiment! However, *hope* is the cordial of the human heart, and I endeavour to cherish it as well as I can.

Notwithstanding the spirit of many of the lyrics of Burns, and the exquisite sweetness and simplicity of others, we cannot but deeply regret that so much of his time and talents was frittered away in compiling and composing for musical collections. There is sufficient evidence both in the edition of Dr. Currie, and in this supplemental volume, that even the genius of Burns could not support him in the monotonous task of writing love verses on heaving bosoms and sparkling eyes, and twisting them into such rhythmical forms, as might suit the capricious evolutions of Scotch reels, ports, and strathspeys. Besides, this constant waste of his fancy and power of verse in small and insignificant compositions, must necessarily have had no little effect in deterring him from undertaking any grave or important task. Let no one suppose that we undervalue the songs of Burns. When his soul was intent on suiting a favourite air with words humorous or tender, as the subject demanded, no poet of our tongue ever displayed higher skill in marrying melody to immortal verse. But the writing of a series of songs for large musical collections, degenerated into a slavish labour, which no talents could support, led to negligence, and above all, diverted the poet from his grand plan of dramatic composition.

To produce a work of this kind, neither perhaps a regular tragedy nor comedy, but something partaking of the nature of both, seems to have been long the cherished wish of Burns. He had even fixed on the subject, which was an adventure in low life, said to have happened to Robert Bruce, while wandering in danger and disguise after being defeated by the English. The Scottish dialect would have rendered such a piece totally unfit for the stage: but those who recollect the masculine and lofty tone of martial spirit which glows in the poem of 'Bannockburn', will sigh to think what the character of the gallant Bruce might have proved under the hand of Burns! It would undoubtedly have wanted that tinge of chivalrous feeling which the manners of the age, no less than the disposition of the monarch, imperiously demanded; but this deficiency would have been more than supplied by a bard who could have drawn from his own perceptions the unbending energy of a hero, sustaining the desertion of friends, the persecution of enemies, and the utmost malice of disastrous fortune. The scene too, being partly laid in humble life, admitted that display of broad humour and exquisite pathos, with which he could interchangeably and at pleasure adorn his cottage views. Nor was the assemblage of familiar sentiments incompatible in Burns with those of the most exalted dignity. In the inimitable tale of 'Tam o' Shanter', he has left us sufficient evidence of his ability to combine the ludicrous with the awful and even the horrible. No poet, with the exception of Shakespeare, ever possessed the power of exciting the most varied and discordant emotions with such rapid transitions. His humorous description of the appearance of Death (in the poem on Dr. Hornbook) borders on the terrific, and the witches' dance, in the 'Kirk of Alloway,' is at once ludicrous and horrible. Deeply must we then regret those avocations which diverted a fancy so varied and so vigorous, joined with language and expression suited to all its changes, from leaving a more substantial monument of his own fame and to the honour of his country.

The next division is a collection of fugitive sentences and common places, extracted partly from the memorandum book of the poet, and partly, we believe, from letters which could not be published in their entire state. Many of these appear to be drawn from a small volume, entitled *Letters to Clarinda, by Robert Burns*, which was printed at Glasgow, but afterwards suppressed. To these, the observations which we offered on the bard's letters in general, apply with additional force: for in such a selection, the splendid patches, the showy, declamatory, figurative effusions of sentimental affectation, are usually the choice of the editor. Respect for the mighty dead, prevents our quoting instances in which Burns has degraded his natural eloquence by these meretricious ornaments. Indeed his stile is sometimes so forced and unnatural, that we must believe he knew to whom he was writing, and that an affectation of enthusiasm in platonic love and devotion, was more likely to be acceptable to the fair Clarinda, than the true language of feeling. The following loose and laboured passage shews, that the passion of *Sylvander* (a name sufficient of itself to damn a whole file of love-letters) had more of vanity, than of real sentiment.

What trifling silliness is the childish fondness of the every-day children of the world! 'Tis the unmeaning toying of the younglings of the fields and forests: but where sentiment and fancy unite their sweets; where taste and delicacy refine; where wit adds the flavour, and good sense gives strength and spirit to all, what a delicious draught is the hour of tender endearment!—beauty and grace in the arms of truth and honour, in all the luxury of mutual love!

The last part of the work comprehends a few original poems. We were rather surprised to find in the van, the beautiful song called

'Evan Banks.' Mr. Cormek ought to have known that this was published by Dr. Currie, in his first edition of Burns' works, and omitted in all those which followed, because it was ascertained to be the composition of Helen Maria Williams, who wrote it at the request of Dr. Wood. Its being found in the hand-writing of Burns, occasioned the first mistake, but the correction of that leaves no apology for a second. The remainder consists of minor poems, epistles, prologues, and songs, by which, if the author's reputation had not been previously established, we will venture to say it would never have risen above the common standard. At the same time there are few of them that do not, upon minute examination, exhibit marks of Burns's hand, though not of his best manner. The following exquisitely affecting stanza contains the essence of a thousand love tales:

> Had we never loved sae kindly
> Had we never loved sae blindly,
> Never met or never parted,
> We had ne'er been broken-hearted.

There are one or two political songs, which for any wit or humour they contain, might have been very well omitted. The satirical effusions of Burns, when they related to persons or subjects removed from his own sphere of observation, were too vague and too coarse to be poignant. We have seen, indeed, some very pointed stanzas in two political ballads . . .; but Mr. Cromek apparently judged them too personal for publication. There are a few attempts at English verse, in which, as usual, Burns falls beneath himself. This is the more remarkable as the sublimer passages of his 'Saturday Night,' 'Vision,' and other poems of celebrity, always swell into the language of classic English poetry. But although in these flights he naturally and almost unavoidably assumed the dialect of Milton and Shakespeare, he never seems to have been completely at his ease when he had not the power of descending at pleasure into that which was familiar to his ear, and to his habits. In the one case, his use of the English was voluntary, and for a short time; but when assumed as a primary and indispensable rule of composition, the comparative penury of rhimes, and the want of a thousand emphatic words which his habitual acquaintance with the Scottish supplied, rendered his expression confined and embarrassed. No man ever had more command of this ancient Doric dialect than Burns. He has left a curious testimony of his skill, in a letter to Mr.

Nicol, published in this volume; an attempt to read a sentence of which, would break the teeth of most modern Scotchmen.

Three or four letters from William Burns, a brother of the poet, are introduced for no purpose that we can guess, unless to shew that he wrote and thought like an ordinary journeyman saddler. We would readily have believed, without positive proof, that the splendid powers of the poet were not imparted to the rest of his family.

We scarcely know, upon the whole, in what terms we ought to dismiss Mr. Cromek. If the reputation of Burns alone be considered, this volume cannot add to his fame; and it is too well fixed to admit of degradation. The Cantata already mentioned, is indeed the only one of his productions not published by Dr. Currie, which we consider as not merely justifying, but increasing his renown. It is enough to say of the very best of those now published, that they take nothing from it. What the public may gain by being furnished with additional means of estimating the character of this wonderful and self-taught genius, we have already endeavoured to state. We know not whether the family of the poet will derive any advantage from this publication of his remains. If so, it is the best apology for their being given to the world; if not, we have no doubt that the editor, as he is an admirer of Chaucer, has read of a certain pardoner, who

> —With his *relics*, when that he fond
> A poor persone dwelling up on lond,
> Upon a day he gat him more moneie
> Than that the persone got in monethes tweie.

41. From an unsigned review in *Universal Magazine*

xi (February 1809), 132–9

The reviewer went on to comment on the spirit of 'turbulent independence' shown in Burns's letters.

Nothing that fell from the pen of Burns can be wholly uninteresting. His genius was powerful, various, and original. He dipt his pencil in the living tints of nature. He depicted what he felt with all those character-istical qualities which stamp the sentiments of the individual with indelible permanency upon what he contemplated. Like Shakespeare, the current of his inspiration was unchecked by the cold niceties of critical perfection: it flowed impetuously onward, sometimes spreading into magnificence and beauty, sometimes meandering in peaceful murmurs, and sometimes rushing with sublime energy over precipices and rocks, forming the thundering cataract or the eddying whirlpool. We know of no modern author who possesses more the *vivida vis animi* than Burns; or who has exerted his genius with greater felicity on such a multiplicity of topics. He was, according as he wished to be, either tender, humorous, moral, energetic, sublime, playful, or in-decorous: he rose and sunk with equal facility. Happy, had the tenor of his life and the bent of his inclination less frequently prompted him to the latter.

42. James Montgomery, from an unsigned review in *Eclectic Review*

v (May 1809), 393–410

James Montgomery (1771–1854), poet, hymn-writer, and miscellaneous prose-writer, included a revised version of part of this review in his *Lectures on Poetry and General Literature* (1835) (see Introduction, p. 33).

In his best pieces, Burns is the poet of truth, of nature, and his native country. His subjects are never remote, abstracted, nor factitious; they are such as *come in his way* and therefore shine in his song, as the clouds that meet the sun in his course are enlightened by his rays; his scenery is always purely Scottish, and represents the very objects that engaged his eye, when the themes with which they are associated were revolving in his mind; his feelings irresistibly impress the heart of the reader, because they are the same that impressed his own, on the spot, and at the time when, those objects were in his sight, and those themes in his thought. Burns wrote not so much from memory as from perception; not after slow deliberation, but from instaneous impulse; the fire that burns through his compositions was not elaborated spark by spark, from mechanical friction, in the closet;—no, it was in the open field, under the cope of heaven, this poetical Franklin caught his lightnings from the cloud while it passed over his head, and he communicated them, too, by a touch, with electrical swiftness and effect. It was literally thus, amidst the inspiration of a thunder-storm, on the wilds of Kenmore, that he composed the 'Address of Bruce to his Soldiers at Bannockburn'.

It was probably fortunate for Burns, that by a partial education his mind was only cleared of the forests, and drained of the morasses, that in a state of unbroken nature intercept the sun, chill the soil, and forbid the growth of generous thought; higher cultivation would unquestionably have called forth richer and fairer harvests, but it would have so softened away the wild and magnificent diversity that makes the objects within the range of his genius resemble the rocks and moorlands, the lakes and glens of his native country, that, instead of being first and unrivalled among the Scottish minstrels, he might with difficulty have maintained a place in the third rank of British poets. It was a further and incalculable advantage to his untamed muse, that she sung her native strains in her native tongue. The Scottish language is of a very peculiar character; its basis was undoubtedly a national dialect now almost obsolete, but its superstructure consists of vulgar idioms, and its embellishments of pure English phrases. Hence the language, as it is *written*, is an arbitrary one, and its force and elegance depend principally upon the skill with which the poet combines its constituent parts, to make a *common chord* of its triple tones; and we may venture to pronounce that style the most harmonious and perfect, in which the national dialect is the *key-note*, and the vulgar and the English are subordinate. The muse of Burns disdained to confine her song to any peculiar accordance of these, but ran, as it suited her subject or her caprice, through the whole diapason of her country scale, and tried her skill in every modulation of which her mother-tongue, copious and flexible beyond any now in use, was capable. Hence we have pieces by Burns in plain English.

[quotes 'A Winter Night', ll. 62–72]

In broad Scottish:-

> Thou never braindg't, an' fech't, an' fliskit,
> But thy auld tail thou wad hae whiskit,
> An spread abreed thy weel-fill'd brisket,
>   Wi' pith and pow'r,
> Till sprittie knows wad rair't and riskit,
>   An' slippet owre.

In the purer or national Scottish:-

> Ay free, aff han', your story tell,
> When wi' a bosom-crony;
> But still keep something to yoursel
> Ye scarcely tell to ony;
> Conceal yourself as weel's ye can
> Fra' critical dissection;
> But keek thro' every other man
> Wi' sharpen'd sly inspection.

But in each of these three styles, words and phrases may be traced borrowed from the other two; and, in his larger and nobler productions, Burns employs them indiscriminately or alternately at pleasure. It follows, that what is now called the Scottish is in fact only a *written* language; there is not a poem of Burns (the *mere*, not *pure*, English ones excepted) composed in a dialect spoken by any class of men in our whole island. This is a curious and in some respects a novel view of a very interesting subject; but we must proceed. There are three other advantages incidental to the use of this dialect, which we shall briefly mention.—1st. The measure of verse may be computed by *quantity*, as well as by *the number of syllables*. The lines, marked with italics, in the following quotation will show this; it would be wilful murder to abridge a letter of one word in them.

> As I stood by yon roofless tower,
> *Where the wa' flower scents the dewy air,*
> *Where the Howlet mourns in her ivy bower,*
> And tells the midnight moon her care,
> The winds were laid, the air was still,
> The stars they shot alang the sky;
> The fox was howling on the hill,
> *And the distant-echoing glens reply.*

2ndly. An undefinable latitude is allowed of using rhyming, jingling, or only alliterative vowel-sounds in dissonant words at the end of the lines: on this we shall not expatiate, as an English ear can neither tolerate, nor comprehend terminations that are truly melodious to a Scottish reader. Finally, this dialect gives exquisite quaintness to humorous, and a simple grace to ordinary, forms of speech; while it renders sublime and terrific imagery yet more striking and dreadful; it seems not a language of this world in the following passage from 'Tam o' Shanter', that miracle of the muse of Burns, in which all his versatile powers are exemplified, through the whole compass of his native tongue, on a subject most gross and abominable, yet supernaturally grand and mysterious.

[quotes 'Tam o' Shanter', ll. 131–42, ending

> —Wi' mair o' horrible and *awfu'*
> Which e'en to name wad be *unlawfu'*]

The elision of the *l* at the end of the two last rhymes is wonderfully expressive of a horror that *suspends the breath* of the speaker.

The high praises which we have bestowed on the poetry of Burns must be confined to his *best pieces*,—his tales, a few of his epistles, his descriptive poems, and most of his songs. His ordinary and his satirical productions, though the worst are stamped with originality and boldness of conceptions, are so debased and defiled with ribaldry and profaneness, that they cannot be perused without shuddering, by any one whose mind is not utterly perverted and polluted. There is a blasphemous boldness in some of his effusions of spleen and malignity against graver personages than himself, which deserves unqualified reprobation; he stabs at the very heart of religion through the sides of hypocrisy; yet the enmity itself which he manifests against her in his frantic moods, proves the power which she held over his mind, even when he was blindfolding, and buffeting, and spitting at her. In misery and misfortune she was his 'forlorn hope', as we learn from many confessions in his letters, written in sickness and sorrow; and we fervently trust that, in his last hours, he who could pray so sweetly for another, as he does for his 'Jean', in the following stanza, prayed effectually for himself.

[quotes 'Epistle to Davie', stanza IX]

We intended to have given specimens of the diversified compositions of Burns; but our limits restrict us, and we shall only offer one example of his *patriotic* strains, which we admire more than even his love-songs.

[quotes 'To W. S*****n', ll. 53–90]

...We have now enough both of the prose and verse of Burns, and much more than *can* endure. In the days of Tarquin, a strange woman came to Rome and offered nine books of the Cumaean Sybil's oracles for sale, at an exorbitant price; which being contemptuously refused, she burned three, and demanded the same sum for the other six. Being again denied, she burnt three more, and still required the price of all nine for the last three. It was given her; and the books were preserved, and revered and consulted for ages by the Roman people. The multifarious works of Robert Burns will share a similar fate. One, older and sager than the Sibyl herself, Time, who tries all things, will offer them to the next generation in their present form; they will be rejected; in the course of fifty years he will have reduced them one third without having diminished their worth; they will still be too bulky; in another century he will curtail them as much more; then, on the remaining third, he will irreversibly fix the original value of the whole; and to posterity *those* 'Reliques' will be inestimable.

43. John Hodgson, from an unsigned review in *Monthly Review*

(December 1809), 399–409

John Hodgson (1786?–1849), who was called to the Bar in 1812, was a frequent contributor to the *Monthly Review* (see Introduction, p. 33).

In Burns's remarks on Scotch songs, (transcribed from an inter-leaved copy in four volumes of the *Scots Musical Museum*, in which they were written by the Poet,) we find ample evidence of his good taste, and a strong illustration of the truth of an old saying, that the best poets are the best critics: but, at the same time, we cannot help perceiving many instances in which nationality has prevailed over judgment; and in which the coarseness and vulgarity of the Scotch dialect (of late so ridiculously compared to the soft and sweetest Doric of Theocritus) is preferred to purer English, only because it is Scotch. We have resolved, however, to leave our readers to discover the exceptionable parts by their own sagacity, and to present them with nothing but the flowers of the collection. This is due to the memory of such a poet as Burns; who perhaps would neither have praised nor published all these pieces, had he yet been able to exercise his judgment on them.—As to his predilection for his native dialect, we shall only observe that in our opinion his best performances are those which are written in the purest English, or in which the Scotch is most easily understood. Which among his songs is superior in animation and delicacy to 'Their groves of green myrtle let foreign lands reckon?' or his tender dirge of 'Man was made to mourn?' or, among many other beautiful pieces equally intelligible to English readers, his sweetly-pathetic stanzas mentioned above—'Ye flowery banks o' bonie Doon?'—The two subjoined stanzas are among his Anglo-Scottish specimens; and to shew how natural this language was to him, we shall only remark that they were written at the age of seventeen:

[quotes 'I dream'd I lay where flowers were springing']

Again how would the beauty of the following extract from his youthful song to his mistress be disfigured by being clothed in the ruder Scottish language, which obscures some of the ballads here printed; and in which ballads (especially those that are not Burns's own) we plainly see that 'repetition indeèd, *and nothing else*, is the soul of poetry.'

> She is not the fairest, although she is fair;
> O' nice education but sma' is her share;
> Her parentage humble as humble can be;
> But I lo'e the dear lassie because she lo'es me.
>
> To beauty what man but maun yield him a prize,
> In her armour of glances, and blushes, and sighs;
> And when wit and refinement ha'e polished her darts,
> They dazzle our een, as they flie to our hearts,
>
> But kindness, sweet kindness, in the fond sparkling e'e,
> Has lustre outshining the diamond to me;
> And the heart beating love, as I'm clasp'd in her arms,
> O, these are my lassie's all-conquering charms!

To the traits of poetical character throughout this volume, as to a subject of very interesting and useful reflection, we have wished to direct the particular attention of our readers. Those which are described in the following letter are striking and impressive:

As I am what the men of the world, if they knew such a man, would call a whimsical mortal, I have various sources of pleasure and enjoyment, which are, in a manner, *peculiar* to myself, or some here and there such other out-of-the-way person. Such is the peculiar pleasure I take in the season of winter, more than the rest of the year. This, I believe, may be partly owing to my misfortunes giving my mind a melancholy cast: but there is something even in the

> Mighty tempest, and the hoary waste
> Abrupt and deep, stretch'd o'er buried earth,

which raises the mind to a serious sublimity, favourable to everything great and noble. There is scarcely any earthly object gives me more—I do not know if I should call it pleasure—but something which exalts me, something which enraptures me—than to walk in the sheltered side of a wood, or high plantation, in a cloudy-winterday, and hear the stormy wind howling among the trees, and raving over the plain. It is my best season for devotion: my mind is wrapt up in a kind of enthusiasm to *Him*, who, in the pompous language of the Hebrew bard, 'walks on the wings of the wind'. In one of these seasons, just after a train of misfortunes, I composed the following:

This poem we must omit, from want of room: but it confirms our opinion that Burns's best style was the English or Anglo-Scottish; as do the correct and spirited lines on Scotland, introduced into an ode to liberty, designed in honour of General Washington's birth-day,—and even above these the subjoined most rapturous love-song, which we cannot forbear to quote:

[quotes 'Yestreen I had a pint o' wine']

After these numerous extracts, we can only refer our readers to the volume itself for many more fragments that are remarkable for either tenderness or vigour; and for a variety of happy and original observations on such subjects as form the usual amusement of a highly poetical imagination:—not to mention several little pieces that are full of sarcasm and humour.

44. Dorothy Wordsworth on Jeffrey's review

1809

Extract from a letter to Thomas De Quincey, 1 May 1809, *The Letters of William and Dorothy Wordsworth*, ed. E. De Selincourt, 2nd ed., II *The Middle Years Part I 1806–1811*, rev. Mary Moorman, p. 326.

This passage reveals both the personal indignation felt in the Wordsworth household at Jeffrey's criticism of Wordsworth, and John Wilson's initial involvement in the Burns debate as a friend of Wordsworth (see Nos 53, 55 and Introduction, p. 38).

This reminds me of the last Edinburgh review which I saw at Mr. Wilson's.[1] There never was such a compound of despicable falsehood, malevolence, and folly as the concluding part of the Review of Burns's Poems (which was, in fact, all that I thought it worth while to read being the only part in which my Brother's works are alluded to). It would be treating Mr. Jeffrey with too much respect to notice any of his *criticisms*; but when he makes my Brother censure himself; by quoting words as from his poems which are not there, I do think it is proper that he should be contradicted and put to shame. I mentioned this to my Brother and he agrees with me; not that he would do it himself; but he thinks it would be well for you, or some other Friend of his to do it for him—but in what way?—I think a letter might be addressed to him in the Edinburgh Papers, and in one or two of the London papers. A private letter to himself would be of no use; and of course he would not *publish* any condemnation of himself in his own Review, if you were to call upon him to do so. I wish you would think about it. Mr. Wilson came to us on Saturday morning and stayed till Sunday afternoon—William read the 'White Doe'; and Coleridge's 'Christabel' to him, with both of which he was much delighted.

[1] Refers to *Edinburgh Review* containing Jeffrey's article on Cromek's *Reliques of Burns*, and to John Wilson (1785-1854), later of *Blackwood's Magazine*.

45. Josiah Walker on Burns

1811

Extract from [Josiah Walker], *Account of the Life and Character of Robert Burns* (Edinburgh, 1811).

Josiah Walker (1761–1831) had been secretary and tutor in the household of the Duke of Athole when Burns visited Blair Castle in 1787, and had briefly met the poet again in Dumfries in 1795. His critical memoir was also published in a two-volume edition of Burns's *Poems* (printed for the Trustees of James Morison) (Edinburgh, 1811), which contained poems and letters omitted by Currie (see Introduction, p. 35).

Though the lofty and energetic spirit of Burns appears to have delighted more in the sublime than in the beautiful; yet, in his delineations of softer and brighter scenery, we shall easily discover the pencil of genius. A summer morning is thus described:

> The rising sun o'er Galston muirs
> Wi' glorious light was glintin,
> The hares were hirplin down the furrs,
> The lavrocks they were chauntin.

Here only three images are introduced, yet more are not required to place the reader where the poet was placed when he wrote. Thomson gives a description of a summer morning, enriched with details, and embellished with splendid elaboration, yet it presents (at least to my mind) nothing which does not offer itself as a natural accompaniment to the *stenographic* sketch, if I may use the metaphor, thrown off by his countryman with such rapid facility. In this passage we have an example of the skill of Burns, in his nice adaptation of words. Of all the terms which any language affords, few could so significantly express the peculiar motion of the hare, when she moves with caution, but without alarm, as the word *hirplin*. In this manner language is extended.

A number of words which are little else than synonimes, to persons
who are at no pains, or who have no power to define and discriminate,
convey to one more anxious for the enjoyment produced by variety
and precision of thought, different shades of significance, which he
separates with ease. He afterwards employs them to express the meaning
which they had conveyed to himself, and they come by his authority
and adoption to be legitimated. In almost every page of Burns we may
find examples of unusual skill in his choice of words. As I have been
accidentally led to point out a term descriptive of peculiar motion, I
shall subjoin a few more of the same class, and if I succeed, under this
restriction, it will naturally be inferred, that, on all subjects, instances of
similar felicity are equally abundant in the works of the poet. 'When
Hughoc he came *doytin by*'.—'Down some *trottin* burn's meander'.
'Awa ye *squatter'd* like a drake.'—'The wheels o' life gae down hill
scrievin'—The two following passages are singularly rich in terms of
the same description:

[quotes 'The Holy Fair', ll. 55–9]

[quotes 'The Auld Farmer's New-Year-morning Salutation', ll. 67–72]

In representations of human character, the power of Burns was no
less conspicuous, than in his portraits of external nature. When describing, with satirical humour, the character of country squires, he
recollects that they are in general disposed to treat their rustic depen-
dents with affable liberality and indulgence, and that there are but a few
unpardonable offences which never fail to kindle their resentment, and
to call forth their power of oppression. These he catches with penetrating observation, and enumerates with happy brevity in six lines, of
which the descriptive truth will be recognised from Caithness to
Cornwall:

> For thae frank, rantin, ramblin billies,
> Fient haet o' them's ill hearted fellows:
> Except for cutting o' their timmer,
> Or speaking lightly o' their limmer,
> Or shooting o' a hare or muirock,
> The ne'er a bit they're ill to poor fock.

Here we have the usual subjects of aristocratic jealousy, and the
common character created by common circumstances in a particular
order of men, expressed with a rapidity and resemblance, which may

be compared to the sudden effect produced by the cast of a mould, rather than to the tardy labour of the pencil. To the same species of characteristic writing, where the description of an individual describes a class, may be referred the poaching sportsman in 'Tam Samson's Elegy.' Few can have passed through life, without meeting some of this numerous family, who are rewarded for their insignificance in the sober departments of gainful industry, by an indisputed supremacy in all the scenes of profitless recreation, which furnish amusements for idle activity.

Another province of the genuine poet is to seize with interesting accuracy, the practices and modes of life which prevail in certain subdivisions of society; and all of those, to which Burns had access, are reflected from the mirror of his writings with the most circumstantial fidelity. In his 'Twa Dogs' and 'Halloween,' we have the interior of a peasant's cottage, with all its appropriate manners and customs, at the season of merry-making; and in the 'Cotter's Saturday night,' we have the same scene, under a more affecting and impressive aspect. 'The Holy Fair' is a representation of practices which arise out of institutions peculiar to a single country, and which, though abundantly open to ridicule, are consecrated by traditionary usage. Those who know the original, must acknowledge it to be a caricature of exquisite humour; and even those who do not, will be diverted by its exhibition of characters and customs, the truth of which derives sufficient evidence from their probability. The nocturnal revels in the alehouse which was the darling resort of Tam o' Shanter, may stand a comparison with the scenes at the Boar's Head tavern, so admirably delineated by Shakespeare; but, in making this comparison, one difference cannot fail to strike us in favour of the immortal dramatist. Falstaff and his associates are characters which we have never met with, yet they are adjusted with such philosophical skill to the varieties possible in human nature— they are made up of parts, which form compounds so congruous, that they are as interesting as if their prototypes were familiarly known. To render a fiction pleasing, it must both resemble and differ from reality. In the happy balance of these two qualities, the excellence of the fiction in a great measure consists; the resemblance giving interest to the difference, as the difference to the resemblance; and in the fictitious characters alluded to, we see this balance admirably managed. But similar inventions were perhaps beyond the enterprise of Burns. All his topers are copies, not compounds, from real life. To pursue this speculation a little farther—though Burns succeeds in making us

sympathize with the mirth and happiness of his hero; though he dis-
poses us to forgive the dissipation which created so much kindness and
cordiality, he would probably have shrunk from an attempt to exhibit
vices less venial, as any thing else than odious or disgusting. It was only
the invincible powers of a Shakespeare, that, in Falstaff, could give a
singular sort of interest to falsehood, debauchery, and cowardice, and
make them, with the aid of wit and sociality, seduce us even into an
indescribable feeling of mirthful and companionable affection.

From the power of Burns, in delineating character, if we ascend to a
higher region of poetry, and try his pretensions to genius by his exhibition of the stronger affections of the mind, we shall still find our
scrutiny successful. Here he had unfortunately no occasion to go far in
search of an original, as in his own breast he might always find some
passion domineering with a force, and indulged with a freedom, which
rendered its operations singularly distinct. Of love he had abundant
experience; and no man was better qualified to describe and discriminate its various emotions, than one who had run through the whole,
from the gentle languishment of dubious and nascent preference, to
the fury of impatient and ungovernable ardour. Nor was his mind more
a stranger to the risings of indignation, the loathings of contempt, the
throes of grief, or the meltings of pity: If the assertion of Roscommon
be just,

> No poet any passion can excite,
> But what they feel transport them, when they write,—

Burns possessed this poetical qualification in no ordinary degree. He
had a title to rely with certainty on communicating the infection, when
the disease was so strong in himself. In opposition to Roscommon, it
may be asked how Shakespeare could delineate to the life the passions
of Hamlet or Othello, when he was neither the Prince of Denmark, nor
the General of Venice; neither the son of a murdered King, nor the
husband of a suspected wife; and when he, therefore, could never have
actually felt the passions excited by circumstances in which he had never
been placed. It must have been from the united force of imagination
and passion. The former was sufficiently powerful to transform him,
for the moment, into the very person of his hero; and the latter, to
make him feel precisely what his hero must have felt. Had either of
these powers been defective, the effect would have been imperfect and
unsatisfactory. Had his imagination been feeble, he could not have gone

out of himself, and assumed the being of another; and had his passions been languid, though he might have placed himself in the proper situation, he would not have been moved by the proper feelings, and would have produced a character very different, and probably far less interesting, than what he had designed.

In like manner Burns could, by the force of his fancy, identify himself with Bruce, at the head of his army, or with the dying soldier in the field of battle; and, by the power of his passions, he could glow with those feelings of patriotism and cravings for glory, which vent themselves in language so appropriate to the situation. It was seldom, however, that he made such efforts. On most occasions he had no need to call in the aid of imagination, or to assume any other character than his own. The events of his life, and the manner in which they had affected him, furnished abundant exercise for his power of displaying the passions. The book of human nature may be read by all human beings, however stationary or obscure: and it is probable that Burns was a better practical scholar, in the workings of the heart, before he quitted the narrow precinct of his native parish, than numbers, whose cool observation had been far more extensive, but at the same time less personal. He who engages deeply in the game of life, will much sooner reach proficiency than one who has studied it at a greater variety of tables, but only as a spectator. Where do love and sorrow breathe their mingled strains in more touching unison, than in the verses addressed 'to Mary in Heaven'? Where does the quiet and complacent warmth of parental affection smile with a more gentle benignity, than in the figure of the mother in 'the Cotter's Saturday Night'? Where can we find a more exhilarating enumeration of the enjoyments of youth, contrasted with their successive extinction as age advances, than in 'the Epistle to J. S.—'? The views of human life which Burns habitually indulged, were dark and cheerless; and in those hours of depression, to which all are occasionally subject, or under the pressure of misfortunes of which we are always ready to shift the blame from ourselves, by charging it to the treachery or injustice of the world, we shall acknowledge the fidelity with which our feelings have been expressed by the bard, in the 'Lament', in 'Despondency' and in those pathetic reflections on the fugacity of pleasure, which are scattered through his writings, and which he is unable to suppress even in the liveliest frolics of his genius. Most of them, too, have a seasoning of tenderness and pity for his fellow creatures, both rational and irrational, by which readers even of the most obtuse sensibility cannot fail to be affected. Nor is this the traditionary cant which one poet inherits from another, and which floats past the attention, as the mere expletive, or professional, style of the art. It has a penetrating and original poignancy, which genius alone can bestow. The poet often touches a new string, with a pathos which instantly awakens a corresponding tone in the heart of his reader. Thus, in his 'Winter Night,' he contrives, by a masterly description of its severity, to lead us gradually on from the sufferings of the innocent songsters, to commiserate those even of the kite and the carrion crow, and to acknowledge that their voracious cruelty has been more than expiated by the merciless lash of the elements.

[quotes 'A Winter Night', ll. 19–30]

It was a daring attempt in Shakespeare to reconcile with probability the gradual submission of Lady Anne to the flattery of Richard; yet Burns shows almost equal confidence in his own powers, when he expects to succeed in claiming our pity for the Devil, or our protection for the tyrants of the grove.

In richness and vigour of imagination, Burns has rarely been surpassed. This power is commonly considered to be the principal constituent of genius, as it is the instrument of invention, and the parent of novelty both in science and art. The sciences and arts, while in a state of progression, appear to advance, rather by sudden and occasional starts, than by regular periodical steps, and to receive their increments, not from the collective efforts of all who engage in them, but from the extraordinary and unexpected exertion of a single mind, by which something that was unknown before is discovered in the one, or executed in the other. To the power of making this solitary exertion, the denomination of genius should, perhaps, in strictness of language, be confined. If the preceding idea be just, it is by the production of novelty that pretensions to genius must be tried: and to this test Burns may, without any apprehension, be subjected. His writings, both in prose and verse, abound with original thoughts, and with images of his own creation. And it must be remembered that an author, whose reading was so limited, might frequently produce, by a second invention, what, unknown to him, had been invented before. Even when a common idea occurs to him, it serves only as a hint to put his fancy in motion, or as the medium through which he passes to some new conception. Thus in his song of 'John Anderson,' the comparison of life to the ascent and declivity of a hill, is common and familiar, but when Burns has begun it, he pursues it beyond the usual limits, and by making his aged couple 'sleep together at the fit,' extends it to an idea which is altogether new, and which, at the same time, harmonizes finely with the serene, affectionate, and pathetic spirit of this beautiful piece. Thus, too, when speaking of the unfitness of genius for ordinary affairs, he employs a trite idea in comparing life to a voyage, but he employs it only as the stem on which he grafts another of his own invention, to illustrate the helpless unskilfulness of poets, whom he calls 'timid *landsmen* on life's stormy main.' In his metaphors he shews himself always ready to rely on the coinage of his own fancy. His fish with ruddy spots are 'bedropt with crimson hail.' The loss of a valuable fellow-citizen, is, 'paying kane to death;' the hour of twelve is 'the keystone of night's black arch;' and the acquisition of immortal fame by a poet, is to 'warsle time, and lay him on his back.'

The conceptions of Burns, it may also be observed, were no less remarkable for their clearness than for their strength. This enabled him to sustain all his similes correctly, and to avoid that incongruity in the progress of the parallel to which less discriminating minds are exposed. We may refer, as examples, to the ludicrous comparisons of Kilmarnock to a cow, in the 'Ordination,' and of the life of the 'Unco Guid' to a mill in the 'Address,' and also to the whole allegorical song of 'John Barleycorn.'

The strength and vivacity of his conceptive faculties may be still better estimated, by the distinctness with which he places himself, and his readers, in fictitious situations. He appears, by a kind of sorcery, to disengage us from the power of the senses, and to transport us to imaginary scenes, where the vision for the time has all the power of actual existence. *Modo me Thebis, modo ponit Athenis.*[1] We feel ourselves become spectators of the 'Holy Fair,' and members of the party at the sports of 'Halloween,' or at the prayers and supper of the 'Cotter.' We find ourselves seated with Tam o' Shanter at the blazing fire of the alehouse, and grow familiarly acquainted with the jovial group. We enter into all the warmth of the fraternal friendship between Tam and the Souter, 'who had been fou for weeks thegither;' and we perceive our spirits rise as the bowl goes round. We accompany the hero through the tempest; we gaze with him at the window of the illuminated ruin, and shudder at the strange mixture of unearthly horror, and heaven defying merriment. Nor can we at once resume our own persons, and withdraw from the contemplation of objects, which by superior vivacity compensate for their want of reality.

[1] 'Now he sets me down in Thebes, now in Athens.' Horace, *Epistles* II.i.213.

The mind of Burns was a magazine of ideas, collected by the activity of his observation, aided by a memory which treasured only what possessed some species of interest. From this affluence of materials, which, by a power of quick association, were always at command, his fancy was ready to frame a variety of pleasing images, and the sensibility which accompanied all his views, supplied that warmth of sentiment with which his writings are so richly seasoned. In these there is nothing indifferent; no frigid description where mind is absent, and feeling asleep; no thought 'which plays round the head but comes not to the heart;' no figurative expression, which serves only to decorate, without increasing the warmth and vigour of what it clothes. Every thing, under the aspect in which he presents it, becomes an object of sympathy, and receives animation from the touch of his pen. Even between his 'Brigs' our hearts make an instant preference. We take part with the venerable and insulted antient, as with the reduced but dignified representative of an honourable ancestry; while we scorn and resent the petulance of its rival, as of the disgusting triumph of upstart ostentation and prosperous vulgarity. In the same manner, we enter into the feelings of his Daisy and his Mouse, his Dogs and his Mare; for on all the subjects of his pencil Burns never failed to spread the hues of passion.

The power ascribed to the music of Timotheus, is ascribable also to the poetry of Burns, which instantly transmits the varied and successive emotions of its author, and infects the reader with all the enthusiasm of his mirth or despondency, his affection or resentment, his applause or derision. Even where he deviates into a strain which we disapprove, we may condemn, but cannot quit him; and generally find the attraction of his talent stronger than the repulsion of his immorality.

His poems have been so frequently, and so judiciously analysed, that any new attempt of a similar kind must be attended with the double danger of repeating stale remarks, or of directing attention to beauties and defects of comparative unimportance. It is fortunate, therefore, that the public has already decided so distinctly for itself, as to render the attempt officious and unbecoming. If the excellence of an author may be estimated by the frequency with which his sentiments are echoed in quotation; if this be the stamp by which the public sanctions the currency of its favourite verses, a high station among the poets has been assigned to Burns for his beauties, without the aid of italics or inverted commas, have become nearly as proverbial, among all by whom the language is understood, as the striking passages of Pope or Milton. Yet, without presuming to assist a choice which has been already made, I shall perhaps be indulged in a few desultory reflections, which, if they miss the assent of the reader, may furnish him with amusement in detecting their futility.

It is remarkable that the writings of Burns, unlike to those of other poets, exhibit few traces of a progressive improvement in his art. The 'Epistle to Davie,' which is the earliest of those compositions, where his powers seem to have been seriously put forth, is little inferior to his latest productions. Its difficult measure, borrowed from 'The Cherry and the Slae,'[1] he probably chose to try his dexterity in rhiming; and it is astonishing that, under this, unusual constraint, he should have clothed his thoughts in expression so natural, flowing, and familiar. This poem, which was written about the period of his father's death, presents an affecting specimen of his reflections, under a singular accumulation of distresses. It seems to be a sort of effort to accustom his thoughts to the very darkest possibilities of evil, and to a recollection of the consolations which will be left, when his anticipations are realised. His consciousness of superior talents, to which his attention, at the time, had perhaps been drawn by their exertion in conversation with his 'brother poet', makes him consider with regret, and not without some of that indignation, which was more congenial to his character, the peculiar discomforts of his situation. These are admirably described in the opening stanza, which represents the northern blast as drifting the snow to the very hearth of his wretched cottage. He then anticipates the period to which he seems so near, when the unequal distribution of external advantages may reach its extreme and when his friend and he may be reduced to the condition of itinerant beggars. The evils of this condition he does not palliate; but soothes himself with the reflection, that, after all the gifts of fortune are gone, those of nature will remain; and that they may still be happy, in the possession of health, taste, ingenuity, and affection, and above all, in the cessation of fear, the chief poisoner of enjoyment, from having reached the lowest point of depression. The lines in which the mendicant poets are imaged, as exulting in the charms of creation, and in the exercise of a talent from which they had derived so little apparent benefit, are extremely pleasing.

[quotes 'Epistle to Davie', stanza IV]

The two last lines are among the few in which the difficulty of the measure produces a little feebleness. In a subsequent stanza, he describes

[1] By Alexander Montgomerie (?1545–?1615).

the advantages to be derived from adversity, with the facility of a practised versifier, and with a philosophy worthy of Epictetus.

[quotes 'Epistle to Davie', ll. 88–98]

He concludes by employing the common fable of Pegasus, to express his fatigue, and the necessity of repose from the exertion he had made; but by the strength of his conception, and his happy choice of epithets, even this hackneyed allegory gains original interest under his management. No writer could set before our eyes, with greater brevity, and at the same time with more distinctness, the picture of a jaded steed at the end of his stage.

Prior to the 'Epistle', Burns had produced 'Poor Maillie,' and 'Winter, a Dirge,' in the introductory stanza of which there is abundant proof of his talent for descriptive poetry. From these first fruits of the genius of Burns, we see that it very suddenly shot up to maturity; and that in the use of the Scottish dialect little subsequent improvement was to be expected. In one department, however, room was still left for a farther progress. By the diligent study, and frequent composition of English verse, he might have attained a wider range of expression, and have thus found more latitude for the originality of his conceptions, and the vagrancy of his fancy, in a language, through the medium of which he would have greatly extended the circle of his admirers. To this he does not appear to have paid very serious attention; and therefore, the last of his English productions, which is a prologue, written eight months before his death, evinces no remarkable accession of power, during the ten preceding years. It is a fair imitation of that style of genteel and chastened sprightliness, which is generally adopted in those dramatic addresses; but when contrasted with the humour of his other poems, it serves to confirm a remark which has frequently been made, that few can give full effect to a witty conception, unless by the language with which they are most familiar, and in which they naturally think. Many Scotchmen, in companies where they can take the aid of their own vernacular dialect, shew a rich vein of humour, which appears to desert them, when restricted to English. This, perhaps more than any constitutional or characteristic indisposition to liveliness, may be the cause why few Scotch writers have been eminent for humour. To the northern division of the empire, English is, in some measure, a foreign tongue, while Irish authors, who often excel in humour, enjoy the advantage of speaking from their cradle, and being accustomed to couch their thoughts, in the language which they are afterwards to write, with little more peculiarity than may be perceived in some of the provincial inhabitants of England. The Irish enjoy a farther advantage, in the similarity of their institutions, ecclesiastical and literary, political and legal, and of the terms and phrases connected with them, to those of the metropolitan country. On such topics a Scotchman might furnish many pleasantries, highly amusing to his countrymen, but equally dull and unmeaning to the English public, (which every subject of the empire is now ambitious of addressing,) from its total ignorance of the professional usages and technical words on which his wit might be exercised.

But to return from this digression—if we do not find in Burns indications of a regular and progressive improvement, we are certainly still farther from finding any thing of a contrary nature. 'Tam o' Shanter,' one of his latest compositions, is also one of the most perfect, and of the best sustained, in the whole collection, combining as an excellent critic has observed, the comic archness or Prior, with the terrific sublimity of Shakespeare. His minor productions nearly of the same period, such as the 'Whistle,' and the poem on *Captain Grose*, evince at least no abatement of his former humour, or ease of expression.

The humour of Burns was original and successful. He had a strong propensity to view under a ludicrous aspect, subjects which he thought zeal or superstition had invested with unnecessary or unquestionable sanctity. When beating for game, he delighted to push to the very confines of propriety, and to sport on the debatable line between sacred and profane. He was indeed scarcely excelled by Lucian himself in that species of humour which is produced by debasing objects of the most serious and solemn magnitude, to the level of easy and indifferent familiarity. In the verses on 'Dr. Hornbook,' where the poet relates his interview and social chat with Death, whose bony figure is drawn with equal drollery and correctness, how is the scythe of that dreaded Being stript of its terrors, when it only serves to suggest this homely and neighbourly address:

> Guid e'en t'ye, friend! hae ye been mawin
> When ither folk are busy sawin?

Nor is the familiarity less, when Death, like the starved Apothecary, pleads his poverty, as an excuse for following an unpopular calling.

> Folk maun do something for their bread,
> And sae maun Death.

This poem has all the excellence of which its description admits; and though humour be its ground-work, it is occasionally streaked with a vein of sublimity, as in the expression, 'It spak right howe,' and in the incident when 'The auld kirk-hammer strak the bell.' This stroke puts the train of risible emotions to flight; and suddenly introduces another, more akin to apprehension, and a recollection of the tremendous personage who had been amusing us with his jokes.

Nor was the power of Burns inferior in that description of humour which exalts insignificant things to a ludicrous dignity. Whether he addresses, or supplies language to inanimate and irrational objects, it is so suitable and unforced, and appears so gravely in earnest, as to render the fable more delusive, and the personification more credible, than is commonly the case in similar attempts. His 'Twa Dogs' exercise their reason with the most sober propriety. His *Ewe* is a sagacious and affectionate matron. His *Louse* a well-scolded intruder. His *Haggis* a fair and portly personage, whose countenance beams good humour and good cheer; and his *Toothach* an imp of torture, practised in all the arts of excruciation. On high pretensions, especially to devotional austerity, Burns had no mercy; nor on that popular weakness which lets fancied reverence for religion beget a sort of coaxing and effeminate tenderness for the person of its ministers. This appears in a variety of his poems, where he applies the scourge of irony with all the force and cordiality of Butler. Even follies which had more of his approbation do not escape entirely: and it is amusing to observe, how dexterously he contrives, by way of a nominal execution of the law, to touch, but not to wound, with the rod; for in his praises of thoughtless dissipation, there is frequently a shade of ridicule, though so thin and slight as to be scarcely perceptible.

In the lyrical effusions of Burns, we find examples of the light and airy, the plaintive and pathetic, and the animating and exalted. The few which he left of the last description are in so noble a spirit that we cannot help regretting the smallness of their number; but he was led by the old Scottish ballads, which he proposed to himself as models, into a preference of the style of Anacreon to that of Tyrtaeus. Without departing from his models, however, he found room for the admission of those tender sentiments to which his heart was always open. Separation from what we love, either by distance of time, or distance of place, is a circumstance of which the recollection most powerfully awakens that 'joy of grief' so often felt by minds of sensibility. In this feeling there is more pleasure from the certainty of what we have formerly enjoyed, than pain, from regretting that it is past. It is partly owing to the consciousness of having secured our natural portion of the blessings of life, that we can look with benignity, and even with superiority, on the young, who are enjoying them at present, but whose portion is still uncertain. This species of sentiment, in which triumph is softened by a 'not unpleasing melancholy,' Horace expresses beautifully in the following lines.

> *Ille potens sui*
> *Laetusque deget, cui licet in diem*
> *Dixisse vixi.*[1]

Or, in the spirited version of Dryden,

> Happy the man, and happy he alone,
> He who can call to-day his own,
> He who, secure within, can say
> Tomorrow do thy worst,—for I have liv'd to-day.

Sentiments akin to that which I have described, harmonizing so happily with the mixture of vivacity and pensiveness, which prevails in the Scottish airs, were also suited to the mind of Burns in which mirth and melancholy were almost co-existent. They accordingly appear, with exquisite effect, in many of his songs, as in 'Auld Lang syne,' and 'John Anderson', where the characters at once regret and exult in the mutual pleasure of former days. It was the felicity of Burns, as it is the province of genius, to exhibit the whole state of the mind by a single expression; and when the two friends recall their 'paidling in the burn,' or the old couple their 'climbing the hill together,' it is impossible not to enter into their feelings of satisfied recollection, shaded by graver thoughts, in the one case, of the troubles by which they had long been separated, and in the other, of the speedy dissolution of their union, for which a common grave is but a melancholy consolation.

In like manner, when the force of affection is softened down by the distance of its objects, to a mild and wistful tenderness of thought, which is disposed to enliven its vivacity, by laying hold of every association, it produces a sentiment congenial to the mind of the poet, and to the music of his country. This sentiment is finely brought out

[1] Horace, *Odes* III. xxix. ll. 41–3.

in 'Of a' the airts the wind can blaw,'—'I look to the west when I gae to my rest,'—'Musing on the roaring ocean,' and several more of the songs. In some, the poet surrenders himself entirely to sadness, without the slightest mixture of gaiety, as in the touching strain of 'Highland Mary,' of which it may be said, in his own words,

> O nocht but love and sorrow join'd
> Sic notes of woe could wauken.

Here the vein of grief is pure from any harsh or reproachful emotion, as he mourns no breach of affection, but merely a blow of Providence. But in the 'Banks of Doon,' a tone of accusation is mingled with that of complaint; and in 'Had I a cave on some wild distant shore,' he rises to a burst of despair so indignant, that for the perfidy of a single individual, he would abandon the whole of her species. He can thus vary the note of amatory anguish, without any failure of execution.

In personating more fortunate lovers, he shows no less ability, and acquaintance with all the shapes and shades of his subject. Whether he pour forth effusions of impassioned admiration, vows of fidelity, or fears for the safety of their object; and whether he assume the male or female character, his expressions are so penetrating and faithful to nature, as to show that his experience in the first of these characters, and his observation of the last, had been equally extensive and exact.

When he gives exclusive indulgence to his perception of the ludicrous, his representations are as amusing by their variety, as they are admirable for their comic truth. In 'Duncan Gray,' we see the fear of prolonging coyness beyond the prudent point, and in 'Last May a braw wooer,' the operation of jealousy, in a vulgar mind, exhibited with amusing archness; while in 'Whistle o'er the lave o't,' and 'Husband, husband, cease your strife,' we have specimens of nuptial antipathy, not surpassed by any thing which this fertile subject has suggested to ancient or modern epigrammatists.

Every reader must have observed with what strokes of delicate and original description, the songs, as well as the other performances of Burns are embellished; and in the former, poetical description is in its proper place, being subservient and auxiliary to sentiment. Thus, in 'Bonny lassie will ye go,' we have this fine picture:

> White o'er the linn the burnie pours,
> And rising weets wi' misty showers
> The birks of Aberfeldie.

And in 'Ca the Ewes,'

> We'll gae down by Clouden side,
> Thro' the hazels spreading wide,
> O'er the waves that sweetly glide,
> To the moon sae clearly.
> Yonder Clouden's silent towers,
> Where at moonshine midnight hours,
> O'er the dewy bending flowers
> Fairies dance sae chearly.

It were endless to enumerate the beauties of these charming ballads; but it is impossible to pass without notice the convivial songs, such as 'Willie brew'd a peck of malt,' in which the whole spirit of good fellowship seems to be concentrated; or the martial odes of 'Wallace,' and 'Farewel, thou fair day,' in which, from their vehemence and grandeur, more than in any of his other compositions, we see the poet placed on the tripod, and swelling with the Pythian afflatus.

The songs of Burns are consecrated by a popularity against the decisions of which it is idle to dispute. From the cottage to the palace, and from the Ganges to the Ohio, they are in the mouths of all by whom the British language is spoken; and the Scottish melodies are now employed to introduce the verses, as the verses formerly sung to them were employed to introduce the music.

Yet with all their excellence, it is perhaps among the songs of Burns that we shall find his least successful attempts as a poet. He seems to have tasked himself to their composition, without waiting for the moment of inspiration, or for that propitious disposition of mind and body, when ideas and expressions meet with co-operating fluency. From those, for example, beginning, 'O saw ye bonny Leslie,' and 'Oh saw ye my dear, my Phely,' had they been anonymous, we should certainly have been led to form no high idea of the powers of the writer. Many of the songs, too, which would have appeared delightful, standing singly, lose a part of their charm when collected, from a monotony in their subjects, images, and thoughts. The subject, in most of them, is the praise or description of a young woman; and though the poet has done his utmost to vary his portraits, they still remain an unavoidable likeness. The recurrence of the same images is also observable. We meet with 'the rose-bud,' 'the daisy,' and the 'scented birks,' the freshness of morning, and the fairness of spring, the 'graceful air,' and the 'een of bonny blue,' with a frequency which weakens their interest: and it may be added, that the efforts of the author to diversify his asseverations of constancy, and his description of love pangs, betray him sometimes into hyperbolical adjurations, and comparisons, with which few of his readers can sympathise. Such, at least in my mind, are some passages of the verses to 'Clarinda,' and of the song 'Where braving angry winter's skies'. . .

Having been so copious in proof and in praise of the genius of Burns, I may be more easily pardoned for noticing some of his literary defects. The most striking of these was incorrectness of taste, and carelessness in exercising the judgment which he possessed. Of the thoughts which occurred to him, he did not instantly perceive, or take any pains to examine, which should be retained, and which rejected; nor could he, without reluctance, sacrifice ingenuity to a sense of decorum, which he had taught himself to deride. He surrendered himself too loosely to the stream of his reflections; and in the act of writing forgot the precaution of stating himself in the situation of a reader. The good sense which guided his conversation, would have been equally serviceable, had he chosen to consult it in guiding his composition; and if he carried in his mind the idea of reciting his poems to a company of all sexes and descriptions, many a passage of too gross and naked a character would have been suppressed. Apologists may urge, that his poems were originally written without any prospect of their publication; and that, to the circle of his acquaintance, from the rusticity of the lower class, and the libertinism of the higher, he knew, by their taste in conversation, the indelicacy of his wit would be half its charm. But it is not to be denied, that, after he had reached a distinction, which must have convinced him that whatever he wrote was written for the public, he shows little amendment, some of his latest productions being as offensive as the earliest.

He was likewise too apt to introduce into a poem, a thought which did not harmonize with the rest, and which interrupts the train of sentiment that had been previously excited. A desire to pay compliments to his friends made him sometimes choose improper and unexpected places for them, without considering how far he would be accompanied by the feelings of his reader. In this manner he disturbs the process of imagination, in the 'Brigs of Ayr,' to praise a favourite fiddler; and he injures the unity of that poem, as well as of his 'Vision,' by mixing real with fancied persons. The effect is nearly the same, as if a painter of some historical event should injudiciously compose his group of portraits of his friends, whether their phisiognomy might suit the characters or not.

In one or two passages, we see Burns grappling with an idea which appears to master him, and which, either from perplexity in the conception, or from a defect of expression, he fails to bring out with distinctness. This is always unpleasing. In works of genius, as in the works of nature, the limit of power should never appear, the imagination being thus led to conceive it much greater than its effects display. A poet should therefore abandon every idea, which he has not expressed both with clearness and with energy; because the boundaries of his ability are thus discovered, and the deception of its indefinite extent removed. Yet, in the two last lines of the following passage, Burns seems to have violated this maxim, for their meaning (to me at least) is far from being obvious:

> And when the bard or hoary sage,
> Charm or instruct the future age,
> They* bind the wild poetic rage
> In energy,
> Or point the inconclusive page
> Full on the eye.'
>
> 'Vision'.

To another stanza the same objection may be made.

> Sages their solemn een may steek,
> And raise a philosophic reek,
> And physically causes seek,
> In clime and season;
> But tell me *Whisky's* name in Greek,
> I'll tell the reason.
>
> 'Earnest Cry and Prayer'.

The bad effect of this stanza is heightened by its position between a passage of exalted pathos, and one of exquisite humour. Other instances of the same kind might be added, but I shall content myself with observing, that, on three different occasions, he endeavours to illustrate, or enliven, his meaning, by comparisons borrowed from a pack of cards, and in each, to my apprehension, he is unsuccessful; with the

---

* The *genii of Kyle*.

additional disadvantage of being compelled, by the rhyme, to pronounce the word *carts*, which to all, but the inhabitants of the south-
west Scotland, will appear a forced and arbitrary accommodation.

Burns, like Milton, Butler, and many others, was sometimes led
to display his knowledge, at the hazard of impairing the progressive
admiration of his reader. We have instances of this in his verses to
'J. S.' where he introduces the technical terms in music; and in the
poem on 'Dr. Hornbook,' where he enumerates the *materia medica* of
the Doctor's shop. He was likewise unseasonable in shewing his
acquaintance with the politics and public characters of the day; as in
the same verses to 'J. S.' where he enfeebles a very animated passage, by
introducing the names of Pitt and Dempster. Such allusions may, no
doubt, please, when they offer some striking illustration of important
characters or events; but for this apology the information of Burns
was too slight and casual; or, as Dr. Blair once observed to me, 'his
politics had too much of the smith's shop.' In several of his productions,
especially in his letters, he occasionally glances at classical and scientific
topics, with an ease and familiarity which may lead some to suspect that
he wished to gain credit for more erudition than he possessed. It must
be remembered, however, that he was an intense, though irregular
reader; and that the knowledge which he had accumulated before the
end of his life, was by no means contemptible.

In the more mechanical part of poetry, or that which relates to
rhyme and measure, Burns permitted himself to be too easily satisfied.
His rhymes, particularly in his songs, are often extremely imperfect,
and his lines sometimes eked out with expletive syllables, which are
offensive to the least fastidious ear. These defects displease the reader,
and depreciate the writer, from the same principle which was stated in
a preceding paragraph. They betray a want of power in the poet to
accomplish what he aims at, and a practical confession that his command of language is not unlimited. If rhymes are employed at all, they
ought to be exact; and, if not so, we conclude that the difficulty of
couching his meaning in the desirable form, is one which the poet was
unable to surmount. When, for example, we meet with sounds so
ill suited as *tocher* and *water*, with such abbreviations as *Caledonie*, or
with 'inspir'd bards,' feebly drawn out from three to five syllables, in
inspired bardies, we see genius driven to its shifts, and suspend that
astonishment and admiration, which we felt, while every difficulty
appeared to sink before it. It is evident that Burns had great confidence
in the facility of his versification, for he boldly undertakes any measure,

236

however arduous or complicated, and, in general, he is singularly successful.

Notwithstanding the demands of metrical convenience, both halves of his couplets are commonly of equal vigour, yet the following lines in 'Tam o' Shanter', may, perhaps, appear an exception, every idea contained in the first being, with a very unimportant difference, repeated in the second:

> Five tomahawks wi' blude red-rusted,
> Five scymitars wi' murder crusted.

Instances of imitation may be discovered in the poems of Burns, but they are neither numerous nor unpleasant. Pretenders to genius are frequently detected by their false judgments of the productions of rival artists, and by envious struggles to lower to their own level, that merit to which they perceive themselves unable to rise. But the characteristic of true genius, is to feel with vehemence, to admire with enthusiasm, and to emulate with vigour and with hope, the excellence of those who have preceded them in their favourite department. If their judgment err at all, it will probably be in ascribing, from excessive admiration of the art, an excess of merit to the artist. In Burns this mark of genius was very perceptible. His love of poetry was such as to call forth a predilection, not very justly measured, for those who, in attempting the practice of it, had shewn themselves affected by the same passion. The poets who fell first into his hands were not the best; but as they were the best he knew, he admired them with his natural ardour; and though he afterwards rose himself far beyond them, they seem to have always retained a portion of his early regard. It is commonly in imitation that genius, if preceded by any near approaches to its own conception of excellence, begins its exertions. It rises first from the ground by the aid and example of others, but, when fairly launched into the air, and made sensible of its own intrinsic buoyancy, exultation in the discovery urges it to a higher flight than had been achieved by its instructors. We need not be surprised, therefore, if in the most original poets, vestiges of imitation are occasionally observed. In Virgil they are frequent; and not less so in Milton, though he was superior in invention perhaps to all other poets. In Burns they are wonderfully rare, when we consider the comparative disadvantages under which he laboured. The great writers just mentioned were, by a regular education, in some measure bred to poetry. The best models were put into their hands: they were taught what to attempt, and what to avoid, and, above all, to beware of the servility of imitation. But Burns set out without a guide: his understanding had to discriminate and form rules for itself: and the spark of his genius, with no gentle breath to cherish it into a flame, waited to be kindled by the passing breeze. He seems always to have been conscious of a strength of talents beyond what he observed around him, but he was ignorant of its extent, and afraid to listen to the persuasions of his consciousness. While other poets, therefore, began with imitating the masters of their art, the first aspirations of Burns were to make some approximation to the songs of the *Evergreen*, or the poems of Ferguson and Ramsay. Yet, though he borrowed from these authors the form of some of his earlier compositions, the moment he began to write, and to feel the impulse of his own original powers, he scorned to be indebted to them for any thing more. Having once entered the path, which they had opened to him, he trod it in a manner entirely his own, and can no more be charged with imitation, in adopting what others had found a convenient vehicle for their thoughts, than the epic or dramatic poets who divide their works after the common example, into books or acts. It might be expected that the ideas of those authors, whom Burns had read with so voracious a relish, at an age when impressions are the strongest, should have blended themselves with his own; and when he began to write, have been insensibly produced as original notions. This has seldom happened; but in a few instances we find a resemblance to prior compositions, strong enough to justify a presumption, that it may have prodeeded from the cause which has been described. On comparing the two following quotations, the similarity of the thought is apparent.

> But gallant Roger, like a soger,
>   Stood, and bravely fought, man;
> I'm wae to tell, at last he fell,
>   But mae down wi' him brought, man.
> At point of death, wi' his last breath,
>   Some standing round in ring, man,
> On's back lying flat, he wav'd his hat,
>   And cried, God save the King, man.
>   SKIRVING.

> But bring a Scotchman frae his hill,
> Clap in his cheek a Highland gill,
> Say, such is Royal George's will,
>   And there's the foe;

238

> He has nae thought but how to kill
>   Twa at a blow.

> Nae cauld faint-hearted doubtings teaze him,
> Death comes, wi' fearless e'e he sees him;
> Wi' bluidy hand, a welcome gies him;
>   And when he fa's,
> His latest draught o' breathing lea'es him
>   In faint huzzas!
>   BURNS.

The first of these passages presents the picture of an individual, and the second that of a class. Both are highly animated; but in warmth of poetical imagery, that of Burns must be allowed the superiority.

There is a considerable similarity between the 'Elegy on Poor Mailie,' and the ballad of the 'Ewie wi' the crooked horn,' though it consists rather in the general strain and spirit of the piece, than in particular passages. The ewes of both poets seem to have been on the same footing of companionable familiarity, and objects of the same domestic tenderness.

The following lines bear a slight resemblance both in the sentiment and in the turn of expression.

> It's no the claes that we hae worn,
> Frae aff her back sae aften shorn,
> The loss o'thae we could hae born* &c.
>   SKINNER.

> It's no the loss o' warl's gear,
> That could sae bitter draw the tear, &c.
>   BURNS.

> Indeed I think that our guidwife
> Will never *get aboon't* ava.
>   SKINNER.

> His heart will never *get aboon*
> His Mailie dead.
>   BURNS.

I once asked Burns, if, in composing the passages which have been quoted, he had not been insensibly indebted to the verses which are compared with them; and he answered (if I rightly recollect) that he suspected he had.

* This ballad is quoted as it was usually sung in Ayrshire about the time of Burns's appearance.

It may be observed, that when Burns employs the English exclusively, even on sublime and serious subjects, he seems to think under constraint; and that the finest of his poems are either wholly in his native dialect, which he could wield at will, or those where he gradually slides into English, only after his fancy had been elevated to a contempt of obstruction, and his ideas had begun to flow in the channel which his mind had selected, while enjoying the utmost ease and freedom in its operations. Of this description are the 'Vision,' and the 'Cotter's Saturday Night.' It may be doubted, however, if the change, even when he excels in both styles, be altogether agreeable; as it implies an acknowledgement that English is the language best suited to the occasion, and that the best has not been uniformly adopted.

Burns once informed me, in describing his mode of composition, that having the advantage of a most exact and retentive memory, he never committed his verses to writing, till he had touched and retouched them in his mind, and had brought them to that state in which he would admit of no farther alteration. This by no means contradicts his assertion that they were 'the effect of easy composition, but of laborious correction.' It only shews that the labour was mentally performed. The same method of composing is said to have been preferred by Gray; and it is remarkable that, notwithstanding all their care, both these poets abound more than most of their eminent contemporaries, with imperfect rhimes. The ear is perhaps less scrupulous than the eye; and a false rhime may have escaped, from the attention not being called to the appearance and orthography of the words, during the process of revision.

The aversion of Burns to adopt alterations which were proposed to him, after having fully satisfied his own taste with the state of his productions, is apparent from his letters. In one passage he says, that he never accepted any of the corrections of the Edinburgh *literati*, except in the instance of a single word. If his admirers should be desirous to to know this *single word*, I am able to gratify them, as I happened to be present when the criticism was made. It was at the table of a gentleman of literary celebrity, who observed that, in two lines of the Holy Fair, beginning, 'For M—speels the holy door,' the last word, which was originally *salvation*, ought, from his description of the preacher, to be *damnation*. This change, both embittering the satire, and introducing a word to which Burns had no dislike, met with his instant and enthusiastic approbation. 'Excellent!' he cried, with great warmth. 'The alteration shall be made; and I hope you will allow me to say in a note, from whose suggestion it proceeds;' a request which the critic, with great good humour, but with equal decision, refused.[1] On the subject of correction, however, Burns was not always so inflexible as he represents himself. We see him frequently yielding to the taste of Mr. Thomson; and he bent, though with 'murmuring reluctance,' even to the 'iron justice' of Dr. Gregory.

In contemplating the genius of Burns, we are naturally disposed to consider whether it could have been successfully directed to some longer and more elaborate work than any which he has left. For various reasons, I am inclined to think that of this there was but little probability. His want of a regular education, and of those habits of periodical study, by which the mind can pause without breaking the continuity of a work, and easily resume it at the point where it had been suspended, would have been unfavourable to his prosecution of an operose or extensive design. His hours of composition were desultory and uncertain. When a favourite idea laid hold of his mind, he would cherish it, till his heated imagination threw it off in verse; and when the paroxysm ceased, he was done with it. The patient and progressive execution of an epic or dramatic work, requires an apprenticeship to the art of writing, a steady discipline of the thoughts, and a power of putting them daily in motion, from the hope of a distant reversion of fame. For such qualifications Burns was by no means remarkable. We can perceive in some of his pieces, that when he had been prevented from finishing them, during the first effervescence of fancy, his original ideas had evaporated; and before he returned to composition, the state of his mind had undergone such a change, as to render the sequel very different from what the outset had led us to expect. This is particularly observable in his 'Brigs of Ayr,' and in the 'Winter Night.' The first of these opens with a description, to which nothing superior can be found in the records of poetry. The spirits of the brigs then begin their controversy, which is no less admirable, but the altercation breaks off, and the poem makes a transition into a different strain. A train of allegorical beings are introduced in a dance upon the ice; and though this part contains some beautiful lines, yet it does not harmonize exactly with what follows; for, had the poet foreseen that his group was to contain personages of so grave and dignified a character, as Learning, Worth, and Peace, he would scarcely have engaged them in the violent and merry movements of a Strathspey.

[1] Cf. Hugh Blair's written suggestion (No. 9), p. 81.

This piece exhibits very plainly the *disjectae membra poetae*, but it is surely deficient in unity of design.

The 'Winter Night,' like the 'Brigs,' sets out with description very powerfully executed, and in language decidedly Scotch, but it passes abruptly to English, and, in my apprehension, to a tone more nearly within the compass of an ordinary poet. On this point, it is with great diffidence I allow my judgement to disagree with that of Dr. Currie; yet it has always appeared to me, that we might conceive the two different portions of this poem to be the work of different authors, or of the same author, at hours when the tide of inspiration had risen to very unequal heights. Other writers are no doubt liable to similar inequalities; but in Burns they were greater, from the superior vehemence, and proportional remission of feeling, under the pressure of which he was urged to composition. When a subject ceased to interest him strongly, it was abandoned for a new one, which possessed this power; and when he did not write with all the *vivida vis animi*, he was apt to let the vigour of his conceptions relax with the vivacity of his emotions, a circumstance which must have weakened his chance of excellence as a dramatic, or even as a didactic poet.

To this view it may be objected, that Ramsay and Bloomfield, without the habits of systematic study, have succeeded in these two departments of composition. But it would be doing Burns injustice, to reduce him to the level of either of those writers, whose genius wanted force to reach the elevation at which the former could occasionally soar, and whose humbler flight could be longer and more steadily maintained. In any species of writing, Burns would certainly have produced passages, to the splendour of which neither Ramsay nor Bloomfield could aspire; but it may be doubted whether he could have finished a work of equal length, and at the same time so uniformly supported, as the 'Gentle Shepherd,' or the 'Farmer's Boy'. A long poem becomes at times a task: and from some of the songs of Burns, which he obliged himself to compose, even under unpropitious circumstances, we may perceive marks of compulsory exertion, by which, if they had occurred in a longer essay, the effect of the finer passages would have been impaired.

In making these remarks, I am led to conjecture what alterations might have been produced on the character and destiny of the poet, if he had been regularly trained as a man of letters. It may, at first sight, have an air of paradoxical absurdity to compare the dissipated and irreverent ploughman of Kyle, with the strict and orthodox moralist of

Litchfield; yet, on farther consideration, the absurdity will perhaps be diminished. In the radical characters of Burns and JOHNSON, there were some points of close resemblance; and though they terminated in a wide disparity, yet we must remember that a slight deviation at the centre becomes great at the circumference; and that, at their outset, they were turned into paths which took a direction almost diametrically opposite. Both were endowed by nature with the same intellectual grasp, with the same richness of imagination, the same tenacity of memory, the same appetite for knowledge, the same preference of exploring human nature, the same colloquial supremacy, the same atrabilious temperament, the same desire to resist it by convivial exertion, the same stern independence, the same national partiality, and the same violence of passion and obstinacy of prejudice. Had Burns spent his boyhood in the shop of a bookseller, or among the members of a cathedral; had he afterwards removed to college with nothing to depend upon, but regularity of conduct and force of application; and had he finally, with all the power of talent this acquired, become a daily labourer in the literary vineyard, it seems by no means unlikely, that the natural resemblance which has been stated, might have been confirmed and increased by the operation of similar causes. In poetry, both humorous and pathetic, he would certainly have been superior to Johnson, and probably equal to him in prose. His conversation would have been distinguished by a piercing insight into the heart, and by pointed and luminous expression; and that predominance which he would have enjoyed, he might have had no scruple occasionally to exert, with tyrannical severity, on an opponent. Neither does it seem at all impossible, that his dark and luxuriant sensibility, under the constant check of learned and virtuous society, and of principles or prejudices derived from early discipline, might have overflown in devotional ardour, religious terrors, and jealous predelictions for the national church, and for the ecclesiastical order of which he would probably have been a member. On the other hand, to borrow illustration from reversing the picture, had Johnson been bred among the lowest peasantry of a district where the prevalence of illicit trade had almost annihilated all medium between a total debauchery of moral feeling, and a puritanical austerity, in which reflecting minds could with difficulty acquiesce, I see little to prevent the supposition that he might have been as remarkable as Burns for extraordinary strength, and frequent misdirection, of native intellect. By some it may be thought that the devotion of Burns to female beauty would have disturbed this process;

but it appears, from all the views of Johnson's character, which we have received, that his appetites were as gross, and his passions as importunate, as those of the poet, though various causes had enabled him to govern them with greater power. Burns indeed was more favoured in personal appearance, and had acquired, by early practice, more of that insinuating gaiety and tenderness, which wind their way to the hearts of the fair; but if he had been immured till twenty-five within the monastic precincts of a college, the shyness and awkwardness, so common in professional scholars, would have diminished his qualifications for a companionable intercourse with women, and his pride would have deterred him from soliciting their favour, while conscious that the disgrace of a repulse was so probable. Even if this had not been its effect, a gallantry begun so late, and under such restraints as have been supposed, would only have supplied that gentleness, in which Johnson was deficient, and might have polished the surface, without altering the substance of the character. We know that, like the strongest plants, the most decided minds preserve, with singular obstinacy, the flexure which art or accident has given them; and I can therefore think it no extravagant conjecture, that the congenial vigour of these two extraordinary men, might, under similar training, in some essential points, have assumed a similar appearance.

The train of reflection having led me to compare Burns with one great modern writer, I am tempted to indulge myself a little farther in this mode of illustration, and to measure him with another, where the parallel will be conducted more by contrariety than by resemblance.

BURNS and COWPER may be regarded as contemporary; for, though the former was much younger than his brother-bard, yet the genius of both burst forth upon the world nearly about the same period. The 'Task' was published in 1784, and the poems of Burns in 1786. Seldom has a greater contrast been exhibited, than by these two masterly writers, in many prominent circumstances of condition and character. Cowper, descended of high and literary lineage, had all the advantage of a careful and complete education: Burns, sprung from the most sordid hovel of a peasant, was deprived, by poverty and accident, of the measure of instruction which even peasants enjoy. The latter was vigorous and robust in body, and in spirit hardy, intrepid, and independent: the former, with a delicate and distempered frame, was timid to excess, tremblingly alive to his own defects, and so dependent for aid, that he leant on the support of elderly females, as beings stronger than himself. Burns was eager to indulge his powers of conversation, even in tumultuous and intemperate scenes: Cowper shrunk from the eye of man, and preferred burying those high endowments of which he was conscious, to encountering even the most correct and gentle society. The former ridiculed every species of fanaticism with a force so unsparing, as scarcely to avoid the sacred root from which these fantastic branches spring: The latter was so impressed by the power of religion, as to let it frequently overwhelm him with visionary terrors, which are the offspring of fanaticism. The one, after an early blaze of reputation, rushed into dangerous pleasures with an ardour which destroyed, in the middle of his career, a constitution apparently formed for long duration. The other, by flying even from the most innocent gratifications, lengthened out a life which was always precarious, and reserved sufficient vigour to earn all his fame at its close. Burns was like a river that sparkles over rocks and rapids, but is soon exhausted by its own impetuosity: Cowper, like a quiet stream, that by long husbanding its scanty strength, in a silent subterraneous channel, comes forth, at last, with unexpected beauty, into open day.

Yet, with all these disparities, their genius possessed many features in common. Both derived the most ardent enjoyment from the sublime and beautiful spectacles of nature, and possessed a peculiar capacity of analysing their delight, by fixing at once on the minute and circumstantial appearances from which it sprung, and both had the power of portraying, in poetical language, the objects which had caused them:— Burns, by a few daring and decisive strokes, and Cowper, by patient touches of more softness, delicacy, and grace. Both seem to have been chiefly enamoured of creation in its wintry attire, and have succeeded with most felicity in catching the characteristics of that gloomy season: Burns delighting in the awful honours of the nocturnal tempest; and Cowper, in all that is pleasing and picturesque in the morning without doors, or soothing and secluded in the evening within. Both felt the acutest sentiment of tenderness for the animal tribes, and strongly interposed their voice for the innocent and persecuted: Burns, in the tone of indignant execration, and Cowper, in that of mild complaint. Both took penetrating views of human character, and their veneration for what worth it possesses, gave them a satirical tendency against its vicious errors, but still preserving the original difference of their characters, it shews itself in Burns with a vigorous coarseness, and in Cowper with an arch and polished *naiveté*. Both were singularly happy in conceiving and in delineating the domestic delights to which they had been severally accustomed; and it is difficult to say whether the interior of Burns's *Cottage*, or of Cowper's *Drawing Room*, has most admirers. They are exquisite pictures, and each most fortunately suited to the pencil which it engaged. Both had a rich vein of humour, and the power of depicting ludicrous manners; as the pleasuring cit of Cowper, and the revelling beggars of Burns, will testify to ages; but, owing to the difference of their taste and education, the former is uniformly chaste in his playfulness, while the latter shews a constant propensity to overstep the bounds of decency.

To illustrate this parallel, some passages from each may be compared. In the following we see the poets describe themselves in the same state of grave and almost involuntary rumination, or in that *twilight* of the mind which corresponded with the dubious illumination of the scene.

First when our drawing-rooms begin to blaze,

——My pleasures too begin. But me, perhaps,
The glowing hearth may satisfy awhile
With faint illumination, that uplifts
The shadow to the ceiling, there by fits
Dancing uncouthly to the quiv'ring flame.
Nor undelightful is an hour to me
So spent in parlour twilight: Such a gloom
Suits well the thoughtful or unthinking mind,
The mind contemplative, with some new theme
Pregnant, or indispos'd alike to all.——

Me oft has fancy, ludicrous and wild,
Sooth'd with a walking dream of houses, towers,
Trees, churches, and strange visages, express'd
In the red cinders, while with poring eye
I gaz'd, myself creating what I saw.
Nor less amus'd, have I, quiescent, watched
The sooty films that play upon the bars,
Pendulous, and foreboding, in the view
Of superstition, prophesying still,
Though still deceiv'd, some stranger's near approach.

COWPER.

——Whan the day had clos'd his e'e,
    Far i' the west,
Ben i' the *spence* right pensively,
    I gaed to rest.
There lanely, by the ingle cheek,
I sat and eyed the spewing reek,

246

That filled wi' hoast-provoking smeek,
  The auld clay biggin,
An' heard the restless rattons squeak
  About the riggin.
All in this motlie, misty clime,
I backward mus'd on wasted time, &c.

BURNS.

The circumstances in both descriptions are finely selected, yet so different amid their similarity, that we can never forget the difference of the poets, either in point of situation; the one appearing in all the *grossierté* of his hovel, and the other in the simple neatness of his parlour; or, in point of character, the innocence of the one rendering his musings tranquil and playful, and the indignant ambition and past imprudence of the other, often leading his mind to self-accusing disquietude.

The poets thus express, each in his own peculiar manner, their opinion of the friendship of fashionable females:

——They are happiest who dissemble best
Their weariness, and they the most polite
Who squander time and treasure with a smile
Even at their own destruction. She that asks
Her dear five hundred friends, contemns them all,
And hates their coming. They, what can they less?
Make just reprisals, and with cringe and shrug,
With bow obsequious, hide their hate of her.

COWPER.

But gentlemen and ladies warst,
Wi' evendown want o' wark are curst,
They loiter, lounging, lank, and lazy,
Tho' deil haet ails them, yet uneasy.
——The ladies arm in arm in clusters,
As great and gracious a' as sisters:
But hear their absent thoughts o' ither,
They're a' run deils and jades thegither.
Whyles, o'er the wee bit cup and platie,
They sip the scandal potion pretty;
Or lee-lang night wi' crabbit leuks,
Pore owre the devil's pictur'd beuks;
Stake on a chance a farmer's stack-yard,
An' cheat like onie unhang'd blackguard.

BURNS.

247

We may compare their manner of introducing the same picturesque object in the following passages:

> The red-breast warbles still, but is content
> With slender notes and more than half suppress'd,
> Pleas'd with his solitude, and flitting light
> From spray to spray, where'er he rests, he shakes
> From many a twig the pendent drops of ice,
> That tinkle in the wither'd leaves below.
>
> COWPER.

> Nae mair the grove with airy concert rings,
> Except perhaps the robin's whistling glee,
> Proud o' the height o' some bit half-lang tree.
>
> BURNS.

To these the reader may add (for the passages are too well known to require quotation) a comparison of the tame-hare, and the woodman's dog of Cowper, with the wounded hare and the shepherd's dog of Burns; and of the delineations of winter scenery with which the works of both abound. From the whole of this estimate, it will probably appear that Burns excels Cowper in genius, less than he is excelled in taste. If therefore the admirers of the one be superior in zeal, those of the other are probably superior in number; both having many friends, but Cowper no foes. The latter, it may likewise be added, writing under a deep conviction of his own demerits, delights to enumerate, with grateful humility, and to dwell on, every little pleasing circumstance of his condition; while Burns, under a contrary impression, betrays, in the effusions of his genius, a stern and haughty discontent with a portion so unworthy of his claims and capacity of enjoyment. The comparison shall be closed by remarking, that both its celebrated subjects occasionally indulge in relaxing the elaboration of their compositions, and sliding into a carelessness which renders some passages very unequal to the excellence of the rest.

46. William Peebles on 'Burnomania'

1811

'Burns Renowned', verse in [William Peebles], *Burnomania: The Celebrity of Robert Burns Considered: In a Discourse Addressed to All Real Christians of Every Denomination. To which are Added, Epistles in Verse, Respecting Peter Pindar, Burns, &c.* (Edinburgh, 1811).

Peebles had been mentioned in several of Burns's satires. In the advertisement to this pamphlet he described 'Peter Pindar' [John Wolcot, 1738–1819] and Burns as 'brother bards of immortality and infamy' (see Introduction, p. 35).

BURNS RENOWNED

Fools make a mock of Sin

Say not, my Friend, there's surely merit,
Superior genius and spirit;
Wit, fancy, music's in the page;
How else explain the ton, the rage?
Alas! we do not understand
Where merit lies, by the demand:
Profanity, the merest trash,
Obscenity and balderdash,
Have venders, purchasers, inspirers;
Have imitators, friends, admirers.

Demanded by the man of fun,
The laughter roars, and has a run:
Ask'd, or not ask'd, the looser scribe,
Or of the prose or rhyming tribe,
Is read, devoured; and money flows
For worse than worthless verse and prose.
And thus the sober-minded mourns:
A Wilkes, a Pindar, Paine, and Burns,
Have venders, purchasers, inspirers,
Have imitators, friends, admirers.

And do you grudge the ploughman's praise,
The Bard of Scotland's far-famed lays;
The man of humour, wit and fun,
Rewards confer'd and honours won;
Whom Caledonia's Hunt of Squires,
Ev'n first nobility, admires;
By fairest ladies brought in view,
By clergymen, and poets too?

Patience a little. Imprimatur
I'll grant your bard for raising laughter;
For wit and humour, to be sure:
Even nonsense' self we might endure,
Quaintly deck'd up in prose and rhyme,
The waste of genius and time.
We might endure, but cannot prize,
Ill nature, impudence, and lies;
Malice that bites in midst of laughing,
And wears the mark of harmless daffing.

But can we bear, and hold the faith,
Sporting with Heaven, and Hell, and Death,
Degrading holy writ; his dreaming
Profanely; and awake blaspheming?

Such vileness sure in darkness lurks;
No, Sir, it shines in splendid works:
Such infamy is no disgrace,
Shameless, it stares you in the face.
—His race is run: the hero dies:
What heaving breasts! what streaming eyes!
The collegies Ambubaiarum
O'er Scotland sound the sad alarum,
Thro' many an elegiac strain,
We ne'er shall see his like again.
Nor is this all: a tribute just
To the great bard, erect a Bust:
Nor is this all: from age to age,
As for a monarch, hero, sage,
Let anniversaries repeat
His glories, celebrate a fete
Imbibe his spirit, sing his songs,
Extol his name, lament his wrongs,
His death deplore, accuse his fate,
And raise him far above the great.

What call you this? Is it Insania?
I'll coin a word, 'tis Burnomania.
His Greenock friends we therefore dub
The Annual Burnomanian Club.

47. The first book on Burns's poetry

1812

Extracts from [G. Gleig], *A Critique on the Poems of Robert Burns* (Edinburgh, 1812), pp. iii, 1–3, 29, 45, 66, 70. This anonymous book, the first on Burns's poetry, was written for a wide public (see Introduction, p. 36).

The author was George Gleig (1753–1840), a Scottish Episcopalian divine who had written on many subjects in periodicals and edited supplementary volumes of the *Encyclopaedia Britannica*.

[Advertisement iii] Nothing like philosophical criticism has been here attempted. If the country gentleman, the farmer, the artisan, and all those who have moved in the same sphere with the poet, shall be led to look into themselves for the truth of these pictures which he has painted in such vivid colours, the object of this publication will be completely answered ... [iv] The philosophical critic and the man of taste are again requested to observe, that no attempt is here made to instruct *them*; and that the sole object of the present publication is to enable men of less cultivated minds to instruct themselves, by the aid of engravings, illustrative of the poetry.

[1–3] Among modern poets, it would be difficult to mention one who has displayed greater originality of genius than BURNS, the Ayrshire Ploughman. The range of his thoughts was not indeed very extensive, nor were the subjects on which he wrote greatly varied; for as the most powerful genius cannot create one simple idea, but must content itself

251

with making different combinations of those which are treasured up in the memory, an illiterate bard, who has not stored his mind by travel and attentive observation, has comparatively but a small number of materials on which to work. Such a bard, however, may possess, in the highest degree, the talents essential to his art.

The province of poetry is to describe, in vivid colours, nature and passion; and the most illiterate man, of a vigorous mind, may describe with accuracy such scenes of nature as he has seen, and such passions as he has experienced either in himself or in others; but he must do more than this to be entitled to the honour of a poet. In genuine poetry, there is something analogous to creation, or at least to the reduction of chaos into form. To describe only individual scenes, is to write *natural history* rather than *poetry*. The poet must be able to analyse the ideas of individual scenes into their constituent parts; to combine these parts into new forms—possible, however, in themselves, and analogous to what he has actually witnessed; and to exhibit, in a striking point of view, the effects as he has known to flow from them, but all such effects as they are naturally capable of producing.

All this may be done by an illiterate poet who has never travelled, as well as by him who has had the benefit of a liberal education, and made the tour of Europe: but it is obvious that the range of the former must be much more limited that the range of the latter. His descriptions, however, if not so varied, may be more vivid; for the learned poet is too apt to intermix what he has read or heard with what he has seen; and the copy of a copy can never produce the same powerful effect with a faithful painting from nature.

Had Burns attempted to paint the face of a country quite different from any that he had ever seen, or to describe the manners of courtiers, he would certainly have failed; or had he possessed, on the other hand, the advantages of a liberal education, it may be doubted whether his language would have been so perfectly adapted to the description of those scenes, with which alone he was thoroughly acquainted. But, by selecting all his subjects from low life as it actually presented itself to his own eyes, and writing in the very language which is spoken by the heroes and heroines of his poems, his powerful imagination has produced an effect, on the mind of every man of taste to whom his language is intelligible, similar to that which his latest biographer, and one of the most judicious of his critics,[1] has declared that the first perusal of his poems produced on him . . .

[1] Josiah Walker.

[29] 'The Vision' has often been mentioned as one of the most elevated of BURNS's poems; and to this character it is perhaps justly entitled, but it is not one of his happiest effusions ... He likewise describes her [Coila's] dress and appearance with great propriety; but he seems to have viewed herself and her actions, to use the words of Dryden, 'through the spectacles of books.'

[45] The 'Saturday Night' is indeed universally felt as the most interesting of all the author's poems.

[66] To attempt to ascertain the particular merit of each of BURNS's Songs would be an endless task. They are on various subjects, and, by the lovers of music, are all admired. Like his other poems, they exhibit such views of their several subjects, whether gay, humorous, or sad, that the reader of taste and feeling fancies everything, of which he is reading, presented to his view.

[70] There are scattered through [the poems] a few images which the more serious reader may reasonably wish away.

48. Henry Crabb Robinson on Burns

1812–29

Extracts from *Henry Crabb Robinson on Books and their Writers*, ed. Edith J. Morley (1938).

Henry Crabb Robinson (1775–1867), journalist and barrister, took a keen interest in poets, especially Goethe and Wordsworth. These are diary entries.

(a) I, pp. 88–9. 29 May 1812

Wordsworth talked very freely of poetry. He praised Burns for his introduction to 'Tam o' Shanter.' He had given a poetical apology for drunkenness by bringing together all the circumstances which can serve to render excusable what is in itself disgusting, thus interesting our feelings and making us tolerant of what would otherwise be not endurable:

[quotes 'Tam o' Shanter', ll. 45–58]

Wordsworth also praised the conclusion of 'Death and Dr. Hornbook'. Wordsworth compared this with the abrupt prevention of the expected battle between Satan and the Archangel in Milton; but this remark did not bring its own evidence with it. I took occasion to apply the praise given to Burns for the passage quoted to Goethe, and this led to my warm praise of him.

(b) I, p. 106. 10 August 1812

In the evening a call at Morgan's. Left books for Coleridge, and then spent two hours very pleasantly with Aders. Read with him Burns's

'Vision' and Goethe's 'Zueignung', the resemblance between which is very striking. It is no slight honour to Burns to have put himself within the reach of a comparison with the great Goethe. And certainly Goethe would recognize a kindred soul in Burns, if not in his earnest and senti-mental, at least in his satirical and wanton pieces. Goethe's 'Zueignung' is exquisitely and elaborately wrought with every grace of verse and style. Burns's 'Vision' is tender and significant. Both of the poets were alike sensible of [their] own worth, though Burns is guilty of a little affectation in placing himself below such an inferior writer as Shenstone. They belong to the most delightful writings of the respective authors. Aders enjoyed heartily 'Tam o' Shanter' and 'Holy Willie's Prayer', etc. I also read to Aders some of Wordsworth, which he did not seem to relish so heartily.

(c) I, p. 182. 16 May 1816

Went to Islington. There I read to the ladies [Mrs. Barbauld and Miss Aikin] Wordsworth's letter on Dr. Currie's *Life of Burns*. Wordsworth is a pure man, and therefore his indulgence for the irregularities of Burns is most amiable. His censure of the exposure as far as Dr. Currie is concerned, at least, just in its general principle, and the moral feeling and delicate taste displayed in this pamphlet are equally delightful.

(d) I, p. 184. 28 May 1816

Godwin is not satisfied with Wordsworth's letter on Burns. It is not disquisitional. Godwin would have written an acute disputation on the evil or good of saying all the evil of great men, which can be said of them with truth. Wordsworth's pamphlet develops a generous feeling only in their favour, and would cover as with a mantle the infirmities of men of great intellectual powers who have rendered themselves objects of admiration to the public.

(e) I, p. 220. 24 February 1818

Heard part of a lecture by Hazlitt at the Surrey Institution. Hazlitt was so contemptuous towards Wordsworth, speaking of his letter about Burns, that I lost my temper and hissed; but I was on the outside of the room. I was led to burst into declamations against Hazlitt which I afterwards regretted, though I uttered nothing but the truth. Hazlitt abused Wordsworth in a vulgar style, imputing to him the mere desire of representing himself as a superior man. I hurried away to attend Mrs. Smith to Coleridge's lecture.

(f) I, p. 223. 10 June 1818

I read in Hazlitt's lectures to-night—the one on Burns, which I heard in part only. He has justly distinguished between the sensual character of Burns, and the moral delicacy of Wordsworth; but it is amusing to observe how the animal vigour of the Scotch peasant is eulogized as if this were glory as well as felicity, while the purity and delicacy of the Philosopher of the Lakes is sneered at as a sort of impotence, and the remarks on Wordsworth's letter about Burns are false and malignant. His strictures on the old ballads are commonplace and insignificant.

(g) I, p. 356. 20 May 1828

I read to-day and within a few days Lockhart's *Life of Burns*, which he meant to be a popular and useful (edifying) work, but he has made it only dull. The fine extracts from Wordsworth's letter to Mr. Gray are like gems adorning a vulgar dress. The book is a spiritless compilation.

(h) I, p. 367. 2 August 1829

[Goethe] was friendly to a degree I cannot account for . . . I inquired concerning his knowledge of Burns. He has no knowledge of the

'Vision'. A most remarkable coincidence between that poem and the 'Zueignung'. Goethe made inquiries of the taste for German literature in England, and I informed him of the several translations as well as of the sudden turn in the *Edinburgh Review*. He evidently enjoyed the prospect of his own extended reputation.

49. Byron on Burns

1813

Extracts from Byron's journal. *Works of Lord Byron, Letters and Journals*, ed. R. E. Prothero (1898), II, pp. 320, 375–7 (see Nos 38, 61 and Introduction, p. 27).

(a) 16 November 1813

Read Burns to-day. What would he have been, if a patrician? We should have had more polish—less force—just as much verse, but no immortality—a divorce and a duel or two, the which had he survived, as his potations must have been less spirituous, he might have lived as long as Sheridan, and outlived as much as poor Brinsley. What a wreck is that man! and all from bad pilotage; for no one had ever better gales, though now and then a little too squally. Poor dear Sherry!

(b) 13 December 1813

Allen . . . has lent me a quantity of Burns's unpublished and never-to-be-published Letters.[1] They are full of oaths and obscene songs. What

[1] John Allen, M.D. (1771–1843).

an antithetical mind!—tenderness, roughness—delicacy, coarseness—
sentiment, sensuality—soaring and grovelling, dirt and deity—all mixed
up in that one compound of inspired clay!

It seems strange; a true voluptuary will never abandon his mind to
the grossness of reality. It is by exalting the earthly, the material, the
physique of our pleasures, by veiling these ideas, by forgetting them
altogether, or, at least, never naming them hardly to one's self, that we
alone can prevent them from disgusting.

50. Scott on Burns

1813–30

See No. 40 and Introduction, pp. 30–3.

(a) To Lord Byron, 6 November 1813. *Letters of Sir Walter Scott*,
ed. H. J. C. Grierson, W. M. Parker and others, 12 vols (1932–7),
III, *1811–1814*, p. 375

The author of the 'Queen's Wake' [James Hogg] will be delighted with
your approbation. He is a wonderful creature for his opportunities, which
were far inferior to those of the generality of Scottish peasants. Burns,
for instance—(not that their extent of talents is to be compared for an
instant)—had an education not much worse than the sons of many
gentlemen in Scotland. But poor Hogg literally could neither read nor
write till a very late period of his life; and when he first distinguished
himself by his poetical talent, could neither spell nor write grammar.

(b) To an unknown correspondent [J. Forbes Mitchell, about the Calton Hill Monument to Burns in Edinburgh?], 3 April 1819. *Ibid.*, V, *1817–1819*, pp. 334–5

I have an high value for the Genius of Burns & beg of you to put me down for five pounds. I wish I could give more with propriety. I heartily subscribe to the opinion that such a notice should be taken of departed Genius, but why should not the thing go farther? We might annually & at no great expense offer a similar tribute of respect to a countryman distinguished for Speculation or Action. There are many who have such a claim on us not only for the Genius they have displayed but for the beneficial & widely extended benefits they have conferred on Mankind. I might mention Smith the Author of the *Wealth of Nations*, Robertson our Classical Historian, Robinson whose talents were of an high order & very many others. A classical Memorial of such men would do us honour—A monument, a statue or even a head, would be sufficient. Let me add that while we offer this tribute to the Poet his son should not be forgotten for I am told he is poor, moral & industrious. But I have already said much more than I intended.

(c) Undated MS. note printed in *Works of Lord Byron, Letters and Journals*, ed. R. E. Prothero (1898), II, p. 376n

Burns, in depth of poetical feeling, in strong shrewd sense to balance and regulate this, in the *tact* to make his poetry tell by connecting it with the stream of public thought and the sentiment of the age, in *commanded* wildness of fancy and profligacy or recklessness as to moral and *occasionally* as to religious matters, was much more like Lord Byron than any other person to whom Lord B. says he had been compared.

A gross blunder of the English public has been talking of Burns as if the character of his poetry ought to be estimated with an eternal recollection that he was a *peasant*. It would be just as proper to say that Lord Byron ought always to be thought of as a *Peer*. Rank in life was nothing to either in his true moments. Then, they were both great Poets. Some silly and sickly affectation connected with the accidents of birth and breeding may be observed in both, when they are not under the influence of 'the happier star.' Witness Burns's prate about independence, when he was an exciseman, and Byron's ridiculous pretence of Republicanism, when he never wrote sincerely about the Multitude without expressing or insinuating the very soul of scorn.

(d) [10 February 1826]. *The Journal of Sir Walter Scott 1825–26*, ed. J. G. Tait (1939), p. 96

This was the man [Byron]—quaint, capricious, and playful, with all his immense genius. He wrote from impulse never from effort and therefore I have always reckoned Burns and Byron the most genuine poetical geniuses of my time and half a century before me. We have however many men of high poetical talent but none of that ever-gushing, and perennial fountain of natural water.

(e) [11 December 1826]. *Ibid.*, p. 290

Long life to thy fame and peace to thy soul, Rob Burns! When I want to express a sentiment which I feel strongly, I find the phrase in Shakespeare—or thee.

(f) To John Richardson, 26 July 1827. *Letters*, X *1826–1828*, p. 264

... [a play about] a Scotch Mephistophiles an incarnation of evil modified according to the peculiar ideas of the people of Scotland at the beginning of the 18th century ... would have been a task for Burns broad pencil which could throw in comic touches among the deepest tragic colouring & was not very strait laced either in thought or expression.

(g) To J. G. Lockhart, 4 March 1828. *Ibid.*, p. 393

I think curious light might be thrown on Burns life from some of his fragments of songs which he threw off like sparkles from a flint when anything struck him. Thus when he was finishing his house at Ellisland he set off with the line of a happy & contented man.

I have a house o' my ain

feeling all the manly consequences as a householder and a husband which a settlement in life which might have been expected to be permanent inspired him with.

(h) 1828. [Scott wrote to Lockhart on 10 April 1827, 'I have some curious untouched matter respecting Burns which I send you inclosed' (*Letters*, X *1826–1828*, p. 185). Lockhart first published the passage in his *Life of Burns* (1828). Text here from J. G. Lockhart, *Life of Scott* (Edinburgh, 1902), pp. 150–2.]

As for Burns, I may truly say, *Virgilium vidi tantum*. I was a lad of fifteen in 1786–7, when he came first to Edinburgh, but had sense and feeling enough to be much interested in his poetry, and would have given the world to know him; but I had very little acquaintance with any literary people, and still less with the gentry of the west country, the two sets that he most frequented. Mr. Thomas Grierson was at that time a clerk of my father's. He knew Burns, and promised to ask him to his lodgings to dinner, but had no opportunity to keep his word, otherwise I might have seen more of this distinguished man. As it was, I saw him one day at the late venerable Professor Fergusson's, where there were several gentlemen of literary reputation, among whom I remember the celebrated Mr. Dugald Stewart. Of course we youngsters sate silent, looked and listened. The only thing I remember which was remarkable in Burns' manner, was the effect produced upon him by a print of Bunbury's, representing a soldier lying dead in the snow, his dog sitting in misery on the one side, on the other his widow, with a child in her arms. These lines were written beneath,—

> Cold on Canadian hills, or Mindens' plain,
> Perhaps that parent wept her soldiers slain:
> Bent o'er her babe, her eye dissolved in dew,
> The big drops, mingling with the milk he drew,
> Gave the sad presage of his future years,
> The child of misery baptized in tears.

Burns seemed much affected by the print, or rather the ideas which it suggested to his mind. He actually shed tears. He asked whose the lines were, and it chanced that nobody but myself remembered that they occur in a half-forgotten poem of Langhorne's, called by the unpromising title of 'The Justice Of The Peace.' I whispered my information to a friend present, who mentioned it to Burns, who rewarded me with a look and a word, which, though of mere civility, I then received, and still recollect, with very great pleasure.

His person was strong and robust: his manners rustic, not clownish; a sort of dignified plainness and simplicity, which received part of its effect perhaps from one's knowledge of his extraordinary talents. His features are represented in Mr. Nasmyth's picture, but to me it conveys the idea that they are diminished as if seen in perspective. I think his countenance was more massive than it looks in any of the portraits. I would have taken the poet, had I not known what he was, for a very sagacious country farmer of the old Scotch school—i.e. none of your modern agriculturists, who keep labourers for their drudgery, but the *douce gudeman* who held his own plough. There was a strong expression of sense and shrewdness in all his lineaments; the eye alone, I think, indicated, the poetical character and temperament. It was large, and of a dark cast, and glowed (I say literally *glowed*) when he spoke with feeling or interest. I never saw such another eye in a human head, though I have seen the most distinguished men in my time. His conversation expressed perfect self-confidence, without the slightest presumption. Among the men who were the most learned of their country, he expressed himself with perfect firmness, but without the least intrusive forwardness; and when he differed in opinion, he did not hesitate to express it firmly, yet at the same time with modesty. I do not remember any part of his conversation distinctly enough to be quoted, nor did I ever see him again, except in the street, where he did not recognise me, as I could not expect he should. He was much caressed in Edinburgh, but (considering what literary emoluments have been since his day) the efforts for his relief were extremely trifling.

I remember on this occasion I mention, I thought Burns' acquaintance with English poetry was rather limited, and also, that having twenty times the abilities of Allan Ramsay and Ferguson, he talked of them with too much humility as his models; there was doubtless national predilection in his estimate.

(i) To J. G. Lockhart, [c. 5–9 June 1828]. *Letters* X *1826–1828*, p. 427

... [the *Life of Burns*] has done you infinite credit. I could give you very good authority where you & I seem to differ but you have chosen the wiser and better view and Burns had a right to have his frailties spared especially *post tantum temporis*. All people applaud it ... A new edition will immediately be wanted.

(j) To J. G. Lockhart, 4 August 1828. *Ibid.*, p. 482

I enclose a letter of Burns to that singular old curmudgeon Lady Winnifred Maxwell or Constable [letter of 16 December 1789] one of the most extravagant figures I ever saw. You will see he plays High Jacobite and on that account the letter is curious. I imagine though his Jacobitism belonged like my own to the fancy rather than the feelings. He was however a great Pittite down to a certain period. [See J. De L. Ferguson, *Letters of Robert Burns* (1931), I, pp. 376–7; II, p. 345.]

(k) To the Earl of Elgin, 20 January 1829. *Ibid.*, XI *1828–1831*, p. 99

The task which Mr. G. [Greenshields] is full of at present seems to be chosen on a false principle,—chiefly adopted from a want of acquaintance with the genuine and proper object of art. The public of Edinburgh have been deservedly amused and delighted with two figures in the characters of Tam o'Shanter and his drunken companion Souter Johnny. The figures were much and justly applauded, and the exhibition being of a kind adapted to every taste, is daily filled. I rather think it is the success of this piece by a man much in his own circumstances, which has inclined Mr. Greenshields to propose cutting a group of grotesque figures from the 'Beggar's Cantata' of the same poet. Now, in the first place, I suspect six figures will form too many for a sculptor to group to advantage. But besides, I deprecate the attempt at such a subject. I do not consider caricature as a proper style for sculpture at all. We have Pan and his Satyrs in ancient sculpture, but the place of these characters in the classic mythology gives them a certain degree of dignity. Besides this, 'the gambol has been shown.' Mr. Thom has produced a group of this particular kind, and instead of comparing what Greenshields might do in this way with higher models, the public would certainly regard him as the rival of Mr. Thom, and give Mr. Thom the preference, on the same principle that the Spaniard says when one man walks first, all the rest must be his followers. At the same time I highly approved of one figure in the group, I mean that of Burns himself. Burns (taking his more contemplative moments) would indeed be a noble study, and I am convinced Mr. G. would do it nobly —as, for example, when Coila describes him as gazing on a snow-storm,—

> I saw grim Nature's visage hoar
> Strike thy young eye.

I suppose it is possible to represent rocks with icicles in sculpture.

Upon the moment I did not like to mention to Mr. G. my objections against a scheme which was obviously a favourite one, but I felt as I did when my poor friend John Kemble threatened to play Falstaff. In the short, the perdurable character of sculpture—the grim and stern severity of its productions,—their size too, and their consequences, confine the art to what is either dignified and noble, or beautiful and graceful: it is, I think, inapplicable to situations of broad humour. A painting of Teniers is very well—it is of a moderate size, and only looked at when we choose; but a group of his drunken boors dancing in stone, as large as life, to a fiddler at the bottom of a drawing-room, would, I think, be soon found intolerable bad company.

['Tam O'Shanter and Soutar Johnny are now exhibiting at No. 40, St. Andrew Square. These Statues are the production of Mr. Thom, a native of Ayrshire, a self-taught Artist, and are intended to be placed on Burns's Monument, near Alloway Kirk . . . These Statues have now been visited by upwards of Nine Thousand of the Inhabitants of Edinburgh'. Advertisements in the *Caledonian Mercury* for 1 and 19 January 1829.]

(l) April 1830. 'Essay on Imitations of the Ancient Ballad'. Text from *Minstrelsy of the Scottish Border*, ed. T. F. Henderson (1932), IV, pp. 15–16

The poet, perhaps, most capable, by verses, lines, even single words, to relieve and heighten the character of ancient poetry, was the Scottish bard Robert Burns. We are not here speaking of the avowed lyrical poems of his own composition, but of the manner in which he re-composed and repaired the old songs and fragments, for the collection of Johnson and others, when, if his memory supplied the theme, or general subject of the song, such as it existed in Scottish lore, his genius contributed that part which was to give life and immortality to the whole. If this praise should be thought extravagant, the reader may compare his splendid lyric, 'My heart's in the Highlands', with the tame and scarcely half-intelligible remains of that song as preserved by Peter Buchan. Or, what is perhaps a still more magnificent example of what we mean: 'Macpherson's Farewell', with all its spirit and gran-deur, as repaired by Burns, may be collated with the original poem called 'Macpherson's Lament', or sometimes the 'Ruffian's Rant'. In Burns's brilliant rifacimento, the same strain of wild ideas is expressed as we find in the original; but with an infusion of the savage and im-passioned spirit of Highland chivalry, which gives a splendour to the composition, of which we do not find a trace in the rudeness of the ancient ditty. I can bear witness to the older verses having been current while I was a child, but I never knew a line of the inspired edition of the Ayrshire bard until the appearance of Johnson's *Museum*.

51. Alexander Peterkin: the reviewers reviewed, with letters by Gilbert Burns and James Gray

1815

Extract from Alexander Peterkin, *A Review of the Life of Robert Burns, and of Various Criticisms on his Character and Writings* (Edinburgh, 1815).

The British copyright of Currie's 1800 edition expired in 1814. The next year Alexander Peterkin (1708–1846), a Scottish lawyer who had edited Fergusson's *Poems*, supervised a reprint of the Currie edition, to which he contributed this long introductory Review—also published separately—and an Appendix containing letters from the poet's brother Gilbert, James Gray, and others, which supported his view that Burns had been traduced (see Introduction, pp. 37–8).

We do not intend, in the following remarks, either to repeat merely what has been already said by others, or to anticipate the contents of the volumes now presented to the public. Our object is to supply defects where these seem to exist—to correct errors, and to expose misrepresentations. To this task, we wish to carry feelings uninfluenced by any unworthy purposes. We engage in it, we trust, with a temper suited to the object; and if we venture to applaud or condemn aught which presents itself for consideration, this shall not be done without exhibiting the evidence on which our opinions rest.

It is a remark too trite perhaps to require repetition, that the writings of Robert Burns, are in Scotland, the most popular of any works of fancy, antient or modern,—that there is scarcely a house in the kingdom which does not contain a copy of his poems,—and that there are few individuals elevated above the clods of the valley, who are not familiar with the productions of his muse. The tendency of works so widely circulated, and so highly esteemed, is evidently a matter of no trivial moment. But the personal character of the poet has, since his death, been in some measure inseparably blended with that of his writings;

and in attempting to form an accurate estimate of the latter, it is necessary to consider the former, and the influence on public feeling which belongs to their united power.

Various individuals, who talk and write with authority, have affected to represent the joint tendency of Burns's personal character and writings as morally pernicious. Much unwarrantable assumption, calumny, and drivelling fanaticism have been wasted, to stain unworthily the memory of Burns; while the sweetest flowers in his writings have yielded to the enemies of his fame the venom which issues from their stings. We do not mean to insinuate, that all the shallow moralizings which we have heard and read are on a level, or spring from malignity; but it is impossible to dissemble our conviction, that a great portion of that debasing passion has been indulged by many at the expence of truth and of Burns. But whether those personages have been animated by correct motives, or the reverse, in the statements which they have rather too rashly hazarded, we think we shall be able, in some very important instances, to show, that those statements are untrue—to strip them of the pure robe which is thrown around them as a disguise—and to expose, in light, the naked deformity of their aspect. We do not dream of asserting that Robert Burns was immaculate and perfect: he was a man, like his censors, and had his failings: but with all his faults he was not a bad man, nor can we silently allow him to be gibbetted to our country-men as 'a blackguard,' tarnished with blemishes which his heart and his conduct never knew. We cannot suffer his foibles to be displayed as the vital part of a character, distinguished for many excellencies; and we aspire to the interesting task of examining, without scruple, the genuine character of Burns and of his writings; and trying, by the test of proof, the moral and literary critiques, which have been put forth with a specious and somewhat ostentatious seeming of reverence for religion and virtue.

Some of the strictures on Burns's Life and Writings, to which we shall advert, have been ascribed to gentlemen of high note among the periodical authors of the day. This matters little. It indeed only serves to rouse a keener purpose of correcting their errors, for which we have not the slightest degree of veneration. We know not even by whom they were written, except in the instances where the names of the authors are given. We are confident that some of them have been misled by erroneous information; and are equally confident they will be happy to see evidence of the truth. But those who have shown by their own unceremonious conduct, that they consider the press free to injure, must learn that it is also free to vindicate, if not to avenge. While we regard the attainments and the talents of some of those whose remarks (according to common report), we are about to subject to a public scrutiny, with all reasonable respect, while, indeed, we cherish for some of them a sincere personal regard, we frankly avow our belief that their unfortunate attempts to stain, will brighten the character of Burns, and that the effects of their hurried and ill-judged lucubrations will perish with the day that gave them birth, and ultimately be lost 'in the blaze of his fame!'

We have not, however, ventured on our present undertaking from any love of controversy, or from any Quixotic passion for literary adventures. We hold the adversaries of Burns to be aggressors; misguided, we are inclined to think, and ready, we trust, in charity, to renounce their errors on satisfactory proof, that they have been misinformed, or have misconstrued the conduct and writings of Burns. But by their public and *voluntary* assertions and reflections of an injurious tendency, they have, successively, thrown down the gauntlet to every Scotchman who takes an interest in the honour of his country, of its literature, and of human nature. We accept the challenge, and will hazard the proof. Nor do we reckon this a very heroical or high achievement: the most 'plebeian' mind in the land is competent to a plain matter-of-fact enquiry, which should assuredly not have been so long delayed, had not the obnoxious critiques appeared too insignificant, separately considered, to merit notice. But from the system of reiterated critical preaching, which has become fashionable in all the recent publications about Burns—from all the slang which has been employed by the busy-bodies of the day, remaining uncontradicted and unexposed, we are afraid that future biographers, might be misled by longer silence, and adopt declamatory ravings as genuine admitted facts. The most celebrated literary journal of which Britain can boast, and of which, as Scotchmen, we are proud, began the cry; all the would-be moralists in newspapers, magazines, and reviews, have taken it up, and have repeated unauthenticated stories as grave truths: at length these have found a resting-place in large and lasting volumes. It is time, therefore, that the torrent of prejudice should be stemmed; and that while it is yet in the power of living men who knew Robert Burns, and can give testimony as to the real qualities of his character and conduct, they should come forth to settle the value of anonymous statements, to tell the truth, and to vindicate his memory from unqualified dishonour . . .

It is not our intention to say much on the subject of Burns's Works, farther than to affirm, that they are eminently friendly to good morals. A proposition, so decidedly in the face of numerous assertions to the contrary, requires a little explanation; and, in giving it, we shall not go over the beaten path, by indulging in high flown panegyrics on his genius. The man that cannot discern the excellencies of Burns's poetry is far beyond the reach of our poor abilities to point them out—and perhaps beyond the consciousness of any thing except mere animal existence.

The writings of Burns may be considered in two points of view: either as indicative of his real personal character, and therefore possessing an influence over society on the score of example—or as having a tendency in their intrinsic qualities to affect the morals of the community in which they circulate. If they are regarded in the first of these lights, we ought to consider strictly, whether, *even* with all their blemishes, *as published since his death*, they afford conclusive evidence, with respect to his character. The writings of no man afford such evidence. It is quite a commonplace fact, that authors, like other men, are very artificial animals—that they are not always what they seem in their writings; and that the force of any presumptions arising as to personal qualities, from the mere complexion of their compositions, whether published or not, must be modified by the circumstances under which these exist. A man may divest himself of all sincerity, and write a book or paper in discordance with his real sentiments. Another may, in a moment of elevation, or thoughtlessness, or confidence, write a letter to an intimate friend, either in jest or under casual and passing emotions, not accordant with the ordinary tenor of his feelings and opinions; and therefore, any inferences as to personal character, deduced from writings of any description, must be drawn with great limitations. Many of Burns's compositions were written in such circumstances as to render it impossible to learn anything very decisive from them concerning his moral feelings—for opposite conclusions may easily be drawn from different parts of his works. To assume dogmatically any positions on the subject is absurd; and to assert that he was irreligious or vicious, or that he must afford a pernicious example, because he satirised some of the fanatical clergy, and wrote private letters to his confidential friends, in which there are occasional deviations from the circumspection observed in the works that he published, is by no means a legitimate mode of induction. The indications of character disclosed in the public and private writings of Burns, to the effect of operating as an example, are so equivocal, therefore, as to afford no satisfactory proof, without a collateral view of his life.

The obvious, the consolatory, and we think the irresistible conclusion to be deduced from the remarks and proof, which we now take the liberty of submitting to the public, is, that Burns has been cruelly wronged. It matters little, whether this evil has arisen from credulity, misinformation, or malicious purpose. It is fit that the error should be corrected,—not merely because it is fair that the dead as well as the living should have justice in every individual instance but because the general interests of society and literature are outraged, if calumny is permitted, in such a case, to circulate in triumphant dogmatism. By calumny we mean injurious accusation without proof. And if ever calumny of the most dastardly kind poisoned public opinion, it has been in the case of Burns. It is not enough to say, that he frequently indulged inconvivial propensities, and therefore was an habitual debauchee, and every way abominable as a man; it is absolute imbecility, savouring of the tabernacle, to say, that because he satirised and painted hypocrisy truly, he was a blasphemer, and a profligate, as an author: and no man shall be permitted to assert, *without evidence* in support of his allegation, that Burns was a worthless wretch, if there be one untrammelled press in Scotland. Some of the *rigidly righteous* tremble at the mere sound of praise to his genius, and seem to think that because he had the failings of humanity, there should be no monument to his memory. It is not to his failings that a monument can be consecrated by any rational being; but to his transcendant genius as the Poet of Nature; for no one who can discover excellence, and distinguish it from the dross of mortality in his own frame, can overlook the high pre-eminence of Burns in all the faculties and feelings which raise man from the dust into the temple of fame. To the broad, the general and unqualified accusations which have been brought against him, we offer a valid defence, that there is no proof: we also give exculpatory evidence of the most satisfying nature, and we retire from public notice, with a perfect conviction, that as Burns *has been tried* he will be acquitted by his country.

SUPPLEMENTARY LETTERS

NO. I.

LETTER FROM MR. GILBERT BURNS

Grant's Braes, *29th September, 1814.*

Sir,

Your letter of the 15th August reached me in due course, informing me of some booksellers in Edinburgh having the intention of publishing a re-print of Dr. Currie's first edition of the Life and Writings of my brother, and that you had undertaken to write some remarks to accompany it, in vindication of my Brother's fame as a poet, and character as man, from the aspersions and misrepresentations thrown upon both from various quarters, particularly by the reviewers of the unfortunate reliques gleaned by Mr. Cromek. To the publication I can have no *personal* objection, but should not wish to countenance it if I thought Messrs Cadell and Davies would justly consider it any encroachment on their right, as I was very much satisfied with the conduct of these gentlemen toward my Brother's family.

That the world should be set right in regard to the misrepresentations above alluded to, especially such as regard my brother's moral character, you will readily believe I ardently wish. Though personally un-acquainted with you, yet from the account I have heard of you from some of my friends who are of your acquaintance, and from knowing that you enjoyed the intimacy of my much esteemed and lamented acquaintance the author of the 'Sabbath,' I am satisfied the task you have undertaken is in good hands.

When any publication appears in the world which has an immoral tendency, it is no doubt the legitimate province of the reviewer to warn the public against its tendency; but even in that case, I do not see what right he has to attack private character, not involved in the works which authors themselves publish, and I am not a little surprised to see men of talents and literary taste, rake up the failings (real or imputed) of the dead, and lacerate the feelings of surviving friends, by presenting an overcharged picture of those failings to the world, and giving currency to every malicious report, founded or unfounded. No person can regret more than I do the tendency of *some* of my Brother's writings to represent irregularity of conduct as a consequence of genius, and sobriety the effect of dulness: but surely more has been said on that subject than the fact warrants: and it ought to be re-membered that the greatest part of his writings, having that tendency, *were not published by himself, nor intended for publication.* But it may like-wise be observed, and every attentive reader of Burns's Works, must have observed, that he frequently presents a caricature of his feelings, and even of his failings—a kind of mock-heroic account of himself and his opinions, which he never supposed could be taken literally. I dare say it never entered into his head, for instance, that when he was speaking in that manner of Milton's Satan, any one should gravely sup-pose that was the model on which he wished to form his own character.

Yet on such rants, which the author evidently intends should be considered a mere play of imagination, joined to some abstract reasoning of the critic, many of the heavy accusations brought against the Poet for bad taste and worse morals, rest. But even where he was really faulty in such representations, it surely required but a moderate portion of that charity which thinketh no evil—of that fraternal feeling, which I should have expected every person of talents and literary taste would have felt for my poor unfortunate brother, to consider them the arguments of a man galled by the honest reproaches of his own mind for occasional deviations from the path of virtue, mustered up as a palliation (dictated by feelings natural to us all,) rather than the effusion of determined profligacy, as they have been most erroneously supposed. That this conclusion was false, I think must appear, independent of other testimony, from the whole events of his life, which have been laid before the public more undisguisedly, than perhaps the life of any other individual has ever been.

Dr. Currie, knowing the events of the later years of my brother's life only from the reports which had been propagated, and thinking it necessary, lest the candour of his work should be called in question to state the substance of these reports, has given a very exaggerated view of the failings of my brother's life at that period, which is certainly to be regretted; but as the Doctor's work was not submitted to me in manuscript, nor, as far as I know, to any of my brother's friends at Dumfries, I had not in my power to set him right in that particular: and considering the excellence of the Doctor's work upon the whole, and how much we owed him, for that stupendous exertion of his benevolence, I never took any notice to him of my disapprobation, or of the inconsistency of this part of his work. But I will not farther anticipate what must have occurred to yourself, and which you will be able to point out with more effect than I can. I am, Sir,

Your most obedient humble servant,
GILBERT BURNS.

To *Mr.* Alex. Peterkin,⎱
   Edinburgh. ⎰

NO. II.

LETTER FROM MR. JAMES GRAY,

FORMERLY IN DUMFRIES, NOW ONE OF THE MASTERS OF THE

HIGH SCHOOL, EDINBURGH.

EDINBURGH, *28th September 1814.*

Dear Sir,

I am happy to learn that you are engaged in a vindication of the character of Burns, from the calumnies contained in some of our most popular literary journals. The fate of this great man has been singularly hard; during the greater part of his life, he was doomed to struggle with adverse fortune, and no friendly hand was stretched forth to shield him from the storm that at last overwhelmed him. It seemed even to have been the object of a jealous and illiberal policy to accelerate his ruin. His enemies have ascribed to him vices foreign to his nature; have exaggerated his failings, and have not even had the justice to relieve the deep shades of imputed depravity, by a single ray of virtue. In their portraits there is none of that disposition of light and shade, in which nature delights. They resemble the works of the caricature painter, in which every beauty is concealed, and every deformity overcharged, rather than the correct likeness of the honest artist, studious of the fidelity of his representation. The truth is, that not one of the periodical writers who have thought fit to pronounce judgement in so decisive a tone, on the moral conduct of the Poet, had the means of forming a fair estimate of his character. They had heard certain reports injurious to his reputation, and they received them without examination as established facts. It is besides to be lamented, that the most respectable of his biographers has in some cases suffered himself to be misled by the slanderous tales of malice or party spirit.

52. A historic Burns supper: 'The memory of Burns', *Edinburgh Evening Courant*

27 January 1816

(Cf. *BC* (1917), XXVI and see Introduction, p. 34.)

We rejoice to find that the feelings of admiration universally enter-tained for the genius of Burns have at length been exhibited in the metropolis of the country which gave him birth in a manner somewhat worthy of that country and of himself. We do not mean to say that the compositions of this illustrious Poet have not received the full measure of applause which is their due, or that that applause has been either tardily or restrictedly bestowed. Scotland has long gloried in the fame of her divinest son; and, equally, in the cottage and the castle, his strains have imparted the most glowing and varied delight. But this silent, this involuntary and inevitable tribute of admiration is too humble for the genius of Burns. He, to whose renown the gratitude and the pride of his country are erecting monuments in every quarter, must be proclaimed with the sounds of exultation and of triumph; and it is to this mode of announcing the feelings of Scotland towards her Bard that we allude when we say that they have *at length* been exhibited in a manner somewhat worthy of his country and of himself.

A meeting of the friends and admirers of Burns was held in this city last year, which was attended by a number of most respectable individuals; but it was not until the present commemoration of the Poet that his memory was celebrated in a manner which could be considered as the indication of a general national feeling. We now think that the country at large is fairly enlisted in this tribute to departed genius, a tribute as much more honourable than that which is paid to the idol of a party as the memory of the Poet is more enduring than that of him who in the more ostentatious walks of life may have carried his blushing honours thickest upon him. Every one remembers 'one

274

Milton, a blind man,' but very few recollect the name of the worthy Prime Minister who bestowed this exquisite epithet upon the Poet of Earth and Heaven, of Time and Eternity.

The Meeting was held on Thursday last at MacEwan's Tavern, in the Royal Exchange, where an extremely good dinner, and plenty of good wine, was given to the guests for a guinea per head. The company exceeded one hundred in number, and comprised a respectable proportion of rank and fashion, and a high display of literary talent. Amongst the former we remarked the Earl of Leven; the Honourable Ramsay Maule, M.P.; Charles Forbes, Esq., M.P.; Alexander Boswell, Esq. of Auchinleck; the Honourable Captain Napier, R.N.; Captain G.C. Mackenzie, R.N.; Captain Gordon, R.N.; Lieutenant-Colonel Wilson, late from the field of Waterloo; with other naval and military characters. In the latter we number Mr. Jeffrey, Mr. John Wilson, and Mr. Walter Scott. Mr. Boswell took the chair, and the Honourable Mr. Maule was croupier. Mr. Scott acted as one of the stewards; assisted by Mr. George Thomson, the well-known correspondent of Burns, and other gentlemen distinguished as the friends or admirers of the Poet.

The company sat down to dinner about six o'clock. When the cloth was removed the fine canon of *Non nobis, Domine* was sung with great effect, by Mess. Elliotts, King, and Evans; after which the following toasts were given, with many others, which springing from the impulse of the moment we lament that we cannot particularise, although those who had the good fortune to be present will not soon forget the happy union in their Chairman of wit, hilarity, and prompt good sense which produced them:—

'The King.'

'The Prince Regent.'

'The Memory of Burns!' in solemn silence was drank by the company standing; after which some beautiful verses, the composition of Mr. Boswell, were recited. These were followed by the Glee, 'Come, Shepherds, we'll follow the Hearse.'

'The Widow and Children of the Poet.'

'The Memory of those who had earliest noticed and befriended, or otherwise distinguished, the Poet—Dr. Blacklock, Mrs. Dunlop, Earl of Glencairn, and Dr. Curry.'

'The Admirers of Burns.'

'Mr. Roscoe.' Glee, 'Where are the Joys,' etc.

'Dunbar, the Chaucer, of Scotland.'

'The Memory of Thomson, Ramsay, and Fergusson.' Glee. 'Lightly tread,' etc.

'Campbell, and the living Poets of Scotland'—drank with loud, prolonged, and marked enthusiasm.

'The Poets of England, from Chaucer to Byron'—received with excessive applauses.

'The Wooden Walls,' Glee, 'Ye Mariners of England.'

'Wellington!'—with enthusiasm and three times three. Glee, 'See, the conquering Hero comes.'

'The Memory of the Heroes of Waterloo.' Song, 'Farewell, thou fair Day.'

Mr. Boswell, being then called upon for a song 'of his own composition,' politely sung one of great beauty and spirit, tributary to the genius of Burns in the first instance; then alluding to the ingenious and respectable Mr. Hogg; and closing in a brilliant tribute to the great Poet present, 'who, a Scotsman himself, made Scotland and Scottish valour the constant themes of his verse.' He concluded by giving, although in his presence, 'Walter Scott!' which was drank amidst peeling applause with three times three. Mr. Scott made a happy and ingenious reply, of which, being averse to mar a curious tale in the telling, we shall not attempt to give the faintest outline.

Mr. Maule then gave 'The Star of the Scottish Bar, Mr. Jeffrey'— drank with loud cheers.

Mr. Scott, in the course of the evening, gave the following toasts:— 'Mr. James Hogg,' whose absence he could almost venture to take upon himself to say could only be occasioned by 'a snow-storm in the headlands'; 'The Memory of the learned and excellent Dr. John Leyden'; 'The Memory of the amiable and ingenious James Grahame.'

Mr. Boswell then proposed the health of 'Mr. George Thomson,' to whose enterprise and exertions chiefly it was owing that the greater number of the exquisite lyrics of Burns had been produced. This toast was drank with loud and prolonged expressions of approbation and cordial concurrence, to which Mr. Thomson replied by a neat and modest address of thanks.

The list of literary toasts was closed with the honoured name of Joanna Baillie; a Scotswoman who yields the palm of poetical excellence to neither sex, and to no country.

Mr. George Burnett, with great propriety and effect, proposed a toast to 'The Memory of the late James Boswell of Auchinleck.' A number of other toasts were given of the most animating and appropriate description; and shortly after 11 o'clock Mr. Boswell (after stating an indisposition of four months' continuance as the cause of his early departure) quitted the chair, which he had filled during the whole evening in the most brilliant and exhilarating manner, carrying with him the cordial good wishes of the many merry hearts he had made, and left behind him.

The chair was then taken by the Honourable R. Maule, who had ably seconded Mr. Boswell as croupier during the day and who maintained the festivity of the meeting till an early hour on Friday morning. Before dismissing the meeting this respectable gentleman took the opportunity of declaring that he should at all times be happy to aid and assist the family of Burns; and farther, that so entirely was he satisfied with the harmony, conviviality, and whole tone and temper of the meeting that he should make a point upon every possible occasion of attending this commemoration during his life. The company then separated at about two o'clock on Friday morning.

Many excellent songs were sung during the evening by private individuals, as well as by the professional gentlemen who were remunerated for their services. Amongst the former we will not deny ourselves the pleasure of mentioning Mr. Russell, of the Theatre, who gratified the meeting by several excellent and appropriate songs which he sung in a manly and effective style. We understand it is determined to have a similar public celebration of the Poet's birthday in Edinburgh every three years; and there can be no doubt that a triennial festival, equally well regulated with that of Thursday last, will ever be most respectably attended.

53. Wordsworth on Burns

1816

(a) Extracts from William Wordsworth, *A Letter to a Friend of Robert Burns: Occasioned by an Intended Republication of the Account of the Life of Burns, by Dr. Currie; and of the Selection made by him from his Letters* (1816).

James Gray, an Edinburgh schoolmaster who had known Burns in Dumfries, sent Wordsworth Peterkin's *Review* (No. 51), and passed on a query from Gilbert Burns about how his brother's name could best be vindicated. This was Wordsworth's reply, published in 1816. Gilbert Burns did not publish a revised edition of Burns's *Works* until 1820, and then it proved to be disappointingly unadventurous (see Nos 16, 29, 33, 44, 51, 70 and Introduction, pp. 37–8).

TO JAMES GRAY, ESQ., EDINBURGH.

Dear Sir,

I have carefully perused the Review of the Life of your friend Robert Burns*, which you kindly transmitted to me; the author has rendered a substantial service to the poet's memory; and the annexed letters are all important to the subject. After having expressed this opinion, I shall not trouble you by commenting upon the publication; but will confine myself to the request of Mr. Gilbert Burns, that I would furnish him with my notions upon the best mode of conducting the defence of his brother's injured reputation; a favourable opportunity being now afforded him to convey his sentiments to the world along with a re-publication of Dr. Currie's book, which he is about to superintend. From the respect which I have long felt for the character of the person who has thus honoured me, and from the gratitude which, as a lover of poetry, I owe to the genius of his departed relative, I should

* *A Review of the Life of Robert Burns*, and of various criticisms on his character and writings, by Alexander Peterkin, 1814.

most gladly comply with this wish; if I could hope that any suggestions of mine would be of service to the cause. But, really, I feel it a thing of much delicacy, to give advice upon this occasion, as it appears to me, mainly, not a question of opinion, or of taste, but a matter of conscience. Mr. Gilbert Burns must know, if any man living does, what his brother was; and no one will deny that he, who possesses this knowledge, is a man of unimpeachable veracity. He has already spoken to the world in contradiction of the injurious assertions that have been made, and has told why he forbore to do this on their first appearance. If it be deemed advisable to reprint Dr. Currie's narrative, without striking but such passages as the author, if he were now alive, would probably oe happy to efface, let there be notes attached to the most obnoxious of them, in which the misrepresentations may be corrected, and the exaggerations exposed. I recommend this course, if Dr. Currie's Life is to be republished, as it now stands, in connexion with the poems and letters, and especially if prefixed to them; but, in my judgement, it would be best to copy the example which Mason has given in his second edition of Gray's works. There, inverting the order which had been properly adopted, when the Life and Letters were new matter, the poems are placed first; and the rest takes its place as subsidiary to them.[1] If this were done in the intended edition of Burn's works. I should strenuously recommend, that a concise life of the poet be prefixed, from the pen of Gilbert Burns, who has already given public proof how well qualified he is for the undertaking. I know no better model as to proportion, and the degree of detail required, nor, indeed, as to the general execution, than the life of Milton by Fenton, prefixed to many editions of the *Paradise Lost*. But a more copious narrative would be expected from a brother; and some allowance ought to be made, in this and other respects, for an expectation so natural.

In this prefatory memoir, when the author has prepared himself by reflecting, that fraternal partiality may have rendered him, in some points, not so trust-worthy as others less favoured by opportunity, it will be incumbent upon him to proceed candidly and openly, as far as such a procedure will tend to restore to his brother that portion of public estimation, of which he appears to have been unjustly deprived. Nay, when we recal to mind the black things which have been written of this great man, and the frightful ones that have been insinuated against him; and, as far as the public knew, till lately, without complaint,

---

[1] Wordsworth refers to the third edition of *The Poems of Mr. Gray* with William Mason's *Memoirs of Gray* (1778), not the second edition, 1775.

remonstrance, or disavowal, from his nearest relatives; I am not sure that it would not be best, at this day, explicitly to declare to what degree Robert Burns had given way to pernicious habits, and, as nearly as may be, to fix the point to which his moral character had been degraded. It is a disgraceful feature of the times that this measure should be necessary; most painful to think that a *brother* should have such an office to perform. But, if Gilbert Burns be conscious that the subject will bear to be so treated, he has no choice; the duty has been imposed upon him by the errors into which the former biographer has fallen, in respect to the very principles upon which his work ought to have been conducted.

I well remember the acute sorrow with which, by my own fire-side, I first perused Dr. Currie's Narrative, and some of the letters, particularly of those composed in the latter part of the poet's life. If my pity for Burns was extreme, this pity did not preclude a strong indignation, of which he was not the object. If, said I, it were in the power of a biographer to relate the truth, the *whole* truth, and nothing *but* the truth, the friends and surviving kindred of the deceased, for the sake of general benefit to mankind, might endure that such heart-rending communication should be made to the world. But in no case is this possible; and, in the present, the opportunities of directly acquiring other than superficial knowledge have been most scanty; for the writer has barely seen the person who is the subject of his tale; nor did his avocations allow him to take the pains necessary for ascertaining what portion of the information conveyed to him was authentic. So much for facts and actions; and to what purpose relate them even were they true, if the narrative cannot be heard without extreme pain; unless they are placed in such a light, and brought forward in such order, that they shall explain their own laws, and leave the reader in as little uncertainty as the mysteries of our nature will allow, respecting the spirit from which they derived their existence, and which governed the agent? But hear on this pathetic and awful subject, the poet himself, pleading for those who have transgressed!

[quotes 'Address to the Unco Guid', ll. 53–64]

How happened it that the recollection of this affecting passage did not check so amiable a man as Dr. Currie, while he was revealing to the world the infirmities of its author? He must have known enough of human nature to be assured that men would be eager to sit in judge-ment, and pronounce *decidedly* upon the guilt or innocence of Burns by his testimony; nay, that there were multitudes whose main interest in the allegations would be derived from the incitements which they found therein to undertake this presumptuous office. And where lies the collateral benefit, or what ultimate advantage can be expected, to counteract the injury that the many are thus tempted to do to their own minds; and to compensate the sorrow which must be fixed in the hearts of the considerate few, by language that proclaims so much, and provokes conjectures as unfavourable as imagination can furnish? Here, said I, being moved beyond what it would become me to express, here is a revolting account of a man of exquisite genius, and confessedly of many high moral qualities, sunk into the lowest depths of vice and misery! But the painful story, notwithstanding its minuteness, is incomplete,—in essentials it is deficient; so that the most attentive and sagacious reader cannot explain how a mind, so well established by knowledge, fell—and continued to fall, without power to prevent or retard its own ruin.

Would a bosom friend of the author, his counsellor and confessor, have told such things, if true, as this book contains? and who, but one possessed of the intimate knowledge which none but a bosom friend can acquire, could have been justified in making these avowals? Such a one, himself a pure spirit, having accompanied, as it were, upon wings, the pilgrim along the sorrowful road which he trod on foot; such a one, neither hurried down by its slippery descents, nor entangled among its thorns, nor perplexed by its windings, nor discomfited by its founderous passages—for the instruction of others—might have delineated, almost as in a map, the way which the afflicted pilgrim had pursued till the sad close of his diversified journey. In this manner the venerable spirit of Isaac Walton was qualified to have retraced the unsteady course of a highly-gifted man, who, in this lamentable point, and in versatility of genius, bore no un-obvious resemblance to the Scottish bard; I mean his friend *Cotton*—whom, notwithstanding all that the sage must have disapproved in his life, he honoured with the title of son. Nothing like this, however, has the biographer of Burns accomplished; and, with his means of information, copious as in some respects they were, it would have been absurd to attempt it. The only motive, therefore, which could authorise the writing and publishing matter so distressing to read—is wanting!

Nor is Dr. Currie's performance censurable from these considerations alone; for information, which would have been of absolute worth if in his capacity of biographer and editor he had known when to stop short, is rendered unsatisfactory and inefficacious through the absence of this reserve, and from being coupled with statement of improbable and irreconcileable facts. We have the author's letters discharged upon us in showers; but how few readers will take the trouble of comparing those letters with each other, and with the other documents of the publication, in order to come at a genuine knowledge of the writer's character!—The life of Johnson by Boswell had broken through many pre-existing delicacies, and afforded the British public an opportunity of acquiring experience, which before it had happily wanted; nevertheless, at the time when the ill-selected medley of Burns's correspondence first appeared, little progress had been made (nor is it likely that, by the mass of mankind, much ever will be made) in determining what portion of these confidential communications escapes the pen in courteous, yet often innocent, compliance—to gratify the several tastes of correspondents; and as little towards distinguishing opinions and sentiments uttered for the momentary amusement merely of the writer's own fancy, from those which his judgement deliberately approves, and his heart faithfully cherishes. But the subject of this book was a man of extraordinary genius; whose birth, education, and employments had placed and kept him in a situation far below that in which the writers and readers of expensive volumes are usually found. Critics upon works of fiction have laid it down as a rule that remoteness of place, in fixing the choice of a subject, and in prescribing the mode of treating it, is equal in effect to distance of time;—restraints may be thrown off accordingly. Judge then of the delusions which artificial distinctions impose, when to a man like Doctor Currie, writing with views so honourable, the *social condition* of the individual of whom he was treating, could seem to place him at such a distance from the exalted reader, that ceremony might be discarded with him, and his memory sacrificed, as it were, almost without compunction. The poet was laid where these injuries could not reach him; but he had a parent, I understand, an admirable woman, still surviving; a brother like Gilbert Burns!—a widow estimable for her virtues; and children, at that time infants, with the world before them, which they must face to obtain a maintenance; who remembered their father probably with the tenderest affection;—and whose opening minds, as their years advanced, would become conscious of so many reasons for admiring him.—Ill-fated child of nature, too frequently thine own enemy,—unhappy favourite of genius, too often misguided,—this is indeed to be 'crushed beneath the furrow's weight!'

Why, sir, do I write to you at this length, when all that I had to express in direct answer to the request, which occasioned this letter, lay in such narrow compass?—Because having entered upon the subject, I am unable to quit it!—Your feelings, I trust, go along with mine; and, rising from this individual case to a general view of the subject, you will probably agree with me in opinion that biography, though differing in some essentials from works of fiction, is nevertheless, like them, an *art*,—an art, the laws of which are determined by the imperfections of our nature, and the constitution of society. Truth is not here, as in the sciences, and in natural philosophy, to be sought without scruple, and promulgated for its own sake, upon the mere chance of its being serviceable; but only for obviously justifying purposes, moral or intellectual.

Silence is a privilege of the grave, a right of the departed: let him, therefore, who infringes that right, by speaking publicly of, for, or against, those who cannot speak for themselves, take heed that he opens not his mouth without a sufficient sanction. *De mortuis nil nisi bonum*, is a rule in which these sentiments have been pushed to an extreme that proves how deeply humanity is interested in maintaining them. And it was wise to announce the precept thus absolutely; both because there exist in that same nature, by which it has been dictated, so many temptations to disregard it,—and because there are powers and influences, within and without us, that will prevent its being literally fulfilled—to the suppression of profitable truth. Penalties of law, conventions of manners, and personal fear, protect the reputation of the living; and something of this protection is extended to the recently dead,—who survive, to a certain degree, in their kindred and friends. Few are so insensible as not to feel this, and not to be actuated by the feeling. But only to philosophy enlightened by the affections does it belong justly to estimate the claims of the deceased on the one hand, and of the present age and future generations, on the other; and to strike a balance between them.—Such philosophy runs a risk of becoming extinct among us, if the coarse intrusions into the recesses, the gross breaches upon the sanctities, of domestic life, to which we have lately been more and more accustomed, are to be regarded as indications of a vigorous state of public feeling—favourable to the maintenance of the liberties of our country.—Intelligent lovers of freedom are from necessity bold and hardy lovers of truth; but, according to the measure in which their love is intelligent, is it attended with a finer discrimination, and a more sensitive delicacy. The wise and good (and all others being lovers of licence rather than of liberty are in fact slaves) respect, as one of the noblest characteristics of Englishmen, that jealousy of familiar approach, which, while it contributes to the maintenance of private dignity, is one of the most efficacious guardians of rational public freedom.

The general obligation upon which I have insisted, is especially binding upon those who undertake the biography of *authors*. Assuredly, there is no cause why the lives of that class of men should be pried into with the same diligent curiosity, and laid open with the same disregard of reserve, which may sometimes be expedient in composing the history of men who have borne an active part in the world. Such thorough knowledge of the good and bad qualities of these latter, as can only be obtained by a scrutiny of their private lives, conduces to explain not only their own public conduct, but that of those with whom they have acted. Nothing of this applies to authors, considered merely as authors. Our business is with their books,—to understand and to enjoy them. And, of poets more especially, it is true—that, if their works be good, they contain within themselves all that is necessary to their being comprehended and relished. It should seem that the ancients thought in this manner; for of the eminent Greek and Roman poets, few and scanty memorials were, I believe, ever prepared; and fewer still are preserved. It is delightful to read what, in the happy exercise of his own genius, Horace chooses to communicate of himself and his friends; but I confess I am not so much a lover of knowledge, independent of its quality, as to make it likely that it would much rejoice me, were I to hear that records of the Sabine poet and his contemporaries composed upon the Boswellian plan, had been unearthed among the ruins of Herculaneum. You will interpret what I am writing, *liberally*. With respect to the light which such a discovery might throw upon Roman manners, there would be reasons to desire it: but I should dread to disfigure the beautiful ideal of the memories of those illustrious persons with incongruous features, and to sully the imaginative purity of their classical works with gross and trivial recollections. The least weighty objection to heterogeneous details, is that they are mainly superfluous, and therefore an incumbrance.

But you will perhaps accuse me of refining too much; and it is, I own, comparatively of little importance, while we are engaged in reading the *Iliad*, the *Eneid*, the tragedies of *Othello* and *King Lear*, whether the authors of these poems were good or bad men; whether they lived happily or miserably. Should a thought of the kind cross our minds, there would be no doubt, if irresistible external evidence did not decide the question unfavourably, that men of such transcendant genius were both good and happy: and if, unfortunately, it had been on record that they were otherwise, sympathy with the fate of their fictitious personages would banish the unwelcome truth whenever it obtruded itself, so that it would but slightly disturb our pleasure. Far otherwise is it with that class of poets, the principal charm of whose writings depends upon the familiar knowledge which they convey of the personal feelings of their authors. This is eminently the case with the effusions of Burns;—in the small quantity of narrative that he has given, he himself bears no inconsiderable part; and he has produced no drama. Neither the subjects of his poems, nor his manner of handling them, allow us long to forget their author. On the basis of his human character he has reared a poetic one, which with more or less distinctness presents itself to view in almost every part of his earlier, and, in my estimation, his most valuable verses. This poetic fabric, dug out of the quarry of genuine humanity, is airy and spiritual:—and though the materials, in some parts, are coarse, and the disposition is often fantastic and irregular, yet the whole is agreeable and strikingly attractive. Plague, then, upon your remorseless hunters after matter of fact (who, after all, rank among the blindest of human beings) when they would convince you that the foundations, of this admirable edifice are hollow; and that its frame is unsound! Granting that all which has been raked up to the prejudice of Burns were literally true; and that it added, which it does not, to our better understanding of human nature and human life (for that genius is not incompatible with vice, and that vice leads to misery—the more acute from the sensibilities which are the elements of genius—we needed not those communications to inform us) how poor would have been the compensation for the deduction made, by this extrinsic knowledge, from the intrinsic efficacy of his poetry—to please, and to instruct!

In illustration of this sentiment, permit me to remind you that it is the privilege of poetic genius to catch, under certain restrictions of which perhaps at the time of its being exerted it is but dimly conscious, a spirit of pleasure wherever it can be found,—in the walks of nature, and in the business of men.—The poet, trusting to primary instincts, luxuriates among the felicities of love and wine, and is enraptured while he describes the fairer aspects of war: nor does he shrink from the company of the passion of love though immoderate—from convivial pleasure though intemperate—nor from the presence of war though savage, and recognized as the hand-maid of desolation. Frequently and admirably has Burns given way to these impulses of nature; both with reference to himself and in describing the condition of others. Who, but some impenetrable dunce or narrow-minded puritan in works of art, ever read without delight the picture which he has drawn of the convivial exaltation of the rustic adventurer, Tam o' Shanter? The poet fears not to tell the reader in the outset that his hero was a desperate and sottish drunkard, whose excesses were frequent as his opportunities. This reprobate sits down to his cups, while the storm is roaring, and heaven and earth are in confusion;—the night is driven on by song and tumultuous noise—laughter and jest thicken as the beverage improves upon the palate—conjugal fidelity archly bends to the service of general benevolence—selfishness is not absent, but wearing the mask of social cordiality—and, while these various elements of humanity are blended into one proud and happy composition of elated spirits, the anger of the tempest without doors only heightens and sets off the enjoyment within.—I pity him who cannot perceive that, in all this, though there was no moral purpose, there is a moral effect.

> Kings may be blest, but Tam was glorious,
> O'er a' the *ills* of life victorious.

What a lesson do these words convey of charitable indulgence for the vicious habits of the principal actor in this scene, and of those who resemble him!—Men who to the rigidly virtuous are objects almost of loathing, and whom therefore they cannot serve! The poet, penetrating the unsightly and disgusting surfaces of things, has unveiled with exquisite skill the finer ties of imagination and feeling, that often bind these beings to practices productive of so much unhappiness to themselves, and to those whom it is their duty to cherish;—and, as far as he puts the reader into possession of this intelligent sympathy, he qualifies him for exercising a salutary influence over the minds of those who are thus deplorably enslaved.

Not less successfully does Burns avail himself of his own character and situation in society, to construct out of them a poetic self,—introduced as a dramatic personage—for the purpose of inspiriting his incidents, diversifying his pictures, recommending his opinions, and giving point to his sentiments. His brother can set me right if I am mistaken when I express a belief, that at the time when he wrote his story of 'Death and Dr. Hornbook,' he had very rarely been intoxicated, or perhaps even much exhilarated by liquor. Yet how happily does he lead his reader into that track of sensations! and with what lively humour does he describe the disorder of his senses and the confusion of his understanding, put to test by a deliberate attempt to count the horns of the moon!

> But whether she had three or four
> He could na' tell.

Behold a sudden apparition that disperses this disorder, and in a moment chills him into possession of himself! Coming upon no more important mission than the grisly phantom was charged with, what mode of introduction could have been more efficient or appropriate?

But, in those early poems, through the veil of assumed habits and pretended qualities, enough of the real man appears to shew that he was conscious of sufficient cause to dread his own passions, and to bewail his errors! We have rejected as false sometimes in the letter, and of necessity as false in the spirit, many of the testimonies that others have borne against him:—but, by his own hand—in words the import of which cannot be mistaken—it has been recorded that the order of his life but faintly corresponded with the clearness of his views. It is probable that he would have proved a still greater poet if, by strength of reason, he could have controlled the propensities which his sensibility engendered; but he would have been a poet of a different class: and certain it is, had that desirable restraint been early established, many peculiar beauties which enrich his verses could never have existed, and many accessary influences, which contribute greatly to their effect, would have been wanting. For instance, the momentous truth of the passage already quoted, 'One point must still be greatly dark,' &c. could not possibly have been conveyed with such pathetic force by any poet that ever lived, speaking in his own voice; unless it were felt that, like Burns, he was a man who preached from the text of his own errors; and whose wisdom, beautiful as a flower that might have risen from seed sown from above, was in fact a scion from the root of personal suffering. Whom did the poet intend should be thought of as occupying that grave over which, after modestly setting forth the moral discernment and warm affections of its 'poor inhabitant', it is supposed to be inscribed that

> ——Thoughtless follies laid him low,
> And stained his name.

Who but himself,—himself anticipating the too probable termination of his own course? Here is a sincere and solemn avowal—a public declaration *from his own will*—a confession at once devout, poetical, and human—a history in the shape of a prophecy! What more was required of the biographer than to have put his seal to the writing, testifying that the foreboding had been realized, and that the record was authentic?—Lastingly is it to be regretted in respect to this memorable being, that inconsiderate intrusion has not left us at liberty to enjoy his mirth, or his love; his wisdom or his wit; without an admixture of useless, irksome, and painful details, that take from his poems so much of that right—which, with all his carelessness, and frequent breaches of self-respect, he was not negligent to maintain for them—the right of imparting solid instruction through the medium of unalloyed pleasure.

You will have noticed that my observations have hitherto been confined to Dr. Currie's book: if, by fraternal piety, the poison can be sucked out of this wound, those inflicted by meaner hands, may be safely left to heal of themselves. Of the other writers who have given their names, only one lays claim to even a slight acquaintance with the author, whose moral character they take upon them publicly to anatomize. The *Edinburgh* reviewer—and him I single out because the author of the vindication of Burns has treated his offences with comparative indulgence, to which he has no claim, and which, from whatever cause it might arise, has interfered with the dispensation of justice—the *Edinburgh* reviewer thus writes:* 'The *leading voice* in Burns's character, and the *cardinal deformity*, indeed, of ALL his productions, was his contempt, or affectation of contempt, for prudence, decency, and regularity, and his admiration of thoughtlessness, oddity, and vehement sensibility: his belief, in short, in the dispensing power of genius and social feeling in all matters of morality and common sense;' adding, that these vices and erroneous notions 'have communicated to a great part of his productions a character of immorality at once contemptible and hateful.' We are afterwards told, that he is *perpetually* making a parade of his thoughtlessness, inflammability, and imprudence; and, in the next paragraph; that he is *perpetually* doing something else; i.e. 'boasting of his own independence.'—Marvellous address in the commission of faults! not less than Caesar shewed in the management of business; who, it is said, could dictate to three secretaries upon three

* From Mr. Peterkin's pamphlet, who vouches for the accuracy of his citations; omitting, however, to apologize for their length.

several affairs, at one and the same moment! But, to be serious. When a man, self-elected into the office of a public judge of the literature and life of his contemporaries, can have the audacity to go these lengths in framing a summary of the contents of volumes that are scattered over every quarter of the globe, and extant in almost every cottage of Scotland, to give the lie to his labours; we must not wonder if, in the plenitude of his concern for the interests of abstract morality, the infatuated slanderer should have found no obstacle to prevent him from insinuating that the poet, whose writings are to this degree stained and disfigured, was 'one of the sons of fancy and of song who spend in vain superfluities the money that belongs of right to the pale industrious tradesman and his famishing infants; and who rave about friendship and philosophy in a tavern, while their wives' hearts,' &c. &c.

It is notorious that this persevering Aristarch*, as often as a work of original genius comes before him, avails himself of that opportunity to re-proclaim to the world the narrow range of his own comprehension. The happy self-complacency, the unsuspecting vain-glory, and the cordial *bonhommie*, with which this part of his duty is performed, do not leave him free to complain of being hardly dealt with if any one should declare the truth, by pronouncing much of the foregoing attack upon the intellectual and moral character of Burns, to be the trespass (for reasons that will shortly appear, it cannot be called the venial trespass) of a mind obtuse, superficial, and inept. What portion of malignity such a mind is susceptible of, the judicious admirers of the poet, and the discerning friends of the man, will not trouble themselves to enquire; but they will wish that this evil principle had possessed more sway than they are at liberty to assign to it; the offender's condition would not then have been so hopeless. For malignity *selects* its diet; but where is to be found the nourishment from which vanity will revolt? Malignity may be appeased by triumphs real or supposed, and will then sleep, or yield its place to a repentance producing dispositions of good will, and desires to make amends for past injury; but vanity is restless, reckless, intractable, unappeasable, insatiable. Fortunate is it for the world when this spirit incites only to actions that meet with an

---

* A friend, who chances to be present while the author is correcting the proof sheets, observes that Aristarchus is libelled by this application of his name, and advises that 'Zoilus' should be substituted. The question lies between spite and presumption; and it is not easy to decide upon a case where the claims of each party are so strong: but the name of Aristarch, who, simple! man would allow no verse to pass for Homer's which he did not approve of, is retained, for reasons that will be deemed cogent.

adequate punishment in derision; such, as in a scheme of poetical justice, would be aptly requited by assigning to the agents, when they quit this lower world, a station in that not uncomfortable limbo—the Paradise of Fools! But, assuredly, we shall have here another proof that ridicule is not the test of truth, if it prevent us from perceiving, that *depravity* has no ally more active, more inveterate, nor, from the difficulty of divining to what kind and degree of extravagance it may prompt, more pernicious than self-conceit. Where this alliance is too obvious to be disputed, the culprit ought not to be allowed the benefit of contempt—as a shelter from detestation; much less should he be permitted to plead, in excuse for his transgressions, that especial malevolence had little or no part in them. It is not recorded, that the ancient, who set fire to the temple of Diana, had a particular dislike to the goddess of chastity, or held idolatry in abhorrence: he was a fool, an egregious fool, but not the less, on that account, a most odious monster. The tyrant who is described as having rattled his chariot along a bridge of brass over the heads of his subjects, was, no doubt, inwardly laughed at; but what if this mock Jupiter, not satisfied with an empty noise of his own making, had amused himself with throwing fire-brands upon the house-tops, as a substitute for lightning; and from his elevation, had hurled stones upon the heads of his people, to shew that he was a master of the destructive bolt, as well as of the harmless voice of the thunder!—The lovers of all that is honourable to humanity have recently had occasion to rejoice over the downfal of an intoxicated despot, whose vagaries furnish more solid materials by which the philosopher will exemplify how strict is the connection between the ludicrously, and the terribly fantastic. We know, also, that Robespierre was one of the vainest men that the most vain country upon earth has produced;—and from this passion, and from that cowardice which naturally connects itself with it, flowed the horrors of his administration. It is a descent, which I fear you will scarcely pardon, to compare these redoubtable enemies of mankind with the anonymous conductor of a perishable publication. But the moving spirit is the same in them all; and, as far as difference of circumstances, and disparity of powers, will allow, manifests itself in the same way; by professions of reverence for truth, and concern for duty—carried to the giddiest heights of ostentation, while practice seems to have no other reliance than on the omnipotence of falsehood.

The transition from a vindication of Robert Burns to these hints for a picture of the intellectual deformity of one who has grossly outraged his memory, is too natural to require an apology: but I fear, sir, that I stand in need of indulgence for having detained you so long. Let me beg that you would impart to any judicious friends of the poet as much of the contents of these pages as you think will be serviceable to the cause; but do not give publicity to any *portion* of them, unless it be thought probable that an open circulation of the whole may be useful.* The subject is delicate, and some of the opinions are of a kind, which, if torn away from the trunk that supports them, will be apt to wither, and, in that state, to contract poisonous qualities; like the branches of the yew, which, while united by a living spirit to their native tree, are neither noxious, nor without beauty; but, being dissevered and cast upon the ground, become deadly to the cattle that incautiously feed upon them.

To Mr. Gilbert Burns, especially, let my sentiments be conveyed, with my sincere respects, and best wishes for the success of his praise-worthy enterprize. And if, through modest apprehension, he should doubt of his own ability to do justice to his brother's memory, let him take encouragement from the assurance that the most odious part of the charges owed its credit to the silence of those who were deemed best entitled to speak; and who, it was thought, would not have been mute, had they believed that they could speak beneficially. Moreover, it may be relied on as a general truth, which will not escape his re-collection, that tasks of this kind are not so arduous as, to those who are tenderly concerned in their issue, they may at first appear to be; for, if the many be hasty to condemn, there is re-action of generosity which stimulates them—when forcibly summoned—to redress the wrong; and, for the sensible part of mankind, *they* are neither dull to under-stand, nor slow to make allowance for, the aberrations of men, whose intellectual powers do honour to their species.

I am, dear sir,
respectfully yours,
WILLIAM WORDSWORTH.

Rydal Mount, January, 1816.

* It was deemed that it would be so, and the letter is published accordingly.

(b) Extract from a letter to John Scott, 11 June 1816. *The Letters of William and Dorothy Wordsworth*, ed. E. De Selincourt, 2nd ed., III *The Middle Years Part II 1812–1820*, rev. M. Moorman and A. G. Hill, pp. 322–3.

John Scott (1784–1821), editor of the *Champion* newspaper, had asked for Wordsworth's views on the clash between genius and morality.

The queries you put to me upon the connection between genius and irregularity of conduct may probably induce me to take up the subject again, and yet it scarcely seems necessary. No man can claim indulgence for his transgressions on the score of his sensibilities, but at the expense of his credit for intellectual powers. All men of *first* rate genius have been as distinguished for dignity, beauty, and propriety of moral conduct. But we often find the faculties and qualities of the mind not well balanced; something of prime importance is left short, and hence confusion and disorder. On the one hand it is well that dunces should not arrogate to themselves a pharisaical superiority, because they avoid the vices and faults which they see men of talent fall into. They should not be permitted to believe that they have more understanding merely on that account, but should be taught that they are preserved probably by having less feeling, and being consequently less liable to temptation. On the other hand, the man of genius ought to know that the cause of his vices is, in fact, his deficiencies, and not, as he fondly imagines, his superfluities and superiorities. All men ought to be judged with charity and forbearance after death has put it out of their power to explain the motives of their actions, and especially men of acute sensibility and lively passions. This was the scope of my letter to Mr. Gray. Burns has been cruelly used, both dead and alive. The treatment which Butler and others have experienced has been renewed in him. He asked for bread—no, he did not *ask* it, he endured the want of it with silent fortitude—and ye gave him a stone. It is worse than ridiculous to see the people of Dumfries coming forward with their pompous mausoleum, they who persecuted and reviled him with such low-minded malignity. Burns might have said to that town when he was dying, 'Ingrata—non possidebis ossa mea!'[1] On this and a thousand other accounts his

[1] 'Ungrateful, you will not possess my bones.' Scipio Africanus (234–183 BC) ordered, these words to be carved on his tomb near Naples after his rejection from Rome.

monument ought to have been placed in or near to Edinburgh, 'stately Edinburgh throned on crags'. How well would such an edifice have accorded with the pastoral imagery near St. Anthony's Well and under Arthur's Seat, while the metropolis of his native country,—to which his writings have done so great honour—with its murmuring sounds, was in distinct hearing![1]

54. Jane Austen on an ardent admirer of Burns

1817

Extract from Jane Austen, *Sanditon*, ed. R. W. Chapman (1925), pp. 88–94.

This is part of chapter 7 of an uncompleted novel begun in 1817, the year of Jane Austen's death. Such poised mockery of an incoherent admirer of Burns underlines by contrast the clumsiness of more direct moralistic criticism of the poet (see Introduction, p. 39).

Miss Denham's Character was pretty well decided with Charlotte. Sir Edward's required longer Observation. He surprised her by quittiny Clara immediately on their all joining & agreeing to walk, & bg addressing his attentions entirely to herself.—Stationing himself close by her, he seemed to mean to detach her as much as possible from the rest of the Party & to give her the whole of his Conversation. He began, in a tone of great Taste & Feeling, to talk of the Sea & the Sea shore— & ran with Energy through all the usual Phrases employed in praise of

---

[1] On 21 April 1819 Wordsworth wrote to J. Forbes Mitchell, declining to contribute to a monument for Burns: 'he has raised for himself a Monument so conspicuous, and of such imperishable materials, as to render a local fabric of Stone superfluous, and therefore comparatively insignificant.' *Letters of William and Dorothy Wordsworth*, 2nd ed., III, *Part II 1812–20*, rev. Moorman and Hill, p. 534.

their Sublimity, & descriptive of the *undescribable* Emotions they excite in the Mind of Sensibility.—The terrific Grandeur of the Ocean in a Storm, its glassy surface in a calm, its Gulls & its Samphire, & the deep fathoms of its Abysses, its quick vicissitudes, its direful Deceptions, its Mariners tempting it in Sunshine & overwhelmed by the sudden Tempest, All were eagerly & fluently touched;—rather commonplace perhaps—but doing very well from the Lips of a handsome Sir Edward, —and she c^d not but think him a Man of Feeling—till he began to stagger her by the number of his Quotations, & the bewilderment of some of his sentences.—'Do you remember, said he, Scott's beautiful Lines on the Sea?—Oh! what a description they convey!—They are never out of my Thoughts when I walk here.—That Man who can read them unmoved must have the nerves of an Assassin!—Heaven defend me from meeting such a Man un-armed.'—'What description do you mean?—said Charlotte. I remember none at this moment, of the Sea, in either of Scott's Poems.'—'Do not you indeed?—Nor can I exactly recall the beginning at this moment—But—you cannot have forgotten his description of Woman.

—Oh! Woman in our Hours of Ease—[1]

Delicious! Delicious!—Had he written nothing more, he w^d have been Immortal. And then again, that unequalled, unrivalled address to Parental affection—

> Some feelings are to Mortals given
> With less of Earth in them than Heaven &c.[2]

But while we are on the subject of Poetry, what think you Miss H. of Burns Lines to his Mary?'[3]
'Oh! there is Pathos to madden one!—If ever there was a Man who *felt*, it was Burns.—Montgomery has all the Fire of Poetry, Wordsworth has the true soul of it—Campbell in his 'pleasures of Hope' has touched the extreme of our Sensations—'Like Angel's visits, few & far between.'[4] Can you conceive any thing more subduing, more melting, more fraught with the deep Sublime than that Line?—But Burns—I confess my sence of his Pre-eminence Miss H.—If Scott *has* a fault, it is the want of Passion.—Tender, Elegant, Descriptive—but *Tame*.—The Man who cannot do justice to the attributes of Woman is my contempt.

[1] *Marmion*, VI, xxx.   [2] 'Lady of The Lake', II, 22.   [3] 'Highland Mary'.
[4] 'Pleasures of Hope', II, 377.

—Sometimes indeed a flash of feeling seems to irradiate him—as in the Lines we were speaking of—"Oh! Woman in our hours of Ease"— But Burns is always on fire.—His Soul was the Altar in which lovely Woman sat enshrined, his Spirit truly breathed the immortal Incence which is her Due.—'I have read several of Burn's Poems with great delight, said Charlotte as soon as she had time to speak, but I am not poetic enough to separate a Man's Poetry entirely from his Character; —& poor Burns's known Irregularities, greatly interrupt my enjoyment of his Lines.—I have difficulty in depending on the *Truth* of his Feelings as a Lover. I have not faith in the *sincerity* of the affections of a Man of his Description. He felt & he wrote & he forgot.' 'Oh! no no —exclaimed Sir Edw: in an extasy. He was all ardour & Truth!—His Genius & his Susceptibilities might lead him into some Aberrations— But who is perfect?—It were Hyper-criticism, it were Pseudo-philosophy to expect from the soul of high toned Genius, the grovellings of a common mind.—The Coruscations of Talent, elicited by impassioned feeling in the breast of Man, are perhaps incompatible with some of the prosaic Decencies of Life;—nor can you, loveliest Miss Heywood—(speaking with an air of deep sentiment)—nor can any Woman be a fair Judge of what a Man may be propelled to say, write or do, by the sovereign impulses of illimitable Ardour.' This was very fine;—but if Charlotte understood it at all, not very moral— & being moreover by no means pleased with his extraordinary stile of compliment, she gravely answered 'I really know nothing of the matter.— This is a charming day. The Wind I fancy must be Southerly.' 'Happy, happy Wind, to engage Miss Heywood's Thoughts!—She began to think him downright silly.—His chusing to walk with her, she had learnt to understand. It was done to pique Miss Brereton. She had read it, in an anxious glance or two on his side—but why he sh^d talk so much Nonsense, unless he could do no better, was unintelligible.—He seemed very sentimental, very full of some Feelings or other, & very much addicted to all the newest-fashioned hard words—had not a very clear Brain she presumed, & talked a good deal by rote.—The Future might explain him further—but when there was a proposition for going into the Library she felt that she had had quite enough of Sir Edw: for one Morn^g, & very gladly accepted Lady D.'s invitation of remaining on the Terrace with her.—The others all left them, Sir Edw: with looks of very gallant despair in tearing himself away, & they united their agreableness—that is, Lady Denham like a true great Lady, talked & talked only of her own concerns, & Charlotte listened.

55. John Wilson in *Blackwood's Magazine*

I, iii (June 1817), 261-6

Extract from 'Observations on Mr. Wordsworth's Letter Relative to a New Edition of Burns' Works. By a Friend of Robert Burns'.

John Wilson (1785-1854) had read part of Jeffrey's essay on Burns to William and Dorothy Wordsworth in 1809 (cf. No. 44). The publication of Wordsworth's 'Letter To A Friend of Burns' drew from him this attack on Wordsworth. Then, with characteristic inconsistency, which his use of pseudonyms concealed from the public, he argued in *Blackwood's* on the other side of the question. (Cf. A. L. Strout, 'John Wilson, "Champion" Of Wordsworth', *Modern Philology* (May 1934), xxxi, 384-6) (see Nos 59, 69 and Introduction, p. 38).

It seems that Mr. Peterkin, in his very heavy and dry Essay, had made several quotations from the Edinburgh and Quarterly Reviews. The last of these articles is far more severe on Burns' failings than the first. But Mr. Wordsworth passes the *Quarterly Review* quietly over; and, with the voice and countenance of a maniac, fixes his teeth in the blue cover of the *Edinburgh*. He growls over it—shakes it violently to and fro—and at last, wearied out with vain efforts at mastication, leaves it covered over with the drivelling slaver of his impotent rage.

But what will be thought of Mr. Wordsworth, when he tells us that he has never *read* the offensive criticism in the *Edinburgh Review*! He has only seen the garbled extract of Mr. Peterkin. What right, then, has he to talk big of injustice done to the dead, when he is himself so deplorably deficient in justice to the living? But Mr. Wordsworth must not be allowed to escape the castigation which his unparalleled insolence deserves. The world is not to be gulled by his hypocritical zeal in the defence of injured merit. It is not Robert Burns for whom he feels,—it is William Wordsworth. All the while that he is exclaiming against the Reviewer's injustice to Burns, he writhes under the lash

which that consummate satirist has inflicted upon himself, and exhibits
a back yet sore with the wounds which have been in vain kept open,
and which his restless and irritable vanity will never allow to close.

We shall not disgrace our pages with any portion of the low and
vulgar abuse which the enraged poet heaps upon the Editor of the
Edinburgh Review. It is Mr. Wordsworth's serious opinion, that that
gentleman is a person of the very weakest intellects—that his malignity
is neutralized by his vanity—that he does not possess one liberal
accomplishment—and that he is nearly *as imbecile as Buonaparte*! Mr.
Wordsworth's friends should not allow him to expose himself in this
way. He has unquestionably written some fine verses in his day; but,
with the exception of some poetical genius, he is, in all respects,
immeasurably inferior, as an intellectual being, to the distinguished
person whom he so foolishly libels.

We wish to have done with this lyrical ballad-monger.

56. Hazlitt lectures on Burns

1818

Extracts from lecture by William Hazlitt (1778–1830), critic and
essayist, 'On Burns, and the Old English Ballads', delivered at the
Surrey Institution in 1818 and published in Hazlitt's *Lectures on the
English Poets* the same year. Text from *Complete Works of William
Hazlitt*, ed. P. P. Howe (1930), V, pp. 127–40 (see No. 62 and
Introduction, p. 38).

He held the plough or the pen with the same firm, manly grasp; nor
did he cut out poetry as we cut out watch-papers, with finical dexterity, nor from the same flimsy materials. Burns was not like Shakespeare in the range of his genius; but there is something of the same
magnanimity, directness, and unaffected character about him. He was

not a sickly sentimentalist, a namby-pamby poet, a mincing metre ballad-monger, any more than Shakespeare. He would as soon hear 'a brazen candlestick tuned, or a dry wheel grate on the axletree.' He was as much of a man—not a twentieth part as much of a poet as Shakespeare. With but little of his imagination or inventive power, he had the same life of mind: within the narrow circle of personal feeling or domestic incidents, the pulse of his poetry flows as healthily and vigorously. He had an eye to see; a heart to feel:—no more. His pictures of good fellowship, of social glee, of quaint humour, are equal to any thing; they come up to nature, and they cannot go beyond it. The sly jest collected in his laughing eye at the sight of the grotesque and ludicrous in manners—the large tear rolled down his manly cheek at the sight of another's distress. He has made us as well acquainted with himself as it is possible to be; has let out the honest impulses of his native disposition, the unequal conflict of the passions in his breast, with the same frankness and truth of description. His strength is not greater than his weakness: his virtues were greater than his vices. His virtues belonged to his genius: his vices to his situation, which did not correspond to his genius.

It has been usual to attack Burns's moral character, and the moral tendency of his writings at the same time; and Mr. Wordsworth, in a letter to Mr. Gray, Master of the High School at Edinburgh, in attempting to defend, has only laid him open to a more serious and unheard-of responsibility. Mr. Gray might very well have sent him back, in return for his epistle, the answer of Holofernes in *Love's Labour's Lost*:—'*Via* Goodman Dull, thou hast spoken no word all this while.' The author of this performance, which is as weak in effect as it is pompous in pretension, shews a great dislike of Robespierre, Buonaparte, and of Mr. Jeffrey, whom he, by some unaccountable fatality, classes together as the three most formidable enemies of the human race that have appeared in his (Mr. Wordsworth's) remembrance; but he betrays very little liking to Burns. He is, indeed, anxious to get him out of the unhallowed clutches of the *Edinburgh* Reviewers (as a mere matter of poetical privilege), only to bring him before a graver and higher tribunal, which is his own; and after repeating and insinuating ponderous charges against him, shakes his head, and declines giving any opinion in so tremendous a case; so that though the judgement of the former critic is set aside, poor Burns remains just where he was, and nobody gains any thing by the cause but Mr. Wordsworth, in an increasing opinion of his own wisdom and purity. 'Out upon this half-faced fellowship!' The author of the *Lyrical Ballads* has thus missed a fine opportunity of doing Burns justice and himself honour. He might have shewn himself a philosophical prose-writer, as well as a philosophical poet. He might have offered as amiable and as gallant a defence of the Muses, as my uncle Toby, in the honest simplicity of his heart, did of the army. He might have said at once, instead of making a parcel of wry faces over the matter, that Burns had written 'Tam o' Shanter,' and that that alone was enough; that he could hardly have described the excesses of mad, hairbrained, roaring mirth and convivial indulgence, which are the soul of it, if he himself had not 'drunk full ofter of the ton than of the well'—unless 'the act and practique part of life had been the mistress of his theorique.' Mr. Wordsworth might have quoted such lines as—

> The landlady and Tam grew gracious,
> Wi' favours secret, sweet, and precious;—

or,

> Care, mad to see a man so happy,
> E'en drown'd himself among the nappy;

and fairly confessed that he could not have written such lines from a want of proper habits and previous sympathy; and that till some great puritanical genius should arise to do these things equally well without any knowledge of them, the world might forgive Burns the injuries he had done his health and fortune in his poetical apprenticeship to experience, for the pleasure he had afforded them. Instead of this, Mr. Wordsworth hints, that with different personal habits and greater strength of mind, Burns would have written differently, and almost as well as *he* does. He might have taken that line of Gay's,

> The fly that sips treacle is lost in the sweets,—

and applied it in all its force and pathos to the poetical character. He might have argued that poets are men of genius, and that a man of genius is not a machine; that they live in a state of intellectual intoxication, and that it is too much to expect them to be distinguished by peculiar *sang froid*, circumspection, and sobriety. Poets are by nature men of stronger imagination and keener sensibilities than others; and it is a contradiction to suppose them at the same time governed only by the cool, dry, calculating dictates of reason and foresight. Mr. Wordsworth might have ascertained the boundaries that part the provinces of reason and imagination:—that it is the business of the understanding to exhibit things in their relative proportions and ultimate consequences—of the imagination to insist on their immediate impressions, and to indulge their strongest impulses; but it is the poet's office to pamper the imagination of his readers and his own with the extremes of present ecstacy or agony, to snatch the swift-winged golden minutes, the torturing hour, and to banish the dull, prosaic, monotonous realities of life, both from his thoughts and from his practice. Mr. Wordsworth might have shewn how it is that all men of genius, or of originality and independence of mind, are liable to practical errors, from the very confidence their superiority inspires, which makes them fly in the face of custom and prejudice, always rashly, sometimes unjustly; for, after all, custom and prejudice are not without foundation in truth and reason, and no one individual is a match for the world in power, very few in knowledge. The world may altogether be set down as older and wiser than any single person in it.

Again, our philosophical letter-writer might have enlarged on the temptations to which Burns was exposed from his struggles with fortune and the uncertainty of his fate. He might have shewn how a poet, not born to wealth or title, was kept in a constant state of feverish anxiety with respect to his fame and the means of a precarious livelihood: that 'from being chilled with poverty, steeped in contempt, he had passed into the sunshine of fortune, and was lifted to the very pinnacle of public favour'; yet even there could not count on the continuance of success, but was, 'like the giddy sailor on the mast, ready with every blast to topple down into the fatal bowels of the deep!' He might have traced his habit of ale-house tippling to the last long precious draught of his favourite usquebaugh, which he took in the prospect of bidding farewel for ever to his native land; and his conjugal infidelities to his first disappointment in love, which would not have happened to him, if he had been born to a small estate in land, or bred up behind a counter!

Lastly, Mr. Wordsworth might have shewn the incompatibility between the Muses and the Excise, which never agreed well together, or met in one seat, till they were unaccountably reconciled on Rydal Mount. He must know (no man better) the distraction created by the opposite calls of business and of fancy, the torment of extents, the plague of receipts laid in order or mislaid, the disagreeableness o exacting penalties or paying the forfeiture; and how all this (together with the broaching of casks and the splashing of beer barrels) must have preyed upon a mind like Burns, with more than his natural sensibility and none of his acquired firmness.

Mr. Coleridge, alluding to this circumstance of the promotion of the Scottish Bard to be 'a gauger of ale-firkins,' in a poetical epistle to his friend Charles Lamb, calls upon him in a burst of heartfelt indignation, to gather a wreath of henbane, nettles, and nightshade,

> To twine
> The illustrious brow of Scotch nobility.

If, indeed, Mr. Lamb had undertaken to write a letter in defence of Burns, how different would it have been from this of Mr. Wordsworth's! How much better than I can even imagine it to have been done!

It is hardly reasonable to look for a hearty or genuine defence of Burns from the pen of Mr. Wordsworth; for there is no common link of sympathy between them. Nothing can be more different or hostile than the spirit of their poetry. Mr. Wordsworth's poetry is the poetry of mere sentiment and pensive contemplation: Burns's is a very highly sublimated essence of animal existence. With Burns, 'self-love and social are the same'—

> And we'll tak a cup of kindness yet,
> For auld lang syne.

Mr. Wordsworth is 'himself alone', a recluse philosopher, or a reluctant spectator of the scenes of many-coloured life; moralising on them, not describing, not entering into them. Robert Burns has exerted all the vigour of his mind, all the happiness of his nature, in exalting the pleasures of wine, of love, and good fellowship: but in Mr. Wordsworth there is a total disunion and divorce of the faculties of the mind from those of the body; the banns are forbid, or a separation is austerely pronounced from bed and board—*a mensâ et thoro*. From the *Lyrical Ballads*, it does not appear that men eat or drink, marry or are given in marriage. If we lived by every sentiment that proceeded out of mouths, and not by bread or wine, or if the species were continued like trees (to borrow an expression from the great Sir Thomas Brown), Mr. Wordsworth's poetry would be just as good as ever. It is not so with

Burns: he is 'famous for the keeping of it up', and in his verse is ever fresh and gay. For this, it seems, he has fallen under the displeasure of the *Edinburgh* Reviewers, and the still more formidable patronage of Mr. Wordsworth's pen.

> This, this was the unkindest cut of all.

I was going to give some extracts out of this composition in support of what I have said, but I find them too tedious. Indeed (if I may be allowed to speak my whole mind, under correction) Mr. Wordsworth could not be in any way expected to tolerate or give a favourable interpretation to Burns's constitutional foibles—even his best virtues are not good enough for him. He is repelled and driven back into himself, not less by the worth than by the faults of others. His taste is as exclusive and repugnant as his genius. It is because so few things give him pleasure, that he gives pleasure to so few people. It is not every one who can perceive the sublimity of a daisy, or the pathos to be extracted from a withered thorn!

To proceed from Burns's patrons to his poetry, than which no two things can be more different. His 'Twa Dogs' is a very spirited piece of description, both as it respects the animal and human creation, and conveys a very vivid idea of the manners both of high and low life. The burlesque panegyric of the first dog,

> His locked, lettered, braw brass collar
> Shew'd him the gentleman and scholar—

reminds one of Launce's account of his dog Crabbe, where he is said, as an instance of his being in the way of promotion, 'to have got among three or four gentleman-like dogs under the Duke's table.' The 'Halloween' is the most striking and picturesque description of local customs and scenery. The 'Brigs of Ayr', the 'Address to a Haggis', 'Scotch Drink,' and innumerable others are, however, full of the same kind of characteristic and comic painting. But his masterpiece in this way is his 'Tam o' Shanter.' I shall give the beginning of it, but I am afraid I shall hardly know when to leave off.

[quotes 'Tam o' Shanter']

Burns has given the extremes of licentious eccentricity and convivial enjoyment, in the story of this scape-grace, and of patriarchal simplicity and gravity in describing the old national character of the Scottish peasantry. 'The Cotter's Saturday Night' is a noble and pathetic picture of human manners, mingled with a fine religious awe. It comes over the mind like a slow and solemn strain of music. The soul of the poet aspires from this scene of low-thoughted care, and reposes, in trembling hope, on 'the bosom of its Father and its God.' Hardly any thing can be more touching than the following stanzas, for instance, whether as they describe human interests, or breathe a lofty devotional spirit.

[quotes 'The Cotter's Saturday Night', ll. 14-45, 55-72, 91-117]

Burns's poetical epistles to his friends are admirable, whether for the touches of satire, the painting of character, or the sincerity of friendship they display. Those to Captain Grose, and to Davie, a brother poet, are among the best:—they are 'the true pathos and sublime of human life.' His prose-letters are sometimes tinctured with affectation. They seem written by a man who has been admired for his wit, and is expected on all occasions to shine. Those in which he expresses his ideas of natural beauty in reference to Alison's 'Essay on Taste,' and advocates the keeping up the remembrances of old customs and seasons, are the most powerfully written. His English serious odes and moral stanzas are, in general, failures, such as the 'The Lament,' 'Man was made to Mourn,' &c. nor do I much admire his 'Scots wha hae wi' Wallace bled'. In this strain of didactic or sentimental moralising, the lines to Glencairn are the most happy, and impressive. His imitations of the old humorous ballad style of Ferguson's songs are no whit inferior to the admirable originals, such as 'John Anderson, my Joe,' and many more. But of all his productions, the pathetic and serious love-songs which he has left behind him, in the manner of the old ballads, are perhaps those which take the deepest and most lasting hold of the mind. Such are the lines to Mary Morison, and those entitled 'Jessy'.

> Here's a health to ane I lo'e dear—
> Here's a health to ane I lo'e dear—
> Thou art sweet as the smile when fond lovers meet,
> And soft as their parting tear—Jessy!
> Altho' thou maun never be mine,
>   Altho' even hope is denied;
> 'Tis sweeter for thee despairing,
>   Than aught in the world beside—Jessy!

The conclusion of the other is as follows.

> Yestreen, when to the trembling string
>   The dance gaed through the lighted ha',
> To thee my fancy took its wing,
>   I sat, but neither heard nor saw.
> Tho' this was fair, and that was bra',
>   And yon the toast of a' the town,
> I sighed and said among them a',
>   Ye are na' Mary Morison.

That beginning, 'Oh gin my love were a bonny red rose,' is a piece of rich and fantastic description. One would think that nothing could surpass these in beauty of expression, and in true pathos: and nothing does or can, but some of the old Scotch ballads themselves. There is in them a still more original cast of thought, a more romantic imagery—the thistle's glittering down, the gilliflower on the old garden-wall, the horseman's silver bells, the hawk on its perch—a closer intimacy with nature, a firmer reliance on it, as the only stock of wealth which the mind has to resort to, a more infantine simplicity of manners, a greater strength of affection, hopes longer cherished and longer deferred, sighs that the heart dare hardly heave, and 'thoughts that often lie too deep for tears.' We seem to feel that those who wrote and sung them (the early minstrels) lived in the open air, wandering on from place to place with restless feet and thoughts, and lending an ever-open ear to the fearful accidents of war or love, floating on the breath of old tradition or common fame, and moving the strings of their harp with sounds that sank into a nation's heart.

57. Keats on Burns

1818-19

Extracts from letters. *Letters of John Keats 1814-1821*, ed. Hyder
E. Rollins (1958), I, pp. 319-20, 331, 322-6; II, p. 78.

Keats also referred to Burns in poems, including the hastily
written 'On Visiting the Tomb of Burns' ('With honour due I
have oft honoured thee'), and the 'Epistle to George Felton
Mathew', ll. 65-71 (see Introduction, p. 40).

(a) To Tom Keats, 7 July 1818

These kirkmen have done Scotland harm—they have banished puns
and laughing and kissing except in cases where the very danger and
crime must make it very fine and gustful. I shall make a full stop at
kissing for after that there should be a better parent-thesis: and go on
to remind you of the fate of Burns. Poor unfortunate fellow—his disposition was southern—how sad it is when a luxurious imagination is
obliged in self defence to deaden its delicacy in vulgarity, and riot in
thing[s] attainable that it may not have leisure to go mad after thing[s]
which are not. No Man in such matters will be content with the
experience of others—It is true that out of suffrance there is no greatness, no dignity; that in the most abstracted Pleasure there is no lasting
happiness: yet who would not like to discover over again that Cleo-
patra was a Gipsey, Helen a Rogue and Ruth a deep one? I have not
sufficient reasoning faculty to settle the doctrine of thrift—as it is
consistent with the dignity of human Society—with the happiness of
Cottagers—All I can do is by plump contrasts—Were the fingers made
to squeeze a guinea or a white hand? Were the Lips made to hold a pen
or a kiss? And yet in Cities Man is shut out from his fellows if he is
poor, the Cottager must be dirty and very wretched if she be not
thrifty—The present state of society demands this and this convinces
me that the world is very young and in a very ignorant state—We live

in a barbarous age. I would sooner be a wild deer than a Girl under the dominion of the kirk, and I would sooner be a wild hog than be the occasion of a Poor Creatures pennance before those execrable elders—

(b) To Tom Keats, 13 July 1818

. . . then we set forward to Burns's town Ayr—the Approach to it is extremely fine—quite outwent my expectations richly meadowed, wooded, heathed and rivuleted—with a grand Sea view, terminated by the black Mountains of the isle of Annan [Arran].[1] As soon as I saw them so nearly I said to myself 'How is it they did not beckon Burns to some grand attempt at Epic'.

(c) To John Hamilton Reynolds, 11, 13 July 1818

. . . One song of Burns's is more worth to you than all I could think for a whole year in his native country—His Misery is a dead weight upon the nimbleness of one's quill—I tried to forget it—to drink Toddy without any care—to write a merry Sonnet—it would not do—he talked with Bitches—he drank with Blackguards, he was miserable—We can see horribly clear in the works of such a man his whole life, as if we were God's spies.

(d) To George and Georgiana Keats, 19 March 1819

The *Blackwood's* review has committed themselves in a scandalous heresy—they have been putting up Hogg the ettrick shepherd against Burns—The senseless villains . . . they ['the scotch'] want imagination —and that is why they are so fond of Hogg, who has a little of it.[2]

[1] For Wordsworth's comment on Burns's failure to describe 'the peaks of Arran', see below p. 403.
[2] Keats refers to *Blackwood's Magazine* (February 1819), iv. See below, No. 59.

58. Burns and Crabbe

1819

Extracts from [J. G. Lockhart], *Peter's Letters to His Kinsfolk* (1819) ('2nd ed.', i.e. 1st), I, 113–36.

Lockhart (1794–1854), a Scottish advocate and man of letters, became editor of the *Quarterly Review* in 1825. He is best known for his *Life* of Scott, his father-in-law (1837–8) (see Nos 63, 66 and Introduction, p. 40).

By the way, this inimitable Cantata is not to be found in Currie's edition, and I suspect you are a stranger even to its name; and yet, had Burns left nothing more than this behind him, I think he would still have left enough to justify all the honour in which his genius is held. There does not exist, in any one piece throughout the whole range of English poetry, such a collection of true, fresh, and characteristic lyrics. Here we have nothing, indeed, that is very high, but we have much that is very tender. What can be better in its way, than the fine song of the Highland Widow, 'wha had in mony a well been douked?'

[quotes 'The Jolly Beggars', ll. 88–100]

And that fine 'Penseroso' close,

> But oh! they catch'd him at the last,
> And bound him in a dungeon fast;
> My curse upon them every one,
> They've hang'd my braw John Highlandman.
> And now, a widow, I must mourn
> Departed joys that ne'er return;
> No comfort—but a hearty can,
> When I think on John Highlandman.

The Little Fiddler, who (in vain, alas!) offers his services to console her, is conceived in the most happy taste.

[quotes 'The Jolly Beggars', ll. 117–28]

But the finest part of the whole, is the old Scottish Soldier's ditty. Indeed, I think there is no question, that half of the best ballads Campbell has written, are the legitimate progeny of some of these lines.

[quotes 'The Jolly Beggars', ll. 29–40, 45–8]

What different ideas of low life one forms even from reading the works of men who paint it admirably. Had Crabbe, for instance, undertaken to represent the carousal of a troop of Beggars in a hedge alehouse, how unlike would his production have been to this Cantata? He would have painted their rags and their dirt with the accuracy of a person who is not used to see rags and dirt very often; he would have seized the light careless swing of their easy code of morality, with the penetration of one who has long been a Master-Anatomist of the manners and the hearts of men. But I doubt very much, whether any one could enter into the true spirit of such a meeting, who had not been, at some period of his life, a partaker in *propria persona*, and almost *par cum paribus*, in the rude merriment of its constituents. I have no doubt that Burns sat for his own picture in the Bard of the Cantata, and had often enough in some such scene as *Poosie Nansie's*—

> —Rising, rejoicing
> Between his twa Deborahs,
> Looked round him and found them,
> Impatient for his chorus.

It is by such familiarity alone that the secret and essence of that charm, which no groupe of human companions entirely wants, can be fixed and preserved even by the greatest of poets—Mr. Crabbe would have described the Beggars like a firm though humane Justice of the Peace—poor Robert Burns did not think himself entitled to assume any such airs of superiority. The consequence is, that we would have understood and pitied the one groupe, but that we sympathize even with the joys of the other. We would have thrown a few shillings to Mr. Crabbe's Mendicants, but we are more than half inclined to sit down and drink them ourselves with the 'orra duds' of those of Burns.

59. John Wilson in *Blackwood's Magazine*

iv (February 1819), 521–9

Extract from 'Some Observations on the Poetry of the Agricultural and that of the Pastoral District of Scotland, illustrated by a Comparative View of the Genius of Burns and the Ettrick Shepherd'.

For Keats's opinion of the comparison between Burns and Hogg, see No. 57d. Hogg reprinted part of this article (on Burns only) in *The Works of Robert Burns*, ed. the Ettrick Shepherd and William Motherwell (1836), V. Wilson reviewed Lockhart's *Life* in 1828. His later criticism of Burns is contained in No. 69, and in *The Land of Burns* [ed. R. Chambers] (Glasgow, 1840) (see No. 55 and Introduction, p. 40).

Religion, then, has made the Scottish people thoughtful and meditative in their intellects—simple and pure in their morals—tender and affectionate in their hearts. But when there is profound thought and awakened sensibility, imagination will not fail to reign; and if this be indeed the general character of a whole people, and should they moreover be blessed with a beautiful country, and a free government, then those higher and purer feelings which, in less happy lands, are possessed only by the higher ranks of society, are brought into free play over all the bosom of society; and it may, without violence, be said, that a spirit of poetry breathes over all its valleys.

Of England, and of the character of her population, high and low, we think with exultation and with pride. Some virtues they perhaps possess in greater perfection than any other people. But we believe, that the most philosophical Englishmen acknowledge that there is a depth of moral and religious feeling in the peasantry of Scotland, not to be found among the best part of their own population. There cannot be said to be any poetry of the peasantry of England. We do not feel any consciousness of national prejudice, when we say, that a great poet could not be born among the English peasantry—bred among them—

and restricted in his poetry to subjects belonging to themselves and their life.

There doubtless are among the peasantry of every truly noble nation, much to kindle the imagination and the fancy; but we believe, that in no country but Scotland does there exist a system of social and domestic life among that order of men, which combines within it almost all the finer and higher emotions of cultivated minds, with a simplicity and artlessness of character peculiar to persons of low estate. The fireside of an English cottage is often a scene of happiness and virtue; but unquestionably, in reading the 'Cottar's Saturday Night' of Burns, we feel, that we are reading the records of a purer, simpler, more pious race; and there is in that immortal poem a depth of domestic joy—an intensity of the feeling of home—a presiding spirit of love— and a lofty enthusiasm of religion, which are all peculiarly Scottish, and beyond the pitch of mind of any other people.

It is not our intention at present, to pursue this interesting subject into its inmost recesses; we may have said enough to awaken the meditations of our readers on the poetical character of our peasantry. Yet, it may not be amiss to say a few words on the difference of poetical feeling and genius in an agricultural and pastoral state of life, —exemplified as that difference appears to be in the poetry of Burns, and his only worthy successor, the Ettrick Shepherd.

And, in the *first* place, it is undeniable, that in an agricultural country, the life of a peasant is a life of severe and incessant labour, leaving him apparently few opportunities for the cultivation and enjoyment either of his moral or intellectual nature. Each hour has its task,—and when the body is enslaved, with difficulty may the soul be free.

In the *second* place, the knowledge which men thus situated are likely to wish to attain, is of a narrow and worldly kind, immediately connected with the means of subsistence, and not linked with objects fitted to awaken much enthusiastic or imaginative feelings. The knowledge absolutely essential to a cottar in an agricultural country is small indeed, and small accordingly it will be found to be in almost all cases. Sobriety and prudence are his chief virtues; but his duties and his cares make no demand on equalities or feelings of a higher kind.

Thirdly, the face of an agricultural country cannot be very kindling to the senses or imagination. It is all subordinated to separate and distinct uses; one great end, namely, production, is constantly obtruded on the mind among all the shews of scenery, and that alone must be fatal to all play of imagination.

Fourthly, the constant and close intercourse between the inhabitants, arising from the density of population, gives to the people a tone of thought alien from all enthusiasm, and consequently from all superstition. Any superstitious forms that may rise up among them will be but slight modifications of feelings excited by the objects of reality, and will possess but a feeble power among the depressing and deadening influences of a life on the whole so unimaginative.

And, *lastly*, it may be asserted, that if such be the character of an agricultural life, the religion of the people will rather be of a sedate and rational kind, than characterized by that fervour, and even passion, without which it is apt to degenerate into a cautionary system of morality, instead of being a kindling, supporting, and elevating faith.

On the whole, therefore, it would seem that it is not to an agricultural country that we are to look for a poetical character in its inhabitants, or for the appearance among them of a great and prevailing poet.

In a pastoral state of society, the scene assumes a very different aspect. For, in the first place, shepherds and men, connected with a pastoral life, are not bowed down 'by bodily labour constant and severe,'—and both the thoughts and the affections have time for indulgence. They have also a more intimate acquaintance with the great and simple forms of nature, and with them are necessarily associated many of their best daily emotions. They hold converse with nature, and become even in the painful prosecution of their necessary labours, unconsciously familiar with her language. Their own language then becomes poetical, and doubtless influences their characters. Their affections become spiritualized along with their imagination—and there is a fine and delicate breath and shadow of superstition over all the character of their best emotions. Their very religion partakes somewhat of the wildness of superstitious fear: the lonely edifice built for the service of God in the mountain solitude is surrounded by spots haunted by the beings of a fairy creed.

It is certain that it has been in the pastoral vallies of the south of Scotland that the poetical genius of our country has been most beautifully displayed; and though the peculiar history of those districts, as well as the circumstances under which their language grew, were especially favourable to the formation and display of poetical feeling, yet we are not to look to such narrow and limited causes as these for the acknowledged superiority of the genius of the shepherds of the south, but rather, as we conceive, to such as have been hinted at above, and are necessarily, in a great degree, common to all pastoral states of society, in all times and in all countries.

When we consider the genius of Burns, we see it manifestly moulded and coloured by his agricultural life. We see in all his earliest poems— and they are by far his finest—a noble soul struggling—labouring with a hard and oppressive fate. He was, from very boy-hood, 'a toil-worn cottar,'—and it was the aim of his noble heart to preserve that dignity which nature gave it, unshaken and unhumbled by the 'weary weight' of his lot. His genius was winged by independence—and in the proud disdain with which he spurned at the fortune that in vain strove to enslave him, it seemed as if his soul rose to a nobler pitch of enthusiasm, and that he more passionately enjoyed his freedom when feeling circled, not bound by unavailing chains.

The hardships and privations that Burns early felt himself born to endure—the constant presence before him of the image of poverty— the conviction of the necessary evils of the poor man's lot—made his whole heart to leap within him when joy, and pleasure, and happiness, opened their arms to receive him. Bliss bursts upon him like a rush of waters—and his soul is at once swept down the flood. Every one must have felt that there is a melancholy air spread over his poetry—as if his creed truly were 'that man was made to mourn', but sudden flashings and illuminations of delight are for ever breaking out;—and in the vehemence, and energy, and triumphant exultation of his language in those moments of inspiration, we feel how dear a thing free and un-mingled happiness is to the children of poverty and sorrow.

It was thus that the calamities of a life of hardship, that bows down ordinary spirits to the earth, elevated and sublimed the genius and character of our immortal poet. It was thus that nothing seemed worthy to engross his attention, but the feelings and the passions of the heart of man. He felt within him visitings of thoughts that wafted him into Elysium—he recognised in those thoughts the awful power of human passion,—and saw that, circumscribed as the sphere was in which he, a poor peasant, was placed, he might yet walk in it with power and glory,—and that he might waken up into strength, freshness, and beauty, those feelings of his lowly brethren that destiny had enfeebled and obscured, and given them an existence in poetry, essentially true to human life, but tinged with that adorning radiance, which emanates only from the poet's soul in the hour of his inspiration.

It is here that we must seek for the true cause of Burns' very limited power of description of external Nature. Certainly, of all poets of the first order, he is the one that has left us the fewest fine pictures of landscape. His senses were gratified with the forms, the blooms, and the odours of nature, and often in the fulness of his convivial delight, he pours out vivid expressions of that rapture and enjoyment. But external nature seems never to have elevated his imagination, or for any length of time to have won him from the dominion of the living world. Where his eye reposed, or his ear listened, there too his soul was satisfied. When he has attempted to generalize, to delineate associations by which nature is connected with the universal feelings of our kind, he sinks to the level of an ordinary versifier. All that vivid and burning vigour, with which he describes his own feelings and passions as a human being in union with human beings, is gone at once; and we witness the unavailing labour of a mind endeavouring to describe what it but imperfectly understands, and but feebly enjoys. There is scarcely a line in his poems written in, or of the Highlands, that would startle us with surprise in the verses of the merest poetaster. His mind had never delivered itself up to such trains of thought. In his evening walks, after a day of toil, the murmur of the stream, the whispering of the breeze, or the song of the blackbird, touched his heart with joy; and beautifully indeed has he blended his sweetest dreams of love and affection with such simple sounds as these; but generally speaking, Nature had no charms for him, unless when she at once recalled to his memory, the image of some human being whom he loved, and the visions of departed happiness. Then indeed, insensate things became instinct with spirit, and spoke the passion of the poet's soul; of which there cannot be a finer instance than in the lines to 'Mary in Heaven,' when the trees, the banks, the streams, the channel of the Ayr, seem all parts of his own being, and the whole of that sylvan scenery is enveloped in an atmosphere of mournful passion.

We have frequently thought that it was fortunate for Burns, that he lived before this age of descriptive poetry. No doubt his original mind would have preserved him from servile imitation; but his admiration of the genius of his great contemporaries might have seduced the train of his emotions from the fireside to the valley, and he might have wasted on the forms of external nature, much of that fervid passion which he has bestowed on the dearer and nearer objects of human love. Had he done so, he would have offered violence to his own soul; for it is plain that he never could have been a truly great poet, except as the low-born poet of lowly life, and that had he resigned any part of his empire over the passions of the human breast, he would have been but an inferior prince in the dominions of pure fancy.

He was, in many respects, born at a happy time; happy for a man of genius like him, but fatal and hopeless to the mere common mind. Much poetry existed in Scotland, but no poet. There was no lavish and prodigal applause of great public favourites, no despotical criticism stretching the leaden sceptre of command over the free thoughts of genius. There were in our popular poetry many exquisite fragments struck off as it were from the great mass of domestic life; many pictures of unfinished, but touching beauty. There was every thing to stimulate, awaken, and excite, little or nothing to depress or discourage. A whole world of life lay before Burns, whose inmost recesses, and darkest nooks, and sunniest eminence he had familiarly trodden from his childhood. All that world, he felt, could be made his own. No conqueror had overrun its fertile provinces, and it was for him to be crowned supreme over all the 'Lyrical singers of that high-souled land.'

The crown that he has won can never be removed from his head. Much is yet left for other poets, even among that life where the spirit of Burns delighted to work;—but he has built monuments on all the high places, and they who follow can only hope to leave behind them some far humbler memorials.

We have said that there is necessarily less enthusiasm, and therefore less superstition in an agricultural than a pastoral country. Accordingly, in the poetry of Burns, there is not much of that wild spirit of fear and mystery which is to be found in the traditions of the south of Scotland. The 'Hallowe'en' is a poem of infinite spirit and vivacity, that brings vividly before us all the merriment of the scene. But there is little or nothing very poetical in the character of its superstitions,—and the poet himself, whose imagination seems never to have been subjected beneath the sway of any creatures but those of flesh and blood, treats the whole subject with a sarcastic good-humour, and sees in it only the exhibition of mere human feelings, and passions, and characters. Even in 'Tam o' Shanter' the principal power lies in the character and situation of that 'drowthy' hero; the Devil himself, playing on his bag-pipes in the window-neuk, is little more than a human piper, rather more burly than common; and while the witches and warlocks are mere old men and women, who continue to dance after 'jigging-time is o'er,' the young witch, 'with the sark of se'enteen hunder linnen,' is

a buxom country lass to all intents and purposes, and considered by
'Tam' in a very alluring but very simple and human light.

Weel done, cutty sark!

The description of the horrors of the scene has always seemed to us
over-charged, and caricatured so as to become shocking rather than
terrible. One touch of Shakespeare's imagination is worth all that
laborious and heavy accumulation of affrightments.

But we are not now seeking to paint a picture of Burns' genius—we
aim only at a general and characteristic sketch. A few words more,
then, on the moral and religious spirit of his poetry, and we have done.

Strong charges have been brought against the general character of
his writings, and by men who, being ministers of the Christian religion,
may be supposed well imbued with its spirit. They have decreed the
poetry of Burns to be hostile to morality and religion. Now, if this be
indeed the case, it is most unaccountable that such compositions should
have become universally popular among a grave, thoughtful, affectionate, and pious peasantry—and that the memory of Burns, faulty
and frail as his human character was, should be cherished by them with
an enthusiastic fondness and admiration, as if they were all bound to
him by ties strong as those of blood itself. The poems of Burns do in
fact form a part of the existence of the Scottish peasantry—the purest
hearts and the most intelligent minds are the best acquainted with
them—and they are universally considered as a subject of rejoicing
pride, as a glory belonging to men in low estate, and which the peasant
feels to confer on him the privilege of equality with the highest in the
land. It would be a gross and irrational libel on the national character
of our people to charge Robert Burns with being an immoral and
irreligious poet.

It is, however, perfectly true, that Burns was led, by accidental and
local circumstances, perhaps too frequently to look, in a ludicrous
point of view, on the absurdities, both of doctrines and forms, that
degraded the most awful rites of religion—and likewise on the follies
and hypocrisies that disgraced the character of some of its most
celebrated ministers. His quick and keen sense of the ludicrous could
not resist the constant temptations which assailed it in the public
exhibitions of these mountebanks; and hence, instead of confining himself to the happier and nobler task of describing religious Observances
and Institutions as they might be, he rioted in the luxury of an almost

315

licentious ridicule of the abject, impious, and humiliating fooleries which, in too many cases, characterized them as they were—while his imagination was thus withdrawn from the virtues and piety of the truly enlightened ministers of Christianity, to the endless and grotesque varieties of professional vice and folly exhibited in the hypocritical pretenders to sanctity, and the strong-lunged bellowers who laid claim to the gifts of grace.

In all this mad and mirthful wit, Burns could hardly fail of sometimes unintentionally hurting the best of the pious, while he was in fact seeking to lash only the worst of the profane; and as it is at all times dangerous to speak lightly about holy things, it is not to be denied, that there are in his poems many most reprehensible passages, and that the ridicule of the human sometimes trespasses with seeming irreverence on the divine. An enemy of Burns might doubtless select from his writings a pretty formidable list of delinquencies of this kind—and by shutting his heart against all the touching and sublime poetry that has made Burns the idol of his countrymen, and brooding with a gloomy malignity on all his infirmities thus brought into one mass, he might enjoy a poor and pitiable triumph over the object of his unchristian scorn. This has been more than once attempted—but without much effect; and nothing can more decidedly prove that the general spirit of Burns' poetry is worthy of the people among whom he was born, than the forgiveness which men of austerest principles have been willing to extend to the manifold errors both of his genius and his life.

But, while we hold ourselves justified in thus speaking of some of his stern and rancorous accusers, we must not shut our eyes to the truth—nor deny, that though Burns has left to us much poetry which sinks, with healing and cheering influence, into the poor man's heart—much that breathes a pure spirit of piety and devotion,—he might have done far more good than he has done—had he delighted less in painting the corruptions of religion, than in delineating her native and in-destructible beauty. 'The Cottar's Saturday Night' shews what he could have done—had he surveyed, with a calm and untroubled eye, all the influences of our religion, carried as they are into the inmost heart of society by our simple and beautiful forms of worship—had marriage—baptism—that other more awful sacrament—death—and funeral—had these and the innumerable themes allied to them, sunk into the depths of his heart, and images of them reascended thence into living and imperishable light.

There is a pathetic moral in the imperfect character of Burns, both as a poet and a man; nor ought they who delight both in him and his works, and rightly hold the anniversary of his birth to be a day sacred in the calendar of genius—to forget, that it was often the consciousness of his own frailties that made him so true a painter of human passions— that he often looked with melancholy eyes to that pure and serene life from which he was, by his own imprudence, debarred—that innocence, purity, and virtue, were to him, in the happiest hours of his inspiration, the fair images of beings whose living presence he had too often shunned —and that the sanctities of religion itself seem still more sanctified when they rise before us in the poetry of a man who was not always withheld from approaching with levity, if not with irreverence, her most holy and mysterious altars.

We should be afraid of turning from so great a national poet as Burns, to a living genius, also born like him in the lower ranks of life, were we not assured that there is a freshness and originality in the mind of the Ettrick Shepherd, well entitling him to take his place immediately after

> Him who walked in glory and in joy,
> Following his plough upon the mountain side.

The truth is, that the respective characters of their poetry are altogether separate and distinct;—and there can be nothing more delightful than to see these two genuine children of Nature following the voice of her inspiration into such different haunts, each happy in his own native dominions, and powerful in his own legitimate rule.

And, in the *first* place, our admirable Shepherd is full of that wild enthusiasm towards external nature, which would seem to have formed so small a part of the poetical character of Burns—and he has been led by enthusiasm to acquire a far wider and far deeper knowledge of her inexhaustible wonders. He too passed a youth of poverty and hardship—but it was the youth of a lonely shepherd among the most beautiful pastoral vallies in the world, and in that solitary life in which seasons of spirit-stirring activity are followed by seasons of contemplative repose, how many years passed over him rich in impressions of sense and in dreams of fancy. His haunts were among scenes

> The most remote, and inaccessible
> By shepherds trod;

317

And living for years in the solitude, he unconsciously formed friendships with the springs—the brooks—the caves—the hills—and with all
the more fleeting and faithless pageantry of the sky, that to him came
in the place of those human affections from whose indulgence he was
debarred by the necessities that kept him aloof from the cottage fire,
and up among the mists on the mountain-top. His mind, therefore, is
stored with images of nature dear to him for the recollections which
they bring—for the restoration of his earlier life. These images he has,
at all times, a delight in pouring out—very seldom, it is true, with
much selection, or skill in the poet's art—so that his pictures in landscape are generally somewhat confused—but in them all there are lines
of light, or strokes of darkness, that at once take the imagination, and
convince us that before a poet's eye had travelled the sunshine or the
shadow. Open a volume of Burns—and then one of the Ettrick
Shepherd—and we shall see how seldom the mind of the one was
visited by those images of external nature which in that of the other
find a constant and chosen dwelling-place.

Secondly, We shall find, that in his delineations of human passions,
Burns drew from himself, or immediately from the living beings that
were 'toiling and moiling' around him; and hence, their vivid truth
and irresistible energy. But the Ettrick Shepherd is, clearly, a man
rather of kind and gentle affections than of agitating passions—and his
poetry, therefore, when it is a delineation of his own feelings, is
remarkable for serenity and repose. When he goes out of himself—
and he does so much more than Burns—he does not paint from living
agents in the transport of their passions—from the men who walk
around him in this our every-day world; but he rather loves to bring
before him, as a shepherd still in his solitude, the far-off images of
human life, dim and shadowy as dreams—and to lose himself in a
world of his own creation, filled with all the visionary phantoms of
poetical tradition.

Accordingly, in his poetry, we have but few complete pictures of
which the intensity of mere human passions or feelings constitutes the
merit and the charm—as in so many of the compositions of Burns; and,
therefore, he never can become so popular a poet, nor does he deserve
to be so. The best poetry of Burns goes, sudden as electricity, to the
heart. Every nerve in our frame is a conductor to the fluid. The best
poetry of the Ettrick Shepherd rather steals into our souls like music;
and, as many persons have no ear for music, so have many persons no
soul for such kind of poetry. Burns addressed himself almost exclusively

to the simplest and most elementary feelings of our nature, as they are exhibited in social and domestic life;—he spoke of things familiar to all, in language familiar to all—and hence his poetry is like 'the casing air', breathed and enjoyed by all. No man dares to be sceptical on the power of his poetry, for passages could be recited against him that would drown the unbeliever's voice in a tumult of acclamation. But we doubt if, from the whole range of the Ettrick Shepherd's writings, one such triumphant and irresistible passage could be produced—one strain appealing, without possibility of failure, to the universal feelings of men's hearts. But it is equally certain that many strains—and those continued and sustained strains too—might be produced from the writings of this extraordinary person, which in the hearts and souls of all men of imagination and fancy—of all men who understand the dim and shadowy associations of recollected feelings—and who can feel the charm of a poetical language, occasionally more delicate and refined, than perhaps was ever before commanded by an uneducated mind—would awaken emotions, if not so strong, certainly finer and more ethereal than any that are inspired by the very happiest compositions of the Bard of Coila.

Indeed we should scarcely hesitate to say that the Ettrick Shepherd had more of pure fancy than Burns. When the latter relinquished his strong grasp of men's passions—or suffered the vivid images of his own experience of life to fade away, he was anything but a great poet—and nothing entirely out of himself had power brightly to kindle his imagination, unless, indeed, it were some mighty national triumph or calamity, events that appealed rather to his patriotism than his poetry. But the Shepherd dreams of the days of old, and of all their dim and wavering traditions. Objects dark in the past distance of time have over him a deeper power than the bright presence of realities—and his genius loves better to lift up the veil which forgetfulness has been slowly drawing over the forms, the scenes, the actions, and the characters of the dead, than to gaze on the motions of the living. Accordingly, there are some images—some strains of feeling in his poetry, more mournful and pathetic—at least, full of a sadness more entrancing to the imagination than any thing we recollect in Burns—but, at the same time, we are aware, that though a few wild airs, from an Eolian harp, perhaps more profoundly affect the soul, at the time when they are swelling, than any other music—yet have they not so permanent a dwelling-place in the memory as the harmonious tunes of some perfect instrument.

But, *thirdly*, we have to remind such of our readers as are well acquainted with the poetry of the Ettrick Shepherd, that to feel the full power of his genius we must go with him

Beyond this visible diurnal sphere,

and walk through the shadowy world of the imagination. It is here, where Burns was weakest, that he is most strong. The airy beings that to the impassioned soul of Burns seemed cold—bloodless—and un-attractive—rise up in irresistible loveliness in their own silent do-mains, before the dreamy fancy of the gentle-hearted Shepherd. The still green beauty of the pastoral hills and vales where he passed his youth, inspired him with ever-brooding visions of fairy-land—till, as he lay musing in his lonely sheiling, the world of phantasy seemed, in the clear depths of his imagination, a lovelier reflection of that of nature—like the hills and heavens more softly shining in the water of his native lake. Whenever he treats of fairy-land, his language insen-sibly becomes, as it were, soft, wild, and aerial—we could almost think that we heard the voice of one of the fairy-folk—still and serene images seem to rise up with the wild music of the versification—and the poet deludes us, for the time, into an unquestioning and satisfied belief in the existence of those 'green realms of bliss' of which he himself seems to be a native minstrel.

In this department of pure poetry, the Ettrick Shepherd has, among his own countrymen at least, no competitor. He is the poet laureate of the Court of Faery—and we have only to hope he will at least sing an annual song as the tenure by which he holds his deserved honours.

The few very general observations which we have now made on the genius of this truly original Poet are intended only as an introduction to our criticisms on his works. It is not uncommon to hear intelligent persons very thoughtlessly and ignorantly say, that the Ettrick Shep-herd no doubt writes very good verses—but that Burns has preoccupied the ground, and is our only great poet of the people. We have perhaps said enough to shew that this is far from being the case—that the genius of the two poets is as different as their life—and that they have, generally speaking, delighted in the delineation of very different objects.

If we have rightly distinguished and estimated the peculiar genius of the 'author of the "Queen's Wake",' we think that he might benefit by attending to some conclusions which seem to flow from our re-marks. He is certainly strongest in description of nature—in the imitation of the ancient ballad—and in that wild poetry which deals with imaginary beings. He has not great knowledge of human nature—nor has he any profound insight into its passions. Neither does he possess much ingenuity in the contrivance of incidents, or much plastic power in the formation of a story emblematic of any portion of human life. He ought, therefore, in our opinion, not to attempt any long poem in which a variety of characters are to be displayed acting on the theatre of the world, and of which the essential merit must lie in the exhibition of those passions that play their parts there; he ought, rather, to bring before us shadowy beings moving across a shadowy distance, and rising up from that world with whose objects he is so familiar, but of which ordinary minds know only enough to regard, with a delightful feeling of surprise and novelty, every indistinct and fairy image that is brought from its invisible recesses. There indeed seems to be a field spread out for him, that is almost all his own. The pastoral vallies of the south of Scotland look to him as their best-loved poet;—all their mild and gentle superstitions have blended with his being;—he is familiar too with all the historical traditions that people them with the 'living dead;' and surely, with all the inestimable advantages of his early shepherd-life, and with a genius so admirably framed to receive and give out the breath of all its manifold inspirations, he may yet make pastoral poetry something more wild and beautiful than it has ever been—and leave behind him a work in which the feelings and habits—the very heart and soul of a shepherd-life, are given to us all breathed over and coloured by the aerial tints of a fairy fancy.

The love of poetry is never bigotted and exclusive, and we should be strongly inclined to suspect its sincerity, if it did not comprehend within the range of its enthusiasm many of the fine productions of the Ettrick Shepherd. We believe that his countrymen are becoming every day more and more alive to his manifold merits—and it would be indeed strange if they who hold annual or triennial festivals in commemoration of their great dead poet should be cold to the claims of the gifted living. It cannot but be deeply interesting to all lovers of genius—and more especially to all proud lovers of the genius of their own Scotland, to see this true poet assisting at the honours paid to the memory of his illustrious predecessor. He must ever be, on such high occasions, a conspicuous and honoured guest; and we all know, that it is impossible better to prove our admiration and love of the character and genius of Burns, than by the generous exhibition of similar sentiments towards the Ettrick Shepherd.

60. Thomas Campbell on Burns

1819

Extract from Thomas Campbell, *Specimens of the British Poets; with Biographical and Critical Notices* (1819), VI, pp. 230–46.

Thomas Campbell (1777–1844), author of 'The Pleasures of Hope', 'Gertrude Of Wyoming', and well-known war-songs, writes here as an exiled Scot about Burns's ability to recreate the past: 'He brings back old Scotland to us.' Campbell also takes issue with Jeffrey (see Introduction, p. 41).

Burns has given an elixir of life to his native dialect. The Scottish 'Tam o' Shanter' will be read as long as any English production of the same century. The impression of his genius is deep and universal; and, viewing him merely as a poet, there is scarcely any other regret connected with his name than that his productions, with all their merit, fall short of the talents which he possessed. That he never attempted any great work of fiction or invention, may be partly traced to the cast of his genius, and partly to his circumstances and defective education. His poetical temperament was that of fitful transports, rather than steady inspiration. Whatever he might have written, was likely to have been fraught with passion. There is always enough of *interest* in life to cherish the feelings of a man of genius; but it requires knowledge to enlarge and enrich his *imagination*. Of that knowledge which unrolls the diversities of human manners, adventures, and characters to a poet's study, he could have no great share; although he stamped the little treasure which he possessed in the mintage of sovereign genius. It has been asserted, that he received all the education which is requisite for a poet: he had learned reading, writing, and arithmetic; and he had dipped into French and geometry. To a poet, it must be owned, the three last of those acquisitions were quite superfluous. His education, it is also affirmed, was equal to Shakspeare's; but, without intending to make any comparison between the genius of the two bards, it should be recollected that Shakspeare lived in an age within the verge

322

of chivalry, an age overflowing with chivalrous and romantic reading; that he was led by his vocation to have daily recourse to that kind of reading; that he dwelt on the spot which gave him constant access to it, and was in habitual intercourse with men of genius. Burns, after growing up to manhood under toils which exhausted his physical frame, acquired a scanty knowledge of modern books, of books tending for the most part to regulate the judgement more than to exercise the fancy. In the whole tract of his reading, there seems to be little that could cherish his inventive faculties. One material of poetry he certainly possessed, independent of books, in the legendary superstitions of his native country. But with all that he tells us of his early love of those superstitions, they seem to have come home to his mind with so many ludicrous associations of vulgar tradition, that it may be doubted if he could have turned them to account in an elevated work of fiction. Strongly and admirably as he paints the supernatural in 'Tam o' Shanter,' yet there, as every where else, he makes it subservient to comic effect. The fortuitous wildness and sweetness of his strains may, after all, set aside every regret that he did not attempt more superb and regular structures of fancy. He describes, as he says, the sentiments which he saw and felt in himself and his rustic compeers around him. His page is a lively image of the contemporary life and country from which he sprung. He brings back old Scotland to us with all her homefelt endearments, her simple customs, her festivities, her sturdy prejudices, and orthodox zeal, with a power that excites, alternately, the most tender and mirthful sensations. After the full account of his pieces which Dr. Currie has given, the English reader can have nothing new to learn respecting them. On one powerfully comic piece Dr. Currie has not disserted, namely, 'The Holy Fair.' It is enough, however, to mention the humour of this production, without recommending its subject. Burns, indeed, only laughs at the abuses of a sacred institution; but the theme was of unsafe approach, and he ought to have avoided it.

He meets us, in his compositions, undisguisedly as a peasant. At the same time, his observations go extensively into life, like those of a man who felt the proper dignity of human nature in the character of a peasant. The writer of some of the severest strictures that ever have been passed upon his poetry* conceives that his beauties are considerably defaced by a portion of false taste and vulgar sentiment, which adhere to him from his low education. That Burns's education, or rather the want of it, excluded him from much knowledge, which

---

* Critique on the character of Burns, in the *Edinburgh Review* [No. 41].

might have fostered his inventive ingenuity, seems to be clear; but his circumstances cannot be admitted to have communicated vulgarity to the tone of his sentiments. They have not the sordid taste of low condition. It is objected to him, that he boasts too much of his own independence; but, in reality, this boast is neither frequent nor obtrusive; and it is in itself the expression of a manly and laudable feeling. So far from calling up disagreeable recollections of rusticity, his sentiments triumph by their natural energy, over those false and fastidious distinctions which the mind is but too apt to form in allotting its sympathies to the sensibilities of the rich and poor. He carries us into the humble scenes of life, not to make us dole out our tribute of charitable compassion to paupers and cottagers, but to make us feel with them on equal terms, to make us enter into their passions and interests, and share our hearts with them as with brothers and sisters of the human species.

He is taxed, in the same place, with perpetually affecting to deride the virtues of prudence, regularity, and decency; and with being imbued with the sentimentality of German novels. Any thing more remote from German sentiment than Burns's poetry could not easily be mentioned. But is he depraved and licentious in a comprehensive view of the moral character of his pieces? The over-genial freedom of a few assuredly ought not to fix this character upon the whole of them. It is a charge which we should hardly expect to see preferred against the author of 'The Cotter's Saturday Night.' He is the enemy, indeed, of that selfish and niggardly spirit which shelters itself under the name of prudence; but that pharisaical disposition has seldom been a favourite with poets. Nor should his maxims, which inculcate charity and can-dour in judging of human frailties, be interpreted as a serious defence of them, as when he says,

> Then gently scan your brother man,
>   Still gentlier sister woman,
> Though they may gang a kennan wrang;
>   To step aside is human.
> Who made the heart, 'tis he alone
>   Decidedly can try us;
> He knows each chord, its various tone,
>   Each spring its various bias.

It is still more surprising, that a critic, capable of so eloquently develop-ing the traits of Burns's genius, should have found fault with his amatory strains for want of polish, and 'of that chivalrous tone of gallantry, which uniformly abases itself in the presence of the object of its devotion.' Every reader must recal abundance of thoughts in his love songs, to which any attempt to superadd a tone of gallantry would not be

> To gild refined gold, to paint the rose,
> Or add fresh perfume to the violet,

but to debase the metal, and to take the odour and colour from the flower. It is exactly this superiority to 'abasement' and polish which is the charm that distinguishes Burns from the herd of erotic songsters, from the days of the troubadours to the present time. He wrote from impulses more sincere than the spirit of chivalry; and even Lord Surrey and Sir Philip Sidney are cold and uninteresting lovers in comparison with the rustic Burns.

The praises of his best pieces I have abstained from re-echoing, as there is no epithet of admiration which they deserve which has not been bestowed upon them. One point must be conceded to the strictures on his poetry, to which I have already alluded, that his personal satire was fierce and acrimonious. I am not, however, disposed to consider his attacks on Rumble John, and Holy Willie, as destitute of wit; and his poem on the clerical settlements at Kilmarnock, blends a good deal of ingenious metaphor with his accustomed humour. Even viewing him as a satirist, the last and humblest light in which he can be regarded as a poet, it may still be said of him,

> His style was witty, though it had some gall;
> Something he might have mended—so may all.

61. Byron on Burns

1821

Extracts from letter of 7 February 1821 to John Murray 'On the Rev. W. L. Bowles's Strictures on the Life and Writings of Pope' (published March 1821). *Works of Byron. Letters and Journals*, ed. R. E. Prothero (1901), v, pp. 541, 560 (see Nos 38, 49 and Introduction, p. 27).

I have myself seen a collection of another eminent, nay, pre-eminent, deceased poet, so abominably gross, and elaborately coarse, that I do not believe that they could be paralleled in our language. What is more strange is, that some of these are couched as *postscripts* to his serious and sentimental letters, to which are tacked either a piece of prose, or some verses, of the most hyperbolical indecency. He himself says, that if 'obscenity' (using a much coarser word) 'be the Sin against the Holy Ghost, he must certainly not be saved'. These letters are in existence, and have been seen by many besides myself; but would his *editor* have been '*candid*' in even alluding to them? Nothing would have even provoked *me*, an indifferent spectator, to allude to them, but this further attempt at the depreciation of Pope . . .

Poets are classed by the power of their performance, and not according to its rank in a gradus. In the contrary case, the forgotten epic poets of all countries would rank above Petrarch, Dante, Ariosto, Burns, Gray, Dryden, and the highest names of various countries.

But if I say that he is very near them [Pope, to Shakespeare and Milton], it is no more than has been asserted of Burns, who is supposed

To rival all but Shakespeare's name below,

I say nothing against this opinion. But of what '*order*', according to the poetical aristocracy, are Burns's poems? There are his *opus magnum*, 'Tam o' Shanter', a *tale*; the 'Cotter's Saturday Night,' a descriptive sketch; some others in the same style: the rest are songs. So much for the *rank* of his *productions*; the rank of *Burns* is the very first of his art.

62. Hazlitt on Burns

1821-5

See No. 56 and Introduction, p. 38.

(a) Extract from 'On Living to Oneself', written in 1821 and published in *Table-Talk*. Text from *Complete Works*, ed. P. P. Howe (1930), viii, p. 100

When a man is dead, they put money in his coffin, erect monuments to his memory, and celebrate the memory of his birthday in set speeches. Would they take any notice of him if he were living? No!—I was complaining of this to a Scotchman who had been attending a dinner and a subscription to raise a monument to Burns. He replied, he would sooner subscribe twenty pounds to his monument than have given it him while living; so that if the poet were to come to life again, he would treat him just as he was treated in fact. This was an honest Scotchman. What *he* said, the rest would do.

(b) Extract from 'Critical List Of Authors'. *Select British Poets* (1824); *Complete Works* (1932), ix, p. 242

One might be tempted to write an elegy rather than a criticism on him. In naïveté, in spirit, in characteristic humour, in vivid description of natural objects and of the natural feelings of the heart, he has left behind him no superior.

(c) Extract from *The Spirit of The Age* (1825). *Complete Works* (1932), xi, p. 60

We would rather have written one song of Burns . . . than all [Scott's] epics.

63. *Blackwood's Magazine* on Burns

xi, lxiii (March) and lxi (July), 1822

xi, lxiii (March) and lxi (July), 1822

(a) [J. G. Lockhart], 'Noctes Ambrosianae. No. I'

Editor ... In reviewing, in particular, what can be done without personality? Nothing, nothing. What are books that don't express the personal characters of their authors; and who can review books, without reviewing those that wrote them?

Odoherty. You get warm, Christopher; out with it.

Editor. Can a man read La Fontaine, Mr. Odoherty, without perceiving his personal good nature? Swift's personal ill-nature is quite as visible. Can a man read Burns without having the idea of a great and a bold man—or Barry Cornwall, without the very uncomfortable feeling of a little man and a timid one? The whole of the talk about personality is, as Fogarty says, cant.

(b) [William Maginn], 'Noctes Ambrosianae. No. IV'

Byron. You prefer Burns, perhaps, now you've been so long a Scotchman, and heard all their eternal puffing of one another.

Odoherty. Poh! poh! I was too old a cat for that straw. Burns wrote five or six good things; 'Tam o' Shanter', 'M'Pherson's Lament', 'Fairwell, thou Fair Earth', 'Mary's Dream', the 'Holy Fair', the 'Stanzas to a Louse on a Lady's Bonnet', and perhaps a few more; but the most of his verses are mere manufacture—the most perfect commonplace about love and bowers, and poverty, and so forth. And as for his prose, why, Gad-a-mercy! 'tis execrable. 'Tis worse than Hogg's worst, or Allan Cunningham's best. His Letters are enough to make a dog sick.

Byron. Come, you are too severe; Burns was a noble fellow, although Jeffrey abused him. But indeed that was nothing. After praising the Cockneys, who cares what he reviles?

Odoherty. Not I.

64. Hew Ainslie on Burns

1822

Extract from *Pilgrimage to the Land of Burns* (1822), a fictionalized account of a trip to the Burns country by three 'tourists', Edie Ochiltree, Jinglin Jock, and the Lang Linker. The *Pilgrimage*, which contains poetry as well as prose, became very popular. Text here from edition by T. C. Latto (1892).

Although in the poems of Robert Burns, the Humour, pathos, and passion, are all of the first order of excellence, yet it is unquestionably owing to his admirable talent at catching 'the manners living as they rise', of overhauling character, and the boldness and freedom with which he ranges through the human breast, which gives to his writings that sort of electricity, which makes every bosom feel the shock, and every spirit a conductor; which sent them through his native land like lightning, and established them therein as the necessaries of life. It is this universal charm that makes his pages glitter in the library of the lord, and lie in the winnock bunker of the labourer, even more honourably thumbed than his venerable co-mates, Boston[1] and Bunyan.

[1] Thomas Boston (1676–1732), religious writer.

65. Allan Cunningham on Burns

1824, 1825

Allan Cunningham (1784–1842), stone-mason, poet, and miscellaneous prose-writer, wrote frequently on Burns (see No. 71, and Introduction, p. 41).

(a) Extract from unsigned article 'Robert Burns and Lord Byron', *London Magazine* (August 1824), 1st ser. x, 117–22.

I have seen Robert Burns laid in his grave, and I have seen George Gordon Byron borne to his; of both I wish to speak, and my words shall be spoken with honesty and freedom. They were great though not equal heirs of fame; the fortunes of their birth were widely dissimilar; yet in their passions and in their genius they approached to a closer resemblance; their careers were short and glorious, and they both perished in the summer of life, and in all the splendour of a reputation more likely to increase than diminish. One was a peasant, and the other was a peer; but Nature is a great leveller, and makes amends for the injuries of fortune by the richness of her benefactions; the genius of Burns raised him to a level with the nobles of the land; by nature if not by birth, he was the peer of Byron. I knew one, and I have seen both; I have hearkened to words from their lips, and admired the labours of their pens, and I am now, and likely to remain, under the influence of their magic songs. They rose by the force of their genius, and they fell by the strength of their passions; one wrote from a love, and the other from a scorn, of mankind; and they both sang of the emotions of their own hearts with a vehemence and an originality which few have equalled, and none surely have surpassed. But it is less my wish to draw the characters of those extraordinary men than to write what I remember of them; and I will say nothing that I know not to be true, and little but what I saw myself.

The first time I ever saw Burns was in Nithsdale. I was then a child, but his looks and his voice cannot well be forgotten; and while I write this I behold him as distinctly as I did when I stood at my father's knee, and heard the bard repeat his 'Tam o' Shanter'. He was tall and of a manly make, his brow broad and high, and his voice varied with the character of his inimitable tale; yet through all its variations it was melody itself. He was of great personal strength, and proud too of displaying it; and I have seen him lift a load with ease, which few ordinary men would have willingly undertaken.

The first time I ever saw Byron was in the House of Lords, soon after the publication of 'Childe Harold'. He stood up in his place on the opposition side, and made a speech on the subject of Catholic freedom. His voice was low, and I heard him but by fits, and when I say, he was witty and sarcastic, I judge as much from the involuntary mirth of the benches as from what I heard with my own ears. His voice had not the full and manly melody of the voice of Burns; nor had he equal vigour of frame, nor the same open expanse of forehead. But his face was finely formed, and was impressed with a more delicate vigour than that of the peasant poet. He had a singular conformation of ear, the lower lobe, instead of being pendulous, grew down and united itself to the cheek and resembled no other ear I ever saw, save that of the Duke of Wellington. His bust by Thorvaldson is feeble and mean; the painting of Phillips is more noble and much more like. Of Burns I have never seen aught but a very uninspired resemblance—and I regret it the more, because he had a look worthy of the happiest effort of art—a look beaming with poetry and eloquence.

The last time I saw Burns in life was on his return from the Browwell of Solway; he had been ailing all spring, and summer had come without bringing health with it; he had gone away very ill and he returned worse. He was brought back, I think, in a covered spring cart, and when he alighted at the foot of the street in which he lived, he could scarce stand upright. He reached his own door with difficulty. He stooped much, and there was a visible change in his looks. Some may think it not unimportant to know, that he was at that time dressed in a blue coat with the undress nankeen pantaloons of the volunteers, and that his neck, which was inclining to be short, caused his hat to turn up behind, in the manner of the shovel hats of the Episcopal clergy. Truth obliges me to add, that he was not fastidious about his dress; and that an officer, curious in the personal appearance and equipments of his company, might have questioned the military nicety of the poet's clothes and arms. But his colonel was a maker of rhyme, and the poet had to display more charity for his commander's verse than the other had to exercise when he inspected the clothing and arms of the careless bard.

From the day of his return till the hour of his untimely death, Dumfries was like a besieged place. It was known he was dying, and the anxiety, not of the rich and the learned only, but of the mechanics and peasants, exceeded all belief. Wherever two or three people stood together, their talk was of Burns and of him alone; they spoke of his history—of his person—of his works,—of his family—of his fame, and of his untimely and approaching fate, with a warmth and an enthusiasm which will ever endear Dumfries to my remembrance. All that he said or was saying—the opinions of the physicians (and Maxwell was a kind and a skilful one), were eagerly caught up and reported from street to street, and from house to house.

His good humour was unruffled, and his wit never forsook him. He looked to one of his fellow volunteers with a smile, as he stood by the bedside with his eyes wet, 'John, don't let the awkward squad fire over me.' He was aware that death was dealing with him; he asked a lady who visited him, more in sincerity than in mirth, what commands she had for the other world—he repressed with a smile the hopes of his friends, and told them he had lived long enough. As his life drew near a close, the eager yet decorous solicitude of his fellow townsmen increased. He was an exciseman it is true—a name odious, from many associations, to his countrymen—but he did his duty meekly and kindly, and repressed rather than encouraged the desire of some of his companions to push the law with severity; he was therefore much beloved, and the passion of the Scotch for poetry made them regard him as little lower than a spirit inspired. It is the practice of the young men of Dumfries to meet in the street during the hours of remission from labour, and by these means I had an opportunity of witnessing the general solicitude of all ranks and of all ages. His differences with them in some important points of human speculation and religious hope were forgotten and forgiven; they thought only of his genius—of the delight his compositions had diffused—and they talked of him with the same awe as of some departing spirit, whose voice was to gladden them no more. His last moments have never been described; he had laid his head quietly on the pillow awaiting dissolution, when his attendant reminded him of his medicine and held the cup to his lip. He started suddenly up, drained the cup at a gulp, threw his hands before him like

a man about to swim, and sprung from head to foot of the bed—fell
with his face down, and expired with a groan.

Of the dying moments of Byron we have no minute nor very
distinct account. He perished in a foreign land among barbarians or
aliens, and he seems to have been without the aid of a determined
physician, whose firmness or persuasion might have vanquished his
obstinacy. His aversion to bleeding was an infirmity which he shared
with many better regulated minds; for it is no uncommon belief that
the first touch of the lancet will charm away the approach of death, and
those who believe this are willing to reserve so decisive a spell for a
more momentous occasion. He had parted with his native land in no
ordinary bitterness of spirit; and his domestic infelicity had rendered
his future peace of mind hopeless—this was aggravated from time to
time by the tales or the intrusion of travellers, by reports injurious to
his character, and by the eager and vulgar avidity with which idle
stories were circulated, which exhibited him in weakness or in folly.
But there is every reason to believe, that long before his untimely
death his native land was as bright as ever in his fancy, and that his
anger conceived against the many for the sins of the few had subsided
or was subsiding. Of Scotland, and of his Scottish origin, he has
boasted in more than one place of his poetry; he is proud to remember
the land of his mother, and to sing that he is half a Scot by birth and a
whole one in his heart. Of his great rival in popularity, Sir Walter
Scott, he speaks with kindness; and the compliment he has paid him
has been earned by the unchangeable admiration of the other. Scott has
ever spoken of Byron as he has lately written, and all those who know
him will feel that this consistency is characteristic. I must, however,
confess, his forgiveness of Mr. Jeffrey was an unlooked-for and unexpected piece of humility and loving kindness, and, as a Scotchman,
I am rather willing to regard it as a presage of early death, and to
conclude that the poet was 'fey', and forgave his arch enemy in the
spirit of the dying Highlander—'Weel, weel, I forgive him, but God
confound you, my twa sons, Duncan and Gilbert, if you forgive him.'
The criticism with which the *Edinburgh Review* welcomed the first
flight which Byron's Muse took, would have crushed and broken any
spirit less dauntless than his own; and for a long while he entertained
the horror of a reviewer which a bird of song feels for the presence of
the raven. But they smoothed his spirit down, first by submission and
then by idolatry, and his pride must have been equal to that which made
the angels fall if it had refused to be soothed by the obeisance of a

reviewer. One never forgets, if he should happen to forgive, an insult or an injury offered in youth—it grows with the growth and strengthens with the strength, and I may reasonably doubt the truth of the poet's song when he sings of his dear Jeffrey. The news of his death came upon London like an earthquake; and though the common multitude are ignorant of literature and destitute of feeling for the higher flights of poetry, yet they consented to feel by faith, and believed, because the newspapers believed, that one of the brightest lights in the firmament of poesy was extinguished for ever. With literary men a sense of the public misfortune was mingled, perhaps, with a sense that a giant was removed from their way; and that they had room now to break a lance with an equal, without fear of being overthrown by fiery impetuosity and colossal strength. The world of literature is now resigned to lower, but perhaps, not less presumptuous poetic spirits. But among those who feared him, or envied him, or loved him, there are none who sorrow not for the national loss, and grieve not that Byron fell so soon, and on a foreign shore.

When Burns died I was then young, but I was not insensible that a mind of no common strength had passed from among us. He had caught my fancy and touched my heart with his songs and his poems. I went to see him laid out for the grave; several eldern people were with me. He lay in a plain unadorned coffin, with a linen sheet drawn over his face, and on the bed, and around the body, herbs and flowers were thickly strewn according to the usage of the country. He was wasted somewhat by long illness; but death had not increased the swarthy hue of his face, which was uncommonly dark and deeply marked—the dying pang was visible in the lower part, but his broad and open brow was pale and serene, and around it his sable hair lay in masses, slightly touched with gray, and inclining more to a wave than a curl. The room where he lay was plain and neat, and the simplicity of the poet's humble dwelling pressed the presence of death more closely on the heart than if his bier had been embellished by vanity and covered with the blazonry of high ancestry and rank. We stood and gazed on him in silence for the space of several minutes—we went, and others succeeded us—there was no justling and crushing, though the crowd was great—man followed man as patiently and orderly as if all had been a matter of mutual understanding—not a question was asked—not a whisper was heard. This was several days after his death. It is the custom of Scotland to 'wake' the body—not with wild howlings and wilder songs, and much waste of strong drink, like our

mercurial neighbours, but in silence or in prayer—superstition says
it is unsonsie to leave a corpse alone; and it is never left. I know not
who watched by the body of Burns—much it was my wish to share
in the honour—but my extreme youth would have made such a
request seem foolish, and its rejection would have been sure.

I am to speak the feelings of another people, and of the customs
of a higher rank, when I speak of laying out the body of Byron for
the grave. It was announced from time to time that he was to be
exhibited in state, and the progress of the embellishments of the poet's
bier was recorded in the pages of an hundred publications. They were
at length completed, and to separate the curiosity of the poor from the
admiration of the rich, the latter were indulged with tickets of admission, and a day was set a-part for them to go and wonder over the
decked room and the emblazoned bier. Peers and peeresses, priests,
poets, and politicians, came in gilded chariots and in hired hacks to
gaze upon the splendour of the funeral preparations, and to see in how
rich and how vain a shroud the body of the immortal had been hid.
Those idle trappings in which rank seeks to mark its altitude above the
vulgar belonged to the state of the peer rather than to the state of the
poet; genius required no such attractions; and all this magnificence
served only to divide our regard with the man whose inspired tongue
was now silenced for ever. Who cared for Lord Byron the peer, and
the privy councillor, with his coronet, and his long descent from
princes on one side, and from heroes on both—and who did not care
for George Gordon Byron the poet, who has charmed us, and will
charm our descendants with his deep and impassioned verse. The
homage was rendered to genius, not surely to rank—for lord can be
stamped on any clay, but inspiration can only be impressed on the
finest metal.

Of the day on which the multitude were admitted I know not in
what terms to speak—I never saw so strange a mixture of silent
sorrow and of fierce and intractable curiosity. If one looked on the
poet's splendid coffin with deep awe, and thought of the gifted spirit
which had lately animated the cold remains, others regarded the whole
as a pageant or a show, got up for the amusement of the idle and the
careless, and criticised the arrangements in the spirit of those who wish
to be rewarded for their time, and who consider that all they condescend to visit should be according to their own taste. There was a
crushing, a trampling, and an impatience, as rude and as fierce as ever I
witnessed at a theatre; and words of incivility were bandied about, and

questions asked with such determination to be answered, that the very mutes, whose business was silence and repose, were obliged to interfere with tongue and hand between the visitors and the dust of the poet. In contemplation of such a scene, some of the trappings which were there on the first day were removed on the second, and this suspicion of the good sense and decorum of the multitude called forth many expressions of displeasure, as remarkable for their warmth as their propriety of language. By five o' clock the people were all ejected—man and woman—and the rich coffin bore tokens of the touch of hundreds of eager fingers—many of which had not been overclean.

The multitude who accompanied Burns to the grave went step by step with the chief mourners; they might amount to ten or twelve thousand. Not a word was heard; and, though all could not be near, and many could not see, when the earth closed on their darling poet for ever, there was no rude impatience shown, no fierce disappointment expressed. It was an impressive and mournful sight to see men of all ranks and persuasions and opinions mingling as brothers, and stepping side by side down the streets of Dumfries, with the remains of him who had sang of their loves and joys and domestic endearments, with a truth and a tenderness which none perhaps have since equalled. I could, indeed, have wished the military part of the procession away —for he was buried with military honours—because I am one of those who love simplicity in all that regards genius. The scarlet and gold—the banners displayed—the measured step, and the military array, with the sound of martial instruments of music, had no share in increasing the solemnity of the burial scene; and had no connexion with the poet. I looked on it then, and I consider it now, as an idle ostentation, a piece of superfluous state which might have been spared, more especially as his neglected and traduced and insulted spirit had experienced no kindness in the body from those lofty people who are now proud of being numbered as his coevals and countrymen. His fate has been a reproach to Scotland. But the reproach comes with an ill grace from England. When we can forget Butler's fate—Otway's loaf—Dryden's old age, and Chatterton's poison-cup, we may think that we stand alone in the iniquity of neglecting pre-eminent genius. I found myself at the brink of the poet's grave, into which he was about to descend for ever—there was a pause among the mourners as if loath to part with his remains; and when he was at last lowered, and the first shovelful of earth sounded on his coffin-lid, I looked up and saw tears on many cheeks where tears were not usual. The volunteers justified the fears of their comrade by three ragged and straggling volleys. The earth was heaped up, the green sod laid over him, and the multitude stood gazing on the grave for some minutes' space, and then melted silently away. The day was a fine one, the sun was almost without a cloud, and not a drop of rain fell from dawn to twilight. I notice this—not from my concurrence in the common superstition—that 'happy is the corpse which the rain rains on,' but to confute a pious fraud of a religious Magazine, which made Heaven express its wrath at the interment of a profane poet, in thunder, in lightning, and in rain. I know not who wrote the story, and I wish not to know; but its utter falsehood thousands can attest. It is one proof out of many, how divine wrath is found by dishonest zeal in a common commotion of the elements, and that men, whose profession is godliness and truth, will look in the face of heaven and tell a deliberate lie.

A few select friends and admirers followed Lord Byron to the grave—his coronet was borne before him, and there were many indications of his rank; but, save the assembled multitude, no indications of his genius. In conformity to a singular practice of the great, a long train of their empty carriages followed the mourning coaches—mocking the dead with idle state, and impeding the honester sympathy of the crowd with barren pageantry. Where were the owners of those machines of sloth and luxury—where were the men of rank among whose dark pedigrees Lord Byron threw the light of his genius, and lent the brows of nobility a halo to which they were strangers? Where were the great Whigs? Where were the illustrious Tories? Could a mere difference in matters of human belief keep those fastidious persons away? But, above all, where were the friends with whom wedlock had united him? On his desolate corpse no wife looked, and no child shed a tear. I have no wish to set myself up as a judge in domestic infelicities, and I am willing to believe they were separated in such a way as rendered conciliation hopeless; but who could stand and look on his pale manly face, and his dark locks which early sorrows were making thin and gray, without feeling that, gifted as he was, with a soul above the mark of other men, his domestic misfortunes called for our pity as surely as his genius called for our admiration. When the career of Burns was closed, I saw another sight—a weeping widow and four helpless sons; they came into the streets in their mournings, and public sympathy was awakened afresh; I shall never forget the looks of his boys, and the compassion which they excited. The poet's life had not been without errors, and such errors, too, as a wife is slow in forgiving;

but he was honoured then, and is honoured now, by the unalienable affection of his wife, and the world repays her prudence and her love by its regard and esteem.

Burns, with all his errors in faith and in practice, was laid in hallowed earth, in the churchyard of the town where he resided; no one thought of closing the church gates against his body, because of the freedom of his poetry, and the carelessness of his life. And why was not Byron laid among the illustrious men of England, in Westminster Abbey? Is there a poet in all the Poets' Corner who has better right to that distinction? Why was the door closed against him, and opened to the carcases of thousands without merit, and without name? Look round the walls, and on the floor over which you tread, and behold them encumbered and inscribed with memorials of the mean and the sordid and the impure, as well as of the virtuous and the great. Why did the Dean of Westminster refuse admission to such an heir of fame as Byron?[1] If he had no claim to lie within the consecrated precincts of the Abbey, he has no right to lie in consecrated ground at all. There is no doubt that the pious fee for sepulture would have been paid—and it is not a small one. Hail! to the Church of England, if her piety is stronger than her avarice.

(b) Extract from Allan Cunningham, ed., *The Songs of Scotland, Ancient and Modern* (1825), i, pp. 230–6.

A lyric poet, with more than the rustic humour and exact truth of Ramsay, with simplicity surpassing Crawford's, and native elegance exceeding Hamilton's, and with a genius which seemed to unite all the distinguishing excellencies of our elder lyrics, appeared in Robert Burns. He was the first who brought deep passion to the service of the lyric Muse, who added sublimity to simplicity, and found grace and elegance among the cottages of his native land. The beauty and the variety of his songs, their tenderness and truth, their pathetic sweetness, their unextinguishable humour, their noble scorn of whatever is mean and vile, and their deep sympathy with the feelings of humble worth, are felt by all, and acknowledged by all. His original power, and his

[1] In 1968 the Very Reverend Eric Abbott, Dean of Westminster Abbey, approved a petition by the Poetry Society for a Byron memorial in the Abbey. The memorial was unveiled on 8 May 1969. See Leslie A. Marchand, *Byron; a Portrait* (1971), p. 478.

happy spirit, were only equalled by his remarkable gift of entering into the characters of our ancient songs, and the skill with which he abated their indelicacy, or eked out their imperfections. No one felt more fondly the presence of beauty, could express admiration, hope, or desire, in more glowing language, or sing of the calm joys of wedded love, or the unbounded rapture of single hearts and mutual affection, with equal force or felicity. All his songs are distinguished more or less by a happy carelessness, by a bounding elasticity of spirit, a singular and natural felicity of expression, by the ardour of an enthusiastic heart, and the vigour of a clear understanding. He had the rare gift of expressing himself according to the rank and condition of mankind, the stateliness of matron pride, the modesty of virgin affection, the querulousness of old age, and the overflowing enthusiasm and vivacity of youth. His simplicity is the simplicity of strength; he is never mean, never weak, seldom vulgar, and but rarely coarse; and his unrivalled power of clothing his thoughts in happy and graceful language never forsakes him. Capricious and wayward as his musings sometimes are, mingling the moving with the comic, and the sarcastic with the solemn, all he says is above the mark of other men—he sheds a redeeming light on all he touches; whatever his eye glances on rises into life and beauty, and stands consecrated and imperishable. His language is familiar, yet dignified, careless, yet concise; and he touches on the most perilous or ordinary themes with a skill so rare and felicitous, that good fortune seems to unite with good taste in carrying him over the mire of rudeness and vulgarity, in which, since his time, so many inferior spirits have wallowed. His love, his enthusiasm, his devotion, his humour, his domestic happiness, and his homeliest joy, is every where characterised by a brief and elegant simplicity, at once easy to him and unattainable to others. No one has such power in adorning the humble, and dignifying the plain, and in extracting sweet and impassioned poetry from the daily occurrences of human life; his simplicity is without childishness, his affection without exaggeration, and his sentiment without conceit.

The influence which the genius of Burns has obtained over the heart of Scotland is indeed great, and promises to be lasting. He alarms, it is true, very sensitive and fastidious persons, by the freedom of his speculations and the masculine vigour of his mode of expression; but these are rather the casual lapses of the Muse, the overflowings of an ardent heart and unwearied fancy, and a love of vivid illustration, than a defect of principle, or an imperfection of taste. Like a fine race-horse, he cannot always stop at the winning post; like a beautiful stream, he sometimes overflows the banks; and his genius resembles more a tree run wild, than one trimmed and pruned to decorate a garden walk. When speaking of his prospect of future fame to a friend, he said he depended chiefly on his songs for the continuance of his name; and his decision seems correct. Not but that I think, in all his earlier poems, he displays greater force and freedom of genius than he any where exhibits in his lyrics; but then these brief and bright effusions are learned by heart—are confided to the memories of the people—and come down from generation to generation without the aid of the press or the pen, to which longer and more deliberate productions must be trusted. In this way alone would many of the best of Burns's songs be preserved, perhaps his humourous lyrics the longest—we naturally prefer mirth to sorrow; the source of tears is deeper than that of laughter; and duller heads and less sensible hearts, which could not partake in his emotions of tenderness and sublimity, would assist in preserving whatever increased the joy of a bridal feast, or the merriment of rustic festivity.

But with all his impassioned eloquence in the presence of beauty, with his power of exciting emotions at will, whether of pleasure or of pity, and with all his delight in what is lovely and inspiring, he had little of that elevated and refined spirit which contemplates beauty with awe, and approaches it with reverence. Of this pure glory and hallowed light his lyrics possess nothing. The midnight tryste and the stolen interview—the rapture to meet, and the anguish to part—the whisper in the dark—and all the lavish spirit of nocturnal enjoyment, correspond more with the warmth than the elevation of love. He looked not on loveliness as on a pure and an awful thing: he drew no magic circle of lofty and romantic thought round those he loved, which could not be passed without lowering them from stations little lower than the angels; but he clasps them in his arms, and lavishes on their condescension all the rapture of unrefined joy. His rapture is without romance; and to the charms of his compositions he has not added that of chivalry. He has no distant mode of salutation—he seeks the couch rather than approaches the footstool of beauty; and the sparkling wine, the private chamber, and the 'pulse's maddening play,' are to him that inspiration which devouter minds have invoked by prayer and humiliation. When one of the ladies who had felt the sorcery of his conversation as well as of his Muse said, with more naïveté than delicacy, that no man's eloquence ever carried her so completely off her feet as that of Burns, she expressed, very happily, that influence which the passionate language of poetry has over a susceptible heart: but still this fails to let us into the secret of the charms he used; and the lady may have lost her self-command by the witchery of a gross as well as an aerial eloquence. But if he was not under the spell of chivalry in the intercourses of love, he was occasionally under an influence which sobered down the selfish impetuosity of passion—which imparted a meekness to his joy, and a reverence to his language. I am willing to believe that a deep feeling of devotion, constant in his youth, and flashing back on him by fits and starts during the period of his short but glorious career, interposed to hallow his thoughts, and restrain that torrent of passion which overflowed in all his productions.

He laid down rules for lyric composition which he did not always observe, and seemed willing to restrain others from pruning the luxuriance, or improving the sentiment, or heightening the story, of ancient song, while he was ready to indulge in it himself. Of the many fine songs which he wrote, a large proportion are either avowedly or evidently conceived in the spirit and executed in the feeling, of others: he retouched many, restored many, and remodelled many; but he retouched few without improving them, restored none without increasing their beauty, and remodelled none without introducing some of those electric touches of delicacy, or humour, or tenderness, for which he is so remarkable. It would extend to a great length the character which I am endeavouring to draw, were I to seek to justify my assertion by an examination into all the sources from which he gathered the materials of song—or to point out fragments which he completed, verses from which he borrowed, or songs which he imitated. He seemed, indeed, to take particular delight in completing the old and imperfect songs of his native country: without much old world lore, with no great thirst of research, without any particular sympathy for the old simple style of our ballads, he has exercised his fancy and displayed his taste among the reliques of ancient song to a greater extent than is generally known. Though nature is exhaustless, I must confess that Burns, who is somewhat little less than nature herself, appears to have felt at last the decay of fancy in the service to which his love of Scottish music called him. To expect that a spirit so wayward could endure, year after year, to measure out lyric verse according to the prescription of all manner of melodies, is to me surprising. That he could stay till he entered into the feeling of the air—till he extracted from bagpipers and fiddlers all their varieties of the melody which was to be united to verse; and then make a notorious sacrifice of vigorous meaning to empty music, and endure the criticism of men, whose skill in the science of sound was less to be disputed than in the science of sense, is one of those instances of condescension and willing humiliation which are unfrequent in the history of Robert Burns.

66. J. G. Lockhart, *Life of Robert Burns*

1828

Extracts from J. G. Lockhart, *Life of Robert Burns* (Edinburgh, 1828). Text from 3rd ed., 'corrected' (1830), pp. 71–2, 80–1, 120–1, 269, 316–28 (see Nos 58, 63 and Introduction, p. 41).

Encouraged by the 'roar of applause' which greeted these pieces ['The Holy Tulzie' and 'Holy Willie's Prayer'], thus orally promulgated and recommended, he produced in succession various satires, wherein the same set of persons were lashed; as, 'The Ordination'; 'The Kirk's Alarm', &c. &c.; and last, and best undoubtedly, 'The Holy Fair', in which, unlike the others that have been mentioned, satire keeps its own place, and is subservient to the poetry of Burns. This was, indeed, an extraordinary performance; no partisan of any sect could whisper that malice had formed its principal inspiration, or that its chief attraction lay in the boldness with which individuals, entitled and accustomed to respect, were held up to ridicule; it was acknowledged, amidst the sternest mutterings of wrath, that national manners were once more in the hands of a national poet; and hardly denied by those who shook their heads the most gravely over the indiscretions of particular passages, or even by those who justly regretted a too prevailing tone of levity in the treatment of a subject essentially solemn, that the Muse of 'Christ's Kirk on the Green' had awakened, after the slumber of ages, with all the vigour of her regal youth, about her, in 'the auld clay biggin' of Mossgiel . . .

342

The 'Cottar's Saturday Night' is perhaps, of all Burns's pieces, the one whose exclusion from the collection, were such things possible now-a-days, would be the most injurious, if not to the genius, at least to the character, of the man. In spite of many feeble lines, and some heavy stanzas, it appears to me, that even his genius would suffer more in estimation, by being contemplated in the absence of this poem, than of any other single performance he has left us. Loftier flights he certainly has made, but in these he remained but a short while on the wing, and effort is too often perceptible; here the motion is easy, gentle, placidly undulating. There is more of the conscious security of power, than in any other of his serious pieces of considerable length; the whole has the appearance of coming in a full stream from the fountain of the heart—a stream that soothes the ear, and has no glare on the surface. It is delightful to turn from any of the pieces which present so great a genius as writhing under an inevitable burden, to this, where his buoyant energy seems not to feel the pressure. The miseries of toil and penury, who shall affect to treat as unreal? Yet they shrink to small dimensions in the presence of a spirit thus exalted at once, and softened, by the pieties of virgin love, filial reverence, and domestic devotion.

That he who thus enthusiastically apprehended, and thus exquisitely painted, the artless beauty and solemnity of the feelings and thoughts that ennoble the life of the Scottish peasant, could witness observances in which the very highest of these redeeming influences are most powerfully and gracefully displayed, and yet describe them in a vein of unmixed merriment—that the same man should have produced the 'Cottar's Saturday Night' and the 'Holy Fair' about the same time—will ever continue to move wonder and regret . . .

Darkly as the career of Burns was destined to terminate, there can be no doubt that he made his first appearance at a period highly favourable for his reception as a British, and, especially as a Scottish poet. Nearly forty years had elapsed since the death of Thomson:—Collins, Gray, Goldsmith, had successively disappeared—Dr. Johnson had belied the rich promise of his early appearance, and confined himself to prose; and Cowper had hardly begun to be recognised as having any considerable pretensions to fill the long-vacant throne in England. At home—without derogation from the merits either of *Douglas* or the *Minstrel*, be it said—men must have gone back at least three centuries to find a Scottish poet at all entitled to be considered as of that high order to which the generous criticism of Mackenzie at once admitted 'the Ayrshire Ploughman'. Of the form and garb of his composition, much, unquestionably and avowedly, was derived from his more immediate predecessors, Ramsay and Ferguson: but there was a bold mastery of hand in his picturesque descriptions, to produce anything equal to which it was necessary to recall the days of 'Christ's Kirk on the Green', and 'Peebles to the Play': and in his more solemn pieces, a depth of inspiration, and a massive energy of language, to which the dialect of his country had been a stranger, at least since 'Dunbar the Mackar'. The Muses of Scotland have never indeed been silent; and the ancient minstrelsy of the land, of which a slender portion had as yet been committed to the safeguard of the press, was handed from generation to generation, and preserved, in many a fragment, faithful images of the peculiar tenderness, and peculiar humour, of the national fancy and character—precious representations, which Burns himself never surpassed in his happiest efforts. But these were fragments; and, with a scanty handful of exceptions, the best of them, at least of the serious kind, were very ancient. Among the numberless effusions of the Jacobite Muse, valuable as we now consider them for the record of manners and events, it would be difficult to point out half a dozen strains, worthy, for poetical excellence alone, of a place among the old chivalrous ballads of the Southern, or even of the Highland Border. Generations had passed away since any Scottish poet had appealed to the sympathies of his countrymen in a lofty Scottish strain . . .

I may mention here, that during the later years of his life, his favourite book, the usual companion of his solitary rambles, was Cowper's 'Task'. It is pleasing to know that these illustrious contemporaries, in spite of the widely different circumstances under which their talents were developed, and the, at first sight, opposite set of opinions which their works express, did justice to each other. No English writer of the time eulogized Burns more generously than Cowper. And in truth they had much in common,

The stamp and clear impression of good sense;

the love of simplicity; the love of nature; sympathy with the poor; humour; pathos; satire; warm and manly hearts; the pride, the independence, and the melancholy of genius . . .

That some men in every age will comfort themselves in the practice of certain vices, by references to particular passages both in the history and in the poetry of Burns, there is all reason to fear; but surely the

general influence of both it calculated, and has been found, to produce far different effects. The university popularity which his writing
have all along enjoyed among one of the most virtuous of nations, is, of
itself, surely, a decisive circumstance. Search Scotland over, from the
Pentland to the Solway, and there is not a cottage-hut so poor and
wretched as to be without its Bible; and hardly one that, on the same
shelf, and next to it, does not treasure a Burns. Have the people
degenerated since their adoption of this new manual? Has their
attachment to the Book of Books declined? Are their hearts less firmly
bound, than were their fathers', to the old faith and the old virtues?
I believe, he that knows the most of the country will be the readiest to
answer all these questions, as every lover of genius and virtue would
desire to hear them answered.

On one point there can be no controversy; the poetry of Burns has
had most powerful influence in reviving and strengthening the national
feelings of his countrymen. Amidst penury and labour, his youth fed
on the old minstrelsy and traditional glories of his nation, and his genius
divined, that what he felt so deeply must belong to a spirit that might
lie smothered around him, but could not be extinguished. The political
circumstances of Scotland were, and had been, such as to starve the
flame of patriotism; the popular literature had striven, and not in vain,
to make itself English; and, above all, a new and a cold system of
speculative philosophy had begun to spread widely among us. A
peasant appeared, and set himself to check the creeping pestilence of
this indifference. Whatever genius has since then been devoted to the
illustration of the national manners, and sustaining thereby of the
national feelings of the people, there can be no doubt that Burns will
ever be remembered as the founder, and, alas! in his own person as the
martyr, of this reformation.

That what is now-a-days called, by solitary eminence, the *wealth*
of the nation, had been on the increase ever since our incorporation
with a greater and wealthier state—nay, that the laws had been improving, and, above all, the administration of the laws, it would be
mere bigotry to dispute. It may also be conceded easily, that the
national mind had been rapidly clearing itself of many injurious
prejudices—that the people, as a people, had been gradually and surely
advancing in knowledge and wisdom, as well as in wealth and security.
But all this good had not been accomplished without rude work. If
the improvement were valuable, it had been purchased dearly. 'The
spring fire', Allan Cunningham says beautifully somewhere, 'which

destroys the furze, makes an end also of the nests of a thousand song-
birds; and he who goes a trouting with line, leaves little of life in the
stream'. We were getting fast ashamed of many precious and beautiful
things, only for that they were old and our own.

It has already been remarked, how even Smollett, who began with
a national tragedy, and one of the noblest of national lyrics, never
dared to make use of the dialect of his own country; and how Moore,
another most enthusiastic Scotsman, followed in this respect, as in
others, the example of Smollett, and over and over again counselled
Burns to do the like. But a still more striking sign of the times is to
be found in the style adopted by both of these novelists, especially
the great master of the art, in their representations of the manners
and characters of their own countrymen. In *Humphrey Clinker*, the
last and best of Smollett's tales, there are some traits of a better kind—
but, taking his works as a whole, the impression it conveys is certainly
a painful, a disgusting one. The Scotchmen of these authors, are the
Jockies and Archies of farce—

Time out of mind the Southrons' mirthmakers—

the best of them grotesque combinations of simplicity and hypocrisy,
pride and meanness. When such men, high-spirited Scottish gentlemen,
possessed of learning and talents, and one of them at least, of splendid
genius, felt, or fancied, the necessity of making such submissions to
the prejudices of the dominant nation, and did so without exciting a
murmur among their own countrymen, we may form some notion of
the boldness of Burns's experiment; and on contrasting the state of
things then with what is before us now, it will cost no effort to appreciate the nature and consequences of the victory in which our poet led
the way, by achievements never in their kind to be surpassed.

'Burns', says Mr. Campbell, 'has given the elixir vitae to his dialect;'
—he gave it to more than his dialect.

The moral influence of his genius has not been confined to his own
countrymen.

'The range of the *pastoral*,' said Johnson, 'is narrow. Poetry cannot dwell upon
the minuter distinctions by which one species differs from another, without
departing from that simplicity of grandeur which *fills the imagination*; nor dis-
sect the latent qualities of things, without losing its *general power of gratifying
every mind by recalling its own conceptions*. Not only the images of rural life, but
the occasions on which they can be properly applied, are few and general. The

state of a man confined to the employments and pleasures of the country, is so little diversified, and exposed to so few of those accidents which produce perplexities, terrors, and surprises, in more complicated transactions, that he can be shown but seldom in such circumstances as attract curiosity. His ambition is without policy, and his love without intrigue. He has no complaints to make of his rival, but that he is richer than himself; nor any disasters to lament, but a cruel mistress or a bad harvest.'*

Such were the notions of the great arbiter of taste, whose dicta formed the creed of the British world, at the time when Burns made his appearance to overturn all such dogmata at a single blow; to convince the loftiest of the noble, and the daintiest of the learned, that wherever human nature is at work, the eye of a poet may discover rich elements of his art—that over Christian Europe, at all events, the purity of sentiment, and the fervour of passion, may be found combined with sagacity of intellect, wit, shrewdness, humour, whatever elevates, and whatever delights the mind, not more easily amidst the most 'complicated transactions' of the most polished societies, than

> In huts where poor men lie.

Burns did not place himself only within the estimation and admiration of those whom the world called his superiors—a solitary tree emerging into light and air, and leaving the parent underwood as low and as dark before. He, as well as any man,

> Knew his own worth, and reverenced the lyre;

but he ever announced himself as a peasant, the representative of his class, the painter of their manners, inspired by the same influences which ruled their bosoms; and whosoever sympathized with the verse of Burns, had his soul opened for the moment to the whole family of man. If, in too many instances, the matter has stopped there—the blame is not with the poet, but with the mad and unconquerable pride and coldness of the worldly heart—'man's inhumanity to man.' If, in spite of Burns, and all his successors, the boundary lines of society are observed with increasing strictness among us—if the various orders of men still, day by day, feel the chord of sympathy relaxing, let us lament over symptoms of a disease in the body politic, which, if it goes on, must find sooner or later a fatal ending: but let us not undervalue the antidote which has all along been checking this strong poison. Who

* *Rambler*, No. 36.

347

can doubt, that at this moment thousands of 'the first-born of Egypt' look upon the smoke of a cottager's chimney with feelings which would never have been developed within their being, had there been no Burns?

Such, it can hardly be disputed, has been and is the general influence of this poet's genius; and the effect has been accomplished, not in spite of, but by means of the most exact contradiction of, every one of the principles laid down by Dr. Johnson in a passage already cited; and, indeed, assumed throughout the whole body of that great author's critical disquisitions. Whatever Burns has done, he has done by his exquisite power of entering into the characters and feelings of individuals; as Heron has well expressed it, 'by the effusion of particular, not general sentiments, and in the picturing out of particular imagery.'

Currie says, that 'if *fiction* be the soul of poetry, as some assert, Burns can have small pretensions to the name of poet.' The success of Burns, the influence of his verse, would alone be enough to overturn all the systems of a thousand definers; but the Doctor has obviously taken *fiction* in far too limited a sense. There are indeed but few of Burns's pieces in which he is found creating beings and circumstances, both alike alien from his own person and experience, and then, by the power of imagination, divining and expressing what forms life and passion would assume with, and under these—but there are some; there is quite enough to satisfy every reader of 'Hallowe'en' the 'Jolly Beggars', and 'Tam o'Shanter', (to say nothing of various particular songs, such as 'Bruce's Address', 'Macpherson's Lament', &c.) that Burns, if he pleased might have been as largely and as successfully an inventor in this way, as he is in another walk, perhaps not so inferior to this as many people may have accustomed themselves to believe; in the art namely, of recombining and newcombining, varying, embellishing, and fixing and transmitting, the elements of a most picturesque experience, and most vivid feelings.

Lord Byron, in his letter on Pope, treats with high and just contempt the laborious trifling which has been expended on distinguishing by air-drawn lines and technical slang-words, the elements and materials of a poetical exertion; and, among other things, expresses his scorn of the attempts that have been made to class Burns among minor poets merely because he has put forth few large pieces and still fewer of what is called the purely imaginative character ... That is poetry of the highest order, which exerts influence of the most powerful order on the hearts and minds of mankind.

Burns has been appreciated duly, and he has had the fortune to be praised eloquently, by almost every poet who has come after him. To accumulate all that has been said of him, even by men like himself, of the first order, would fill a volume—and a noble monument, no question, that volume would be—the noblest, except what he has left us in his own immortal verses, which—were some dross removed, and the rest arranged in a chronological order—would, I believe, form, to the intelligent, a more perfect and vivid history of his life, than will ever be composed out of all the materials in the world besides . . .

The cantata of the 'Jolly Beggars', which was not printed at all until some time after the poet's death, and has not been included in the editions of his works until within these few years, cannot be considered as it deserves, without strongly heightening our regret that Burns never lived to execute his meditated drama. That extraordinary sketch, coupled with his later lyrics in a higher vein, is enough to show that in him we had a master capable of placing the musical drama on a level with the loftiest of our classical forms. *Beggar's Bush*, and *Beggar's Opera*, sink into tameness in the comparison; and indeed, without profanity to the name of Shakspeare, it may be said, that out of such materials, even his genius could hardly have constructed a piece in which imagination could have more splendidly predominated over the outward shows of things—in which the sympathy-awakening power of poetry could have been displayed more triumphantly under circumstances of the greatest difficulty. That remarkable performance by the way, was an early production of the Mauchline period; I know nothing but the 'Tam o' Shanter' that is calculated to convey so high an impression of what Burns might have done.

As to Burns's want of education and knowledge, Mr. Campbell may not have considered, but he must admit, that whatever Burns's opportunities had been at the time when he produced his first poems, such a man as he was not likely to be a hard reader, (which he certainly was), and a constant observer of men and manners, in a much wider circle of society than almost any other great poet has ever moved in, from three-and-twenty to eight-and-thirty, without having thoroughly removed any pretext for auguring unfavourably on that score, of what he might have been expected to produce in the more elaborate departments of his art, had his life been spared to the usual limits of humanity. In another way, however, I cannot help suspecting that Burns's enlarged knowledge both of men and books, produced an unfavourable effect, rather than otherwise, on the exertions, such as they were, of his later years. His generous spirit was open to the impression of every kind of excellence; his lively imagination, lending its own vigour to whatever it touched, made him admire even what other people try to read in vain; and after travelling, as he did, over the general surface of our literature, he appears to have been somewhat startled at the consideration of what he himself had, in comparative ignorance, adventured, and to have been more intimidated than encouraged by the retrospect. In most of the new departments in which he made some trial of his strength, (such, for example, as the moral epistle in Pope's vein, the *heroic* satire, &c.), he appears to have soon lost heart, and paused. There is indeed one magnificent exception in 'Tam O'Shanter'—a piece which no one can understand without believing, that had Burns pursued that walk, and poured out his stores of traditionary lore, embellished with his extraordinary powers of description of all kinds, we might have had from his hand a series of national tales, uniting the quaint simplicity, sly humour, and irresistible pathos of another Chaucer, with the strong and graceful versification, and masculine wit and sense of another Dryden.

This was a sort of feeling that must have in time subsided. But let us not waste words in regretting what might have been, where so much is. Burns, short and painful as were his years, has left behind him a volume in which there is inspiration for every fancy, and music for every mood; which lives, and will live in strength and vigour—'to soothe', as a generous lover of genius has said—'the sorrows of how many a lover, to inflame the patriotism of how many a soldier, to fan the fires of how many a genius, to disperse the gloom of solitude, appease the agonies of pain, encourage virtue, and show vice its ugliness';[1]—a volume in which, centuries hence, as now, wherever Scotsman may wander, he will find the dearest consolation of his exile. Already, in the language of Childe Harold, has

> Glory without end
> Scattered the clouds away; and on that name attend
> The tears and praises of all time.

[1] Sir Egerton Brydges.

67. Thomas Carlyle on Lockhart's *Life of Burns*

December 1828

Extract from unsigned review in *Edinburgh Review*, xlviii, no. xcvi.

Text here from reprint by Chapman and Hall (1854), pp. 1–88. This was the most influential critical essay on Burns of its period. There is a separate study by John Muir, *Carlyle on Burns* (Glasgow, 1898). On the relationship of Carlyle (1795–1881) with Jeffrey, see P. Morgan, 'Carlyle, Jeffrey and the *Edinburgh Review*', *Neophilologus* (July 1970), liv. no. 3 (See Nos 39, 66 and Introduction, pp. 41–3).

Burns first came upon the world as a prodigy; and was, in that character, entertained by it, in the usual fashion, with loud, vague, tumultuous wonder, speedily subsiding into censure and neglect; till his early and most mournful death again awakened an enthusiasm for him, which, especially as there was now nothing to be done, and much to be spoken, has prolonged itself even to our own time. It is true, the 'nine days' have long since elapsed; and the very continuance of this clamour proves that Burns was no vulgar wonder. Accordingly, even in sober judgments, where, as years passed by, he has come to rest more and more exclusively on his own intrinsic merits, and may now be wellnigh shorn of that casual radiance, he appears not only as a true British poet, but as one of the most considerable British men of the eighteenth century. Let it not be objected that he did little. He did much, if we consider where and how. If the work performed was small, we must remember that he had his very materials to discover; for the metal he worked in lay hid under the desert moor, where no eye but his had guessed its existence; and we may almost say, that with his own hand he had to construct the tools for fashioning it. For he found himself in deepest obscurity, without help, without instruction, without model, or with models only of the meanest sort. An educated man stands, as it were, in the midst of a boundless arsenal and magazine, filled with all the weapons and engines which man's skill has been able to devise from the earliest time; and he works, accordingly, with a strength borrowed from all past ages. How different is *his* state who stands on the outside of that storehouse, and feels that its gates must be stormed, or remain forever shut against him! His means are the commonest and rudest; the mere work done is no measure of his strength. A dwarf behind his steam-engine may remove mountains; but no dwarf will hew them down with the pickaxe; and he must be a Titan that hurls them abroad with his arms.

It is in this last shape that Burns presents himself. Born in an age the most prosaic that Britain had yet seen, and in a condition the most disadvantageous, where his mind, if it accomplished aught, must accomplish it under the pressure of continual bodily toil, nay of penury and desponding apprehension of the worst evils, and with no furtherance but such knowledge as dwells in a poor man's hut, and the rhymes of a Ferguson or Ramsay for his standard of beauty, he sinks not under all these impediments: through the fogs and darkness of that obscure region, his lynx eye discerns the true relations of the world and human life; he grows into intellectual strength, and trains himself into intellectual expertness. Impelled by the expansive movement of his own irrepressible soul, he struggles forward into the general view; and with haughty modesty lays down before us, as the fruit of his labour, a gift, which Time has now pronounced imperishable. Add to all this, that his darksome, drudging childhood and youth was by far the kindliest era of his whole life; and that he died in his thirty-seventh year: and then ask, If it be strange that his poems are imperfect, and of small extent, or that his genius attained no mastery in its art? Alas, his Sun shone as through a tropical tornado; and the pale Shadow of Death eclipsed it at noon! Shrouded in such baleful vapours, the genius of Burns was never seen in clear azure splendour, enlightening the world: but some beams from it did, by fits, pierce through; and it tinted those clouds with rainbow and orient colours, into a glory and stern grandeur, which men silently gazed on with wonder and tears!

We are anxious not to exaggerate; for it is exposition rather than admiration that our readers require of us here; and yet to avoid some tendency to that side is no easy matter. We love Burns, and we pity him; and love and pity are prone to magnify. Criticism, it is sometimes thought, should be a cold business; we are not so sure of this; but, at all events, our concern with Burns is not exclusively that of critics. True and genial as his poetry must appear, it is not chiefly as a poet, but as a man, that he interests and affects us. He was often advised to write a tragedy: time and means were not lent him for this; but through life he enacted a tragedy, and one of the deepest. We question whether the world has since witnessed so utterly sad a scene; whether Napoleon himself, left to brawl with Sir Hudson Lowe, and perish on his rocks, 'amid the melancholy main,' presented to the reflecting mind such a 'spectacle of pity and fear' as did this intrinsically nobler, gentler and perhaps greater soul, wasting itself away in a hopeless struggle with base entanglements, which coiled closer round him, till only death opened him an outlet. Conquerors are a class of men with whom, for most part, the world could well dispense; nor can the hard intellect, the unsympathising loftiness and high but selfish enthusiasm of such persons inspire us in general with any affection; at best it may excite amazement; and their fall, like that of a pyramid, will be beheld with a certain sadness and awe. But a true Poet, a man in whose heart resides some effluence of Wisdom, some tone of the 'Eternal Melodies,' is the most precious gift that can be bestowed on a generation: we see in him a freer, purer development of whatever is noblest in ourselves; his life is a rich lesson to us; and we mourn his death as that of a benefactor who loved and taught us.

Such a gift had Nature, in her beauty, bestowed on us in Robert Burns; but with queenlike indifference she cast it from her hand, like a thing of no moment; and it was defaced and torn asunder as an idle bauble, before we recognised it. To the ill-starred Burns was given the power of making man's life more venerable, but that of wisely guiding his own life was not given. Destiny,—for so in our ignorance we must speak,—his faults, the faults of others, proved too hard for him; and that spirit, which might have soared could it but have walked, soon sank to the dust, its glorious faculties trodden under foot in the blossom; and died, we may almost say, without ever having lived. And so kind and warm a soul; so full of inborn riches, of love to all living and lifeless things! How his heart flows out in sympathy over universal Nature; and in her bleakest provinces discerns a beauty and a meaning! The 'Daisy' falls not unheeded under his ploughshare; nor the ruined nest of that 'wee, cowering, timorous beastie,' cast forth, after all its provident pains, to 'thole the sleety dribble, and cranreuch cauld.' The 'hoar visage' of Winter delights him; he dwells with a sad and oft-returning fondness in these scenes of solemn desolation; the voice of the tempest becomes an anthem to his ears; he loves to walk in the sounding woods, for 'it raises his thoughts to *Him that walketh on the wings of the wind*.' A true Poet-soul, for it needs but to be struck, and the sound it yields will be music! But observe him chiefly as he mingles with his brother men. What warm, all comprehending fellow-feeling; what trustful, boundless love; what generous exaggeration of the object loved! His rustic friend, his nut-brown maiden, are no longer mean and homely, but a hero and a queen, whom he prizes as the paragons of Earth. The rough scenes of Scottish life, not seen by him in any Arcadian illusion, but in the rude contradiction, in the smoke and soil of a too harsh reality, are still lovely to him: Poverty is indeed his companion, but Love also, and Courage; the simple feelings, the worth, the nobleness, that dwell under the straw roof, are dear and venerable to his heart: and thus over the lowest provinces of man's existence he pours the glory of his own soul; and they rise, in shadow and sunshine, softened and brightened into a beauty which other eyes discern not in the highest. He has a just self-consciousness, which too often degenerates into pride; yet it is a noble pride, for defence not for offence; no cold suspicious feeling, but a frank and social one. The Peasant Poet bears himself, we might say, like a King in exile: he is cast among the low, and feels himself equal to the highest; yet he claims no rank, that none may be disputed to him. The forward he can repel, the supercilious he can subdue; pretensions of wealth or ancestry are of no avail with him; there is a fire in that dark eye, under which the 'insolence of condescension' cannot thrive. In his abasement, in his extreme need, he forgets not for a moment the majesty of Poetry and Manhood. And yet, far as he feels himself above common men, he wanders not apart from them, but mixes warmly in their interests; nay, throws himself into their arms, and, as it were, entreats them to love him. It is moving to see how, in his darkest despondency, this proud being still seeks relief from friendship; unbosoms himself, often to the unworthy; and, amid tears, strains to his glowing heart a heart that knows only the name of friendship. And yet he was 'quick to learn;' a man of keen vision, before whom common disguises afforded no concealment. His understanding saw through the hollowness even of accomplished deceivers; but there was a generous credulity in his heart. And so did our Peasant shew himself among us; 'a soul like an AEolian harp, in whose strings the vulgar wind, as it passed through them, changed itself into articulate melody.' And this was he for whom the world found no fitter business than quarrelling with smugglers and vintners, computing excise-dues upon tallow, and gauging alebarrels! In such toils was that mighty Spirit sorrowfully wasted: and a hundred years may pass on, before another such is given us to waste.

All that remains of Burns, the Writings he has left, seem to us, as we hinted above, no more than a poor mutilated fraction of what was in him; brief, broken glimpses of a genius that could never shew itself complete; that wanted all things for completeness: culture, leisure, true effort, nay even length of life. His poems are, with scarcely any exception, mere occasional effusions; poured forth with little premeditation; expressing, by such means as offered, the passion, opinion, or humour of the hour. Never in one instance was it permitted him to grapple with any subject with the full collection of his strength, to fuse and mould it in the concentrated fire of his genius. To try by the strict rules of Art such imperfect fragments, would be at once unprofitable and unfair. Nevertheless, there is something in these poems, marred and defective as they are, which forbids the most fastidious student of poetry to pass them by. Some sort of enduring quality they must have: for, after fifty years of the wildest vicissitudes in poetic taste, they still continue to be read; nay, are read more and more eagerly, more and more extensively; and this not only by literary virtuosos, and that class upon whom transitory causes operate most strongly, but by all classes, down to the most hard, unlettered and truly natural class, who read little, and especially no poetry, except because they find pleasure in it. The grounds of so singular and wide a popularity, which extends, in a literal sense, from the palace to the hut, and over all regions where the English tongue is spoken, are well worth enquiring into. After every just deduction, it seems to imply some rare excellence in these works. What is that excellence?

To answer this question will not lead us far. The excellence of Burns is, indeed, among the rarest, whether in poetry or prose; but at the same time, it is plain and easily recognised: his *Sincerity*, his indisputable air of Truth. Here are no fabulous woes or joys; no hollow fantastic sentimentalities; no wiredrawn refinings, either in thought or feeling: the passion that is traced before us has glowed in a living heart; the opinion he utters has risen in his own understanding, and been a light to his own steps. He does not write from hearsay, but from sight and experience; it is the scenes that he has lived and laboured amidst, that he describes: those scenes, rude and humble as they are, have kindled beautiful emotions in his soul, noble thoughts, and definite resolves; and he speaks forth what is in him, not from any outward call of vanity or interest, but because his heart is too full to be silent. He speaks it with such melody and modulation as he can; 'in homely rustic jingle;' but it is his own, and genuine. This is the grand secret for finding readers and retaining them: let him who would himself move and convince others, be first moved and convinced himself. Horace's rule, *Si vis me flere*, is applicable in a wider sense than the literal one. To every poet, to every writer, we might say: Be true, if you would be believed. Let a man but speak forth with genuine earnestness the thought, the emotion, the actual condition of his own heart; and other men, so strangely are we all knit together by the tie of sympathy, must and will give heed to him. In culture, in extent of view, we may stand above the speaker, or below him; but in either case, his words, if they are earnest and sincere, will find some response within us; for in spite of all casual varieties in outward rank, or inward, as face answers to face, so does the heart of man to man.

This may appear a very simple principle, and one which Burns had little merit in discovering. True, the discovery is easy enough; but the practical appliance is not easy; is indeed the fundamental difficulty which all poets have to strive with, and which scarcely one in the hundred ever fairly surmounts. A head too dull to discriminate the true from the false; a heart too dull to love the one at all risks, and to hate the other in spite of all temptations, are alike fatal to a writer. With either, or, as more commonly happens, with both, of these deficiencies, combine a love of distinction, a wish to be original, which is seldom wanting, and we have Affectation, the bane of literature, as Cant, its elder brother, is of morals. How often does the one and the other front us, in poetry, as in life! Great poets themselves are not always free of this vice; nay, it is precisely on a certain sort and degree of greatness that it is most commonly ingrafted. A strong effort after excellence will sometimes solace itself with a mere shadow of success; he who has much to unfold, will sometimes unfold it imperfectly. Byron, for instance, was no common man: yet if we examine his poetry with this view, we shall find it far enough from faultless. Generally speaking, we should say that it is not true. He refreshes us, not with the divine fountain, but too often with vulgar strong waters, stimulating indeed to the taste, but soon ending in dislike, or even nausea. Are his Harolds and Giaours, we would ask, real men; we mean, poetically consistent and conceivable men? Do not these characters, does not the character of their author, which more or less shines through them all, rather appear a thing put on for the occasion; no natural or possible mode of being, but something intended to look much grander than nature? Surely, all these stormful agonies, this volcanic heroism, superhuman contempt and moody desperation, with so much scowling, and teeth-gnashing, and other sulphurous humour, is more like the brawling of a player in some paltry tragedy, which is to last three hours, than the bearing of a man in the business of life, which is to last three score and ten years. To our minds, there is a taint of this sort, something which we should call theatrical, false, affected, in every one of these otherwise so powerful pieces. Perhaps 'Don Juan', especially the latter parts of it, is the only thing approaching to a *sincere* work, he ever wrote; the only work where he shewed himself, in any measure, as he was; and seemed so intent on his subject as, for moments, to forget himself. Yet Byron hated this vice; we believe, heartily detested it: nay, he had declared formal war against it in words. So difficult is it even for the strongest to make this primary attainment, which might seem the simplest of all: to *read its own consciousness without mistakes*, without errors involuntary or wilful! We recollect no poet of Burns's susceptibility who comes before us from the first, and abides with us to the last, with such a total want of affectation. He is an honest man, and an honest writer. In his successes and his failures, in his greatness and his littleness, he is ever clear, simple, true, and glitters with no lustre but his own. We reckon this to be a great virtue; to be, in fact, the root of most other virtues, literary as well as moral.

Here, however, let us say, it is to the Poetry of Burns that we now allude; to those writings which he had time to meditate, and where no special reason existed to warp his critical feeling, or obstruct his endeavour to fulfil it. Certain of his Letters, and other fractions of prose composition, by no means deserve this praise. Here, doubtless, there is not the same natural truth of style; but on the contrary, something not only stiff, but strained and twisted; a certain high-flown inflated tone, the stilting emphasis of which contrasts ill with the firmness and rugged simplicity of even his poorest verses. Thus no man, it would appear, is altogether unaffected. Does not Shakspeare himself sometimes premeditate the sheerest bombast! But even with regard to these Letters of Burns, it is but fair to state that he had two excuses. The first was his comparative deficiency in language. Burns, though for most part he writes with singular force, and even gracefulness, is not master of English prose, as he is of Scottish verse; not master of it, we mean, in proportion to the depth and vehemence of his matter. These Letters strike us as the effort of a man to express something which he has no organ fit for expressing. But a second and weightier excuse is to be found in the peculiarity of Burns's social rank. His correspondents are often men whose relation to him he has never accurately ascertained; whom therefore he is either forearming himself against, or else unconsciously flattering, by adopting the style he thinks will please them. At all events, we should remember that these faults, even in his letters, are not the rule, but the exception. Whenever he writes, as one would ever wish to do, to trusted friends and on real interests, his style becomes simple, vigorous, expressive, sometimes even beautiful. His letters to Mrs. Dunlop are uniformly excellent.

But we return to his Poetry. In addition to its Sincerity, it has another peculiar merit, which indeed is but a mode, or perhaps a means, of the foregoing: this displays itself in his choice of subjects; or rather in his indifference as to subjects, and the power he has of making all subjects interesting. The ordinary poet, like the ordinary man, is forever seeking in external circumstances the help which can be found only in himself. In what is familiar and near at hand, he discerns no form or comeliness: home is not poetical but prosaic; it is in some past, distant, conventional heroic world, that poetry resides; were he there and not here, were he thus and not so, it would be well with him. Hence our innumerable host of rose-coloured Novels and iron-mailed Epics, with their locality not on the earth, but somewhere nearer to the Moon. Hence our Virgins of the Sun, and our Knights of the Cross, malicious Saracens in turbans, and copper-coloured Chiefs in wampum, and so many other truculent figures from the heroic times or the heroic climates, who on all hands swarm in our poetry. Peace be with them! But yet, as a great moralist proposed preaching to the men of this century, so would we fain preach to the poets, 'a sermon on the duty of staying at home.' Let them be sure that heroic ages and heroic climates can do little for them. That form of life has attraction for us, less because it is better or nobler than our own, than simply because it is different; and even this attraction must be of the most transient sort. For will not our own age, one day, be an ancient one; and have as quaint a costume as the rest; not contrasted with the rest, therefore, but ranked along with them, in respect of quaintness? Does Homer interest us now, because he wrote of what passed beyond his native Greece, and two centuries before he was born; or because he wrote what passed in God's world, and in the heart of man, which is the same after thirty centuries? Let our poets look to this: is their feeling really finer, truer, and their vision deeper than that of other men,—they have nothing to fear, even from the humblest subject; is it not so,—they have nothing to hope, but an ephemeral favour, even the highest.

The poet, we imagine, can never have far to seek for a subject: the elements of his art are in him, and around him on every hand; for him the Ideal world is not remote from the Actual, but under it and within it: nay, he is a poet, precisely because he can discern it there. Wherever there is a sky above him, and a world around him, the poet is in his place; for there too is man's existence, with its infinite longings and small acquirings; its ever-thwarted, ever-renewed endeavours; its unspeakable aspirations, its fears and hopes that wander through Eternity; and all the mystery of brightness and of gloom that it was ever made of, in any age or climate, since man first began to live. Is there not the fifth act of a Tragedy in every death-bed, though it were a peasant's, and a bed of heath? And are wooings and weddings obsolete, that there can be Comedy no longer? Or are men suddenly grown wise, that Laughter must no longer shake his sides, but be cheated of his Farce? Man's life and nature is, as it was, and as it will ever be. But the poet must have an eye to read these things, and a heart to understand them; or they come and pass away before him in vain. He is a *vates*, a seer; a gift of vision has been given him. Has life no meanings for him, which another cannot equally decipher; then he is no poet, and Delphi itself will not make him one.

In this respect, Burns, though not perhaps absolutely a great poet, better manifests his capability, better proves the truth of his genius, than if he had, by his own strength, kept the whole Minerva Press going, to the end of his literary course. He shews himself at least a poet of Nature's own making; and Nature, after all, is still the grand agent in making poets. We often hear of this and the other external condition being requisite for the existence of a poet. Sometimes it is a certain sort of training; he must have studied certain things, studied for instance 'the elder dramatists,' and so learned a poetic language; as if poetry lay in the tongue, not in the heart. At other times, we are told, he must be bred in a certain rank, and must be on a confidential footing with the higher classes; because, above all things, he must see the world. As to seeing the world, we apprehend this will cause him little difficulty, if he have but eyesight to see it with. Without eyesight, indeed, the task might be hard. The blind or the purblind man 'travels from Dan to Beersheba, and finds it all barren.' But happily every poet is born *in* the world; and sees it, with or against his will, every day and every hour he lives. The mysterious workmanship of man's heart, the true light and the inscrutable darkness of man's destiny, reveal themselves not only in capital cities and crowded saloons, but in every hut and hamlet where men

ROBERT BURNS

have their abode. Nay, do not the elements of all human virtues and
all human vices; the passions at once of a Borgia and of a Luther,
lie written, in stronger or fainter lines, in the consciousness of every
individual bosom, that has practised honest self-examination? Truly,
this same world may be seen in Mossgiel and Tarbolton, if we look
well, as clearly as it ever came to light in Crockford's, or the Tuileries
itself.

But sometimes still harder requisitions are laid on the poor aspirant
to poetry; for it is hinted that he should have *been born* two centuries
ago; inasmuch as poetry, about that date, vanished from the earth, and
became no longer attainable by men! Such cobweb speculations have,
now and then, overhung the field of literature; but they obstruct not
the growth of any plant there: the Shakspeare or the Burns, unconsciously and merely as he walks onward, silently brushes them away. Is
not every genius an impossibility till he appear? Why do we call him
new and original, if *we* saw where his marble was lying, and what
fabric he could rear from it? It is not the material but the workman that
is wanting. It is not the dark place that hinders, but the dim eye. A
Scottish peasant's life was the meanest and rudest of all lives, till Burns
became a poet in it, and a poet of it; found it a *man's* life, and therefore
significant to men. A thousand battle-fields remain unsung; but the
Wounded Hare has not perished without its memorial; a balm of mercy
yet breathes on us from its dumb agonies, because a poet was there.
Our *Halloween* had passed and repassed, in rude awe and laughter,
since the era of the Druids; but no Theocritus, till Burns, discerned in it
the materials of a Scottish Idyl: neither was the *Holy Fair* any Council
of Trent, or Roman Jubilee, but nevertheless, *Superstition* and *Hypocrisy*
and *Fun* having been propitious to him, in this man's hand it became a
poem, instinct with satire and genuine comic life. Let but the true poet
be given us, we repeat it, place him where and how you will, and true
poetry will not be wanting.

Independently of the essential gift of poetic feeling, as we have now
attempted to describe it, a certain rugged sterling worth pervades whatever Burns has written: a virtue, as of green fields and mountain
breezes, dwells in his poetry; it is redolent of natural life, and hardy
natural men. There is a decisive strength in him, and yet a sweet native
gracefulness: he is tender, he is vehement, yet without constraint or too
visible effort; he melts the heart, or inflames it, with a power which
seems habitual and familiar to him. We see that in this man there was
the gentleness, the trembling pity of a woman, with the deep earnestness,

the force and passionate ardour of a hero. Tears lie in him, and consuming fire; as lightning lurks in the drops of the summer cloud. He has a resonance in his bosom for every note of human feeling; the high and the low, the sad, the ludicrous, the joyful, are welcome in their turns to 'his lightly-moved and all-conceiving spirit.' And observe with what a fierce prompt force he grasps his subject, be it what it may! How he fixes, as it were, the full image of the matter in his eye; full and clear in every lineament; and catches the real type and essence of it, amid a thousand accidents and superficial circumstances, no one of which misleads him! Is it of reason; some truth to be discovered? No sophistry, no vain surface-logic detains him; quick, resolute, unerring, he pierces through into the marrow of the question; and speaks his verdict with an emphasis that cannot be forgotten. Is it of description; some visual object to be represented? No poet of any age or nation is more graphic than Burns: the characteristic features disclose themselves to him at a glance; three lines from his hand, and we have a likeness. And, in that rough dialect, in that rude, often awkward metre, so clear and definite a likeness! It seems a draughtsman working with a burnt stick; and yet the burin of a Retzch is not more expressive or exact.

Of this last excellence, the plainest and most comprehensive of all, being indeed the root and foundation of *every* sort of talent, poetical or intellectual, we could produce innumerable instances from the writings of Burns. Take these glimpses of a snow-storm from his 'Winter Night' (the italics are ours):

> When biting Boreas, fell and doure,
> *Sharp shivers* thro' the leafless bow'r,
> And Phoebus *gies a short-liv'd glowr*
> *Far south the lift,*
> *Dim-dark'ning thro' the flaky show'r*
> *Or whirling drift:*
> Ae night the storm the steeples rock'd,
> Poor labour sweet in sleep was lock'd,
> While burns *wi' snawy wreeths upchock'd,*
> *Wild-eddying whirl,*
> Or thro' the mining outlet lock'd,
> Down headlong hurl.

Are there not 'descriptive touches' here? The describer *saw* this thing; the essential feature and true likeness of every circumstance in it; saw, and not with the eye only. 'Poor labour locked in sweet sleep;' the dead stillness of man, unconscious, vanquished, yet not unprotected, while such strife of the material elements rages, and seems to reign supreme in loneliness: this is of the heart as well as of the eye!—Look also at his image of a thaw, and prophesied fall of the *Auld Brig*:

[quotes 'The Brigs of Ayr', ll. 113-26, 'And dash the gumlie jaups up to the pouring skies']

The last line is in itself a Poussin-picture of that Deluge! The welkin has, as it were, bent down with its weight; the 'gumlie jaups' and the 'pouring skies' are mingled together, it is a world of rain and ruin.— In respect of mere clearness and minute fidelity, the *Farmer's* commendation of his *Auld Mare*, in plough or in cart, may vie with Homer's Smithy of the Cyclops, or yoking of Priam's Chariot. Nor have we forgotten stout *Burn-the-wind* and his brawny customers, inspired by *Scotch Drink*: but it is needless to multiply examples. One other trait of a much finer sort we select from multitudes of such among his *Songs*. It gives, in a single line, to the saddest feeling the saddest environment and local habitation:

> *The pale Moon is setting beyond the white wave,*
> *And Time is setting wi' me, O;*
> Farewell, false friends! false lover, farewell!
> I'll nae mair trouble them nor thee, O.

   This clearness of sight we have called the foundation of all talent; for in fact, unless we *see* our object, how shall we know how to place or prize it, in our understanding, our imagination, our affections? Yet it is not in itself, perhaps, a very high excellence; but capable of being united indifferently with the strongest, or with ordinary powers. Homer surpasses all men in this quality: but strangely enough, at no great distance below him are Richardson and Defoe. It belongs, in truth, to what is called a lively mind; and gives no sure indication of the higher endowments that may exist along with it. In all the three cases we have mentioned, it is combined with great garrulity; their descriptions are detailed ample and lovingly exact; Homer's fire burst through, from time to time, as if by accident; but Defoe and Richardson have no fire. Burns, again, is not more distinguished by the clearness than by the impetuous force of his conceptions. Of the strength, the piercing emphasis with which he thought, his emphasis of expression may give a humble but the readiest proof. Who ever uttered sharper sayings than his; words more memorable, now by their burning vehemence, now by their cool vigour and laconic pith? A single phrase depicts a whole subject, a whole scene. We hear of 'a gentleman that derived his patent of nobility direct from Almighty God.' Our Scottish forefathers in the battlefield struggled forward 'red-wat-shod:' in this one word, a full vision of horror and carnage, perhaps too frightfully accurate for Art!

In fact, one of the leading features in the mind of Burns is this vigour of his strictly intellectual perceptions. A resolute force is ever visible in his judgments, and in his feelings and volitions. Professor Stewart says of him, with some surprise: 'All the faculties of Burns's mind were, as far as I could judge, equally vigorous; and his predilection for poetry was rather the result of his own enthusiastic and impassioned temper, than of a genius exclusively adapted to that species of composition. From his conversation I should have pronounced him to be fitted to excel in whatever walk of ambition he had chosen to exert his abilities'. But this, if we mistake not, is at all times the very essence of a truly poetical endowment. Poetry, except in such cases as that of Keats, where the whole consists in a weak-eyed maudlin sensibility, and a certain random tunefulness of nature, is no separate faculty, no organ which can be superadded to the rest, or disjoined from them; but rather the result of their general harmony and completion. The feelings, the gifts that exist in the Poet, are those that exist, with more or less development, in every human soul: the imagination, which shudders at the Hell of Dante, is the same faculty, weaker in degree, which called that picture into being. How does the Poet speak to men, with power, but by being still more a man than they? Shakspeare, it has been well observed, in the planning and completing of his tragedies, has shewn an Understanding, were it nothing more, which might have governed states, or indited a *Novum Organum*. What Burns's force of understanding may have been, we have less means of judging: it had to dwell among the humblest objects; never saw Philosophy; never rose, except by natural effort and for short intervals, into the region of great ideas. Nevertheless, sufficient indication, if no proof sufficient, remains for us in his works: we discern the brawny movements of a gigantic though untutored strength, and can understand how, in conversation, his quick sure insight into men and things may, as much as aught else about him, have amazed the best thinkers of his time and country.

But, unless we mistake, the intellectual gift of Burns is fine as well as strong. The more delicate relations of things could not well have escaped his eye, for they were intimately present to his heart. The logic of the senate and the forum is indispensable, but not all-sufficient; nay, perhaps the highest Truth is that which will the most certainly elude it. For this logic works by words, and 'the highest,' it has been said, 'cannot be expressed in words.' We are not without tokens of an openness for this higher truth also, of a keen though uncultivated sense for it, having existed in Burns. Mr. Stewart, it will be remembered, 'wonders,' in the passage above quoted, that Burns had formed some distinct conception of the 'doctrine of association.' We rather think that far subtler things than the doctrine of association had from of old been familiar to him. Here for instance:

'We know nothing,' thus writes he, 'or next to nothing, of the structure of our souls, so we cannot account for those seeming caprices in them, that one should be particularly pleased with this thing, or struck with that, which, on minds of a different cast, makes no extraordinary impression. I have some favourite flowers in spring, among which are the mountain-daisy, the harebell, the foxglove, the wild-brier rose, the budding birch, and the hoary hawthorn, that I view and hang over with particular delight. I never hear the loud solitary whistle of the curlew in a summer noon, or the wild mixing cadence of a troop of grey plover in an autumnal morning, without feeling an elevation of soul like the enthusiasm of devotion or poetry. Tell me, my dear friend, to what can this be owing? Are we a piece of machinery, which, like the Æolian harp, passive, takes the impression of the passing accident; or do these workings argue something within us above the trodden clod? I own myself partial to such proofs of those awful and important realities: a God that made all things, man's immaterial and immortal nature, and a world of weal or wo beyond death and the grave.'

Force and fineness of understanding are often spoken of as something different from general force and fineness of nature, as something partly independent of them. The necessities of language so require it; but in truth these qualities are not distinct and independent: except in special cases, and from special causes, they ever go together. A man of strong understanding is generally a man of strong character; neither is delicacy in the one kind often divided from delicacy in the other. No one, at all events, is ignorant that in the Poetry of Burns, keenness of insight keeps pace with keenness of feeling; that his *light* is not more pervading than his *warmth*. He is a man of the most impassioned temper; with passions not strong only, but noble, and of the sort in which great virtues and great poems take their rise. It is reverence, it is love towards all Nature that inspires him, that opens his eyes to its beauty, and makes heart and voice eloquent in its praise. There is a true old saying, that 'Love furthers knowledge:' but above all, it is the living essence of that knowledge which makes poets; the first principle of its existence, increase, activity. Of Burns's fervid affection, his generous all-embracing Love, we have spoken already, as of the grand distinction of his nature, seen equally in word and deed, in his life and in his Writings. It were easy to multiply examples. Not man only, but all that environs man in the material and moral universe, is lovely in his sight: 'the hoary hawthorn,' the 'troop of grey plover,' the 'solitary curlew,' all are dear to him; all live in this Earth along with him, and to all he is knit as in mysterious brotherhood. How touching is it, for instance, that, amidst the gloom of personal misery, brooding over the wintry desolation without him and within him, he thinks of the 'ourie cattle' and 'silly sheep,' and their sufferings in the pitiless storm!

[quotes 'A Winter Night', ll. 14–24]

The tenant of the mean hut, with its 'ragged roof and chinky wall,' has a heart to pity even these! This is worth several homilies on Mercy: for it is the voice of Mercy herself. Burns, indeed, lives in sympathy; his soul rushes forth into all realms of being; nothing that has existence can be indifferent to him. The very Devil he cannot hate with right orthodoxy:

> But fare you weel, auld Nickie-ben;
> O wad ye tak a thought and men!
> Ye aiblins might,—I dinna ken,—
>   Still hae a stake;
> I'm wae to think upo' yon den,
>   Even for your sake!

'*He* is the father of curses and lies,' said Dr. Slop; 'and is cursed and damned already.'—'I am sorry for it,' quoth my uncle Toby! A Poet without Love were a physical and metaphysical impossibility.

But has it not been said in contradiction to this principle, that 'Indignation makes verses?' It has been so said, and is true enough: but the contradiction is apparent, not real. The Indignation which makes verses is, properly speaking, an inverted Love; the love of some right, some worth, some goodness, belonging to ourselves or others, which has been injured, and which this tempestuous feeling issues forth to defend and avenge. No selfish fury of heart, existing there as a primary feeling, and without its opposite, ever produced much Poetry: otherwise, we suppose, the Tiger were the most musical of all our choristers. Johnson said, he loved a good hater; by which he must have meant, not so much one that hated violently, as one that hated wisely; hated baseness from love of nobleness. However, in spite of Johnson's paradox, tolerable enough for once in speech, but which need not have been so often adopted in print since then, we rather believe that good men deal sparingly in hatred, either wise or unwise: nay that a 'good' hater is still a desideratum in this world. The Devil, at least, who passess for the chief and best of that class, is said to be nowise an amiable character.

Of the verses which Indignation makes, Burns has also given us specimens: and among the best that were ever given. Who will forget his 'Dweller in yon Dungeon dark;' a piece that might have been chaunted by the Furies of Æschylus? The secrets of the infernal Pit are laid bare; a boundless baleful 'darkness visible:' and streaks of hell-fire quivering madly in its black haggard bosom!

> Dweller in yon Dungeon, dark,
> Hangman of Creation, mark!
> Who in widow's weeds appears,
> Laden with unhonoured years,
> Noosing with care a bursting purse,
> Baited with many a deadly curse?

Why should we speak of 'Scots wha hae wi' Wallace bled;' since all know of it, from the king to the meanest of his subjects? This dithyrambic was composed on horseback; in riding in the middle of tempests, over the wildest Galloway moor, in company with a Mr. Syme, who, observing the poet's looks, forbore to speak,—judiciously enough for a man composing 'Bruce's Address' might be unsafe to trifle with. Doubtless this stern hymn was singing itself, as he formed it, through the soul of Burns: but to the external ear, it should be sung with the throat of the whirlwind. So long as there is warm blood in the heart of Scotchman or man, it will move in fierce thrills under this war-ode; the best, we believe, that was ever written by any pen.

Another wild stormful Song, that dwells in our ear and mind with a strange tenacity, is 'Macpherson's Farewell'. Perhaps there is something in the tradition itself that cooperates. For was not this grim Celt, this shaggy Northland Cacus, that 'lived a life of sturt and strife, and died by treacherie,' was not he too one of the Nimrods and Napoleons of the earth, in the arena of his own remote misty glens, for want of a clearer and wider one? Nay, was there not a touch of grace given him? A fibre of love and softness, of poetry itself, must have lived in his savage heart: for he composed that air the night before his execution;

on the wings of that poor melody, his better soul would soar away above oblivion, pain and all the ignominy and despair which, like an avalanche, was hurling him to the abyss! Here also, as at Thebes, and in Pelops' line, was material Fate matched against man's Freewill; matched in bitterest though obscure duel; and the ethereal soul sank not, even in its blindness, without a cry which has survived it. But who, except Burns, could have given words to such a soul; words that we never listen to without a strange half-barbarous, half-poetic fellow-feeling?

> Sae rantingly, sae wantonly,
> Sae dauntingly gaed he;
> He play'd a spring, and danced it round,
> Below the gallows tree.

Under a lighter disguise, the same principle of Love, which we have recognised as the great characteristic of Burns, and of all true poets, occasionally manifests itself in the shape of Humour. Everywhere, indeed, in his sunny moods, a full buoyant flood of mirth rolls through the mind of Burns; he rises to the high, and stoops to the low, and is brother and playmate to all Nature. We speak not of his bold and often irresistible faculty of caricature; for this is Drollery rather than Humour: but a much tenderer sportfulness dwells in him; and comes forth here and there, in evanescent and beautiful touches; as in his 'Address to the Mouse,' or the 'Farmer's Mare,' or in his 'Elegy on poor Mailie,' which last may be reckoned his happiest effort of this kind. In these pieces there are traits of a Humour as fine as that of Sterne; yet altogether different, original, peculiar,—the Humour of Burns.

Of the tenderness, the playful pathos, and many other kindred qualities of Burns's Poetry, much more might be said; but now, with these poor outlines of a sketch, we must prepare to quit this part of our subject. To speak of his individual Writings adequately and with any detail, would lead us far beyond our limits. As already hinted, we can look on but few of these pieces as, in strict critical language, deserving the name of Poems: they are rhymed eloquence, rhymed pathos, rhymed sense; yet seldom essentially melodious, aerial, poetical. 'Tam o' Shanter' itself, which enjoys so high a favour, does not appear to us, at all decisively, to come under this last category. It is not so much a poem, as a piece of sparkling rhetoric; the heart and body of the story still lies hard and dead. He has not gone back, much less carried us back, into that dark, earnest, wondering age, when the tradition was believed, and when it took its rise; he does not attempt, by any new-modelling of his supernatural ware, to strike anew that deep mysterious chord of human nature, which once responded to such things, and which lives in us too, and will forever live, though silent now, or vibrating with far other notes, and to far different issues. Our German readers will understand us, when we say, that he is not the Tieck but the Musäus of this tale. Externally it is all green and living; yet look closer, it is no firm growth, but only ivy on a rock. The piece does not properly cohere: the strange chasm which yawns in our incredulous imaginations between the Ayr public-house and the gate of Tophet, is nowhere bridged over, nay the idea of such a bridge is laughed at; and thus the Tragedy of the adventure becomes a mere drunken phantasmagoria, or many-coloured spectrum painted on ale-vapours, and the Farce alone has any reality. We do not say that Burns should have made much more of this tradition; we rather think that, for strictly poetical purposes, not much *was* to be made of it. Neither are we blind to the deep, varied, genial power displayed in what he has actually accomplished; but we find far more 'Shakspearean' qualities, as these of 'Tam o' Shanter have been fondly named, in many of his other pieces; nay, we incline to believe, that this latter might have been written, all but quite as well, by a man who, in place of genius, had only possessed talent.

Perhaps we may venture to say, that the most strictly poetical of all his 'poems' is one which does not appear in Currie's Edition; but has been often printed before and since, under the humble title of 'The Jolly Beggars.' The subject truly is among the lowest in Nature; but it only the more shews our Poet's gift in raising it into the domain of Art. To our minds, this piece seems thoroughly compacted; melted together, refined; and poured forth in one flood of true *liquid* harmony. It is light, airy, soft of movement; yet sharp and precise in its details; every face is a portrait; that *raucle carlin*, that *wee Apollo*, that *Son of Mars*, are Scottish, yet ideal; the scene is at once a dream, and the very Ragcastle of 'Poosie-Nansie.' Farther, it seems in a considerable degree complete, a real self-supporting Whole, which is the highest merit in a poem. The blanket of the Night is drawn asunder for a moment; in full, ruddy, flaming light, these rough tatterdemalions are seen in their boisterous revel; for the strong pulse of Life vindicates its right to gladness even here; and when the curtain closes, we prolong the action, without effort; the next day as the last, our *Caird* and our *Balladmonger*, are singing and soldering their 'brats and callets' are hawking, begging, cheating; and some other night, in new combinations, they will wring from Fate another hour of wassail and good cheer. Apart from the universal sympathy with man which this again bespeaks in Burns, a genuine inspiration and no inconsiderable technical talent are manifested here. There is the fidelity, humour, warm life and accurate painting and grouping of some Teniers, for whom hostlers and carousing peasants are not without significance. It would be strange, doubtless, to call this the best of Burns's writings: we mean to say only, that it seems to us the most perfect of its kind, as a piece of poetical composition strictly so called. In the *Beggars' Opera*, in the *Beggar's Bush*, as other critics have already remarked, there is nothing which, in real poetic vigour, equals this *Cantata*; nothing, as we think, which comes within many degrees of it.

But by far the most finished, complete and truly inspired pieces of Burns, are without dispute, to be found among his *Songs*. It is here that, although through a small aperture, his light shines with least obstruction; in its highest beauty, and pure sunny clearness. The reason may be, that Song is a brief simple species of composition; and requires nothing so much for its perfection, as genuine poetic feeling, genuine music of heart. Yet the Song has its rules equally with the Tragedy; rules which in most cases are poorly fulfilled, in many cases are not so much as felt. We might write a long essay on the Songs of Burns; which we reckon by far the best that Britain has yet produced: for, indeed, since the era of Queen Elizabeth, we know not that, by any other hand, aught truly worth attention has been accomplished in this department. True, we have songs enough 'by persons of quality;' we have tawdry, hollow, wine-bred madrigals; many a rhymed speech 'in the flowing and watery vein of Ossorius the Portugal Bishop,' rich in sonorous words, and, for moral, dashed perhaps with some tint of a sentimental sensuality; all which many persons cease not from endeavouring to sing; though for most part, we fear, the music is but from the throat outwards or at best from some region far enough short of the *Soul*: not in which, but in a certain inane Limbo of the Fancy, or even in some vaporous debateable-land on the outskirts of the Nervous System, most of such madrigals and rhymed speeches seem to have originated. With the Songs of Burns we must not name these things. Independently of the clear, manly, heartfelt sentiment that ever pervades *his* poetry, his Songs are honest in another point of view: in form, as well as in spirit. They do not *affect* to be set to music, but they actually and in themselves are music; they have received their life, and fashioned themselves together, in the medium of Harmony, as Venus rose from the bosom of the sea. The story, the feeling, is not detailed, but suggested; not *said*, or spouted, in rhetorical completeness and coherence; but *sung*, in fitful gushes, in glowing hints, in fantastic breaks, in *warblings* not of the voice only, but of the whole mind. We consider this to be the essence of a song; and that no songs since the little careless catches, and, as it were, drops of song, which Shakspeare has here and there sprinkled over his Plays, fulfil this condition in nearly the same degree as most of Burns's do. Such grace and truth of external movement, too, pre-supposes in general a corresponding force and truth of sentiment and inward meaning. The Songs of Burns are not more perfect in the former quality than in the latter. With what tenderness he sings, yet with what vehemence and entireness! There is a piercing wail in his sorrow, the purest rapture in his joy; he burns with the sternest ire, or laughs with the loudest or sliest mirth; and yet he is sweet and soft, 'sweet as the smile when fond lovers meet, and soft as their parting tear!' If we further take into account the immense variety of his sub-jects; how, from the loud flowing revel in 'Willie brew'd a Peck o' Maut,' to the still, rapt enthusiasm of sadness for 'Mary in Heaven;' from the glad kind greeting of 'Auld Langsyne,' or the comic archness of 'Duncan Gray,' to the fire-eyed fury of 'Scots wha hae wi' Wallace bled,' he has found a tone and words for every mood of man's heart,—it will seem a small praise if we rank him as the first of all our Song-writers; for we know not where to find one worthy of being second to him.

It is on his Songs, as we believe, that Burns's chief influence as an author will ultimately be found to depend: nor, if our Fletcher's aphorism is true, shall we account this a small influence. 'Let me make the songs of a people,' said he, 'and you shall make its laws.' Surely, if ever any Poet might have equalled himself with Legislators on this ground, it was Burns. His Songs are already part of the mother-tongue, not of Scotland only but of Britain, and of the millions that in all ends of the earth speak a British language. In hut and hall, as the heart un-folds itself in many-coloured joy and woe of existence, the *name*, the *voice* of that joy and that woe, is the name and voice which Burns has given them. Strictly speaking, perhaps no British man has so deeply affected the thoughts and feelings of so many men, as this solitary and altogether private individual, with means apparently the humblest.

In another point of view, moreover, we incline to think that Burns's influence may have been considerable: we mean, as exerted specially on the Literature of his country, at least on the Literature of Scotland. Among the great changes which British, particularly Scottish literature, has undergone since that period, one of the greatest will be found to consist in its remarkable increase of nationality. Even the English writers, most popular in Burns's time, were little distinguished for their literary patriotism, in this its best sense. A certain attenuated cosmopolitanism had, in good measure, taken the place of the old insular home-feeling; literature was, as it were, without any local environment; was not nourished by the affections which spring from a native soil. Our Grays and Glovers seemed to write almost as if *in vacuo*; the thing written bears no mark of place; it is not written so much for Englishmen, as for men, or rather, which is the inevitable result of this, for certain Generalisations which philosophy termed men. Goldsmith is an exception: not so Johnson; the scene of his *Rambler* is little more English than that of his *Rasselas*. But if such was, in some degree, the case with England, it was, in the highest degree, the case with Scotland. In fact, our Scottish literature had, at that period, a very singular aspect unexampled, so far as we know, except perhaps at Geneva, where the same state of matters appears still to continue. For a long period after Scotland became British, we had no literature: at the date when Addison and Steele were writing their *Spectators*, our good John Boston was writing, with the noblest intent, but alike in defiance of grammar and philosophy, his *Fourfold State of Man*. Then came the schisms in our National Church, and the fiercer schisms in our Body Politic: Theologic ink, and Jacobite blood, with gall enough in both cases, seemed to have blotted out the intellect of the country; however, it was only obscured, not obliterated. Lord Kames made nearly the first attempt at writing English; and ere long, Hume, Robertson, Smith, and a whole host of followers, attracted hither the eyes of all Europe. And yet in this brilliant resuscitation of our 'fervid genius,' there was nothing truly Scottish, nothing indigenous, except, perhaps, the natural impetuosity of intellect, which we sometimes claim, and are sometimes upbraided with, as a characteristic of our nation. It is curious to remark that Scotland, so full of writers, had no Scottish culture, nor indeed any English; our culture was almost exclusively French. It was by studying Racine and Voltaire, Batteux and Boileau, that Kames had trained himself to be critic and philosopher; it was the light of Montesquieu and Mably that guided Robertson in his political speculations; Quesnay's lamp that kindled the lamp of Adam Smith. Hume was too rich a man to borrow; and perhaps he reacted on the French more than he was acted on by them: but neither had he aught to do with Scotland; Edinburgh, equally with La Flèche, was but the lodging and laboratory, in which he not so much morally *lived*, as metaphysically *investigated*. Never, perhaps was there a class of writers, so clear and well-ordered, yet so totally destitute, to all appearance, of any patriotic affection, nay of any human affection whatever. The French wits of the period were as unpatriotic: but their general deficiency in moral principle, not to say their avowed sensuality and unbelief in all virtue, strictly so called, render this accountable enough. We hope, there is a patriotism founded on something better than prejudice; that our country may be dear to us, without injury to our philosophy; that in loving and justly prizing all other lands, we may prize justly, and yet love before all others, our own stern Motherland, and the venerable Structure of social and moral Life, which Mind has through long ages been building up for us there. Surely there is nourishment for the better part of man's heart in all this: surely the roots, that have fixed themselves in the very core of man's being, may be so cultivated as to grow up not into briers, but into roses, in the field of his life! Our Scottish sages have no such propensities: the field of their life shews neither briers nor roses; but only a flat, continuous thrashing-floor for Logic, whereon, all questions, from the 'Doctrine of Rent' to the 'Natural History of Religion,' are thrashed and sifted with the same mechanical impartiality!

With Sir Walter Scott at the head of our literature, it cannot be denied that much of this evil is past, or rapidly passing away: our chief literary men, whatever other faults they may have, no longer live among us like a French Colony, or some knot of Propaganda Missionaries; but like natural-born subjects of the soil, partaking and sympathising in all our attachments, humours and habits. Our literature no longer grows in water but in mould, and with the true racy virtues of the soil and climate. How much of this change may be due to Burns, or to any other individual, it might be difficult to estimate. Direct literary imitation of Burns was not to be looked for. But his example, in the fearless adoption of domestic subjects, could not but operate from afar; and certainly in no heart did the love of country ever burn with a warmer glow than in that of Burns: 'a tide of Scottish prejudice,' as he modestly calls this deep and generous feeling, 'had been poured along his veins; and he felt that it would boil there till the flood-gates shut in eternal rest.' It seemed to him, as if *he* could do so little for his country, and yet would so gladly have done all. One small province stood open for him,—that of Scottish Song; and how eagerly he entered on it, how devotedly he laboured there! In this toilsome journeyings, this object never quits him; it is the little happy-valley of his careworn heart. In the gloom of his own affliction he eagerly searches after some lonely brother of the muse, and rejoices to snatch one other name from the oblivion that was covering it! These were early feelings, and they abode with him to the end:

> ——A wish (I mind its power),
> A wish, that to my latest hour
> Will strongly heave my breast;
> That I, for poor auld Scotland's sake,
> Some useful plan or book could make,
> Or sing a sang at least.
> The rough bur Thistle spreading wide
>   Amang the bearded bear,
> I turn'd my weeding-clips aside,
>   And spared the symbol dear.

But to leave the mere literary character of Burns, which has already detained us too long. Far more interesting than any of his written works, as it appears to us, are his acted ones: the Life he willed, and was fated, to lead among his fellow men. These Poems are but little rhymed fragments scattered here and there in the grand unrhymed Romance of his earthly existence; and it is only when intercalated in this at their proper places, that they attain their full measure of significance. And this too, alas, was but a fragment. The plan of a mighty edifice had been sketched, some columns, porticos, firm masses of building stand completed; the rest more or less clearly indicated; with many a far-stretching tendency which only studious and friendly eyes can now trace towards the purposed termination. For the work is broken off in the middle, almost in the beginning; and rises among us, beautiful and sad at once unfinished and a ruin! If charitable judgment was necessary in estimating his Poems, and justice required that the aim and the manifest power to fulfil it must often be accepted for the fulfilment; much more is this the case in regard to his Life, the sum and result of all his endeavours where his difficulties came upon him not in detail only, but in mass; and so much has been left unaccomplished, nay was mistaken, and altogether marred.

Properly speaking, there is but one era in the life of Burns, and that the earliest. We have not youth and manhood, but only youth: for, to the end, we discern no decisive change in the complexion of his character; in his thirty-seventh year, he is still, as it were, in youth. With all that resoluteness of judgment, that penetrating insight, and singular maturity

373

of intellectual power, exhibited in his writings, he never attains to any clearness regarding himself; to the last, he never ascertains his peculiar aim, even with such distinctness as is common among ordinary men; and therefore never can pursue it with that singleness of will, which insures success and some contentment to such men. To the last, he wavers between two purposes: glorying in his talent, like a true poet, he yet cannot consent to make this his chief and sole glory, and to follow it as the one thing needful, through poverty or richness, through good or evil report. Another far meaner ambition still cleaves to him; he must dream and struggle about a certain 'Rock of Independence;' which, natural and even admirable as it might be, was still but a warring with the world, on the comparatively insignificant ground of his being more completely or less completely supplied with money, than others; of his standing at a higher or at a lower altitude in general estimation than others. For the world still appears to him, as to the young, in borrowed colours: he expects from it what it cannot give to any man; seeks for contentment, not within himself, in action and wise effort, but from without, in the kindness of circumstances, in love, friendship, honour, pecuniary ease. He would be happy, not actively and in himself, but passively and from some ideal cornucopia of Enjoyments, not earned by his own labour, but showered on him by the beneficence of Destiny. Thus, like a young man, he cannot gird himself up for any worthy well-calculated goal, but swerves to and fro, between passionate hope and remorseful disappointment: rushing onwards with a deep tempestuous force, he surmounts or breaks asunder many a barrier; travels, nay advances far, but advancing only under uncertain guidance, is ever and anon turned from his path; and to the last, cannot reach the only true happiness of a man, that of clear decided Activity in the sphere for which, by nature and circumstances, he has been fitted and appointed.

We do not say these things in dispraise of Burns; nay, perhaps, they but interest us the more in his favour. This blessing is not given soonest to the best; but rather, it is often the greatest minds that are latest in obtaining it; for where most is to be developed, most time may be required to develop it. A complex condition has been assigned to him from without; as complex a condition from within: no 'pre-established harmony' existed between the clay soil of Mossgiel and the empyrean soul of Robert Burns; it was not wonderful that the adjustment between them should have been long postponed, and his arm long cumbered, and his sight confused, in so vast and discordant an economy as he had been appointed steward over. Byron was, at his death, but a year younger than Burns; and through life, as it might have appeared, far more simply situated: yet in him too, we can trace no such adjustment, no such moral manhood; but at best, and only a little before his end, the beginning of what seemed such.

By much the most striking incident in Burns's Life is his journey to Edinburgh; but perhaps a still more important one is his residence at Irvine, so early as in his twenty-third year. Hitherto his life had been poor and toilworn; but otherwise not ungenial, and, with all its distresses, by no means unhappy. In his parentage, deducting outward circumstances, he had every reason to reckon himself fortunate, His father was a man of thoughtful, intense, earnest character, as the best of our peasants are; valuing knowledge, possessing some, and, what is far better and rarer, open-minded for more: a man with a keen insight and devout heart; reverent towards God, friendly therefore at once, and fearless towards all that God has made; in one word, though but a hard-handed peasant, a complete and fully unfolded *Man*. Such a father is seldom found in any rank in society; and was worth descending far in society to seek. Unfortunately, he was very poor; had he been even a little richer, almost never so little, the whole might have issued far otherwise. Mighty events turn on a straw; the crossing of a brook decides the conquest of the world. Had this William Burns's small seven acres of nursery-ground anywise prospered, the boy Robert had been sent to school; had struggled forward, as so many weaker men do, to some university; come forth not as a rustic wonder, but as a regular well-trained intellectual workman, and changed the whole course of British Literature,—for it lay in him to have done this! But the nursery did not prosper; poverty sank his whole family below the help of even our cheap school-system: Burns remained a hard-worked ploughboy, and British literature took its own course. Nevertheless, even in this rugged scene there is much to nourish him. If he drudges, it is with his brother, and for his father and mother, whom he loves, and would fain shield from want. Wisdom is not banished from their poor hearth, nor the balm of natural feeling: the solemn words, *Let us worship God*, are heard there from a 'priest-like father;' if threatenings of unjust men throw mother and children into tears, these are tears not of grief only, but of holiest affection; every heart in that humble group feels itself the closer knit to every other; in their hard warfare they are there together, a 'little band of brethren.' Neither are such tears, and the deep beauty that dwells in them, their only portion. Light visits the hearts as it does the eyes of all living: there is a force, too, in this youth, that enables him to trample on misfortune; nay, to bind it under his feet to make him sport. For a bold, warm, buoyant humour of character has been given him; and so the thick-coming shapes of evil are welcomed with a gay, friendly irony, and in their closest pressure he bates no jot of heart or hope. Vague yearnings of ambition fail not, as he grows up; dreamy fancies hang like cloud-cities around him; the curtain of Existence is slowly rising, in many-coloured splendour and gloom: and the auroral light of first love is gilding his horizon, and the music of song is on his path; and so he walks

> ——in glory and in joy,
> Behind his plough, upon the mountain side![1]

We ourselves know, from the best evidence, that up to this date Burns was happy; nay, that he was the gayest, brightest, most fantastic, fascinating being to be found in the world; more so even than he ever afterwards appeared. But now, at this early age, he quits the paternal roof; goes forth into looser, louder, more exciting society; and becomes initiated in those dissipations, those vices which a certain class of philosophers have asserted to be a natural preparative for entering on active life; a kind of mud-bath, in which the youth is, as it were, necessitated to steep, and, we suppose, cleanse himself, before the real toga of Manhood can be laid on him. We shall not dispute much with this class of philosophers; we hope they are mistaken: for Sin and Remorse so easily beset us at all stages of life, and are always such indifferent company, that it seems hard we should, at any stage, be forced and fated not only to meet, but to yield to them, and even serve for a term in their leprous armada. We hope it is not so. Clear we are, at all events, it cannot be the training one receives in this Devil's-service, but only our determining to desert from it, that fits us for true manly Action. We become men, not after we have been dissipated, and disappointed in the chase of false pleasure; but after we have ascertained, in any way, what impassable barriers hem us in through this life, how mad it is to hope for contentment to our infinite soul from the *gifts* of this extremely finite world; that a man must be sufficient for himself; and that for suffering and enduring there is no remedy but striving and doing. Manhood begins when we have in any way made truce with Necessity; begins even when we have surrendered to Necessity, as the most part only

[1] Wordsworth, 'Resolution And Independence', No. 33a.

do; but begins joyfully and hopefully only when we have reconciled ourselves to Necessity; and thus, in reality, triumphed over it, and felt that in Necessity we are free. Surely, such lessons as this last, which, in one shape or other, is the grand lesson for every mortal man, are better learned from the lips of a devout mother, in the looks and actions of a devout father, while the heart is yet soft and pliant, than in collision with the sharp adamant of Fate, attracting us to shipwreck us, when the heart is grown hard, and may be broken before it will become contrite! Had Burns continued to learn this, as he was already learning it, in his father's cottage, he would have learned it fully, which he never did; and been saved many a lasting aberration, many a bitter hour and year of remorseful sorrow.

It seems to us another circumstance of fatal import in Burns's history, that at this time too he became involved in the religious quarrels of his district; that he was enlisted and feasted, as the fighting man of the New-Light Priesthood, in their highly unprofitable warfare. At the tables of these free-minded clergy, he learned much more than was needful for him. Such liberal ridicule of fanaticism awakened in his mind scruples about Religion itself; and a whole world of Doubts, which it required quite another set of conjurors than these men to exorcise. We do not say that such an intellect as his could have escaped similar doubts, at some period of his history; or even that he could, at a later period, have come through them altogether victorious and unharmed: but it seems peculiarly unfortunate that this time, above all others, should have been fixed for the encounter. For now, with principles assailed by evil example from without, by 'passions raging like demons' from within, he had little need of sceptical misgivings to whisper treason in the heat of the battle, or to cut off his retreat if he were already defeated. He loses his feeling of innocence; his mind is at variance with itself; the old divinity no longer presides there; but wild Desires and wild Repentance alternately oppress him. Ere long, too, he has committed himself before the world; his character for sobriety, dear to a Scottish peasant as few corrupted worldlings can even conceive, is destroyed in the eyes of men; and his only refuge consists in trying to disbelieve his guiltiness, and is but a refuge of lies. The blackest desperation now gathers over him, broken only by red lightnings of remorse. The whole fabric of his life is blasted asunder; for now not only his character, but his personal liberty, is to be lost; men and Fortune are leagued for his hurt; 'hungry Ruin has him in the wind.' He sees no escape but the saddest of all: exile from his loved country, to a country in every sense inhospitable and abhorrent to him. While the 'gloomy night is gathering fast,' in mental storm and solitude, as well as in physical, he sings his wild farewell to Scotland:

> Farewell my friends, farewell my foes!
> My peace with these, my love with those:
> The bursting tears my heart declare;
> Adieu, my native banks of Ayr!

Light breaks suddenly in on him in floods; but still a false transitory light, and no real sunshine. He is invited to Edinburgh; hastens thither with anticipating heart; is welcomed as in a triumph, and with universal blandishment and acclamation; whatever is wisest, whatever is greatest or loveliest there, gathers round him, to gaze on his face, to shew him honour, sympathy, affection. Burns's appearance among the sages and nobles of Edinburgh must be regarded as one of the most singular phenomena in modern Literature; almost like the appearance of some Napoleon among the crowned sovereigns of modern Politics. For it is nowise as 'a mockery king', set there by favour, transiently and for a purpose, that he will let himself be treated; still less is he a mad Rienzi, whose sudden elevation turns his too weak head: but he stands there on his own basis; cool, unastonished, holding his equal rank from Nature herself; putting forth no claim which there is not strength *in* him, as well as about him, to vindicate. Mr. Lockhart has some forcible observations on this point:

It needs no effort of imagination, (says he), to conceive what the sensations of an isolated set of scholars (almost all either clergymen or professors) must have been, in the presence of this big-boned, black-browed, brawny stranger, with his great flashing eyes, who, having forced his way among them from the plough-tail at a single stride, manifested in the whole strain of his bearing and conversation a most thorough conviction, that in the society of the most eminent men of his nation, he was exactly where he was entitled to be; hardly deigned to flatter them by exhibiting even an occasional symptom of being flattered by their notice; by turns calmly measured himself against the most cultivated understandings of his time in discussion; overpowered the *bon-mots* of the most celebrated convivialists by broad floods of merriment, impregnated with all the burning life of genius; astounded bosoms habitually enveloped in the thrice-piled folds of social reserve, by compelling them to tremble,—nay, to tremble visibly,—beneath the fearless touch of natural pathos; and all this without indicating the smallest willingness to be ranked among those professional ministers of excitement, who are content to be paid in money and smiles for doing what the spectators and auditors would be ashamed of doing in their own persons, even if they had the power of doing it; and last, and probably worst of all, who was known to be in the habit of enlivening societies which they would have scorned to approach, still more frequently than their own, with eloquence no less magnificent; with wit, in all likelihood still more daring; often enough, as the superiors whom he fronted without alarm might have guessed from the beginning, and had ere long no occasion to guess, with wit pointed at themselves.

The further we remove from this scene, the more singular will it seem to us: details of the exterior aspect of it are already full of interest. Most readers recollect Mr. Walker's personal interviews with Burns as among the best passages of his Narrative: a time will come when this reminiscence of Sir Walter Scott's, slight though it is, will also be precious. . . .

The conduct of Burns under this dazzling blaze of favour; the calm, unaffected, manly manner in which he not only bore it, but estimated its value, has justly been regarded as the best proof that could be given of his real vigour and integrity of mind. A little natural vanity, some touches of hypocritical modesty, some glimmerings of affectation, at least some fear of being thought affected, we could have pardoned in almost any man; but no such indication is to be traced here. In his unexampled situation the young peasant is not a moment perplexed; so many strange lights do not confuse him, do not lead him astray. Nevertheless, we cannot but perceive that this winter did him great and lasting injury. A somewhat clearer knowledge of men's affairs, scarcely of their characters, it did afford him; but a sharper feeling of Fortune's unequal arrangements in their social destiny it also left with him. He had seen the gay and gorgeous arena, in which the powerful are born to play their parts; nay had himself stood in the midst of it; and he felt more bitterly than ever, that here he was but a looker-on, and had no part or lot in that splendid game. From this time a jealous indignant fear of social degradation takes possession of him; and perverts, so far as aught could pervert, his private contentment, and his feelings towards his richer fellows. It was clear to Burns that he had talent enough to make a fortune, or a hundred fortunes, could he but have rightly willed this; it was clear also that he willed something far different, and therefore could not make one. Unhappy it was that he had not power to choose the one, and reject the other; but must halt forever between two opinions, two objects; making hampered advancement towards either. But so is it with many men: we 'long for the merchandise, yet

379

would fain keep the price;' and so stand chaffering with Fate, in vexatious altercation, till the night come, and our fair is over!

The Edinburgh Learned of that period were in general more noted for clearness of head than for warmth of heart: with the exception of the good old Blacklock, whose help was too ineffectual, scarcely one among them seems to have looked at Burns with any true sympathy, or indeed much otherwise than as at a highly curious *thing*. By the great also he is treated in the customary fashion; entertained at their tables and dismissed: certain modica of pudding and praise are, from time to time, gladly exchanged for the fascination of his presence; which exchange once effected, the bargain is finished, and each party goes his several way. At the end of this strange season, Burns gloomily sums up his gains and losses, and meditates on the chaotic future. In money he is somewhat richer; in fame and the show of happiness, infinitely richer; but in the substance of it, as poor as ever. Nay poorer; for his heart is now maddened still more with the fever of worldly Ambition; and through long years the disease will rack him with unprofitable sufferings, and weaken his strength for all true and nobler aims.

What Burns was next to do or to avoid; how a man so circumstanced was now to guide himself towards his true advantage, might at this point of time have been a question for the wisest. It was a question too, which apparently he was left altogether to answer for himself: of his learned or rich patrons it had not struck any individual to turn a thought on this so trivial matter. Without claiming for Burns the praise of perfect sagacity, we must say, that his Excise and Farm scheme does not seem to us a very unreasonable one; that we should be at a loss, even now, to suggest one decidedly better. Certain of his admirers have felt scandalised at his ever resolving to *gauge*; and would have had him lie at the pool, till the spirit of Patronage stirred the waters, that so, with one friendly plunge, all his sorrows might be healed. Unwise counsellors! They know not the manner of this spirit; and how, in the lap of most golden dreams, a man might have happiness, were it not that in the interim he must die of hunger! It reflects credit on the manliness and sound sense of Burns that he felt so early on what ground he was standing; and preferred self-help, on the humblest scale, to dependence and inaction, though with hope of far more splendid possibilities. But even these possibilities were not rejected in his scheme: he might expect, if it chanced that he *had* any friend, to rise, in no longer period, into something even like opulence and leisure; while again, if it chanced that he had no friend he could still live in security; and for the rest, he 'did not intend to borrow honour from any profession.' We reckon that his plan was honest and well-calculated: all turned on the execution of it. Doubtless it failed; yet not, we believe, from any vice inherent in itself. Nay, after all, it was no failure of external means, but of internal, that overtook Burns. His was no bankruptcy of the purse, but of the soul; to his last day, he owed no man anything.

Meanwhile he begins well: with two good and wise actions. His donation to his mother, munificent from a man whose income had lately been seven pounds a-year, was worthy of him, and not more than worthy. Generous also, and worthy of him, was the treatment of the woman whose life's welfare now depended on his pleasure. A friendly observer might have hoped serene days for him: his mind is on the true road to peace with itself: what clearness he still wants will be given as he proceeds; for the best teacher of duties, that still lie dim to us, is the Practice of those we see, and have at hand. Had the 'patrons of genius,' who could give him nothing, but taken nothing from him, at least nothing more! The wounds of his heart would have healed, vulgar ambition would have died away. Toil and Frugality would have been welcome, since Virtue dwelt with them; and Poetry would have shone through them as of old: and in her clear ethereal light, which was his own by birthright, he might have looked down on his earthly destiny, and all its obstructions, not with patience only, but with love.

But the patrons of genius would not have it so. Picturesque tourists,* all manner of fashionable danglers after literature and, far worse, all manner of convivial Maecenases, hovered round him in his retreat; and his good as well as his weak qualities secured them influence over him. He was flattered by their notice; and his warm social nature made it impossible for him to shake them off, and hold on his way apart from them. These men, as we believe, were proximately the means of his ruin. Not that they meant him any ill, they only meant themselves a

---

* There is one little sketch by certain 'English gentlemen' of this class, which, though adopted in Currie's Narrative, and since then repeated in most others, we have all along felt an invincible disposition to regard as imaginary: 'On a rock that projected into the stream, they saw a man employed in angling, of a singular appearance. He had a cap made of fox-skin on his head, a loose greatcoat fixed round him by a belt, from which depended an enormous Highland broad-sword. It was Burns.'

Now, we rather think, it was *not* Burns. For, to say nothing of the fox-skin cap, the loose and quite Hibernian watchcoat with the belt, what are we to make of this 'enormous Highland broad-sword' depending from him? More especially, as there is no word of parish constables on the outlook to see whether, as Dennis phrases it, he had an eye to his own midriff or that of the public! Burns, of all men, had the least need, and the least tendency, to seek for distinction, either in his own eyes, or those of others, by such poor mummeries.

little good; if he suffered harm, let *him* look to it! But they wasted his precious time and his precious talent; they disturbed his composure, broke down his returning habits of temperance and assiduous contented exertion. Their pampering was baneful to him; their cruelty, which soon followed, was equally baneful. The old grudge against Fortune's in-equality awoke with new bitterness in their neighbourhood; and Burns had no retreat but to the 'Rock of Independence,' which is but an air-castle, after all, that looks well at a distance, but will screen no one from real wind and wet. Flushed with irregular excitement, exasperated alternately by contempt of others, and contempt of himself, Burns was no longer regaining his peace of mind, but fast losing it forever. There was a hollowness at the heart of his life, for his conscience did not now approve what he was doing.

Amid the vapours of unwise enjoyment, of bootless remorse, and angry discontent with Fate, his true loadstar, a life of Poetry, with Poverty, nay with Famine if it must be so, was too often altogether hidden from his eyes. And yet he sailed a sea, where without some such loadstar there was no right steering. Meteors of French Politics rise before him, but these were not *his* stars. An accident this, which hastened, but did not originate, his worst distresses. In the mad contentions of that time, he comes in collision with certain official Superiors; is wounded by them; cruelly lacerated, we should say, could a dead mechanical implement, in any case, be called cruel: and shrinks, in indignant pain, into deeper self-seclusion, into gloomier moodiness than ever. His life has now lost its unity: it is a life of fragments; led with little aim, beyond the melancholy one of securing its own continuance,—in fits of wild false joy when such offered, and of black despondency when they passed away. His character before the world begins to suffer: calumny is busy with him; for a miserable man makes more enemies than friends. Some faults he has fallen into, and a thousand misfortunes; but deep criminality is what he stands accused of, and they that are *not* without sin cast the first stone at him! For is he not a well-wisher of the French Revolution, a Jacobin, and therefore in that one act guilty of all? These accusations, political and moral, it has since appeared, were false enough: but the world hesitated little to credit them. Nay, his convivial Maecenases themselves were not the last to do it. There is reason to believe that, in his later years, the Dumfries Aristocracy had partly withdrawn themselves from Burns, as from a tainted person, no longer worthy of their acquaintance. That painful class, stationed, in all provincial cities, behind the outmost breastwork of Gentility, there to stand siege and do battle against the intrusions of Grocerdom and Grazierdom, had actually seen dishonour in the society of Burns, and branded him with their veto; had, as we vulgarly say, *cut* him! We find one passage in this Work of Mr. Lockhart's, which will not out of our thoughts:

A gentleman of that county, whose name I have already more than once had occasion to refer to, has often told me that he was seldom more grieved, than when riding into Dumfries one fine summer evening about this time to attend a county ball, he saw Burns walking alone, on the shady side of the principal street of the town, while the opposite side was gay with successive groups of gentlemen and ladies, all drawn together for the festivities of the night, not one of whom appeared willing to recognise him. The horseman dismounted, and joined Burns, who on his proposing to cross the street said: 'Nay, nay young friend, that's all over now'; and quoted, after a pause, some verses of Lady Grizzel Baillie's pathetic ballad:

> His bonnet stood ance fu' fair on his brow,
> His auld ane look'd better than mony ane's new;
> But now he lets's wear ony way it will hing.
> And casts himsell dowie upon the corn-bing.
>
> O were we young, as we ance hae been,
> We sud hae been galloping down on yon green,
> And linking it ower the lily-white lea!
> *And werena my heart light I wad die.*

It was little in Burns's character to let his feelings on certain subjects escape in this fashion. He, immediately after reciting these verses, assumed the sprightliness of his most pleasing manner; and taking his young friend home with him, entertained him very agreeably till the hour of the ball arrived.

Alas! when we think that Burns now sleeps 'where bitter indignation can no longer lacerate his heart,'[*] and that most of those fair dames and frizzled gentlemen already lie at his side,—where the breastwork of gentility is quite thrown down,—who would not sigh over the thin delusions and foolish toys that divide heart from heart, and make man unmerciful to his brother!

It was not now to be hoped that the genius of Burns would ever reach maturity, or accomplish aught worthy of itself. His spirit was jarred in its melody; not the soft breath of natural feeling, but the rude hand of Fate, was now sweeping over the strings. And yet what harmony was

---

[*] *Ubi saeva indignatio cor ulteriùs lacerare nequit.*—Swift's Epitaph.

in him, what music even in his discords! How the wild tones had a charm for the simplest and the wisest; and all men felt and knew that here also was one of the Gifted! 'If he entered an inn at midnight, after all the inmates were in bed, the news of his arrival circulated from the cellar to the garret; and ere ten minutes had elapsed, the landlord and all his guests were assembled!' Some brief pure moments of poetic life were yet appointed him, in the composition of his Songs. We can understand how he grasped at this employment; and how too, he spurned all other regard for it but what the labour itself brought him. For the soul of Burns, though scathed and marred, was yet living in its full moral strength, though sharply conscious of its errors and abasement: and here, in his destitution and degradation, was one act of seeming nobleness and self-devotedness left even for him to perform. He felt too, that with all the 'thoughtless follies' that had 'laid him low,' the world was unjust and cruel to him, and he silently appealed to another and calmer time. Not as a hired soldier, but as a patriot would he strive for the glory of his country: so he cast from him the poor sixpence a-day, and served zealously as a volunteer. Let us not grudge him this last luxury of his existence; let him not have appealed to us in vain! The money was not necessary to him; he struggled through without it: long since, these guineas would have been gone, and now the high-mindnessness of refusing them will plead for him in all hearts forever.

We are here arrived at the crisis of Burns's life; for matters had now taken such a shape with him as could not long continue. If improvement was not to be looked for, Nature could only for a limited time maintain this dark and maddening warfare against the world and itself. We are not medically informed whether any continuance of years was, at this period, probable for Burns; whether his death is to be looked on as in some sense an accidental event, or only as the natural consequence of the long series of events that had proceeded. The latter seems to be the likelier opinion; and yet it is by no means a certain one. At all events, as we have said, *some* change could not be very distant. Three gates of deliverance, it seems to us, were open for Burns: clear poetical activity; madness; or death. The first, with longer life, was still possible, though not probable; for physical causes were beginning to be concerned in it: and yet Burns had an iron resolution; could he but have seen and felt, that not only his highest glory, but his first duty, and the true medicine for all his woes, lay here. The second was still less probable; for his mind was ever among the clearest and firmest. So the milder third gate was opened for him: and he passed, not softly, yet speedily, into that still country, where the hail-storms and fire showers do not reach, and the heaviest-laden wayfarer at length lays down his load!

Contemplating this sad end of Burns, and how he sank unaided by any real help, uncheered by any wise sympathy, generous minds have sometimes figured to themselves, with a reproachful sorrow, that much might have been done for him; that by counsel, true affection and friendly ministrations, he might have been saved to himself and the world. We question whether there is not more tenderness of heart than soundness of judgement in these suggestions. It seems dubious to us whether the richest, wisest, most benevolent individual could have lent Burns any effectual help. Counsel, which seldom profits any one, he did not need; in his understanding, he knew the right from wrong, as well perhaps as any man ever did; but the persuasion, which would have availed him, lies not so much in the head as in the heart, where no argument or expostulation could have assisted much to implant it. As to money again, we do not believe that this was his essential want; or well see how any private man could, even presupposing Burns's consent, have bestowed on him an independent fortune, with much prospect of decisive advantage. It is a mortifying truth, that two men in any rank of society could hardly be found virtuous enough to give money, and to take it as a necessary gift, without injury to the moral entireness of one or both. But so stands the fact; Friendship, in the old heroic sense of that term, no longer exists; except in the cases of kindred or other legal affinity, it is in reality no longer expected, or recognised as a virtue among men. A close observer of manners has pronounced 'Patronage,' that is, pecuniary or other economic furtherance, to be 'twice cursed;' cursing him that gives, and him that takes! And this, in regard to outward matters also, it has become the rule, as in regard to inward it always was and must be the rule, that no one shall look for effectual help to another; but that each shall rest contented with what help he can afford himself. Such, we say, is the principle of modern Honour; naturally enough growing out of that sentiment of Pride, which we inculcate and encourage as the basis of our whole social morality. Many a poet has been poorer than Burns; but no one was ever prouder: we may question whether, without great precautions, even a pension from Royalty would not have galled and encumbered, more than actually assisted him.

Still less, therefore, are we disposed to join with another class of Burns's admirers, who accuse the higher ranks among us of having ruined Burns by their selfish neglect of him. We have already stated our doubts whether direct pecuniary help, had it been offered, would have been accepted, or could have proved very effectual. We shall readily admit, however, that much was to be done for Burns; that many a poisoned arrow might have been warded from his bosom; many an entanglement in his path cut asunder by the hand of the powerful; and light and heat, shed on him from high places, would have made his humble atmosphere more genial; and the softest heart then breathing might have lived and died with some fewer pangs. Nay, we shall grant further, and for Burns it is granting much, that, with all his pride, he would have thanked, even with exaggerated gratitude, any one who had cordially befriended him: patronage unless once cursed, needed not to have been twice so. At all events, the poor promotion he desired in his calling might have been granted: it was his own scheme, therefore likelier than any other to be of service. All this it might have been a luxury, nay it was a duty, for our nobility to have done. No part of all this, however, did any of them do; or apparently attempt, or wish to do: so much is granted against them. But what then is the amount of their blame? Simply that they were men of the world, and walked by the principles of such men; that they treated Burns, as other nobles and other commoners had done other poets; as the English did Shakspeare; as King Charles and his Cavaliers did Butler, as King Philip and his Grandees did Cervantes. Do men gather grapes of thorns; or shall we cut down our thorns for yielding only a *fence* and haws? How, indeed, could the 'nobility and gentry of his native land' hold out any help to this 'Scottish Bard, proud of his name and country'? Were the nobility and gentry so much as able rightly to help themselves? Had they not their game to preserve; their borough interests to strengthen; dinners, therefore, of various kinds to eat and give? Were their means more than adequate to all this business, or less than adequate? Less than adequate in general; few of them in reality were richer than Burns; many of them were poorer; for sometimes they had to wring their supplies, as with thumbscrews, from the hard land; and, in their need of guineas, to forget their duty of mercy; which Burns was never reduced to do. Let us pity and forgive them. The game they preserved and shot, the the dinners they ate and gave, the borough interests they strengthened, the *little* Babylons they severally builded by the glory of their might, are all melted or melting back into the primeval Chaos, as man's merely selfish endeavours are fated to do: and here was an action, extending, in virtue of its worldly influence, we may say, through all time; in virtue of its moral nature, beyond all time; in virtue of its moral nature, beyond all time, being immortal as the Spirit of Goodness itself; this action was offered them to do, and light was not given them to do it. Let us pity and forgive them. But better than pity, let us go and *do otherwise*. Human suffering did not end with the life of Burns; neither was the solemn mandate, 'Love one another, bear one another's burdens,' given to the rich only, but to all men. True, we shall find no Burns to relieve, to assuage by our aid or our pity; but celestial natures, groaning under the fardels of a weary life, we shall still find; and that wretched-ness which Fate has rendered *voiceless* and *tuneless* is not the least wretched, but the most.

Still, we do not think that the blame of Burns's failure lies chiefly with the world. The world, it seems to us, treated him with more, rather than with less kindness than it usually shews to such men. It has ever, we fear, shewn but small favour to its Teachers: hunger and nakedness, perils and reviling, the prison, the cross, the poison-chalice have, in most times and countries been the market-price it has offered for Wisdom, the welcome with which it has greeted those who have come to enlighten and purify it. Homer and Socrates, and the Christian Apostles, belong to old days; but the world's Martyrology was not completed with these. Roger Bacon and Galileo languish in priestly dungeons; Tasso pines in the cell of a madhouse; Camoens dies begging on the streets of Lisbon. So neglected, so 'persecuted they the Prophets,' not in Judea only, but in all places where men have been. We reckon that every poet of Burns's order is, or should be, a prophet and teacher to his age; that he has no right to expect great kindness from it, but rather is bound to do it great kindness; that Burns, in particular, experienced fully the usual proportion of the world's goodness; and that the blame of his failure, as we have said, lies not chiefly with the world.

Where then does it lie? We are forced to answer: With himself; it is his inward, not his outward misfortunes that bring him to the dust. Seldom, indeed, is it otherwise; seldom is a life morally wrecked but the grand cause lies in some internal mal-arrangement, some want less of good fortune than of good guidance. Nature fashions no creature without implanting in it the strength needful for its action and duration; least of all does she so neglect her masterpiece and darling, the poetic soul. Neither can we believe that it is in the power of *any* external circumstances utterly to ruin the mind of a man; nay, if proper wisdom be given him; even so much as to affect its essential health and beauty. The sternest sum-total of all worldly misfortunes is Death; nothing more *can* lie in the cup of a human woe; yet many men, in all ages, have triumphed over Death, and led it captive; converting its physical victory into a moral victory for themselves, into a seal and immortal consecration for all that their past life had achieved. What has been done, may be done again; nay, it is but the degree and not the kind of such heroism that differs in different seasons; for without some portion of this spirit, not of boisterous daring, but of silent fearlessness, of Self-denial in all its forms, no good man, in any scene or time, has ever attained to be good.

We have already stated the error of Burns; and mourned over it, rather than blamed it. It was the want of unity in his purposes, of consistency in his aims; the hapless attempt to mingle in friendly union the common spirit of the world with the spirit of poetry, which is of a far different and altogether irreconcilable nature. Burns was nothing wholly; and Burns could be nothing, no man formed as he was can be anything, by halves. The heart, not of a mere hot-blooded, popular Verse-monger, or poetical *Restaurateur*, but of a true Poet and Singer, worthy of the old religious heroic times, had been given him; and he fell in an age, not of heroism and religion, but of scepticism, selfishness and triviality, when true Nobleness was little understood, and its place supplied by a hollow, dissocial, altogether barren and unfruitful principle of Pride. The influences of that age, his open, kind, susceptible nature, to say nothing of his highly untoward situation, made it more than usually difficult for him to cast aside, or rightly subordinate; the better spirit that was within him ever sternly demanded its rights, its supremacy: he spent his life in endeavouring to reconcile these two; and lost it, as he must lose it, without reconciling them.

Burns was born poor; and born also to continue poor, for he would not endeavour to be otherwise: this it had been well could he have once for all admitted, and considered as finally settled. He was poor, truly; but hundreds even of his own class and order of minds have been poorer, yet have suffered nothing deadly from it, nay, his own Father had a far sorer battle with ungrateful destiny than his was; and he did not yield to it, but died courageously warring, and to all moral intents prevailing, against it. True, Burns had little means, had even little time for poetry, his only real pursuit and vocation; but so much the more precious was what little he had. In all these external respects his case was hard; but very far from the hardest. Poverty, incessant drudgery and much worse evils, it has often been the lot of Poets and wise men to strive with, and their glory to conquer. Locke was banished as a traitor; and wrote his *Essay on the Human Understanding* sheltering himself in a Dutch garret. Was Milton rich or at his ease when he composed *Paradise Lost*? Not only low, but fallen from a height; not only poor, but impoverished; in darkness and with dangers compassed round, he sang his immortal song, and found fit audience, though few. Did not Cervantes finish his work, a maimed soldier and in prison? Nay, was not the *Araucana*, which Spain acknowledges as its Epic, written without even the aid of paper; on scraps of leather, as the stout fighter and voyager snatched any moment from that wild warfare?

And what then had these men, which Burns wanted? Two things; both which, it seems to us, are indispensable for such men. They had a true, religious principle of morals; and a single not a double aim in their activity. They were not self-seekers and self-worshippers; but seekers and worshippers of something far better than Self. Not personal enjoyment was their object; but a high, heroic idea of Religion, of Patriotism, of heavenly Wisdom in one or the other form, ever hovered before them; in which cause, they neither shrank from suffering, nor called on the earth to witness it as something wonderful; but patiently endured, counting it blessedness enough so to spend and be spent. Thus the 'golden-calf of Self-love,' however curiously carved, was not their Deity; but the Invisible Goodness, which alone is man's reasonable service. This feeling was as a celestial fountain, whose streams refreshed into gladness and beauty all the provinces of their otherwise too desolate existence. In a word, they willed one thing, to which all other things were subordinated and made subservient; and therefore they accomplished it. The wedge will rend rocks; but its edge must be sharp and single: if it be double the wedge is bruised in pieces and will rend nothing.

Part of this superiority these men owed to their age; in which heroism and devotedness were still practised, or at least not yet disbelieved in: but much of it likewise they owed to themselves. With Burns again it was different. His morality, in most of its practical points, is that of a mere worldly man; enjoyment, in a finer or coarser shape, is the only thing he longs and strives for. A noble instinct sometimes raises him above this; but an instinct only, and acting only for moments. He has no Religion; in the shallow age, where his days were cast, Religion has not discriminated from the New and Old Light *forms* of Religion; and was, with these, becoming obsolete in the minds of men. His heart, indeed, is alive with a trembling adoration, but there is no temple in his understanding. He lives in darkness and in the shadow of doubt. His religion, at best, is an anxious wish; like that of Rabelais, 'a great Perhaps.'

He loved Poetry warmly, and in his heart; could he but have loved it purely, and with his whole undivided heart, it had been well. For Poetry, as Burns could have followed it, is but another form of Wisdom, of Religion; is itself Wisdom and Religion. But this also was denied him. His poetry is a stray vagrant gleam, which will not be extinguished within him, yet rises not to be the true light of his path, but is often a wildfire that misleads him. It was not necessary for Burns to be rich, to be, or to seem, 'independent;' but it *was* necessary for him to be at one with his own heart; to place what was highest in his nature highest also in his life; 'to seek within himself for that consistency and sequence, which external events would forever refuse him.' He was born a poet; poetry was the celestial element of his being, and should have been the soul of his whole endeavours. Lifted into that serene aether, whither he had wings given him to mount, he would have needed no other elevation; poverty, neglect and all evil, save the desecration of himself and his Art, were a small matter to him; the pride and the passions of the world lay far beneath his feet; and he looked down alike on noble and slave, on prince and beggar, and all that wore the stamp of man, with clear recognition, with brotherly affection, with sympathy, with pity. Nay, we question whether for his culture as a Poet, poverty and much suffering for a season were not absolutely advantageous. Great men, in looking back over their lives, have testified to that effect. 'I would not for much,' says Jean Paul, 'that I had been born richer'. And yet Paul's birth was poor enough; for, in another place, he adds: 'The prisoner's allowance is bread and water; and I had often the latter.' But the gold that is refined in the hottest furnace comes out the purest; or, as he has himself expressed it, 'the canary-bird sings sweeter the longer it has been trained in a darkened cage.'

A man like Burns might have divided his hours between poetry and virtuous industry; industry which all true feeling sanctions, nay prescribes, and which has a beauty; for that cause, beyond the pomp of thrones: but to divide his hours between poetry and rich men's banquets was an ill-starred and inauspicious attempt. How could he be at ease at such banquets? What had he to do there, mingling his music with the coarse roar of altogether earthly voices; brightening the thick smoke of intoxication with fire lent him from heaven? Was it his aim to *enjoy* life? Tomorrow he must go drudge as an Exciseman! We wonder not that Burns became moody, indignant, and at times an

offender against certain rules of society; but rather that he did not grow
utterly frantic, and run *amuck* against them all. How could a man, so
falsely placed, by his own or others' fault, ever know contentment or
peaceable diligence for an hour? What he did, under such perverse
guidance, and what he forbore to do, alike fill us with astonishment at
the natural strength and worth of his character.

Doubtless there was a remedy for this perverseness: but not in others;
only in himself; least of all in simple increase of wealth and worldly
'respectability'. We hope we have now heard enough about the efficacy
of wealth for poetry, and to make poets happy. Nay, have we not seen
another instance of it in these very days? Byron, a man of an endowment
considerably less ethereal than that of Burns, is born in the rank not of
a Scottish ploughman, but of an English peer: the highest worldly
honours, the fairest worldly career, are his by inheritance; the richest
harvest of fame he soon reaps, in another province, by his own hand.
And what does all this avail him? Is he happy, is he good, is he true?
Alas, he has a poet's soul, and strives towards the Infinite and the
Eternal; and soon feels that all this is but mounting to the house-top
to reach the stars! Like Burns, he is only a proud man; might, like
him, have 'purchased a pocket-copy of Milton to study the character
of Satan;' for Satan also is Byron's grand exemplar, the hero of his
poetry, and the model apparently of his conduct. As in Burns's case
too, the celestial element will not mingle with the clay of earth; both
poet and man of the world he must not be; vulgar Ambition will not
live kindly with poetic Adoration; he *cannot* serve God and Mammon.
Byron, like Burns, is not happy; nay, he is the most wretched of all
men. His life is falsely arranged: the fire that is in him is not a strong,
still, central fire, warming into beauty the products of a world; but
it is the mad fire of a volcano; and now,—we look sadly into the
ashes of a crater, which ere long will fill itself with snow!

Byron and Burns were sent forth as missionaries to their generation,
to teach it a higher Doctrine, a purer Truth; they had a message to
deliver, which left them no rest till it was accomplished; in dim throes
of pain, this divine behest lay smouldering within them; for they knew
not what it meant, and felt it only in mysterious anticipation, and they
had to die without articulately uttering it. They are in the camp of the
Unconverted; yet not as high messengers of rigorous though benignant
truth, but as soft flattering singers, and in pleasant fellowship, will they
live there: they are first adulated, then persecuted; they accomplish
little for others, they find no peace for themselves, but only death and

the peace of the grave. We confess, it is not without a certain mournful awe that we view the fate of these noble souls, so richly gifted yet ruined to so little purpose with all their gifts. It seems to us there is a stern moral taught in this piece of history,—*twice* told us in our own time! Surely to men of like genius, if there be any such, it carried with it a lesson of deep impressive significance. Surely it would become such a man, furnished for the highest of all enterprises, that of being the Poet of his Age, to consider well what it is that he attempts, and in what spirit he attempts it. For the words of Milton are true in all times, and were never truer than in this: 'He, who would write heroic poems, must make his whole life a heroic poem.' If he cannot first so make his life, then let him hasten from this arena; for neither its lofty glories, nor its fearful perils, are fit for him. Let him dwindle into a modish ballad-monger; let him worship and besing the idols of the time, and the time will not fail to reward him. If, indeed, he can endure to live in that capacity! Byron and Burns could not live as idol-priests, but the fire of their own hearts consumed them; and better it was for them that they could not. For it is not in the favour of the great or of the small, but in a life of truth, and in the inexpugnable citadel of his own soul, that a Byron's or a Burns's strength must lie. Let the great stand aloof from him, or know how to reverence him. Beautiful is the union of wealth with favour and furtherance for literature; like the costliest flower-jar enclosing the loveliest amaranth. Yet let not the relation be mistaken. A true poet is not one whom they can hire by money or flattery to be a minister of their pleasures, their writer of occasional verses, their purveyor of table-wit; he cannot be their menial, he cannot even be their partisan. At the peril of both parties, let no such union be attempted! Will a Courser of the Sun work softly in the harness of a Dray-horse? His hoofs are of fire, and his path is through the heavens, bringing light to all lands; will he lumber on mud highways, dragging ale for earthly appetites from door to door?

But we must stop short in these considerations, which would lead us to boundless lengths. We had something to say on the public moral character of Burns; but this also we must forbear. We are far from regarding him as guilty before the world, as guiltier than the average; nay from doubting that he is less guilty than one of ten thousand. Tried at a tribunal far more rigid than that where the *Plebiscita* of common civic reputations are pronounced, he has seemed to us even there less worthy of blame than of pity and wonder. But the world is habitually unjust in its judgements of such men; unjust on many grounds, of which this one may be stated as the substance: It decides, like a court of law, by dead statutes; and not positively but negatively, less on what is done right, than on what is or is not done wrong. Not the few inches of deflection from the mathematical orbit, which are so easily measured, but the *ratio* of these to the whole diameter, constitutes the real aberration. This orbit may be a planet's, its diameter the breadth of the solar system; or it may be a city hippodrome; nay the circle of a gin-horse, its diameter a score of feet or paces. But the inches of deflection only are measured: and it is assumed that the diameter of the gin-horse, and that of the planet, will yield the same ratio when compared with them! Here lies the root of many a blind, cruel condemnation of Burnses, Swifts, Rousseaus, which one never listens to with approval. Granted, the ship comes into harbour with shrouds and tackle damaged; the pilot is blame-worthy; he has not been all-wise and all-powerful: but to know *how* blameworthy, tell us first whether his voyage has been round the Globe, or only to Ramsgate and the Isle of Dogs.

With our readers in general, with men of right feeling anywhere, we are not required to plead for Burns. In pitying admiration he lies enshrined in all our hearts, in a far nobler mausoleum than that one of marble; neither will his Works, even as they are, pass away from the memory of men. While the Shakspeares and Miltons roll on like mighty rivers through the country of Thought, bearing fleets of traffickers and assiduous pearlfishers on their waves; this little Valclusa Fountain will also arrest our eye: for this also is of Nature's own and most cunning workmanship, bursts from the depths of the earth, with a full gushing current, into the light of day; and often will the traveller turn aside to drink of its clear waters, and muse among its rocks and pines!

68. Macaulay from an unsigned review, *Edinburgh Review*

xlvii, 93 (January 1828), 15

Review by the historian, poet, and essayist T. B. Macaulay (1800–59) of *The Poetical Works of John Dryden.*

We have attempted to show that, as knowledge is extended and as the reason develops itself, the imitative arts decay. We should, therefore, expect that the corruption of poetry would commence in the educated classes of society. And this, in fact, is almost constantly the case. The few great works of imagination which appear in a critical age are, almost without exception, the works of uneducated men. Thus, at a time when persons of quality translated French romances, and when the universities celebrated royal deaths in verses about tritons and fauns, a preaching tinker produced the *Pilgrim's Progress.* And thus a ploughman startled a generation which had thought Haley and Beattie great poets with the adventures of Tam o' Shanter.

69. 'Christopher North' in *Blackwood's Magazine*

1829–34

Extracts from 'Christopher North' [John Wilson], 'Noctes Ambrosianae'; text here from *The Works of Professor Wilson*, ed. his son-in-law Professor Ferrier (Edinburgh, 1855–8) (see Nos 55, 59 and Introduction, p. 39).

(a) April 1829. *Works* II, pp. 229–31

North. My dear James, every word I have now uttered may be mere nonsense.—I cannot tell. But do you see my drift?

Shepherd. Na. I see you like a veshel tryin to beat up against a strong wund and a strong tide, and driftin awa to leeward, till it's close in upon the shore, and about to gang stern foremost in amang the rocks and the breakers. Sae far I see your drift, and nae farther. You'll soon fa' ower on your beam ends, and become a total wreck.

North. Well, then, mark my drift, James. We idolise Genius, to the neglect of the worship of Virtue. To our thoughts, Genius is all in all— Virtue absolutely nothing. Human nature seems to be glorified in Shakespeare, because his intellect was various and vast, and because it comprehended a knowledge of all the workings, perhaps, of human being. But if there be truth in that faith to which the Christian world is bound, how dare we, on that ground, to look on Shakespeare as almost greater and better than Man? Why, to criticise one of his works poorly, or badly, or insolently, is it held to be blasphemy? Why? Is Genius so sacred, so holy a thing, *per se*, and apart from Virtue? Folly all! One truly good action performed is worth all that ever Shakespeare wrote. Who is the Swan of Avon in comparison to the humblest being that ever purified his spirit in the waters of eternal life?

Shepherd. Speak awa! I'll no interrupt you—but whether I agree wi' you or no's anither question.

North. Only listen, James, to our eulogies on genius. How virtue must veil her radiant forehead before that idol! How the whole world speaks out her ceaseless sympathy with the woes of Genius! How silent as frost, when Virtue pines! Let a young poet poison himself in wrathful despair—and all the muses weep over his unhallowed bier. Let a young Christian die under the visitation of God, who weeps? No eye but his mother's. We know that such deaths are every day—every hour,—but the thought affects us not—we have no thought—and heap after heap is added, unbewailed, to city or country churchyard. But let a poet, forsooth, die in youth—pay the debt of nature early—and Nature herself, throughout her elements, must in her turn pay tribute to his shade.

Shepherd. Dinna mak me unhappy, sir—dinna mak me sae very unhappy, sir, I beseech you—try and explain awa what you hae said, to the satisfaction o' our hearts and understandings.

North. Impossible. We are base idolaters. 'Tis infatuation—not religion. Is it Genius, or is it Virtue, that shall send a soul to heaven?

Shepherd. Virtue—there's nae denying that;—virtue, sir—virtue.

North. Let us then feel, think, speak, and act, as if we so believed. Is Poetry necessary to our salvation? Is *Paradise Lost* better than the New Testament?

Shepherd. Oh! dinna mak me unhappy. Say again that Poetry is religion.

North. Religion has in it the finest and truest spirit of poetry, and the finest and truest spirit of poetry has in it the spirit of religion. But—

Shepherd. Say nae mair—say nae mair. I'm satisfied wi' that—

North. Oh! James, it makes my very soul sick within me to hear the puny whinings poured by philosophical sentimentalists over the failings —the errors—the vices of genius! There has been, I fear, too much of that traitorous dereliction of the only true faith, even in some eloquent eulogies on the dead, which I have been the means of giving to the world. Have you not often felt that when reading what has been said about our own immortal Burns?

Shepherd. I have in my calmer moments.

North. While the hypocritical and the base exaggerated all that illustrious man's aberrations from the right path, nor had the heart to acknowledge the manifold temptations strewed around his feet,— —the enthusiastic and the generous ran into the other extreme, and weakly—I must not say wickedly—strove to extenuate them into mere trifles—in too many instances to deny them altogether; and when too flagrant to be denied, dared to declare that we were bound to forget and forgive them on the score of the poet's genius—as if genius, the guardian of virtue, could ever be regarded as the pander to vice, and the slave of sin. Thus they were willing to sacrifice morality, rather than that the idol set up before their imagination should be degraded; and did far worse injury, and offered far worse insult, to Virtue and Religion, by thus slurring over the offences of Burns against both, than ever was done by those offences themselves—for Burns bitterly repented what they almost canonised; and the evil practice of one man can never do so much injury to society, as the evil theory of a thousand. Burns erred greatly and grievously; and since the world knows that he did, as well from friends as from foes, let us be lenient and merciful to him, whose worth was great; but just and faithful to that law of right, which must on no consideration be violated by our judgments, but which must maintain and exercise its severe and sovereign power over all transgressions, and more especially over the transgressions of those to whom nature has granted endowments that might have been, had their possessors nobly willed it, the ministers of unmingled good to themselves and the whole human race.

Shepherd. You've written better about Burns, yoursel, sir, nor onybody else breathin. That you hae—baith better and aftener—and a' friends of the poet ought to be grateful to Christopher North.

North. That is true praise coming from my Shepherd. But I have fallen into the error I now reprehend.

Shepherd. There's a set o' sumphs that say periodical literature has degraded the haill literature o' the age. They refer us to the standard warks o' the auld school.

North. There is intolerable impertinence in such opinions—and disgusting ignorance. Where is the body of philosophical criticism, of which these prigs keep prating, to be found? Aristotle's *Poetics* is an admirable manual—as far as it goes—but no more than a manual—outlines for a philosophical lecturer to fill up into a theory. Quintilian is fuller—but often false and oftener feeble—and too formal by far. Longinus was a man of fine enthusiasm, and wrote from an awakened spirit. But he was not a master of principles—though to a writer so eloquent I shall not deny the glory of deserving that famous panegyric—

And is himself the Great Sublime he draws.

(b) April 1830. *Works* II, p. 326

North. The first astronomers were shepherds—
Shepherd. Ay, Chaldean shepherds like mysel—but no a mother's
son o' them could hae written the Manuscripp.[1] Ha, ha, ha!
Tickler. What a misty evening!
Shepherd. Nae wonder—wi' thirteen soups a' steamin up to the skies!
O but the Orrery is sublime the noo, in its shroud! Naethin like hotch-
potch for geein a dim grandeur to the stars. See, yonder Venus—peer-
less planet—shining like the face o' a virgin bride through her white
nuptial veil! He's a grim chiel yon Saturn. Nae wonder he devourit his
weans—he has the coontenance o' a cannibal. Thank you, Mr. Awmrose
for opening the door—for this current o' air has swept awa the mists
frae heaven, and gien us back the beauty o' the celestial spheres.
North (*aside to the English Opium-Eater*). You hear, Mr. De Quincey,
how he begins to blaze even before broth.
English Opium-Eater (*aside to North*). I have always placed Mr. Hogg,
in genius, far above Burns. He is indeed 'of imagination all compact'.
Burns had strong sense—and strong sinews—and brandished a pen
pretty much after the same fashion as he brandished a flail. You never
lose sight of the thresher—
Shepherd. Dinna abuse Burns, Mr. De Quinshy. Neither you nor
ony ither Englishman can thoroughly understaun' three sentences o'
his poems—
English Opium-Eater (*with much animation*). I have for some years
past longed for an opportunity to tear into pieces that gross national
delusion, born of prejudice, ignorance, and bigotry, in which, from
highest to lowest, all literary classes of Scotchmen are as it were in-
carnated—to wit, a belief strong as superstition, that all their various
dialects must be as unintelligible, as I grant that most of them are
uncouth and barbarous, to English ears—even to those of the most
accomplished and consummate scholars. Whereas, to a Danish,
Norwegian, Swedish, Saxon, German, French, Italian, Spanish—and
let me add, Latin and Greek scholar, there is not even a monosyllable
that—

---

[1] Refers to 'The Chaldee Manuscript', a scurrilous article in *Blackwood's* of October
1817, suppressed when the magazine was re-issued. On its authorship, see *PMLA*, lxv
(September 1950).

Shepherd. What's *a gowpen o' glaur?*

English Opium-Eater. Mr. Hogg—Sir, I will not be interrupted—

Shepherd. You cannot tell. It's just twa neif-fu's o' clarts.*

North. James—James—James!

Shepherd. Kit—Kit—Kit. But beg your pardon, Mr. De Quinshy—afore denner I'm aye unco snappish. I admit you're a great grammarian. But kennin something o' a language by bringin to bear upon't a' the united efforts o' knowledge and understaunin'—baith first-rate—is ae thing, and feeling every breath and every shadow that keeps playin ower a' its syllables, as if by a natural and born instinct, is anither; the first you may aiblins hae—naebody likelier,—but to the second, nae man may pretend that hasna had the happiness and the honour o' havin been born and bred in bonny Scotland. What can ye ken o' Kilmeny?

English Opium-Eater (smiling graciously). 'Tis a ballad breathing the sweetest, simplest, wildest spirit of Scottish traditionary song—music, as of some antique instrument long lost, but found at last in the Forest among the decayed roots of trees, and touched, indeed, as by an instinct, by the only man who could reawaken its sleeping chords—the Ettrick Shepherd.

Shepherd. Na—if you say that sincerely—and I never saw a broo smoother wi' truth than your ain—I maun qualify my former apothegm and alloo you to be an exception frae the general rule. I wush, sir, you would write a Glossary o' the Scottish Language. I ken naebody fitter.

North. Our distinguished guest is aware that this is 'All Fool's Day,' —and must, on that score, pardon these court-dresses. We consider them, my dear sir, appropriate to this Anniversary.

(c) January 1831. *Works* II, p. 118

Shepherd. Mr. North, if Mr. Muir was sittin on that empty chair there, wi' the laddie kissin the lassie embroidered on the inside o' the back o't—Patie and Roger, I jalouse—I would just say till him, wi' a pleesant vice, and kind een, and a launch about my mouth,—Mister Muir, you're under a great mistak. Nae man o' a high order o' mind, either thinks or feels through 'an unreal medium.' But I'll tell you, sir, what

* Two handfuls of mud.

he does—he thinks and feels through a *fine* medium. He breathes the *pure* air o' the mountain-tap—and he sees through the *clear* air a' the dwallins o' man—and richt through their roofs intil their hearths and their hearts. Did Burns feel and think through an unreal medium, Mister Muir, when—

> 'In glory and in joy,
> Following his plough upon the mountain-side,'

his soul saw the Cottar's Saturday Night, and in words gave the vision imperishable life?

North. James—

> 'You are attired
> With sudden brightness, like a man inspired,'

Shepherd. Na, na—'tis but the glow o' the fire on ma face. Yet ma heart's a' on a low—for as sure as God is in heaven, and that he has gien us his word on earth, that Picture is a Picture of the Truth, and Burns, in drawing it, saw, felt, and thocht through that *real medium*, in which alone all that is fairest, loveliest, brichtest, best in creation, is made apparent to the eyes o' genius, or permanent in its immortal works.

North. Ca' ye that pitchin your talk on a laigh key? 'Tis at the tap o' the gawmut.

Shepherd. Hoo can you, Mister Muir, sit there and tell me that men o' a high order o' mind sune get sae enamoured o' the eemages o' ideal good and beauty, that they consider all that is beneath that standard unworthy o' their care? Let me come ower and sit beside you for a few minutes. There, dinna be feared—I'm no a grain angry—and I'm sitting, you see, my dear sir, wi' my airm ower the back o' your chair.

North. Don't press so close upon Mr. Moore, James—

Shepherd. Mister Muir's makin nae complents, sir.—It is 'men o' a *laigh* order o' genius,' ma freen, that is subject to sic degeneracy and adulteration. A puny, sickly, sensibility there is which is averse frae all the realities of life; and Byron or somebody else spoke well when he said that Sterne preferred whining ower a dead ass to relieving a living mother—But wha was Sterne? As shallow a sentimentalist as ever grat —or rather tried to greet. O, sir! but it's a degrawdin sicht to humanity, yon—to see the shufflin sinner tryin to bring the tears intil his een, by rubbin the lids wi' the pint o' his pen, or wi' the feathers on the shank, and when it a' winna do, takin refuge in a blank, sae—or hidin his head amang a set o' asterisks, sae ****; or boltin aff the printed page a' thegither and disappearin in ae black blotch!

North. Sterne had genius, James.

Shepherd. No ae grain, sir.

North. Some—not a little—

Shepherd. Weel, weel—be it sae—a' that I mean to aver is, that had he been 'o' the first order o' minds,' he would not hae preferred whining ower a dead ass to relieving a living mother; but if news had been suddenly brocht to him that his mother was ill, he wad hae hired a livin horse, and aff to her house like a flash o' lichtin, flingin himsel out o' the saiddle to the danger o' his neck, up-stairs to her bedside, and doun upon his knees, beseeching God for her recovery, and willing to die for her sake, so that she who gave birth micht yet live, nor be taken from the licht of day and buried amang the tombs!

North. Don't press, my dear James, so heavily on Mr. Moore's shoulder.

Shepherd. Mister Muir's makin nae complents—There's mysel, sirs—I shanna pretend to say whether I'm a man o' the higher order o' genius or no; but—

North. Yes, James, you are; for you wrote *Kilmeny*.

Shepherd. But if I haena ten thousand times the quantity o' genius, that ever Sterne had, may this be the last jug, sirs, that ever we three drink thegither—

(d) August 1834. *Works* IV, pp. 102–3

North. 'the dowie holms o' Yarrow!'

Shepherd. In theirsels they're no dowie—but as cheerfu' as ony ever sang ower by the laverock—and mony a lintie is heard liltin merrily in the broom. But Poetry and Passion changed their character at their ain wild wull—tauld the silver Yarrow to rin red wi' lovers' bluid—and ilka swelling turf, fit for the Fairies' play, to look like a grave where a human flower was buried! Sic power has genie transfigurin a' nature in its grief!

North. Write you no songs now, James?

Shepherd. Nane! Isna five hunder or mair sangs aneuch? I shanna say ony o' mine's are as gude as some sax or aucht o' Burns's —for about that number of Robbie's are o' inimitable perfection. It was heaven's wull that in them he should transcend a' the minnesingers o' this warld. But they're too perfectly beautifu' to be envied by mortal man— therefore let his memory in them be hallowed for evermair.

North. A noble sentiment.

Shepherd. At least a natural ane, and flowin frae a heart elevated at ance and purified by the sangs o' ane, let us trust, noo a seraph.

North. Peace to the soul of the Poet.

Shepherd. Peace and glory that fadeth not away! His sins were a' born o' his body—that is dust—and if they tainted his immortal soul— and oh! wae's me! mournfully and mysteriously I fear that sair did they sae—what's the mornin-dew or the well on the mountain to what has washed out a' thae stains, and made it purer noo than even the innocent daisy that on this earth—ay, even when toilin at his wark at ance like a slave and a king—his kindled heart changed into a flower o' heaven!

North. I wish Allan Cunningham were with us.

Shepherd. And sae maist fervently do I.

Tickler. And I.

North. Some of Allan's songs, too, James, will not die.

Shepherd. Mony a bonny thing does—some o' them, as it would seen, o' theirsels, without onything hurtin them, and as if even gracious Nature, though loth, consented to allow them to fade awa into forget-fulness; and that will happen, I fear, to no a few o' baith his breathins and mine—but that ithers will surveeve, even though Time should try to ding them doun wi' his heel into the yird, as sure am I as that the nicht sky shall never lose a single star till the mornin o' the Day o' Doom.

North. Ramsay, Fergusson, Bruce, Burns, Hogg, Cunningham . . .

(e) November 1834. *Works* IV, p. 174

North. Allan Cunningham, and William Motherwell, and you, my dear James, have caught the true spirit of the old traditionary strain— and, seek the wide world, where will there be found such a lyrical lark as he whom, not in vain, you three have aspired to emulate— sweet Robbie Burns?

Shepherd. That's richt, sir. I was wrang in ever hintin ae word in disparagement o' Burns's 'Cottar's Saturday Night'. But the truth is, you see, that the subjeck's sae heaped up wi' happiness, and sae charged wi' a' sorts o' sanctity—sae national and sae Scottish—that beautifu' as the poem is—and really, after a', naething can be mair beautifu'—there's nae satisfyin either peasant or shepherd by only delineation o't, though drawn in lines o' licht, and shinin equally wi' genius and wi' piety. That's it. Noo, this is Saturday nicht at Tibbie's—and, though we've been gey funny, there has been naething desecratin in our fun, and we'll be a' attendin' divine service the morn—me in Yarrow, and you, Mr. North, and Mr. Tickler, and the lave o' you, in Ettrick kirk.

North. And, James, we can nowhere else hear Christianity preached in a more fervent and truthful spirit.

70. Wordsworth on Burns

1843

Note dictated by Wordsworth to Isabella Fenwick in 1843, concerning ' "There!" said a Stripling', an Itinerary poem written in 1833 and published in 1835. *Poetical Works of William Wordsworth*, ed. E. De Selincourt and Helen Darbishire (1947), IV, p. 408 (see Nos 16, 29, 33, 44, 53 and Introduction, p. 28).

Mosgiel was thus pointed out to me by a young man on the top of a coach on my way from Glasgow to Kilmarnock. It is remarkable that, though Burns lived some time here, and during much the most productive period of his poetical life, he nowhere adverts to the splendid prospects stretching towards the sea and bounded by the peaks of Arran on one part, which in clear weather he must have had daily before his eyes.[1] Yet this is easily explained. In one of his poetical effusions he speaks of describing 'fair Nature's face' as a privilege on which he sets

[1] Compare Keats's comment, above, p. 306.

a high value; nevertheless, natural appearances rarely take a lead in his poetry. It is as a human being, eminently sensitive and intelligent, and not as a Poet, clad in his priestly robes and carrying the ensigns of sacerdotal office, that he interests and affects us. Whether he speaks of rivers, hills, and woods, it is not so much on account of the properties with which they are absolutely endowed, as relatively to local patriotic remembrances and associations, or as they ministered to personal feelings, especially those of love, whether happy or otherwise;—yet it is not *always* so. Soon after we had passed Mosgiel Farm we crossed the Ayr, murmuring and winding through a narrow woody hollow. His line—'Auld hermit Ayr strays through his woods'—came at once to my mind with Irwin, Lugar, Ayr, and Doon,—Ayrshire streams over which he breathes a sigh as being unnamed in song; and surely his own attempts to make them known were as successful as his heart could desire.

71. Allan Cunningham on Burns

1834

Extracts from *The Works of Robert Burns with his Life*, ed. Allan Cunningham (1834), I, pp. 13–87, 364–82 (see No. 65 and Introduction, p. 41).

The 'Halloween' is a happy mixture of the dramatic and the descriptive, and bears the impress of the manners, customs, and superstitions of the people. We see the scene, and are made familiar with the actors; we not only see them busied in the mysteries of the night, but we hear their remarks; nor can we refrain from accompanying them on their solitary and perilous errands to 'Winnow wechts of naething, sow hemp-seed, pull kale-stocks, eat apples at the glass;' or, more romantic still, 'wet the left sleeve of the shirt where three lairds' lands meet at a burn.' The whole poem hovers between the serious and the ludicrous: in delineating the superstitious beliefs and mysterious acts of the evening, Burns keeps his own opinion to himself. The scene is laid in the last night of harvest, as the name implies, at a husbandman's fireside, whose corn is gathered into the stack-yard and the barn; and the hands which aided in the labour are met—

> To burn their nits, and pou their stocks,
> An' haud their Halloween.'

They seem not unaware that while they are merry, or looking into futurity, fairies are dancing on Cassilis-Downons, and witches are mounted on their 'ragweed nags', hurrying to some wild rendezvous, or concerting with the author of mischief fresh woes for man. It is the most equal of all the Poet's compositions.

A singular poem, and in its nature personal, was also the offspring of the same year. This is 'Death and Doctor Hornbook'. The hero of the piece was John Wilson, schoolmaster of the parish of Tarbolton: a person of blameless life, fond of argument, opinionative, and obstinate. At a maston-meeting, it seems he provoked the Poet by questioning some of his positions in a speech stuffed with Latin phrases and allusions to pharmacy. The future satire dawned on Burns at the moment, for he exclaimed twice, 'Sit down, Doctor Hornbook!' On his way home he seated himself on the parapet of a bridge near 'Willie's Mill', and in the moonlight began to reflect on what had passed. It then occurred to him that Wilson had added to the moderate income of his school the profit arising from the sale of a few common medicines; this suggested an interview with 'Death', and all the ironical commendations of the Dominie which followed. He composed the poem on his perilous seat, and when he had done, fell asleep; he was awakened by the rising sun, and, on going home, committed it to paper. It exhibits a singular union of fancy and humour; the attention is arrested at once by the difficulty felt in counting the horns of the moon, and we expect something to happen when his shadowy majesty comes upon the stage, relates his experience in 'nicking the thread and choking the breath,' and laments how his scythe and dart are rendered useless by the skill of Dr. Hornbook. On the appearance of the poem, Wilson found the laugh of Kyle too much for him—

> The weans held out their fingers laughin.

405

So he removed to Glasgow, where he engaged with success in other pursuits. He lives, but loves no one better for naming the name of the Poet, or making any allusion to the poem. Burns repeated the satire to his brother during the afternoon of the day on which it was composed. 'I was holding the plough,' said Gilbert, 'and Robert was letting the water off the field beside me.'

The patriotic feelings of the Bard were touched when he took up the song of 'Scotch Drink' against the government of the day, and uttered his 'Earnest cry and prayer to the Scottish representatives in the House of Commons.' Yet bitter as he sometimes is, and overflowing with humorous satire, these poems abound with natural and noble images; nay, he scolds himself into a pleasant mood, and scatters praise on the 'chosen Five-and-Forty', with much skill and discrimination. His praise of whiskey is strangely mingled with sadness:

[quotes 'Scotch Drink', ll. 25–36]

A country forge with a blazing fire, an anxious blacksmith, and a welding-heat, will rise to the fancy readily on reading these inimitable stanzas:—

[quotes 'Scotch Drink', ll. 55–66]

Nor is there wanting stanzas of a more solemn kind to bring trembling to our mirth. The Scotsman dying on a battle-field with the sound of victory in his ear, is a noble picture:—

> Nae cauld faint-hearted doubtings tease him,
> Death comes!—wi' fearless eye he sees him,
> Wi' bloody hand a welcome gies him,
>   An' when he fa's
> His latest draught o' breathin lea'es him
>   In faint huzzas.

He steps at once from the serious to the comic: his description of Mother Scotland sitting on her mountain throne, her diadem a little awry, her eyes reeling, and the heather below becoming moist during her prolonged libations, is equally humorous and irreverent. Those who may suspect that all this singing about liquor arose from a love of it, will be glad to hear that when Nanse Tinnock was told that Burns proposed to toast the Scotch members in her house 'nine times a week', she exclaimed, 'Him drink in my house! I hardly ken the colour o' his coin.'

The year 1785 was a harvest-season of verse with Burns. Some of his poems he hesitated for a while to make public; others he copied, and scattered amongst his friends. Of these one of the most remarkable is 'The Jolly Beggars.' This drama, which I cannot help considering the most varied and characteristic of the Poet's works, was unknown, save to some west country acquaintances, till after his death, when it came unexpectedly out. The opening seems uttered by another muse than Coila—the sound is of the elder days of verse; but the moment the curtain draws up and shows the actors, the spirit of Burns appears kindling and animating all. It is impossible to deny his presence:—

[quotes 'Love and Liberty', ll. 15–28]

The scene of this rustic drama lies in Mauchline, and the actors are strolling vagrants, who having acquired meal and money by begging, pilfering, and slight-of-hand, assemble in Posie Nansie's to 'toom their pocks and pawn their duds,' and

> Gie ae night's discharge to care,

over the gill-stoup and the quaigh. They hold a sort of Beggar's Saturday-night—sing songs, utter sentiments, and lay down the loose laws of the various classes they represent. The characters are numerous— All these, and more, sing and shout and talk and act in character; and unite in giving effect to the chorus of a song which claims, for the jovial ragged ring, exemption from the cares which weigh down the sedate and the orderly, and a happiness which refuses to wait on the train-attended carriage, or on the sober bed of matrimony. The curtain drops as they all shout,

> A fig for those by law protected,
> Liberty's a glorious feast,
> Courts for cowards were erected,
> Churches built to please the priest.

There is nothing in the language which, for life and character, approaches this singular 'cantata.' The *Beggar's Opera* is a burial compared to it; it bears some resemblances to the *Wallenstein's Camp* of Schiller, as translated by Lord Francis Leveson Gower; the same variety, and the same licence of action and speech distinguished both . . .

Frequent bursts of religious feeling and a fine spirit of morality, are visible in much that Burns wrote; yet only one of his poems is expressly dedicated to devotion—'The Cottar's Saturday Night.' The origin of this noble strain is related by his brother:—

Robert had frequently remarked to me that he thought there was something peculiarly venerable in the phrase, 'Let us worship God,' used by a decent sober head of a family introducing family worship. The hint of the plan and title of the poem were taken from Fergusson's 'Farmer's Ingle.' When Robert had not some pleasure in view, in which I was not thought fit to participate, we used frequently to walk together when the weather was favourable on the Sunday afternoon, those precious breathing times to the labouring part of the community, and enjoyed such Sundays as would make us regret to see their number abridged. It was in one of these walks that I first had the pleasure of hearing the Author repeat the 'Cottar's Saturday Night.'

The poem is a picture of cottage devotion, by a hand more solicitous about accuracy than effect; for no one knew better than Burns that invention could not heighten, nor art embellish a scene in which man holds intercourse with heaven. His natural good taste told him that his work-day burning impetuosity of language and intrepid freedom of illustration were unsuitable here; he calmed down his style into an earnest and touching simplicity, which has been mistaken by critics for tameness; but the strength of the poem is proved by the numerous and beautiful images, all of a devotional character, which it impresses on the mind. Religion is the leading feature of the whole; but love in its virgin state, and patriotism in its purity, mingle with it, and give a gentle tinge, rather than a decided colour, to the performance. The scene is peculiar to Scotland. With what natural art the Poet introduces us to the cottar, and to his happy home, and gradually prepares us, by a succession of solemn images, for the opening of the bible and the pouring out of prayer! . . . The admonition of this good man to his children is, to be obedient to those above them; to mind their labours, nor be idle when unobserved; and chiefly to fear the Lord, and duly, morn and night, implore his aid and counsel. While this is going on, a gentle rap is heard at the door, and a strappan youth, who 'takes the mother's e'e,' is introduced by Jenny as a neighbour lad, who, among other things, had undertaken to see her safely home. The visit is well taken, for he is neither wild nor worthless, but come of honest parents, and is, moreover, blate and bashful, and for inward joy can scarce behave himself. The mother knows well what make him so grave; the father converses about horses and ploughs, while the supper-table is spread, and milk from her only cow, and a 'well-hained cheese', of a peculiar flavour, and a twelvemonth old 'sin' lint was in the bell,' are placed by the frugal and happy mother before the lothful stranger.

> The cheerfu' supper done, wi' serious face
>   They round the ingle form a circle wide,
> The sire turns o'er, wi' patriarchal grace,
>   The big ha'bible, ance his father's pride:
> His bonnet reverently is laid aside,
>   His lyart haffets wearing thin and bare,
> Those strains that once did sweet in Zion glide,
>   He wales a portion with judicious care,
> And 'let us worship God,' he says with solemn air.

The canker-tooth of the most envious criticism cannot well fasten on a work in every respect so perfect; nor, in expatiating upon it, are we going out of the direct line of biography: it is known to be, in part, a picture of the household of William Burness . . . As a poet, Burns stands in the first rank: his conceptions are original; his thoughts new and weighty; his manner unborrowed; and even his language is his own. He owes no honour to his subjects, for they are all of an ordinary kind, such as humble life around him presented; he sought neither in high station nor in history for matter to his muse, and yet all his topics are simple, natural, and to be found without research. The Scottish bards who preceded him selected subjects which obtained notice from their oddity, and treated them in a way singular and outré. The verses of the first and fifth James, as well as those of Ramsay and Fergusson are chiefly a succession of odd and ludicrous pictures, as true as truth itself, and no more. To their graphic force of delineation Burns added sentiment and passion, and an elegant tenderness and simplicity. He took topics familiar to all; the Daisy grew on the lands he ploughed; the Mouse built her nest on his own stubble-field; the Haggis smoked on his own board; the Scotch Drink which he sung was distilled on the banks of Doon; the Dogs that conversed so wittily and wisely were his own collies; Tam O'Shanter was a merry husbandman of his own acquaintance; and even the 'De'il himsel' was familiar to all, and had often alarmed, by his eldritch croon and the marks of his cloven foot, the pastoral people of Kyle. Burns was the first who taught the world that in lowly subjects high poetry resided. Touched by him, they were lifted at once into an humble topic, as the sap of spring ascends a tree to endow it with beauty and fragrance.

Burns is our chief national Poet; he owes nothing of the structure of his verse or of the materials of his poetry to other lands—he is the off-spring of the soil; he is as natural to Scotland as the heath is to her hills, and all his brightness, like our nocturnal aurora, is of the north. Nor has he taken up fleeting themes; his song is not of the external manners and changeable affectations of man—it is of the human heart—of the mind's hopes and fears, and of the soul's aspirations. Others give us the outward form and pressure of society—the court-costume of human nature—the laced lapelle and the epauletted shoulder. He gives us flesh and blood; all he has he holds in common with mankind; yet all is national and Scottish. We can see to whom other bards have looked for inspiration—like fruit of the finest sort, they smack of the stock on which they were grafted. Burns read Young, Thomson, Shenstone, and Shakspeare; yet there is nothing of Young, Thomson, Shenstone, or Shakspeare about him; nor is there much of the old ballad. His light is of nature, like sunshine, and not reflected. When, in after life, he tried imitation, his 'Epistle to Grahame of Fintray' shewed satiric power and polish little inferior to Dryden.

He is not only the truest and best of Scottish poets, but, in ease, fire, and passion, he is second to none save Shakespeare. I know of no one besides, whose verse flows forth so sparkling and spontaneous. On the lines of other bards, we see the marks of care and study—now and then they are happy, but they are often elaborated out and brightened like a key by frequent handling. Burns is seldom or never so —he wrote from the impulse of nature—he wrote because his passions raged like so many demons till they got in vent in rhyme. Others sit and solicit the muse, like a coy mistress, to be kind; she came to Burns 'unsent for', like the 'bonnie lass' in the song, and showered her favours freely. The strength was equal to the harmony; rugged westlin words were taken from the lips of the weaver and the ploughman, and adorned with melody and feeling; and familiar phrases were picked up from shepherds and mechanics, and rendered as musical as is Apollo's lute.—

'I can think of no verse since Shakespeare's,' said Pitt to Henry Addington, 'which came so sweetly and at once from nature. "Out of the eater came forth meat."'—the premier praised whom he starved. Burns was not a poet by fits and starts; the mercury of his genius stood always at the inspired point; like the fairy's drinking-cup, the fountain of his fancy was ever flowing and ever full. He had, it is true, set times and seasons when the fruits of his mind were more than usually abundant; but the songs of spring were equal to those of summer—

those of summer were not surpassed by those of autumn; the quantity might be different, the flavour and richness were ever the same.

His variety is equal to his originality. His humour, his gaiety, his tenderness, and his pathos come all in a breath; they come freely, for they come of their own accord; nor are they huddled together at random, like doves and crows in a flock; the contrast is never offensive; the comic slides easily into the serious, the serious into the tender, and the tender into the pathetic. The witch's cup, out of which the wondering rustic drank seven kinds of wine at once, was typical of the muse of Burns. It is this which has made him welcome to all readers.—
'No poet,' says Scott, 'with the exception of Shakespeare, ever possessed the power of exciting the most varied and discordant emotions with such rapid transitions.'

Notwithstanding the uncommon ease and natural elegance of his musings—the sweet and impassioned tone of his verse, critics have not been wanting who perceived in his works the humility of his origin. His poems, I remember well enough, were considered by many, at first, as the labours of some gentleman who assumed the rustic for the sake of indulging in satire; their knowledge was reckoned beyond the reach, and their flights above the power, of a simple ploughman. Something of this belief may be seen in Mrs. Scott of Wauchope's letter; and when it was known for a truth that the author was a ploughman, many lengthy discussions took place concerning the way in which the Poet had acquired his knowledge. Ayr race-course was pointed out as the likely scene of his studies of high life, where he found what was graceful and elegant. When Jeffrey wrote his depreciating criticism, he forgot that Burns had studied politeness in the very school where he himself was polished:—

I've been at drunken writers' feasts,

claims a scholarship which the critic might have respected. If sharp epigrams, familiar gallantry, love of independence, and a leaning to the tumid be, as that critic assures us, true symptoms of vulgar birth, then Swift was a scavenger, Rochester a coalheaver, Pope a carman, and Thomson a boor. He might as well see lowness of origin in the James Stuart who wrote 'Christ's Kirk on the green,' as in the Robert Burns who wrote 'Tam O'Shanter.' The nature which Burns infused into all he wrote deals with internal emotions: feeling is no more vulgar in a ploughman than in a prince.

In all this I see the reluctance of an accomplished scholar to admit the merits of a rustic poet who not only claimed, but took, the best station on the Caledonian Parnassus. It could be no welcome sight to philosophers, historians, and critics to see a peasant, fragrant from the furrow, elbowing his way through their polished ranks to the highest place of honour, exclaiming,—

What's a' your jargon o' your school?

Some of them were no doubt astonished and incensed; nature was doing too much; they avenged themselves by advising him to leave his vulgar or romantic fancies and grow classical. His best songs they called random flights; his happiest poems the fruit of a vagrant impulse; they accounted him an accident—'a wild colt of a comet'—a sort of splendid error; and refused to look upon him as a true poet, raised by the kindly warmth of nature; for they thought nothing beautiful which was not produced or adorned by learning.

Burns is a thorough Scotchman; his nationality, like cream on milk, floats on the surface of all his works; it mingles in his humour as well as in his tenderness; yet it is seldom or never offensive to an English ear; there is nothing narrow-souled in it. He rejoices in Scotland's ancient glory and in her present strength; he bestows his affection on her heathery mountains, as well as on her romantic vales; he glories in the worth of her husbandmen, and in the loveliness of her maidens. The brackeny glens and thistly brae-sides of the North are more welcome to his sight than are the sunny dales of Italy, fragrant with ungathered grapes; its men, if not quite divinities, are more than mortal; and the women are clothed in beauty, and walk in a light of their own creating; a haggis is food fit for gods; brose is a better sort of ambrosia; 'wi' twopenny we fear nae evil;' and whiskey not only makes us insensible to danger, but inspires noble verse and heroic deeds. There is something at once ludicrous and dignified in all this: to excite mingled emotions was the aim of the Poet. Besides a love of country, there is an intense love of freedom about him; not the savage joy in the boundless forest and the unlicensed range, but the calm determination and temperate delight of a reflecting mind. Burns is the bard of liberty —not that which sets fancy free and fetters the body; he resists oppression—he covets free thought and speech—he scorns slavish obedience to the mob as much as he detests tyranny in the rulers. He spoke out like a bold-inspired person; he knew his word would have weight with the world, and sung his 'Man's a man for a' that,' as a watch-word to future generations—as a spell against slavery.

The best poems of Burns are about rural and pastoral life, and relate the hopes, joys, and aspirations of that portion of the people falsely called the humble, as if grandeur of soul were a thing 'born in the purple,' and not the free gift and bounty of heaven. The passions and feelings of man are disguised, not changed, in polished society; flesh and blood are the same beneath hoddin' gray as beneath three-piled velvet. This was what Burns alluded to when he said he saw little in the splendid circles of Edinburgh which was new to him. His pictures of human life and of the world are of a mental as well as national kind. His 'Twa Dogs' prove that happiness is not unequally diffused: 'Scotch Drink' gives us fireside enjoyments; the 'Earnest Cry and Prayer' shows the keen eye which humble people cast on their rulers; the 'Address to the Deil' indulges in religious humanities, in which sympathy overcomes fear; 'The Auld Mare,' and 'The Address to Maillie,' enjoin, by the most simple and touching examples, kindness and mercy to dumb creatures; 'The Holy Fair' desires to curb the licentiousness of those who seek amusement instead of holiness in religion; 'Man was made to Mourn' exhorts the strong and the wealthy to be mindful of the weak and the poor; 'Halloween' shows us superstition in a domestic aspect; 'Tam O'Shanter' adorns popular belief with humourous terror, and helps us to laugh old dreads away; 'The Mouse,' in its weakness, contrasts with man in his strength, and preaches to us the instability of happiness on earth; while 'The Mountain Daisy' pleads with such moral pathos the cause of the flowers of the field sent by God to adorn the earth for man's pleasure, that our feet have pressed less ungraciously on the 'wee modest crimson-tipped flower,' since his song was written.

Others of his poems have a still grander reach. 'The Vision' reveals the Poet's plan of Providence, proves the worth of eloquence, bravery, honesty and beauty, and that even the rustic bard himself is an useful and ornamental link in the great chain of being. 'The Cottar's Saturday Night' connects us with the invisible world, and shows, that domestic peace, faithful love, and patriotic feelings are of earthly things most akin to the joys of heaven; while the divine 'Elegy on Mathew Henderson' unites human nature in a bond of sympathy with the stars of the sky, the fowls of the air, the beasts of the field, the flowery vale, and the lonely mountain. The hastiest of his effusions has a wise aim; and the eloquent Currie perceived this when he spoke of the 'sublime morality of Burns.'

Had Burns, in his poems, preached only so many moral sermons, his audience might have been a select, but it would have been a limited one. The sublimest truths, like the surest medicines, are sometimes uneasy to swallow: for this the Poet provided an effectual remedy; he associated his moral counsel with so much tenderness and pathos, and garnished it all about with such exquisite humour, that the public, like the giant drinking the wine in Homer, gaped, and cried, 'More! this is divine!' If a reader has such a limited soul as to love humour only, why Burns is his man—he has more of it than any modern poet: should he covet tenderness, he cannot read far in Burns without finding it to his mind; should he desire pathos, the Scottish Peasant has it of the purest sort; and if he wish for them altogether, let him try no other Bard—for in what other poet will he find them woven more naturally into the web of song? It is by thus suiting himself to so many minds and tastes, that Burns has become such a favourite with the world; if, in a strange company, we should chance to stumble in quoting him, an English voice, or an Irish one, corrects us; much of the business of life is mingled with his verse; and the lover, whether in joy or sorrow, will find that Burns has anticipated every throb of his heart:—

> Every pulse along his veins,
> And every roving fancy.

He was the first of our northern poets who brought deep passion and high energy to the service of the muse, who added sublimity to simplicity, and found loveliness and elegance dwelling among the cottages of his native land. His simplicity is graceful as well as strong; he is never mean, never weak, never vulgar, and but seldom coarse. All he says is above the mark of other men: his language is familiar, yet dignified; careless, yet concise; and he touches on the most ordinary—nay, perilous themes, with a skill so rare and felicitous, that good fortune seems to unite with good taste in helping him through the Slough of Despond, in which so many meaner spirits have wallowed. No one has greater power in adorning the humble, and dignifying the plain—no one else has so happily picked the sweet fresh flowers of poesy from among the thorns and brambles of the ordinary paths of existence.

'The excellence of Burns', says Thomas Carlyle—a true judge, 'is, indeed, among the rarest, whether in poetry or prose; but at the same time it is plain and easily recognized—his sincerity—his indisputable air of truth . . .'

It must be mentioned, in abatement of this high praise, that Burns occasionally speaks with too little delicacy. He violates without necessity the true decorum of his subject, and indulges in hidden meanings and allusions, such as the most tolerant cannot applaud. Nor is this the worst; he is much too free in his treatment of matters holy. He ventures to take the Deity to task about his own passions, and the order of nature, in a way less reverent than he employs when winning his way to woman's love. He has, in truth, touches of profanity which make the pious shudder. In the warmth of conversation such expressions might escape from the lips; but they should not have been coolly sanctioned in the closet with the pen. These deformities are not, however, of frequent occurrence; and, what is some extenuation, they are generally united to a noble or natural sentiment. He is not profane or indecorous for the sake of being so: his faults, as well as his beauties, come from an overflowing fulness of mind.

His songs have all the beauties, and none of the faults, of his poems. As compositions to be sung, a finer and more scientific harmony, and a more nicely-modulated dance of words were required, and Burns had both in perfection. They flow as readily to the music as if both the air and verse had been created together, and blend and mingle like two uniting streams. The sentiments are from nature; and they never, in any instance, jar or jangle with the peculiar feeling of the music. While humming the air over during the moments of composition, the words came and took their proper places, each according to the meaning of the air: rugged expressions could not well mingle with thoughts inspired by harmony.

In his poems Burns supposes himself in the society of men, and indulges in reckless sentiments and unmeasured language: in his songs he imagines himself in softer company: when woman's eye is on him he is gentle, persuasive, and impassioned; he is never boisterous; he seeks not to say fine things, yet he never misses saying them; his compliments are uttered of free will, and all his thoughts flow naturally from the subject. There is a natural grace and fascination about his songs; all is earnest and from the heart: he is none of your millinery bards who deal in jewelled locks, laced garments, and shower pearls and gems by the bushel on youth and beauty. He makes bright eyes, flushing cheeks: the music of the tongue, and the pulses' maddening play do all. Those charms he knew came from heaven, and not out of the tire-woman's basket, and would last when fashions changed. It is remarkable that the most naturally elegant and truly impassioned songs

in the language were written by a ploughman-lad in honour of the
rustic lasses around him.

If we regard the songs of Burns as so many pastoral pictures, we will
find that he has an eye for the beauties of nature as accurate and as
tasteful as the happiest landscape painter. Indeed, he seldom gives us a
finished image of female loveliness without the accompaniment of
blooming flowers, running streams, waving woods, and the melody of
birds: this is the frame-work which sets off the portrait. He has recourse
rarely to embellishments borrowed from art; the lighted hall and the
thrilling strings are less to him than a walk with her he loves by some
lonely rivulet's side, when the dews are beginning to glisten on the
lilies and weigh them down, and the moon is moving out unconsciously above them. In all this we may recognize a true poet—one who
felt that woman's loveliness triumphed over these fragrant accom-
paniments, and who regarded her still as the 'blood royal of life,' the
brightest part of creation.

Those who desire to feel, in their full force, the songs of Burns, must
not hope it from scientific singers in the theatres. The right scene is the
pastoral glen; the right tongue for utterance is that of a shepherd lass;
and the proper song is that which belongs to her present feelings. The
gowany glen, the nibbling sheep, the warbling birds, and the running
stream give the inanimate, while the singer herself personates the
living, beauty of the song. I have listened to a country girl singing one
of his songs, while she spread her webs to bleach by a running stream—
ignorant of her audience—with such feeling and effect as were quite
overpowering. This will keep the fame of Burns high among us; should
the printer's ink dry up, ten thousand melodious tongues will preserve
his songs to remote generations.

The variety, too, of his lyrics is equal to their truth and beauty. He
has written songs which echo the feelings of every age and condition
in life. He personates all the passions of man and all the gradations of
affection. He sings the lover hastening through storm and tempest to
see the object of his attachment—the swelling stream, the haunted
wood, and the suspicious parents are all alike disregarded. He paints
him again on an eve of July, when the air is calm, the grass fragrant,
and no sound is abroad save the amorous cry of the partridge, enjoying
the beauty of the evening as he steals by some unfrequented way to the
trysting thorn, whither his mistress is hastening; or he limns him on a
cold and snowy night, enjoying a brief parley with her whom he loves,
from a cautiously opened window, which shews her white arm and

bright eyes, and the shadow perhaps of a more fortunate lover, which accounts for the marks of feet impressed in the snow on the way to her dwelling. Nor is he always sighing and vowing; some of his heroes answer scorn with scorn, are saucy with the saucy, and proud with the proud, and comfort themselves with sarcastic comments on woman and her fickleness and folly; others drop all allegiance to that fantastic idol beauty, and while mirth abounds, and 'the wine-cup shines in light,' find wondrous solace. He laughs at the sex one moment, and adores them the next—he ridicules and satirizes—he vows and entreats —he traduces and he deifies—all in a breath. Burns was intimate with the female heart, and with the romantic mode of courtship practised in the pastoral districts of Caledonia. He was early initiated into all the mysteries of rustic love, and had tried his eloquence with such success among the maidens of the land, that one of them said, 'Open your eyes and shut your ears with Rob Burns, and there's nae fear o' your heart; but close your eyes and open your ears, and you'll lose it.'

Of all lyric poets he is the most prolific and various. Of one hundred and sixty songs which he communicated to Johnson's *Museum*, all, save a score or so, are either his composition, or amended with such skill and genius as to be all but made his own. For Thomson he wrote little short of a hundred. He took a peculiar pleasure in ekeing out and amending the old and imperfect songs of his country. He has exercised his fancy and taste to a greater extent that way than antiquarians either like or seem willing to acknowledge. Scott, who performed for the ballads of Scotland what Burns did for many of her songs, perceived this . . . No one has ever equalled him in these exquisite imitations: he caught up the peculiar spirit of the old song at once; he thought as his elder brother in rhyme thought, and communicated an antique sentiment and tone to all the verses which he added. Finer feeling, purer fancy, more exquisite touches of nature, and more vigorous thoughts were the result of this intercourse. Burns found Scottish song like a fruit-tree in winter, not dead, though unbudded; nor did he leave it till it was covered with bloom and beauty. He sharpened the sarcasm, deepened the passion, heightened the humour, and abated the indelicacy of his country's lyrics . . .

A want of chivalry has been instanced as a radical fault in the lyrics of Burns. He certainly is not of the number who approach beauty with much awe or reverence, and who raise loveliness into an idol for man to fall down and worship. The polished courtesies and romantic affectations of high society had not found their way among the maidens

P

of Kyle; the midnight tryste, and the stolen interview—the rapture to meet, and the anguish to part—the secret vow, and the scarce audible whisper, were dear to their bosoms; and they were unacquainted with moving in parallel lines, and breathing sighs into roses, in the affairs of the heart. To draw a magic circle of affection round those he loved, which could not be passed without lowering them from the station of angels, forms no part of the lyrical system of Burns' poetic wooing: there is no affectation in him; he speaks like one unconscious of the veneered and varnished civilities of artificial life; he feels that true love is unacquainted with fashionable distinctions, and in all he has written has thought but of the natural man and woman, and the uninfluenced emotions of the heart. Some have charged him with a want of delicacy —an accusation easily answered; he is rapturous, he is warm, he is impassioned—his heart cannot contain its ecstasies; he glows with emotion as a crystal goblet with wine; but in none of his best songs is there the least indelicacy. Love is with him a leveller; passion and feeling are of themselves as little influenced by fashion and manners as the wind is in blowing, or the sun in shining; chivalry, and even notions of delicacy, are changeable things; our daughters speak no longer with the free tongues of their great-grandmothers, and young men no longer challenge wild lions, or keep dangerous castles in honour of their ladies' eyes.

The prose of Burns has much of the original merit of his poetry; but it is seldom so pure, no natural, and so sustained. It abounds with bright bits, fine out-flashings, gentle emotions, and uncommon warmth and ardour. It is very unequal; sometimes it is simple and vigorous; now and then inflated and cumbrous; and he not seldom labours to say weighty and decided things, in which a 'double double toil and trouble' sort of labour is visible. 'But hundreds even of his most familiar letters'—I adopt the words of Wilson—'are perfectly artless, though still most eloquent compositions. Simple we may not call them, so rich are they in fancy, so overflowing in feeling, and dashed off in every other paragraph with the easy boldness of a great master, conscious of his strength even at times when, of all things in the world, he was least solicitous about display; while some there are so solemn, so sacred, so religious, that he who can read them with an unstirred heart can have no trust, no hope, in the immortality of the soul.' Those who desire to feel him in his strength must taste him in his Scottish spirit. There he spoke the language of life: in English, he spoke that of education; he had to think in the former before he could express himself in the latter. In the language in which his mother sung and nursed him he excelled; a dialect reckoned barbarous by scholars, grew classic and elevated when uttered by the tongue of ROBERT BURNS.

72. James Hogg on Burns

1836

Extract from *Works of Robert Burns*, ed. The Ettrick Shepherd and Wiliam Motherwell (Glasgow, 1836), V, pp. 1–10, 176–83, 244–5, 278–82.

James Hogg (1770–1835), poet and author of *The Private Memoirs and Confessions of a Justified Sinner*, belonged to the *Blackwood's* group of writers. His 'Robin's Awa!' strikes a truer note than most poetic tributes to Burns (see Introduction, p. 23).

So I am set down to write a memoir of the life of ROBERT BURNS. I wish from my soul that as many lives of that singular man had been written *during his lifetime* as have been of myself, and then we should have known all of the bard and the man that behoved us to know; for really this everlasting raking up of the ashes of the illustrious dead, in search of collateral evidence relating to things about which we have no concern and ought not to know, is too bad.

It has always been my opinion, that mankind have as little right to dive into the private actions of a poet as those of any other individual. It is by a man's general behaviour in society that he is to be judged. But with regard to his private frailties and failings, these are between God and his own heart, and we have nothing to do with them. Why then should the distinguished bard be an exemption from this general and rational principle,—he who of all men is the most exposed to erratic wanderings, but without whose strong passions and ardent feelings, he could never have been the splendid meteor of our admiration, or the being of our high concern? Therefore, of all other retrospects, a narrow one into the private failings of a deceased poet, is the most unfair. No, no; mankind have nothing ado with them. For what he has produced under the sanction of his name to the public, his character is answerable, both to the existing public and posterity; but no farther. Be his private failings benevolently buried with the ardent dust that nourished them, and the silent tear of regret shed over them. They were between the soul of the bard and the God who made him. Let any man consider how he would like to have all his private amours, follies, political and selfish intrigues, raked together and exposed to public view. Let even the most cautious and specious of our sex consider of this, and think of the catalogue. The very thought is awful . . .

I wish no one had ever meddled with the life of Burns save Dr. Currie and Mr. Lockhart; for the work of the latter, though altogether inimitable, and the most impressive memoir that perhaps ever was written, is rather a supplement to the former than a concise history of the poet's life from beginning to end. For Dr. Currie I have the highest veneration; nor can I discover, for all the blame attached to him by whole herds of reviewers and self-important biographers, that any one sentence which he published has yet been disproved; or, if any thing may be objected to, it is only in the expressions used. I would be cautious how I endeavoured to prove Dr. Currie's exaggerations in any thing, as he certainly had advantages which no other has subsequently possessed, with the exception of Mr. Gilbert Burns, whose edition has only rendered confusion more confounded. Dr. Currie had his documents from those who could not be mistaken. The proof sheets of the passages reprobated were transmitted to his friends and approven. Why then carp at them now? It has been said they ought to have been left out: so think I; but Dr. Currie thought otherwise, and was known to have expressed himself otherwise, saying, that there were so many thousands living who were intimately acquainted with the character and failings of Burns, that if he had drawn a veil over these altogether, his memorial would have been viewed as any thing but a genuine life of the poet—as only a sly piece of sophistry, which would have done more evil than good.

Walker wrote well on the subject, but disclosed little. Peterkin, fiercely, without proving or disapproving any thing. The late Rev. Mr. Gray took up the subject with great enthusiasm, but though my beloved friend and brother-in-law, I had least dependence on him of any of them. He had such a profusion of sophistry in the defence of genius that it was boundless as well as insurmountable. His mind was an anomaly; his admiration of poetical genius running to such an extreme height that before it all faults and failings vanished, and instead of degrading the man, rather lent a splendour to his character. The errors of men of genius that were passing daily before our eyes he would not admit of, but logically proved them to have no existence. If I chanced to recount any of my own foibles or mistakes to my intimate friends, Gray denied them, asserting that the things were impossible, for it was not in my nature to do them, and would leave all the party but myself convinced that the things were not true, and that I was only trying to mislead them.

He always however confessed one awful night with Burns, but only one. He would never give me the detail even in friendship, but answered me with, 'No, no, that cannot be detailed. But it was not his blame, poor fellow! he was led into it by a few scoundrels of Englishmen, who had made it up among them to entice our great lyrical poet (who so far outshone all their own countrymen) to degrade himself, and they effected it by leading him from one mischief to another. But the aberration cost him dear both in health and spirits.'

Even this excuse I was naturally inclined to hold equivocal. I could not conceive English gentlemen guilty of such a combination, and have little doubt that they were so happy with Burns that they could not part with him. This I think more likely than that the Englishmen had previously laid a plan to entrap him. As far as my experience goes, I cannot conceive an English gentleman drawn to a Scottish poet by aught save admiration and attachment.

As for Mr. Wordsworth, his was the most uncalled-for ebullition of pompous absurdity that ever was penned. Mr. Gray being most anxious to further Gilbert Burns's edition, requested of Wordsworth something that could appear in the work, and lend the lustre of his name to it. The poet complied, sat down and penned his letter; but perceiving that it was a masterpiece, that Gilbert Burns might not reap the sole benefit of such a gem, he published it by itself first in a pamphlet. The publication of this pamphlet drew from the matchless pen of a contemporary[1] some remarks which seem to have come from the very heart's core, and which are so prophetic as well as so illustrative of the subject I am on, that I am compelled to give a few extracts.

[1] John Wilson.

After some prefatory explanation, he says,

We conceive that Mr. Wordsworth has made a slight mistake in saying that
Gilbert Burns has done him the honour of requesting his advice. This does not
appear to have been the case: the request was made by Mr. Gray, not by Mr.
Burns, who, we have reason to know, was scarcely aware of Mr. Wordsworth's
existence; had never read a line of his poetry; and had formed no idea, good,
bad, or indifferent, of his character.

In the second place, it appears that this letter was, at first, a private communication to Mr. Gray; and it is a pity it did not remain so; for we think that
there is great indelicacy, vanity, and presumption, in this coming forward with
printed and *published* advice to a man who, most assuredly, stands in no need of
it.

Mr. Wordsworth says in a note, that it was deemed necessary to publish this
letter and give it an open circulation. We wish to ask Mr. Wordsworth *who
deemed it would be so*? Did Gilbert Burns so deem? did Mr. Gray so deem? or
was it only Mr. Wordsworth that so deemed? We believe that the latter
gentleman alone recommended its publication.

It is natural for us to ask what peculiarly fits Mr. Wordsworth to give advice
on this subject. He has never lived in Scotland; he knows nothing about Burns;
he very imperfectly understands the language in which Burns writes; he has not
even read those publications which are supposed to be unjust to his memory;
yet, in the midst of all this portentous ignorance, and in the face of these manifest disqualifications, he has the effrontery to offer advice to Gilbert Burns, one
of the most intelligent and strong-minded men alive, on a subject nearest and
dearest to his heart, which he had doubtless contemplated in every possible light,
and of which he must know many deeply interesting particulars unthought of
by the world. What would Mr. Wordsworth think of the understanding of a
correspondent who would publish an advice to him when to go on with his
poem of the Excursion and how to conduct it?

The ingenious writer from whom these scraps were selected many
years ago, says, in another place, with great truth and energy:

When Mr. Wordsworth brings his specific charge against Dr. Currie, accusing
him of narrating Burns's errors and misfortunes without affording the reader
any information concerning their source or cause,—this error of the biographer,
he says, gave him 'acute sorrow,' excited 'strong indignation,—moved him
beyond what it became him to express.' Now, really Mr. Wordsworth might
have spared himself all this unnecessary emotion; for the truth is, that no man can
with his eyes open read Dr. Currie's life of Burns, and the multitude of letters
from and to the poet which his edition contains, without a clear, distinct, and
perfect knowledge of all the causes from which the misfortunes and errors of

that mighty genius sprung. His constant struggles with poverty through boy-hood, youth, and manhood,—the warmth and vehemence of his passions,—his sudden elevation to fame and celebrity,—the disappointment of his hopes,—the cruel and absurd debasement of his occupation,—the temptations which assailed him from every quarter,—his gradual and increasing indulgences,—the prickings of heart and soul which consequently oppressed him,—his keen re-morse for every violation of duty which his uncorrupted conscience often forced him to feel more acutely than the occasion might demand,—the pure and lofty aspirations after a nobler kind of life, which often came like a sun-burst on his imagination,—his decay of health and spirit,—the visitations of melancholy, despondency, and despair, which at the close of his eventful life he too often endured;—this, and much more than all this, Mr. Wordsworth might have learned from the work he pretends to despise; and with such knowledge laid before the world, shame to the man who thus dares to calumniate the dead, and to represent as the ignorant, illiberal, and narrow-minded enemy to genius, him who was its most ardent admirer; its most strenuous, enlightened, and successful defender.

Moreover, Mr. Wordsworth should have reflected that the life and character of Burns had, long before Dr. Currie's edition, been the theme of universal discussion; that he had lived in the eye of the world; that innumerable anecdotes of his conversation, habits, propensities, and domestic economy were floating through society; that thousands existed who knew him and the general tenor of his life;—and that, therefore, had his biographer preserved that strict silence regarding his personal character which Dr. Currie's accusers recommend, he would thereby have seemed to sanction the world's belief in all the false or exaggerated stories in circulation about that extraordinary man; to have shrunk from the relation of facts which he could not justify; and to have drawn a veil over enormities which he could not but condemn.

In conclusion, one word to *all* those officious gentlemen who are now so idly bestirring themselves in the revival of an obsolete subject. The world are agreed about the character and genius of Burns. None but the most narrow-minded bigots think of his errors and frailties but with sympathy and indulgence; none but the blindest enthusiasts can deny their existence. It is very possible that his biographers and critics may have occasionally used epithets and expressions too peremptory and decisive; but, on the whole, the character of the bard has had ample justice. There is no need for any one now-a-days to say what Burns was, or what he was not. This he has himself told us a hundred times in immortal language; and the following most pathetic and sublime stanza ought to silence both his friends and his enemies,—if enemies there can indeed be to a man so nobly endowed. For while with proud consciousness, he there glories in the virtues which God has bestowed on him, there, too, does he with compunctious visitings of nature own, in prostration of spirit, that the light which led him astray was not always light from Heaven.

> The poor inhabitant below,
> Was quick to learn and wise to know,
> And keenly felt the friendly glow
>   And softer flame;
> But thoughtless follies laid him low
>   And stained his name.

Having thus settled with Wordsworth, turn we to the Rev. Hamilton Paul.★ There is a hero for you. Any man will stand up for a friend, who, while he is manifestly in the right, is suffering injuries from the envy or malice of others; but how few like Mr. Paul have the courage to step forward and defend a friend whether he is right or wrong; and even to show his determination, when he feels that the bard is farthest wrong, to persist that there he was most mainly right. I remember that, when Mr. Paul's work appeared, I could not help admiring it greatly, not for its internal merits, but for the spirit in which it was executed. After the fame of the poet had arisen to its acme, and had been acknowledged by all ranks, there were a thousand venomed shafts prepared against his memory, and the foulest insinuations promulgated both regarding his character and the tendency of his poetry, when he himself was no more to defend them. It was then that the Rev. Hamilton Paul stood forward as the champion of the deceased bard, and in the face of every obloquy which he knew would be poured upon him from every quarter as a divine of the Church of Scotland, and of which he brought down on himself a liberal portion; yet he would neither be persuaded to flinch from the task, nor yet to succumb, or eat in a word afterwards. The cantings of hypocrisy only rendered him more bold and audacious, and he maintains the perfect and pure morality of Burns' satirical poetry to this day. I must acknowledge that I admire that venerable parson although differing from him on many points.

From all this it will be seen that my main dependence for facts will

★ Burns's *Poems*, with life by the Rev. Hamilton Paul, 1819. [Bold in defence of Burns, but lacking critical originality.]

be on Dr. Currie and Mr. Lockhart, whose joint labours I shall endeavour to condense as much as possible, without leaving out any circumstance worthy of preservation. But in the meantime, wherever I can procure any thing highly original or deeply interesting, and better than I could express it myself, respecting our bard, I deem it my duty to interweave such in this edition . . . When I took up [Carlyle's] article, which occurs in one of the numbers of the *Edinburgh Review*, I meant only to give a few, a very few quotations, which I thought beautifully and strongly illustrative of the literary character of Burns; but, as I proceeded, I perceived that I could neither do justice to the poet nor the writer, without inserting the main substance of the essay; and though what I have written, both in the memoir and the notes, be often quite adverse to the sentiments copied here, I must still make a few further remarks upon it.

In the first place, with regard to the merits of 'Tam o' Shanter,' we are completely at odds, which he denies to be poetical, or even a poem at all. Now, I account it a glorious poem, and highly poetical. I do not think that ever Burns intended to strike anew any of the deep mysterious chords of superstition in the human heart; but that he meant it merely as a bold, humorous description of some really natural scenes in common life, and some perfectly ludicrous supernatural ones; and that he accomplished to a tee, what he intended. I therefore think it was much too bad, in this ingenious writer, to term it 'a mere drunken phantasmagoria painted on ale vapours.' But here I am not afraid to make my appeal to the public. Again Mr. Carlisle, with all his enthusiasm about Burns, and about poetry in general, frequently talks of the failure of Burns, and regards him as a poet of great capability, who had accomplished nothing.* I am astonished at such a sentiment ever having been cherished by this writer, and far more, that he should have suffered it to drop from his pen, after, too, admitting the truth of Fletcher's axiom. What poet has accomplished so much, or half so much, for Scotland as Burns,—in the renovation and new-modelling of her whole lyrical department,—and who has given a polish, a melody, and a zest, to our pastoral and love songs which they never before possessed? and yet Mr. Carlisle speaks freely of the failure of Burns, as an understood and acknowledged verity. He says likewise,

---

* Hold, Mr. Hogg; fair play!—Mr. Carlisle's sentiment is not that Burns accomplished nothing, far from it; but only that what he did accomplish was nothing to what he might have accomplished, had his capacious mind been under a purer influence, and his mighty powers been more worthily directed [Note by William Motherwell].

that the most strictly poetical of all his works is the 'Jolly Beggars'!
Good that . . .

'Robin's Awa!'

AIR—'There will never be peace till Jamie comes hame'.

BY THE ETTRICK SHEPHERD

Ae night, i' the gloaming, as late I pass'd by,
A lassie sang sweet as she milkit her kye,
An' this was her sang, while the tears down did fa'—
O there's nae bard o' nature sin' Robin's awa!
The bards o' our country, now sing as they may,
The best o' their ditties but maks my heart wae;
For at the blithe strain there was ane beat them a',—
O there's nae bard o' nature sin' Robin's awa!

Auld Wat he is wily and pleases us fine,
Wi' his lang-nebbit tales an' his ferlies langsyne;[1]
Young Jack is a dreamer[2], Will sings like a craw[3],
An' Davie[4] an' Delta[5], are dowy an' slaw;
Trig Tam frae the Heelands was aince a braw man[6];
Poor Jamie he blunders an' sings as he can[7];
There's the Clerk an' the Sodger, the Newsman an' a',
They but gar me greet sairer for him that's awa!

'Twas he that could charm wi' the wauff o' his tongue,
Could rouse up the auld an' enliven the young,
An' cheer the blithe hearts in the cot an' the ha',—
O there's nae bard o' nature sin' Robin's awa!
Nae sangster amang us has half o' his art,
There was nae fonder lover an' nae kinder heart;
Then wae to the wight wha wad wince at a flaw.
To tarnish the honours of him that's awa!

If he had some fauts I cou'd never them see,
They're nae to be sung by sic gilpies as me,
He likit us weel, an' we likit him a',—
O there's nae sicken callan sin' Robin's awa!
When'er I sing late at the milkin my kye,
I look up to heaven an' say with a sigh,
Although he's now gane, he was king o' them a',—
Ah! there's nae bard o' nature sin' Robin's awa!

[1] Sir Walter Scott.   [2] Keats.   [3] Wordsworth.   [4] Unidentified.
[5] D. M. Moir.   [6] Thomas Campbell.   [7] Hogg himself.

73. Thomas De Quincey looks back

1837

Extracts from 'Autobiography of an English Opium-Eater', *Tait's Magazine* (February 1837), new series IV, pp. 71–3, by Thomas De Quincey (1785–1859), essayist, critic, and author of *Confessions of an English Opium-Eater* (1822). Text here from 'A Liverpool Coterie', *The Collected Writings of Thomas De Quincey. New and Enlarged Edition*, ed. David Masson (Edinburgh, 1899), II, pp. 130–7.

Dr. Currie was so much occupied with his professional duties that of him I saw but little. His edition of Burns was just then published (I think in that very month), and in everybody's hands. At that time, he was considered not unjust to the memory of the man, and (however constitutionally phlegmatic, or with little enthusiasm, at least in external show) not much below the mark in his appreciation of the poet.

So stood matters some twelve or fourteen years; after which period a 'craze' arose on the subject of Burns, which allowed no voice to be heard but that of zealotry and violent partisanship. The first impulse to this arose out of an oblique collision between Lord Jeffrey and Mr. Wordsworth; the former having written a disparaging critique upon Burns's pretensions—a little, perhaps, too much coloured by the fastidiousness of long practice in the world, but, in the main, speaking some plain truths on the quality of Burns's understanding, as expressed in his epistolary compositions. Upon which, in his celebrated letter to Mr. James Gray, the friend of Burns, himself a poet, and then a master in the High School of Edinburgh, Mr. Wordsworth commented with severity, proportioned rather to his personal resentments towards Lord Jeffrey than to the quantity of wrong inflicted upon Burns. Mr. Wordsworth's letter, in so far as it was a record of embittered feeling, might have perished; but, as it happened to embody some profound criticisms, applied to the art of biography, and especially to the delicate task of following a man of original genius through his personal

427

infirmities or his constitutional aberrations— this fact, and its relation to Burns and the author's name, have all combined to embalm it. Its momentary effect, in conjunction with Lord Jeffrey's article, was to revive the interest (which for some time had languished under the oppression of Sir Walter Scott and Lord Byron) in all that related to Burns. Fresh *Lives* appeared in a continued succession, until, upon the death of Lord Byron in 1824, Mr. Allan Cunningham, who had personally known Burns, so far as a boy *could* know a mature man, gave a new impulse to the interest, by an impressive paper in which he contrasted the circumstances of Burns's death with those of Lord Byron's, and also the two funerals—both of which, one altogether, and the other in part, Mr. Cunningham had personally witnessed. A man of genius, like Mr. Cunningham, throws a new quality of interest upon all which he touches; and, having since brought fresh research and the illustrative power of the arts to bear upon the subject, and all this having gone on concurrently with the great modern revolution in literature—that is, the great extension of a *popular* interest, through the astonishing reductions of price—the result is, that Burns has, at length, become a national and, therefore, in a certain sense, a privileged subject; which, in a perfect sense, he was *not*, until the controversial management of his reputation had irritated the public attention. Dr. Currie did not address the same alert condition of the public feeling, nor, by many hundred degrees, so *diffused* a condition of any feeling which might imperfectly exist, as a man must consciously address in these days, whether as the biographer or the critic of Burns. The lower-toned enthusiasm of the public was not of a quality to irritate any little enthusiasm which the worthy Doctor might have felt. The public of that day felt with regard to Burns exactly as with regard to Bloomfield—not that the quality of his poems was then the staple of the interest, but the extraordinary fact that a ploughman or a lady's shoemaker should have written any poems at all. The sole difference in the two cases, as regarded by the public of that day, was that Burns's case was terminated by a premature, and, for the public, a very sudden death: this gave a personal interest to his case which was wanting in the other; and a direct result of this was that his executors were able to lay before the world a series of his letters recording his opinions upon a considerable variety of authors, and his feelings under many ordinary occasions of life.

Dr. Currie, therefore, if phlegmatic, as he certainly was, must be looked upon as upon a level with the public of his own day—a public how different, different by how many centuries, from the world of this present 1837! One thing I remember which powerfully illustrates the difference. Burns, as we all know, with his peculiarly wild and almost ferocious spirit of independence, came a generation too soon. In this day, he would have been forced to do that, clamorously called upon to do that, and would have found his pecuniary interest in doing that, which in his own generation merely to attempt doing loaded him with the reproach of Jacobinism. It must be remembered that the society of Liverpool wits on whom my retrospect is now glancing were all Whigs—all, indeed, fraternizers with French Republicanism. Yet so it was that—not once, not twice, but daily almost, in the numerous conversations naturally elicited by this Liverpool monument to Burns's memory—I heard every one, clerk or layman, heartily agreeing to tax Burns with ingratitude and with pride falsely directed, because he sate uneasily or restively under the bridle-hand of his noble self-called '*patrons*.' Aristocracy, then, the essential spirit of aristocracy—this I found was not less erect and clamorous amongst partisan democrats—democrats who were such merely in a party sense of supporting his Majesty's Opposition against his Majesty's Servants—than it was or could be among the most bigoted of the professed feudal aristocrats. For my part, at this moment, when all the world was reading Currie's monument to the memory of Burns and the support of his family, I felt and avowed my feeling most loudly—that Burns was wronged, was deeply, memorably wronged. A £10 bank note, by way of subscription for a few copies of an early edition of his poems—this is the outside that I could ever see proof given of Burns having received anything in the way of *patronage*; and doubtless this would have been gladly returned, but from the dire necessity of dissembling.

Lord Glencairn is the 'patron' for whom Burns appears to have felt the most sincere respect. Yet even he—did he give him more than a seat at his dinner table? Lord Buchan again, whose liberalities are by this time pretty well appreciated in Scotland, exhorts Burns, in a tone of one preaching upon a primary duty of life, to exemplary gratitude towards a person who had given him absolutely nothing at all. The man has not yet lived to whose happiness it was more essential that he should live unencumbered by the sense of obligation; and, on the other hand, the man has not lived upon whose independence as professing benefactors so many people practised, or who found so many others ready to ratify and give value to their pretences.* Him, whom beyond

* Jacobinism—although the seminal principle of all political evil in all ages alike of advanced civilization—is natural to the heart of man, and, in a qualified sense, may be

most men nature had created with the necessity of conscious independence, all men besieged with the assurance that he was, must be, ought
to be dependent; nay, that it was his primary duty to be grateful for
his dependence. I have not looked into any edition of Burns, except
once for a quotation, since this year 1801—when I read the whole of
Currie's edition, and had opportunities of meeting the editor—and
once subsequently, upon occasion of a fifth or supplementary volume
being published. I know not, therefore, how this matter has been
managed by succeeding editors, such as Allan Cunningham, far more
capable of understanding Burns's situation, from the previous struggles
of their own honourable lives, and Burns's feelings, from something
of congenial power.

I, in this year, 1801, when in the company of Dr. Currie, did not
forget, and, with some pride I say that I stood alone in remembering,
the very remarkable position of Burns: not merely that, with his genius,
and with the intellectual pretensions generally of his family, he should
have been called to a life of early labour, and of labour unhappily not
prosperous, but also that he, by accident about the proudest of human
spirits, should have been by accident summoned, beyond all others, to
eternal recognitions of some mysterious gratitude which he owed to
some mysterious patrons little and great, whilst yet, of all men, perhaps,
he reaped the least obvious or known benefit from any patronage that
has ever been put on record. Most men, if they reap little from patronage, are liberated from the claims of patronage, or, if they are summoned
to a galling dependency, have at least the fruits of their dependency.
But it was this man's unhappy fate—with an early and previous
irritability on this very point—to find himself saddled, by his literary
correspondents, with all that was odious in dependency, whilst he had
every hardship to face that is most painful in unbefriended poverty.

On this view of the case, I talked, then, being a schoolboy, with and

---

meritorious. A good man, a high-minded man, in certain circumstances, *must* be a
Jacobin in a certain sense. The aspect under which Burns's Jacobinism appears is striking;
there is a thought which an observing reader will find often recurring, which expresses its
peculiar bitterness. It is this: the necessity which in old countries exists for the labourer
humbly to beg *permission* that he may labour. To eat in the sweat of a man's brow,—that
is bad; and that is a curse, and pronounced such by God. But, when *that* is all, the labourer
is by comparison happy. The second curse makes *that* a jest: he must sue, he must sneak,
he must fawn like an Oriental slave, in order to win his fellow-man, in Burns's indignant
words, 'to give him *leave* to toil.' That was the scorpion thought that was for ever shooting its sting into Burns's meditations, whether forward-looking or backward-looking;
and, that considered, there arises a world of allowance for that vulgar bluster of independence which Lord Jeffrey, with so much apparent reason, charges upon his prose writings.

against the first editor of Burns:—I did not, and I do not, profess to admire the letters (that is, the prose), all or any, of Burns. I felt that they were liable to the charges of Lord Jeffrey, and to others beside; that they do not even express the natural vigour of Burns's mind, but are at once vulgar, tawdry, coarse, and commonplace; neither was I a person to affect any profound sympathy with the general character and temperament of Burns, which has often been described as 'of the earth, earthy'—unspiritual—animal—beyond those of most men equally intellectual. But still I comprehended his situation; I had for ever ringing in my ears, during that summer of 1801, those groans which ascended to heaven from his over-burthened heart—those harrowing words, '*To give him leave to toil*,' which record almost a reproach to the ordinances of God—and I felt that upon him, amongst all the children of labour, the primal curse had fallen heaviest and sunk deepest. Feelings such as these I had the courage to express: a personal compliment, or so, I might now and then hear; but all were against me on the *matter*. Dr. Currie said—'Poor Burns! such notions had been his ruin'; Mr. Shepherd continued to draw from the subject some scoff or growl at Mr. Pitt and the Excise; the laughing tailor told us a good story of some proud beggar; Mr. Clarke proposed that I should write a Greek inscription for a cenotaph which he was to erect in his garden to the memory of Burns;—and so passed away the solitary protestation on behalf of Burns's jacobinism, together with the wine and the roses, and the sea-breezes of that same Verton, in that same summer of 1801. Mr. Roscoe is dead, and has found time since then to be half forgotten; Dr. Currie, the physician, has been found 'unable to heal himself'; Mr. Shepherd of Gatacre is a name and a shadow; Mr. Clarke is a shadow without a name; the tailor, who set the table in a roar, is dust and ashes; and three men at the most remain of all who in those convivial meetings held it right to look down upon Burns as upon one whose spirit was rebellious overmuch against the institutions of man, and jacobinical in a sense which 'men of property' and master manufacturers will never brook, albeit democrats by profession.

74. J. G. Whittier: an American poet's debt to Burns

1840

Extract from 'Burns. On receiving a sprig of heather in blossom', *The Complete Poetical Works of Whittier*, ed. H. E. Scudder (Boston, 1894), pp. 196–7.

John Greenleaf Whittier (1807–1892) has sometimes been called 'the American Burns'. The label can be misleading, as Whittier's poetic originality was different in kind from that of Burns; but his admiration for the Scottish poet lasted from boyhood until hs death.

I call to mind the summer day,
    The early harvest mowing,
The sky with sun and clouds at play,
    And flowers with breezes blowing.

I hear the blackbird in the corn,
    The locust in the haying;
And, like the fabled hunter's horn,
    Old tunes my heart is playing.

How oft that day, with fond delay,
    I sought the maple's shadow,
And sang with Burns the hours away,
    Forgetful of the meadow!

Bees hummed, birds twittered, overhead
    I heard the squirrels leaping,
The good dog listened while I read,
    And wagged his tail in keeping.

I watched him while in a sportive mood
    I read 'The Twa Dogs' story,
And half believed he understood
    The poet's allegory.

Sweet day, sweet songs! The golden hours
  Grew brighter for that singing,
From brook and bird and meadow flowers
  A dearer welcome bringing.

New light on home-seen Nature beamed,
  New glory over Woman;
And daily life and duty seemed
  No longer poor and common.

I woke to find the simple truth
  Of fact and feeling better
Than all the dreams that held my youth
  A still repining debtor:

That Nature gives her handmaid, Art,
  The themes of sweet discoursing;
The tender idyls of the heart
  In every tongue rehearsing . . .

With clearer eyes I saw the worth
  Of life among the lowly;
The Bible at his Cotter's hearth
  Had made my own more holy . . .

Not his the song whose thunderous chime
  Eternal echoes render;
The mournful Tuscan's haunted rhyme,
  And Milton's starry splendour!

But who his human heart has laid
  To Nature's bosom nearer?
Who sweetened toil like him, or paid
  To love a tribute dearer?

Through all his tuneful art, how strong
  The human feeling gushes!
The very moonlight of his song
  Is warm with smiles and blushes!

75. Ralph Waldo Emerson: an American tribute

1840, 1859

Ralph Waldo Emerson (1803–82), philosopher, poet, and prolific essayist, was an admirer of the works of Burns and Scott, and a friend of Thomas Carlyle.

(a) Extract from a journal entry of December 1840 which identifies the error in directing moral criticism indiscriminately at poets of Burns's stature; text from *The Journals of Ralph Waldo Emerson*, eds A. W. Plumstead and Harrison Hayford (Cambridge, Mass., 1969), VII, 1838–42, p. 410.

If you criticize a fine genius as Burns or Goethe, the odds are that you are quite out of your reckoning, and are only whipping your own false portrait of the man. For there is something spheral & infinite in every man, especially in every genius, which if you can come very near him, sports with all your limitations. For rightly every man is but a channel through which the God floweth, & whilst I thought I was criticizing him, I was blaspheming my own Soul.

(b) Extract from a frequently reprinted speech given at a Centenary Burns dinner in Boston on 25 January 1859. Emerson seeks to explain why 'The people who care nothing for literature and poetry care for Burns'. Text from volume XI of the Centenary Edition of the Complete Works of Ralph Waldo Emerson, ed. E. W. Emerson (Boston and New York, 1911), pp. 440–3.

His organic sentiment was absolute independence, and resting as it should on a life of labour. No man existed who could look down on him. They that looked into his eyes saw that they might look down the sky as easily. His muse and teaching was common sense, joyful, aggressive, irresistible. Not Latimer, nor Luther struck more telling blows against false theology than did this brave singer. The Confession of Augsburg, the Declaration of Independence, the French Rights of Man, and the 'Marseillaise', are not more weighty documents in the history of freedom than the songs of Burns. His satire has lost none of its edge. His musical arrows yet sing through the air. He is so substantially a reformer that I find his grand plain sense in close chain with the greatest masters,—Rabelais, Shakespeare in comedy, Cervantes, Butler, and Burns. If I should add another name, I find it only in a living countryman of Burns.[1]

He is an exceptional genius. The people who care nothing for literature and poetry care for Burns. It was indifferent—they thought who saw him—whether he wrote verse or not: he could have done anything else as well. Yet how true a poet he is! And the poet, too, of poor men, of gray hodden and the guernsey coat and the blouse. He has given voice to all the experiences of common life; he has endeared the farmhouse and cottage, patches and poverty, beans and barley; ale, the poor man's wine; hardship; the fear of debt; the dear society of weans and wife, of brothers and sisters, proud of each other, knowing so few and finding amends for want and obscurity in books and thoughts. What a love of Nature, and, shall I say it? of middle-class Nature. Not like Goethe, in the stars, or like Byron, in the ocean, or Moore, in the luxurious East, but in the homely landscape which the poor see around them,—bleak leagues of pasture and stubble, ice and sleet and rain and snow-choked brooks; birds, hares, field-mice, thistles and heather, which he daily knew. How many 'Bonny Doons' and 'John Anderson my jo's' and 'Auld lang synes' all around the earth have his verses been applied to! and his love-songs still woo and melt the youths and maids; the farmwork, the country holiday, the fishing-cobble are still his debtors to-day.

And as he was thus the poet of the poor, anxious, cheerful, working humanity, so had he the language of low life. He grew up in a rural district, speaking a *patois* unintelligible to all but natives, and he has made the Lowland Scotch a Doric dialect of fame. It is the only example in history of a language made classic by the genius of a single man. But more than this. He had that secret of genius to draw from the bottom of society the strength of its speech, and astonish the ears of the

[1] Thomas Carlyle.

polite with these artless words, better than art, and filtered of all offence through his beauty. It seemed odious to Luther that the devil should have all the best tunes; he would bring them into the churches; and Burns knew how to take from friars and gypsies, blacksmiths and drovers, the speech of the market and street, and clothe it with melody . . . The memory of Burns,—every man's, every boy's and girl's head carried snatches of his songs, and they say them by heart, and, what is strangest of all, never learned them from a book, but from mouth to mouth. The wind whispers them, the birds whistle them, the corn, barley, and bulrushes hoarsely rustle them, nay, the music-boxes at Geneva are framed and toothed to play them; the hand-organs of the Savoyard in all cities repeat them, and the chimes of bells ring them in the spires. They are the property and the solace of mankind.

APPENDIX A

The publication of Burns's poems and songs, 1786–1800

The following summary shows that Burns's early critical reputation was inevitably affected by the different forms in which his poems and songs were published (see Introduction, pp. 3–14).

(1) Principal editions of Burns's poems

Poems, chiefly in the Scottish Dialect (Kilmarnock 1786); (Edinburgh 1787) (enlarged, 2 issues); (London 1787); (Edinburgh 1793) (enlarged, 2 vols); (Edinburgh 1974, 2 vols); Edinburgh 1797, 2 vols); (Edinburgh 1798, 2 vols); (Edinburgh 1800, 2 vols). See review of Egerer by G. R. Roy in *Modern Philology*, vol. 64, no. 4, May 1967, pp. 357–61.

There were also numerous pirated editions and reprints.

(2) A selection of poems first printed in chapbooks, as broadsides, or in other unorthodox forms

'The calf', 1787 (chapbook); 'The Ayrshire Garland', [Dumfries, 1789?] (anonymous broadside); 'The Prayer Of Holy Willie, A Canting, Hypocritical, Kirk Elder' (1789) (anonymous); 'Tam o' Shanter', *Edinburgh Herald*, 18 March 1791 (then as a footnote in *The Antiquities of Scotland*, by Francis Grose(1791), vol. 2, pp. 199–201); 'The Jolly-Beggars: A Cantata' (1799) (chapbook); *The Merry Muses of Caledonia* (1799) (edition, without Burns's name, of which only two copies are known to survive).

(3) Song-collections which include work by Burns

The Scots Musical Museum, edited by James Johnson, Edinburgh [6 vols issued serially 1787, 1788, 1790, 1792, 1796, 1803]. Burns was virtual editor of vols 2–5 and contributed almost a third of the total of six hundred songs in the edition, as well as collecting many others. His name does not appear on the title-pages. In the texts and indexes of volumes 1–4 it is given beside only a small number of his contributions: much use is made of initials. His name occurs more frequently in the volume of 1796, published shortly after his death; but it becomes prominent only in volume 6, 1803, and in re-issues in that year of all the earlier volumes. Attributions are much more numerous in texts and indexes in the set of 1803, and 'Written for this Work by Robert Burns' takes the place of the earlier laconic attribution.

A Select Collection of Original Scottish Airs, edited by George Thomson [5 vols, issued serially 1793–1818. Vol. I, 1793; vol. II, 1799. A sixth vol. without songs by Burns, 1825]. Fifty-nine songs written or altered by Burns were first printed in this work. His name first appeared on the title-page of a 1798 re-issue of volume I.

A Selection of Scots Songs harmonized by P. Urbani, vol. 2 (Edinburgh [1794]). The first publication of 'O my Love's like a red, red rose', described in the Advertisement as being 'by a celebrated Scot's poet'.

(4) First collected edition.

The Works of Robert Burns; with an Account of his Life, and a Criticism on his Writings. To which are prefixed, Some Observations on The Character and Condition of the Scottish Peasantry, Edited by James Currie, 4 vols (Liverpool, 1800). This edition was the first to bring together the main group of poems and a large number of songs.

APPENDIX B

Burns in America: a late nineteenth-century view

Some reasons for Burns's popularity in America (see above, pp. 44–6) are discussed in 'Burns in America', which appeared in volume VI of *Burnsiana*, ed J. D. Ross (Paisley and London, 1897), pp. 27–9. The essay is by John G. Dow, a Scottish immigrant to Madison, Wisconsin.

A Scotsman coming to live in this country is agreeably surprised by the American love of Burns's poetry. Burns in America is known, revered and loved in a degree not surpassed by his most enthusiastic anniversary-holders in Ayr or Edinburgh. There is in this country a familiarity with the poet's writings more widely spread, if not more minute than one finds among Scotsmen in their own country.

In America, when the ubiquitous Scot leaves his native country, his patriotism grows, if anything, stronger and more sensitive. Amid strange scenes, strange faces, and alien tongues, memories of the Old Country grow warm in his heart, and the old familiar accent becomes very dear to him. Then it is that Burns's poetry, and more especially his songs, offer a rallying ground for troops of affectionate reminiscences and vague emotions that arise from instincts of the blood. For Burns's poetry is not merely a reflex of the country life of Scotland as he found it in all its beauty and ugliness—its mingled faith and superstition, piety and irreverence, sobriety and drunkenness, integrity and hypocrisy. It gathers up and preserves a full heritage of national memories, and embodies them, while it interprets those evasive moods and tones of national life and character which for centuries have constituted the individuality of the race and nation. Burns's poetry, therefore, means ever so much more to the Scot abroad than it means to the Scot at home. Hence in America among Scotsmen, and those who claim Scotch descent, Burns is more lovingly, as well as more extensively, read than he is in the land of his nativity.

But Scotch blood explains only a little of the American regard for Burns. In this country he receives a profounder and sincerer homage than any that springs from the sentimental claims of race and nationality—a homage that is rendered, not by reason, but in spite of much that is intrinsic in the poet's character and work; a homage that takes us beyond the limited range of Burns's patriotism, and reveals the true horizon of the poet's greatness. Notwithstanding his excessive Scotchness Burns has struck home to the American heart as no other outside writer has done before or since, and won from a practical, but essentially non-poetic, people an appreciative homage which is the most eloquent tribute yet accorded to his genius . . .

The literary, like the political revolution of the 18th century, consisted chiefly in the assertion and establishment of the dignity of individual man; it lay also in a return to the healing powers of nature, and in both of these respects the Napoleon of this revolution was Robert Burns. Nature was his high priestess in song; and when equality and fraternity were being branded with blood and fire on the face of Europe, Burns gathered as into a burning focus the whole human sentiment of the revolution in 'A man's a man for a' that'. This was a voice straight from the democracy, speaking for the democracy with an unexampled directness and dignity—the voice of one who stood on his own rock of independence, and esteeming every man at his mere intrinsic worth, proclaimed the new creed and gospel of humanity.

In this Burns is more in sympathy with American than with Scottish life. The principle of individual worth and the spirit of independence which are to us in this country commonplaces of our daily lives are not so familiar in Scotland of to-day, and in the days of Burns they were startling in their novelty. It is true that Burns seemed to have failed miserably, that he was silently crushed out and down by the allied respectabilities of social caste, whose extinction he so proudly heralded. But despite his apparent failure there is in the life and poetry of this herald of the dawn an immortal record of the true majesty of manhood. Therein lies the great ethic of his work, therein lies his just claim to sit among the great and beneficent spirits of the human race.

Bibliography

This short select bibliography is of works listing editions of Burns or indicating sources of critical comment on his poetry, primarily in the period 1786–1837. It also includes Burns's Commonplace Books and Letters, which reveal his attitude towards criticism.

Burns Chronicle (1892–). Annual publication of the Burns Federation, Kilmarnock. Contains material relating to all aspects of the poet's work and reputation.

BENTMAN, R., 'The Romantic Poets and Critics on Robert Burns', *Texas Studies in Literature and Language,* VI (1964). Presents evidence of interest in Burns in early nineteenth-century Britain.

DAICHES, D., introd., *Robert Burns's Commonplace Book 1783–1785* (1965). Facsimile edition. Reproduces Burns's early views on poetry, song, and criticism.

EGERER, J. W., 'Burns and "Guid Black Prent"', in *The Age of Johnson: Essays Presented to C. B. Tinker* (1949). Suggests that his experience of publication discouraged Burns.

EGERER, J. W., *A Bibliography of Robert Burns* (1964). Lists most editions, though not criticism.

FERGUSON, J. D. (ed.), *The Letters of Robert Burns,* 2 vols (1931).

FERGUSON, J. D., 'Some aspects of the Burns legend', *Philological Quarterly,* xi (1932). Comments on early idolaters and moral censors.

JACK, W., 'Burns' 1787 Edinburgh Unpublished Commonplace Book', *MacMillan's Magazine,* March–November 1879. Includes Burns's views on men of letters in Edinburgh.

JACK, W., *Burns In Other Tongues* (1896). Lists translations.

KINGHORN, A. M., 'The literary and historical origins of the Burns myth', *Dalhousie Review,* xxxix (1959). Argues that Burns misled critics of his first edition.

MACKINTOSH, W., *Burns in Germany* (1928).

MACVIE, J., *The Burns Federation: A Bi-Centenary Review* (1959). Traces history of Burns Clubs.

PAINTER, A. M., 'American editions of the poems of Burns before 1800', *Library*, 4th series xii (1932).

RENWICK, W. L., *Burns as Others saw him* (1959). Reprints impressions of those who met the poet.

ROSS, J. D. (ed.), *The Story of the Kilmarnock Burns* (1933). Gives facts of publication of 1786 edition.

ROY, G. R., 'French critics of Robert Burns to 1893', *Revue de Littérature Comparée*, xxxviii (1964). Comprehensive.

SNYDER, F. B., *The Life of Robert Burns* (1932). Takes issue with earlier biographers and critics.

THORNTON, R. D., *James Currie the Entire Stranger & Robert Burns* (1963). Defends the man who prepared the first collected edition.

WERKMEISTER, L., 'Robert Burns and the London daily press', *Modern Philology*, lxiii (1966). Shows that several poems were sent to newspapers.

Select Index

III AUTHORS WHOSE WORK IS COMPARED BY CRITICS AND REVIEWERS WITH THAT OF BURNS

IV SHORT TITLES OR FIRST LINES OF POEMS AND SONGS BY BURNS WHICH ARE DISCUSSED OR QUOTED